second editio...

READINGS ...
PHYSICAL ...

THOMAS W...
Professor of A...
Simon Fraser U...

Prentice-Hall, Inc., Englewood Cliffs, New Jersey

ISBN: 13–7594707–0

Library of Congress Catalog Number: 75–166981

10 9 8 7 6 5 4 3 2 1

PRINTED IN THE UNITED STATES OF AMERICA

Prentice-Hall International, Inc., *London*
Prentice-Hall of Australia, Pty. Ltd., *Sydney*
Prentice-Hall of Canada, Ltd., *Toronto*
Prentice-Hall of India Private Limited, *New Delhi*
Prentice-Hall of Japan, Inc., *Tokyo*

CONTENTS

PREFACE

This book is designed for the student whose interest or curiosity has led him into an introductory course in physical anthropology. The readings included provide a broader outlook upon this subject for the increasing number of introductory students who want to go beyond the limits and generalizations of the course outline. This demand for more specialized coverage has encouraged the development of the following selection of articles. My only regret is that the limitations of space have forced many important omissions.

Articles have been chosen, whenever possible, to demonstrate how the evidence and tools of physical anthropology are used. Descriptions of the fossil forms and narrations of the important discoveries are better left to classroom presentation. In the lectures, evidence can be described and demonstrated to the students, and the backgrounds of individuals, as well as the circumstances of their original discoveries, can be thoroughly discussed. By contrast, a properly selected series of articles can give the student additional information on how the scientist uses and interprets evidence to arrive at his conclusions. In this way, the articles will not only broaden the student's general knowledge of the field but will also lead him into critical analysis.

Complete coverage is a courageous goal, but the current diversification and expansion of the field of physical anthropology and the greater demand for interdisciplinary coverage has made it impractical to treat all branches of the field in a book such as this. So, limited as most of us are to a one-semester introductory course, it seems fitting to concentrate on the more classic areas of physical anthropology.

The book is divided into an introductory article and nine general sections which can be used in sequence or rearranged to suit particular needs.

Each section includes one or more articles by leading anthropologists whose selections demonstrate a particular emphasis or interpretation that is representative of the basic literature of the field. Many are recent articles, chosen because they reflect important new theoretical trends and dynamic new approaches to traditional research problems. A few selections, culled from earlier publications, have withstood the test of time; classics now in the field literature, they continue to delineate critical problem areas and remain valid reading for students who wish to sample the full range of research in physical anthropology. It is easy, when planning a book of this kind, to be dazzled by the new and freshly-printed. And there is an unfortunate tendency among editors of academic anthologies to select for inclusion only the most recently-published articles. I understand and share the desire to offer current material, but I object—as do my students—to the exclusion of still-valid data on the basis of age alone. The purpose of a book of readings is to gather, within a single accessible volume, the *best available* research statements—of whatever vintage. The present selection blends the old with the new in an attempt to pull together the most authoritative summaries of current work in physical anthropology. With the combination of classroom lectures and these representative readings, the student is given the opportunity to acquire a realistic understanding of what physical anthropology is, and of what physical anthropologists do in the laboratory and in the field.

In order to acquaint the student with authors responsible for the more important general books in physical anthropology, I have included a list of general references at the end of Chapter One. For students whose interest is sparked by specific historical or research topics, supplementary readings are suggested at the close of individual chapters.

As editor, I assume full responsibility for the choice of articles within these pages; selections were organized around my own introductory course. However, I am indebted to many for their kind assistance. I should like to thank the authors who have consented to be represented here, as well as their editors and publishers who gave permission to reprint the articles. Many of my students gave valuable suggestions; B. Miles Gilbert and Lawrence G. Quade looked upon my selections from the student's viewpoint and argued winningly for the inclusion of certain articles. Mr. Richard F. Dempewolff, editor of *Science Digest* magazine, once again lent assistance; his continued interest in my own work and in that of other anthropologists is greatly appreciated. Mr. Robert Fenyo of Prentice-Hall is an energetic and imaginative editor whose genuine enthusiasm for the field of physical anthropology makes any publication project an enjoyable one.

And special thanks must go to my wife and closest friend, Sharon, a busy free-lance writer who often and cheerfully abandoned her own work in order to type and edit introductory paragraphs and to handle the prolific correspondence that is so much a part of a book of this kind.

Thomas W. McKern, Ph.D.

one

INTRODUCTION

Physical anthropology, as a true discipline, dates back to the latter part of the nineteenth century. Although many of the problems that the early scientists faced remain with us today, the approaches to these problems and the techniques for solving them have changed. Whether we can call today's physical anthropology "new" or whether the present situation represents the normal developmental progress of a young science is not as important as understanding why changes have taken place and what some of the essential changes have been. Washburn's article does just this and illustrates the more dynamic aspects of a growing science.

The New Physical Anthropology

S. L. Washburn

Recently, evolutionary studies have been revitalized and revolutionized by an infusion of genetics into paleontology and systematics. The change is fundamentally one of point of view, which is made possible by an understanding of the way the genetic constitution of populations changes. The new systematics is concerned primarily with process and with the mechanism of evolutionary change, whereas the older point of view was chiefly concerned with sorting the results of evolution. Physical anthropology is now undergoing the same sort of change. Population genetics presents the anthropologist with a clearly formulated, experimentally verified, conceptual scheme. The application of this theory to the primates is the immediate task of physical anthropology.

In the past, physical anthropology has been considered primarily as a technique. Training consisted in learning to take carefully defined measurements and in computing indices and statistics. The methods of observation, measurement, and comparison were essentially the same, whether the object of the study was the description of evolution, races, growth, criminals, constitutional types, or army personnel. Measurements were adjusted for various purposes, but measurement of the outside of the body, classification, and correlation, remained the anthropologist's primary tools. The techniques of physical anthropology were applied to a limited group of problems, and any definition or statement of traditional anthropology must include both the metrical methods and the problems for which the methods were used. Further, anthropology was characterized by theories, or rather by a group of attitudes and assumptions.

From Transactions of the New York Academy of Sciences *13 series II, (1951): 298–304; reprinted by permission of the author and publisher.*

There has been almost no development of theory in physical anthropology itself, but the dominant attitude may be described as static, with emphasis on classification based on types. Any such characterization is oversimplified, and is intended only to give an indication of the dominant techniques, interests, and attitudes of the physical anthropologist. Except for emphasis on particular animals, physical anthropology shared much with the zoology of the times when it developed. Much of the method was developed before the acceptance of the idea of evolution, and all of it before the science of genetics.

Physical anthropology should change, just as systematic zoology has changed. The difficulties which accompany the necessary modifications can be greatly reduced if their nature is clearly understood. Naturally, in a time of rapid flux there will be numerous doubts and disagreements as to what should be done. This is natural, and what I have to offer is a tentative outline to indicate how parts of the new physical anthropology may differ from the old.

The old physical anthropology was primarily a technique. The common core of the science was measurement of external form with calipers. The new physical anthropology is primarily an area of interest, the desire to understand the process of primate evolution and human variation by the most efficient techniques available.

The process of evolution, as understood by the geneticist, is the same for all mammals. The genetic composition of a population may be described in terms of gene frequencies. The modification of these frequencies results in evolution which is caused by *selection,* mutations, drift, and migrations. Mutations and migrations introduce new genetic elements into the population. But selection on the phenotype, adapting animals to their environment, is the primary cause of alteration in gene frequencies.

This is essentially a return to Darwinism, but with this important difference: Darwin wrote in a pregenetic era. Therefore, he did not understand the mechanism which makes possible the production of variation and the possibility of selection. Since Darwin's ideas could not be proved in detail by the techniques available in his time, the concept of selection did not become fully effective. Therefore, some pre-evolutionary ideas continued in full force. More Linnaean species were described from types after Darwin than before. The idea of evolution created interest in species, but the species were described in pre-evolutionary terms. Further, it is possible for people to hold a variety of theories in place of, or in addition to, Darwin's. For example, Lamarckian ideas have continued right down to today. Orthogenesis has been widely believed and irreversibility has been regarded as a law.

It has been claimed that evolution should be described in terms of nonadaptive traits, yet this is impossible if evolution is largely due to selection. The first great achievement of the synthesis of genetics, paleontology, and systematics is in clearing away a mass of antiquated theories and attitudes which permeate the writings of the older students of evolution. Further, the new evolutionary theory shows which aspects of past work are worth using, extending, and strengthening. This is possible because much of the mechanism of evolutionary change is now understood, clearly formulated, and *experimentally verified*. The logic of Darwin's great theory could only become fully effective when techniques had been developed to prove that selection was right and that other ideas of evolution were wrong. A change in theory, no matter how popular, is not enough. The new ideas must be implemented by effective techniques.

If a new physical anthropology is to differ effectively from the old, it must be more than the adoption of a little genetic terminology. It must change its ways of doing things to conform with the implications of modern evolutionary theory. For example, races must be based on the study of populations. There is no way to justify the division of a breeding population into a series of racial types. It is not enough to state that races should be based on genetic traits; races which cannot be reconciled with genetics should be removed from consideration. If we consider the causes of changes in gene frequency as outlined above, and if we are concerned with the process of evolution, the task of the anthropologist becomes clear. He has nothing to offer on mutation, but can make contributions with regard to migration, drift, and selection.

The migrations of man made possible by culture have vastly confused the genetic picture. Before selection can be investigated, it is necessary to know how long a people has been in an area and under what conditions they have been living. For example, the spread of European people, of Bantu speakers, or of Eskimo, all have changed the distribution of the blood groups. The interpretation of the genetic situation demands an understanding of history. Whether people became adapted to cold by selection or by change in their way of life completely alters the interpretation of the distribution of physical traits. This has been widely recognized by anthropologists, and the solution of this difficulty requires the active collaboration of archeologists, ethnologists, linguists, and students of the physical man.

Drift is related to population size, and this depends on the way of life. Again, as in the case of migration, the situation in which drift may have taken place cannot be specified by the physical anthropologist alone, but requires the active collaboration of many specialists. The adoption of modern evolutionary theory will force a far closer and more realistic collaboration between the branches of anthropology than ever before.

Although much of the present distribution of races may be explained by migration and although drift probably accounts for some differences, selection must be the explanation of long-term evolutionary trends and of many patterned variations as well. Anthropologists have always stressed the importance of adaptation in accounting for the differences between apes and men, and sometimes have used the idea in interpreting racial divergences. But suggestions of adaptations are not enough. It is easy to guess that a form is adaptive, but the real problem is to determine the precise nature of a particular adaptation. The work in which I have been interested is designed to demonstrate the relation of form to function. My feeling has been that it is impossible to do more than guess about this matter using traditional anthropological measurements, and that the literature is already too full of uncontrolled speculations. Therefore, I would like to take this opportunity to present an outline, a beginning, of an analysis of the human body into complexes which may vary independently.

In this work, the guiding principle has been that the major force in evolution is selection of functional complexes. A variety of methods has been used to demonstrate the adaptive complexes. The four major methods for factoring complexes out of the body are: (1) comparison and evolution; (2) development; (3) variability; and (4) experiment. All these have been used by numerous investigators, but, to the best of my knowledge, they have not been combined into a working system. All must be used to gain an understanding of the human body.

The major regions of the body seem to have had remarkable independence in recent evolutionary history. The complex to attain its present pattern first is that of the arms and thorax. This complex is associated with arm swinging in the trees, the way of life called "brachiation." It is association with a reduction in the deep back muscles and in the number of lumbar vertebrae and consequent shortening of the trunk and elongation of all parts of the upper extremity, adaptation of the joints and muscles to greater pronation, supination in the forearm, and flexion and abduction at the shoulder. Many changes in the positions of viscera are associated with the shorter trunk. We share this complex with the living gibbons and apes. The bipedal complex was the next to develop and seems to have been fundamentally human in the South African man-apes. The major changes are in the ilium and in the gluteal muscles. Just as in the arm, the change is in a bone-muscle complex, which makes a different way of life possible. The head seems to have attained essentially its present form during the fourth glacial advance, perhaps 50,000 years ago. The brain continued to enlarge until the end of the last interglacial period, and the face decreased in size for some time after that. The great increase in the size of the brain and decrease in the face were after the use of tools.

Evolution, in a sense, has dissected the body for us, and has shown that great changes may occur in arms and trunk, pelvis and legs, and brain case, or face, accompanied by little change in the rest of the body. The first two complexes to change are related to brachiation and bipedal locomotion. The final changes in the head may well be related to changed selection after the use of tools.

To carry the analysis further, it is necessary to deal with one of the areas suggested by this preliminary dividing of the body. Let us consider the face, and especially the lower jaw. The coronoid process varies with the temporal muscle. The angle of the jaw varies with the masseter and internal pterygoid muscle. The tooth-supporting area varies with the teeth. The main core of the jaw is affected by hormones which do not affect the other parts, as shown in acromegaly. Alizarin dye, which stains the growing bone, reveals the pattern of growth. The split-line technique (Benninghoff) shows the mechanical arrangement.

After making an analysis of this kind, comparisons of a different sort are possible. The simple statement, that a trait is or is not there, is replaced by the attempt to understand under what conditions it might be present. For example, if the simian shelf is developed in monkeys and apes when the jaws are long and the anterior teeth large, then the South African man-apes and other fossil men would not be expected to have such a shelf. The dental characters necessary to bring out the expression of the shelf are absent in all. It can be argued that we have the potential for a simian shelf but that we do not have the necessary tooth and jaw size to make it evident. Trying to understand the process which produces a trait leads to very different evaluations than does a listing of presence or absence.

In the light of this sort of information, let us look at the skull of an Eocene lemur, *Notharctus*. The jaw is long, in conformity with the length of the teeth. It is low, and there is a large angular region. This region has been described as lemuroid. If this angle has remained there for 50 million years, however, over countless generations of lemurs, it must have more of a function than to mark the jaw as primitive or to help us in identifying lemur jaws. If the mandible of a remarkably similar modern leum (genus *Lemur*) is examined, it is found that the internal pterygoid muscle inserts at the end of the angle, but that the masseter muscle inserts only on the lateral side of the ascending ramus, leaving the angle bare of muscle. An internal pterygoid muscle inserting in this position is a protruder of the jaw. The function of the angle of the lemur jaw is to provide insertion for a large, functionally important muscle. The dependence of the angular process on the internal pterygoid and the exact function of the internal pterygoid need to be experimentally verified.

The only point to be stressed now is that the theory that such a process is of adaptive significance, and that it is maintained by selection, leads one to look for a functional complex. If such a process is regarded simply as a taxonomic aid, or as nonfunctional, no guide is available for research or future understanding.

The post-orbital bar of this same lemur again illustrates the advantage of assuming, until it is proved otherwise, that a part is functionally important. Originally, the complete bony ring around the orbit may have been for protection or for some other unknown function. Once the ring is established, however, the skeletal framework for radial modification of the skull is present. The change from the lemur skull, with a wide interorbital region, to the monkey skull, with reduced olfactory mechanism and reduced interorbital space, is mechanically possible because pressure, tension, and buttressing of the sides of the face is provided by the complete rings of bone around the orbits. Structures which probably develop as part of a protective mechanism were pre-adaptive for a reorganization of the face.

Classic Neanderthal man differs from other fossil men in that the angle of the lower jaw is poorly developed, the part of the malar bone associated with the origin of the largest part of the masseter muscle is small, and the lateral part of the browridge is less sharply demarcated. All these differences may be related, and certainly the association of the small angle and malar suggests that the masseter muscle was small compared to the temporal muscle. Differences of this sort should be described in terms of the variation in the groups being compared. Since similar differences may be found in living men, the development of appropriate quantitative, descriptive methods is merely a matter of time and technique. The procedure is: (1) diagnose the complex; (2) develop methods appropriate to describe variations in it; and (3) try to discover the genetic background of these variations.

So far, we are still engaged in finding the complexes, but even at this level it is possible to make suggestions about fossil men. Probably some Mongoloid groups will have the highest frequency of the big masseter complex, and some of the Negro groups the lowest. This is merely stating some traditional physical anthropology in a somewhat different way by relating statements about the face to those on the lower jaw and relating both to a large and important muscle. It differs from the traditional in the technique of analysis and avoids speculation of the sort which says that the characteristics of the Mongoloid face are due to adaptation to cold.

In this preliminary analysis of the lower jaw, the attempt has been made to divide a single bone into relatively independent systems and to show that the differences make sense in terms of differing adaptations. Eventually, it may be possible to understand the genetic mechanisms involved. If this type of analysis is at all correct, it is theoretically impossible to make any progress in genetic understanding by taking the traditional measurements on the mandible. They are all complex resultants of the interrelation of two or more of the variables. The measurements average the anatomy in such a way that it is as futile to look for the mode of inheritance of the length of the jaw as it is to look for the genes of the cephalic index.

The implications for anthropology of this type of analysis may be made clearer by some comparisons of the skulls of monkeys. If the skulls of adult male and adult female vervets are compared, many differences may be seen. The male skull is larger in all dimensions, particularly those of the face. If, however, an adult female is compared to a juvenile male with the same cranial capacity and the same weight of temporal muscle, all the differences disappear, except that in the size of the canine tooth. What would appear to be a very large number of unrelated differences, if traditional methods were used, are only aspects of one fundamental difference in the size of the face. If a large-faced monkey is compared with a small-faced one, both of the genus *Cercopithecus*, there appear to be many differences. Yet again, if animals of the same cranial capacity and the same temporal muscle size are compared, almost all the measurements are the same. The species difference is in quantity of face, although this appears in many different forms. If these two skulls were fossil men, differing in the same way, and if they were treated by the usual anthropological methods, they would be found to differ in numerous observations, measurements, and indices. Yet one may be transformed into the other by a simple reduction in mass of face, including teeth, bones, muscles. Perhaps many fossils are far less different than we have supposed. The methods used created the number of differences, just as a metrical treatment of these monkeys would make the adults appear very distinct.

The purpose of this paper has been to call attention to the changes which are taking place in physical anthropology. Under the influence of modern genetic theory, the field is changing from the form it assumed in the latter part of the nineteenth century into a part of modern science. The change is essentially one of emphasis. If traditional physical anthropology was 80 per cent measurement and 20 per cent concerned with heredity, process, and anatomy, in the new physical anthropology the proportions may be approximately reversed. I have stressed the impact of genetics on anthropology, but the process need not be all one way. If the form of the human face can be thoroughly analyzed, this will open the way to understanding its development, the interpretation of abnormalities and malocclusion, and may lead to advances in genetics, anatomy, and medicine. Although evolution is fascinating in itself, the understanding of the functional anatomy which may be gained from it is of more than philosophical importance. The kind of systemic anatomy in which bones, muscles, ligaments, etc., are treated separately became obsolete with the publication of the *Origin of Species* in 1859. The anatomy of life, of integrated function, does not know the artificial boundaries which still govern the dissection of a corpse. The new physical anthropology has much to offer to anyone interested in the structure or evolution of man, but this is only a beginning. To build it, we must collaborate with social scientists, geneticists, anatomists, and paleontologists. We need new ideas, new methods, new workers. There is nothing we do today which will not be done better tomorrow.

GENERAL REFERENCES

BRACE, LORING C., and MONTAGU, M. F. ASHLEY. *Man's Evolution: an Introduction to Physical Anthropology*. New York: Macmillan, 1965.

COMAS, JUAN. *Manual of Physical Anthropology*. Springfield, Ill.: Charles C. Thomas, 1960.

HARRISON, R. J., and MONTAGNA, W. *Man*. New York: Appleton-Century-Crofts, 1969.

HOWELLS, W. W. *Mankind in the Making*. Garden City, N.Y.: Doubleday, 1959.

HULSE, F. S. *The Human Species: an Introduction to Physical Anthropology*. New York: Random House, 1964.

MCKERN, SHARON S., and MCKERN, THOMAS W. *Tracking Fossil Man: an Adventure in Human Evolution*. New York: Praeger, 1970.

———. *Human Origins: an Introduction to Physical Anthropology*. Englewood Cliffs, N.J.: Prentice-Hall, Inc., 1969.

PFEIFFER, JOHN E. *The Emergence of Man*. New York: Harper & Row, 1969.

two

HUMAN EVOLUTION

Darwin, in his Origin of Species *(1859), introduced a theory which attempted to explain the development and variation of life forms. It is noteworthy that he did not include man in his first treatise. It was not until later, on the basis of demonstrated similarities of anatomy and physiology, that he decided the same mechanisms which affected animal populations could also be applied to human groups. Man was not a special creation, and his relationship, especially to the rest of the primates, could not be denied. Of course, Darwin's theory of evolution was merely a beginning, a basis for further study. Many of his conclusions were neither understood nor accepted until the science of genetics was established years later. Modern scientists have turned the "theory of evolution" into "evolutionary theory." With the exception of de Camp's brief but highly-readable historical treatment, the following selections illustrate a number of new approaches to that theory.*

Evolution: Still on Trial After 100 Years

L. Sprague de Camp

On October 16, 1968, the Supreme Court of the United States was winding up a case that had begun in 1965 when Susan Epperson, a young, pretty biology teacher from Little Rock, Arkansas, tried to have the Rotenberry Act—Arkansas' "monkey law"—declared unconstitutional. This act forbade teaching in public schools or colleges ". . . the theory or doctrine that mankind ascended or descended from a lower order of animals. . . ."

Eugene Warren, the attorney for the Arkansas teacher, had already asserted that the law was unconstitutionally vague. It did not define "teach." It could mean "to proselyte."

Moreover, continued Warren, Arkansas used a standard biology textbook, Otto & Towle's *Modern Biology,* which recounts the evolution of life and of man. This placed teachers in an anomalous position. Some told pupils: "It is illegal to read this next chapter," knowing that this was the surest way to get the students to study the material. If the law were broadly construed, it would be illegal even to refer pupils to a standard dictionary or encyclopedia, all of which have articles on evolution.

When the State of Arkansas presented its case, the Supreme Court's austere justices saw fit to have a little fun with the young and embarrassed assistant attorney general for Arkansas, Don Langston. Chief Justice Earl Warren asked if a state might outlaw the mention of geometry.

Justice Stewart added: "What if Arkansas would forbid the theory that the world is round?"

Grins and discreet laughter spread around the courtroom. The hearing was over in half an hour.

From Science Digest *67, no. 3 (March 1970): 17–21.*

The Epperson case was the closing battle in a war of ideas, which had raged in the United States for a century. In the 1870s, American Protestant leaders became aware of two disturbing developments. For one, many European scholars were scrutinizing the Bible more closely than ever. They concluded that it was not, as Christians had long assumed, a book dictated by God and therefore to be accepted without question. Some came to believe it to be, instead, an anthology of ancient myths, legends, history, law, philosophy, sermons and poems.

The other development was the spread of Charles Darwin's theory of evolution by natural selection, which included the idea that man had descended from some apelike or monkeylike primate. Men had speculated about evolution at least since the time of Anaximandros of Miletos in the sixth century B.C. In his *Origin of Species* of 1859, Darwin not only presented a mass of evidence proving the evolution of all living things but also advanced a convincing explanation of why evolution took place. His theory of natural selection—the "survival of the fittest"—is Darwinism in the strictest sense.

During the last quarter of the 19th century, the spread of Darwin's doctrine aroused conservative religious leaders to denounce the doctrine and to seek, sometimes successfully, to deprive evolutionist preachers of their pulpits and professors of their classrooms. In 1895, the Niagara Bible Conference issued a statement which demanded a literal belief in the Book of Genesis—Adam, Eve, Serpent and all—and it brought the Bible into head-on collision with Darwinism. In 1907 the millionaire brothers, Lyman and Milton Stewart, founded the Los Angeles Bible Institute and chose a committee to codify the tenets of the faithful. The result was a dozen pamphlets, issued in 1910 as *The Fundamentals* and circulated by the Stewarts' generosity. These publications gave the name of "Fundamentalism" to the growing anti-evolutionary movement.

Also known as the "Adamist" movement, it expanded swiftly after the First World War. Of its many leaders, the most prominent—and in many ways the most attractive—was William Jennings Bryan (1860–1925): lawyer, politician, orator, Sunday-school teacher, lecturer, editor, anti-liquor crusader, thrice-defeated candidate for President, one-time Secretary of State and prominent Presbyterian layman.

Not unintelligent, Bryan, however, was wholly superficial, with unshakable faith in slogans as solutions to problems and unable to grasp any idea that conflicted with his preconceived opinions.

Then in 1925, the farmer-legislator John Washington Butler introduced into Tennessee's House of Representatives an anti-evolutionary bill, which passed both houses with little discussion and was signed by the governor on March 21. On April 4, the Chattanooga *Daily Times* announced that the American Civil Liberties Union (ACLU) would finance a case to test the constitutionality of the Butler Act.

Next day, an argument arose in Robinson's Drug Store in the small town of Dayton, in southeastern Tennessee. The disputants were Walter White, superintendent of the Rhea County schools; Sue K. Hicks, a young lawyer; and George W. Rappleyea, a young New Yorker who managed a bankrupt local coal company. Rappleyea, one of the few evolutionists in town, opposed the law; White and Hicks favored it.

Why not, said Rappleyea, have the proposed test case right here? It would put Dayton on the map! He appealed to White: "Well, we will make it a sporting proposition. As it is, the law is not enforced. If you win, it will be enforced. If I win, the law will be repealed."

He soon won over Hicks and White. For a victim they chose their friend John Thomas Scopes, a 24-year-old science teacher in the Dayton High School. Unmarried, modest and popular, Scopes was the obvious candidate. Summoned to the drug store, Scopes was talked into accepting his role. Rappleyea wired the ACLU about his plan. Receiving a favorable reply, he swore out a warrant against Scopes.

The young teacher retained two Tennessean attorneys to defend him. Then Hicks wrote Bryan, offering him a place on the prosecution. When Bryan accepted, Clarence Darrow, America's best-known defense attorney and a noted agnostic, offered his services and those of his friend Dudley Field Malone, a New York divorce lawyer. They were joined by Arthur Garfield Hays, attorney for the ACLU. Several more attorneys volunteered, without pay, for one side or the other.

The trial did indeed put Dayton on the map. Over 100 journalists arrived, including two Britons and the celebrated literary gadfly H. L. Mencken. This agile critic so infuriated the townsfolk by describing them in his dispatches to the Baltimore *Sun* as "gaping primates" and "anthropoid rabble" that he narrowly escapted a coat of tar and feathers.

In blistering heat, the trial began July 10. The Fundamentalist judge, John T. Raulston, tried to run a fair trial, but this proved difficult because of the circus atmosphere and because the judge himself was more than a little bewildered.

The defense had persuaded a dozen scholars and scientists to come to Dayton as expert witnesses for the defense. When, however, the defense proposed to call these witnesses to prove that evolution was a well-established fact and that it did not necessarily conflict with a liberal, allegorical reading of the Bible, the prosecution objected. A day was spent on the question, with eloquent speeches. Then Raulston ruled out the scientific witnesses. Darrow lost his temper and insulted the judge, who cited him for contempt.

On the afternoon of the 20th, fearing for the safety of the picturesquely ugly old courthouse building, Raulston moved the trial out on the courthouse lawn. Then the defense played its trump—Bryan himself was called as a witness. Bryan agreed to testify, and for an hour and a half Darrow grilled him about the Bible and the origins of man and civilization: Did the whale swallow Jonah? Had Joshua stopped the earth from spinning? Where had Cain obtained his wife? Bryan sweated and evaded but was forced to admit ignorance of many subjects on which he had pontificated. Darrow trapped him into conceding that the earth might be millions of years old, not a mere few thousand.

Lastly, how did the Serpent walk before God told it to go on its belly? Did it hop on its tail? The crowd guffawed. Bryan rose, shaking his fist and screaming: "The only purpose of Mr. Darrow here is to slur at the Bible. . . ." Darrow roared back; the excited spectators teetered on the verge of a riot. With a smash of his gavel, Raulston adjourned court.

On the 21st, Raulston expunged the Bryan-Darrow debate from the record and called in the jury, which had been exiled from the courtroom through most of the trial. Darrow hinted that he wanted a guilty verdict, to make possible an appeal. The jury obliged, and Raulston fined Scopes $100.

The hosts dispersed. Five days after the trial, Bryan died quietly in his sleep in Dayton. Scopes became a graduate student at the University of Chicago and eventually a petroleum geologist. He confessed later that he had never actually taught the evolutionary lesson; he had been too busy that day coaching the football team.

The defense appealed to the Supreme Court of Tennessee. On January 15, 1927, this court remanded the case to the lower court and advised the district attorney to drop prosecution saying: "We see nothing to be gained by prolonging the life of this bizarre case." The district attorney complied, leaving the law intact and Scopes unpunished.

The year following the Scopes trial saw a surge of anti-evolutionary activity, with a host of Adamist societies, heated local controversies and the occasional disciplining of an evolutionist teacher. A law similar to the Butler Act was passed in Mississippi. Many states were persuaded to adopt textbooks that tactfully ignored the evolutionary question.

During 1927, however, the Fundamentalist movement began to flag. Its last triumph was the Rotenberry Act in Arkansas, passed by referendum when it failed to get through the legislature. During the following decades, anti-evolutionary sentiment slowly dwindled as millions learned about geological eras and prehistoric life from books, articles and movies.

On November 12, 1968, Justice Fortas delivered the opinion of the Supreme Court in *Epperson* v. *Arkansas*. The majority held that, since the purpose of the Rotenberry Act was to forbid any teaching that gainsaid the Creation myth of Genesis, the act established a religious doctrine, as forbidden by the First and Fourteenth Amendments. Therefore, "The judgment of the Supreme Court of Arkansas is *reversed*." Three justices filed separate but concurring opinions. Justice Black thought the law should have been struck down for vagueness; Justice Harlan objected to some of the peripheral discussion; Justice Stewart thought that the law, by levying criminal penalties on a mere expression of opinion, violated the guaranties of freedom of speech.

So ended the Monkey War. The remaining anti-evolutionary statute, Mississippi's, is unlikely either to be enforced or to be adjudicated. Adamist sentiment remains strong in parts of the country, especially in the South and West. Conservative members of the California State Board of Education, appointed by Governor Reagan, have recently objected to the schools' teaching evolution as a "fact" rather than as a mere "theory." In the present state of knowledge, this is a little like demanding that the roundness of the earth be taught as mere "theory."

The Evolution of Living Systems

Ernst Mayr

The number, kind, and diversity of living systems is overwhelmingly great, and each system, in its particular way, is unique. In the short time available to me, it would be quite futile to try to describe the evolution of viruses and fungi, whales and sequoias, or elephants and hummingbirds. Perhaps we can arrive at valid generalizations by approaching the process in a rather unorthodox way. Living systems evolve in order to meet the challenge of the environment. We can ask, therefore, what *are* the particular demands that organisms have to meet? The speakers preceding me have already focused attention on some of these demands.

The first challenge is to cope with a continuously changing and immensely diversified environment, the resources of which, however, are not inexhaustible. Mutation, the production of genetic variation, is the recognized means of coping with the diversity of the environment in space and time. Let us go back to the beginning of life. A primeval organism in need of a particular complex molecule in the primordial "soup" in which he lived, gained a special advantage by mutating in such a way that, after having exhausted this resource in his environment, he was able to synthesize the needed molecule from simpler molecules that were abundantly available. Simple organisms such as bacteria or viruses, with a new generation every 10 or 20 minutes and with enormous populations consisting of millions and billions of individuals, may well be able to adjust to the diversity and to the changes of the environment by mutation alone. In addition, they have numerous mechanisms of phenotypic adaptation. A capacity for mutation is perhaps the most important evolutionary characteristic of the simplest organisms.

From Proceedings of the National Academy of Sciences *51 (1964): 934–41; reprinted by permission of the author and the publisher.*

More complex organisms, those with much longer generation times, much smaller population size, and particularly with a delicately balanced coadapted genotype, would find it hazardous to rely on mutation to cope with changes in the environment. The chances that the appropriate mutation would occur at the right time so that mutation alone could simply appropriate genetic variability for sudden changes in the environment of such organisms are virtually nil. What, then, is the prerequisite for the development of more complex living systems? It is the ability of different organisms to exchange "genetic information" with each other, the process the geneticist calls recombination, more popularly known as *sex*. The selective advantage of sex is so direct and so great that we can assume it arose at a very early stage in the history of life. Let us illustrate this advantage by a single example. A primitive organism able to synthesize amino acid *A*, but dependent on the primordial soup for amino acid, *B*, and another organism able to synthesize amino acid *B*, but dependent on the primordial soup for amino acid *A*, by genetic recombination would be able to produce offspring with the ability to synthesize both amino acids and thus able to live in an environment deficient in both of them. Genetic recombination can speed up evolutionary change enormously and assist in emancipation from the environment.

Numerous mechanisms evolved in due time to make recombination increasingly precise in every respect. The result was the evolution of elaborately constructed chromosomes; of diploidy through two homologous chromosome sets, one derived from the father, the other from the mother; of an elaborate process of meiosis during which homologous chromosomes exchange pieces so that the chromosomes of father and mother are transmitted to the grandchildren not intact, but as newly reconstituted chromosomes with a novel assortment of genes. These mechanisms regulate genetic recombination among individuals, by far the major source of genotypic variability in higher organisms.

The amount of genetic diversity within a single interbreeding population is regulated by a balance of mechanisms that favor inbreeding and such that favor outbreeding. The extremes, in this respect, are much greater among plants and lower animals than among higher animals. Extreme inbreeding (self-fertilization) and extreme outbreeding (regular hybridization with other species) are rare in higher animals. Outbreeders and inbreeders are drastically different living systems in which numerous adaptations are correlated in a harmonious manner.

The result of sexuality is that ever-new combinations of genes can be tested by the environment in every generation. The enormous power of the process of genetic recombination by sexual reproduction becomes evident if we remember that in sexually reproducing species no two individuals are genetically identical. We must admit, sex is wonderful!

However, even sex has its drawbacks. To make this clear, let me set up for you the model of a universe consisting entirely of genetically different individuals that are *not* organized into species. Any individual may engage in genetic recombination with any other individual in this model. New gene complexes will be built up occasionally, as a result of chance, that have unique adaptive advantages. Yet, because in this particular evolutionary system there is no guarantee that such an exceptional individual will engage in genetic recombination *only* with individuals having a similarly adaptive genotype, it is inevitable that this exceptionally favorable genotype will eventually be destroyed by recombination during reproduction.

How can such a calamity be avoided? There are two possible means, and nature has adopted both. One method is to abandon sexual reproduction. Indeed we find all through the animal kingdom, and even more often among plants, a tendency to give up sexuality temporarily or permanently in order to give a successful genotype the opportunity to replicate itself unchanged, generation after generation, taking advantage of its unique superiority. The history of the organic world makes it clear, however, that such an evolutionary opportunist reaches the end of his rope sooner or later. Any sudden change of the environment will convert his genetic advantage into a handicap and, not having the ability to generate new genetic variability through recombination, he will inevitably become extinct.

The other solution is the "invention," if I may be pardoned for using this anthropomorphic term, of the biological species. The species is a protective system guaranteeing that only such individuals interbreed and exchange genes as have largely the same genotypes. In this system there is no danger that breakdown of genotypes will result from genetic recombination, because all the genes present in the gene pool of a species have been previously tested, through many generations, for their ability to recombine harmoniously. This does not preclude considerable variability within a species. Indeed, all our studies make us realize increasingly how vast is the genetic variability within even comparatively uniform species. Nevertheless, the basic developmental and homeostatic systems are the same, in principle, in all members of a species.

By simply explaining the biological meaning of species, I have deliberately avoided the tedious question of how to define a species. Let me add that the species can fulfill its function of protecting well-integrated, harmonious genotypes only by having some mechanisms (called "isolating mechanisms") by which interbreeding with individuals of other species is prevented.

In our design of a perfect living system, we have now arrived at a system that can cope with the diversity of its environment and that has the means to protect its coadapted, harmonious genotype. As described, this well-balanced system seems so conservative as to offer no opportunity for the origin of additional new systems. This conclusion, if true, would bring us into a real conflict with the evolutionary history of the world. The paleontologists tell us that the number of species has increased steadily during geological time and that the multiplication of species, in order to compensate for the extinction of species, must occur at a prodigious rate. If the species is as well-balanced, well-protected, and as delicate as we have described it, how can one species be divided into two? This serious problem stumped Darwin completely, and evolutionists have argued about it for more than one hundred years.

Eventually it was shown that there are two possible solutions, or perhaps I should say two normally occurring solutions. The first mode occurs very frequently in plants, but is rare in the animal kingdom. It consists in the doubling of the chromosome set so that the new individual is no longer a diploid with two sets of homologous chromosomes, but, let us say, a tetraploid with four sets of chromosomes, or if the process continues, a higher polyploid with an even higher chromosome number. The production of a polyploid constitutes instantaneous speciation; it produces in a single step an incompatibility between the parental and the daughter species.

The other mode of speciation is simplicity itself. Up to now, we have spoken of the species as something rigid, uniform, and monolithic. Actually, natural species, particularly those that are widespread, consist like the human species of numerous local populations and races, all of them differing more or less from each other in their genetic composition. Some of these populations, particularly those at the periphery of the species range, are completely isolated from each other and from the main body of the species. Let us assume that one of these populations is prevented for a long time from exchanging genes with the rest of the species, because the isolating barrier—be it a mountain range, a desert, or a waterway—is impassable. Through the normal processes of mutation, recombination, and selection, the gene pool of the isolated population becomes more and more different from that of the rest of the species, finally reaching a level of distinctness that normally characterizes a different species. This process, called "geographic speciation," is by far the most widespread mode of speciation in the animal kingdom and quite likely the major pathway of speciation also in plants.

Before such an incipient species qualifies as a genuine new species, it must have acquired two properties during its genetic rebuilding. First, it must have acquired isolating mechanisms that prevent it from interbreeding with the parental species when the two again come into contact. Secondly, it must also have changed sufficiently in its demands on the environment, in its niche utilization (as the ecologist would say), so that it can live side by side with mother and sister species without succumbing to competition.

KINDS OF LIVING SYSTEMS

In our discussion of the evolution of living systems, I have concentrated, up to now, on major unit processes or phenomena, such as the role of mutation, of genetic recombination and sex, of the biological species, and of the process of speciation. These processes give us the mechanisms that make diversification of the living world possible, but they do not explain why there should be such an enormous variety of life on earth. There are surely more than three million species of animals and plants living on this earth, perhaps more than five million. What principle permits the coexistence of such a wealth of different kinds? This question troubled Darwin, and he found an answer for it that has stood the test of time. Two species, in order to coexist, must differ in their utilization of the resources of the environment in a way that reduces competition. During speciation there is a strong selective premium on becoming different from pre-existing species by trying out new ecological niches. This experimentation in new adaptations and new specializations is the principal evolutionary significance of the process of speciation. Once in a long while one of these new species finds the door to a whole new adaptive kingdom. Such a species, for instance, was the original ancestor of the most successful of all groups of organisms, the insects, now counting more than a million species. The birds, the bony fishes, the flowering plants, and all other kinds of animals and plants, all originated ultimately from a single ancestral species. Once a species discovers an empty adaptive zone, it can speciate and radiate until this zone is filled by its descendants.

To avoid competition, organisms can diverge in numerous ways. Dr. Hutchinson has already mentioned size. Not only has there been a trend toward large size in evolution, but also other species and genera, often in the same lines, have evolved toward decreased size. Small size is by no means always a primitive trait.

Specialization for a very narrow niche is perhaps the most common evolutionary trend. This is the characteristic approach of the parasites. Literally thousands of parasites are restricted to a single host, indeed restricted to a small part of the body of the host. There are, for instance, three species of mites that live on different parts of the honey bee. Such extreme specialization is rare if not absent in the higher plants, but is characteristic for insects and explains their prodigious rate of speciation. The deep sea, lightless caves, and the interstices between sand grains along the seashore are habitats leading to specialization.

The counterpart of the specialist is the generalist. Individuals of such species have a broad tolerance to all sorts of variations of climate, habitat, and food. It seems difficult to become a successful generalist, but the very few species that can be thus classified are widespread and abundant. Man is the generalist par excellence with his ability to live in all latitudes and altitudes, in deserts and in forest, and to subsist on the pure meat diet of the Eskimos or on an almost pure vegetable diet. There are indications that generalists have unusually diversified gene pools and, as a result, produce rather high numbers of inferior genotypes by genetic recombination. Widespread and successful species of Drosophila seem to have more lethals than rare or restricted species. It is not certain that this observation can be applied to man, but this much is certain, that populations of man display much genetic variation. In man we do not have the sharply contrasting types ("morphs") that occur in many polymorphic populations of animals and plants. Instead we find rather complete intergradation of mental, artistic, manual, and physical capacities (and their absence). Yet, whether continuous or discontinuous, genetic variation has long been recognized as a useful device by which a species can broaden its tolerance and enlarge its niche. That the same is true for man is frequently forgotten. Our educators, for instance, have tended far too long to ignore man's diversity and have tried to force identical educational schedules on highly diverse talents. Only within recent years have we begun to realize that equal opportunity calls for differences in education. Genetically different individuals do not have equal opportunities unless the environment is diversified.

Every increase in the diversity of the environment during the history of the world has resulted in a veritable burst of speciation. This is particularly easily demonstrated for changes in the biotic environment. The rise of the vertebrates was followed by a spectacular development of trematodes, cestodes, and other vertebrate parasites. The insects, whose history goes back to the Paleozoic nearly 400 million years ago, did not really become a great success until the flowering plants (angiosperms) evolved some 150 million years ago. These plants provided such an abundance of new adaptive zones and niches that the insects entered a truly explosive stage in their evolution. By now three quarters of the known species of animals are insects, and their total number (including undiscovered species) is estimated to be as high as two or three million.

PARENTAL CARE

Let me discuss just one additional aspect of the diversity of living systems, care of the offspring. At one extreme we have the oysters that do nothing whatsoever for their offspring. They cast literally millions of eggs and male gametes into the sea, providing the opportunity for the eggs to be fertilized. Some of the fertilized eggs will settle in a favorable place and produce new oysters. The statistical probability that this will happen is small, owing to the adversity of the environment, and although a single full-grown oyster may product more than 100 million eggs per breeding season, it will have on the average only one descendant. That numerous species of marine organisms practice this type of reproduction, many of them enormously abundant and many of them with an evolutionary history going back several hundred million years, indicates that this shotgun method of thrusting offspring into the world is surprisingly successful.

How different is reproduction in species with parental care! This always requires a drastic reduction in the number of offspring, and it usually means greatly enlarged yolk-rich eggs, it means the development of brood pouches, nests, or even internal placentae, and it often means the formation of a pair-bond to secure the participation of the male in the raising of the young. The ultimate development along this line of specialization is unquestionably man, with his enormous prolongation of childhood.

Behavioral characteristics are an important component of parental care, and our treatment of the evolution of living systems would be incomplete if we were to omit reference to behavior and to the central nervous system. The germ plasm of a fertilized egg contains in its DNA a coded genetic program that guides the development of the young organism and its reactions to the environment. However, there are drastic differences among species concerning the precision of the inherited information and the extent to which the individual can benefit from experience. The young in some species appear to be born with a genetic program containing an almost complete set of ready-made, predictable responses to the stimuli of the environment. We say of such an organism that his behavior is unlearned, innate, instinctive, that his behavior program is closed. The other extreme is provided by organisms that have a great capacity to benefit from experience, to learn how to react to the environment, to continue adding "information" to their behavior program, which consequently is an open program.

Let us look a little more closely at open and closed programs and their evolutionary potential. We are all familiar with the famous story of imprinting explored by Konrad Lorenz. Young geese or ducklings just hatched from the egg will adopt as parent any moving object (but preferably one making appropriate noises). If hatched in an incubator, they will follow their human caretaker and not only consider him their parent but consider themselves as belonging to the human species. For instance, upon reaching sexual maturity they may tend to display to and count a human individual rather than another goose. The reason for this seemingly absurd behavior is that the hatching gosling does not have an inborn knowledge of the Gestalt of its parent; all it has is readiness to fill in this Gestalt into its program. Its genetically coded program is open; it provides for a readiness to adopt as parent the first moving object seen after hatching. In nature, of course, this is invariably the parent.

Let us contrast this open program with the completely closed one of another bird, the parasitic cowbird. The mother cowbird, like the European cuckoo, lays her eggs in the nests of various kinds of songbirds such as yellow warblers, vireos, or song sparrows, then to abandon them completely. The young cowbird is raised by its foster parents, and yet, as soon as he is fledged, he seeks other young cowbirds and gathers into large flocks with them. For the rest of his life, he associates with members of his own species. The Gestalt of his own species is firmly imbedded in the genetic program with which the cowbird is endowed from the very beginning. It is—at least in respect to species recognition—a completely closed program. In other respects, much of the behavioral program of the cowbird is open, that is, ready to incorporate experiences by learning. Indeed, there is probably no species of animals, not even among the protozoans, that does not, at least to some extent, derive benefit from learning processes. On the whole, and certainly among the higher vertebrates, there has been a tendency to replace rigidly closed programs by open ones or, as the student of animal behavior would say, to replace rigidly instinctive behavior by learned behavior. This change is not a change in an isolated character. It is part of a whole chain reaction of biological changes. Since man is the culmination of this particular evolutionary trend, we naturally have a special interest in this trend. Capacity for learning can best be utilized if the young is associated with someone from whom to learn, most conveniently his parents. Consequently there is strong selection pressure in favor of extending the period of childhood. And since parents can take care of only a limited number of young, there is selection in favor of reducing the number of offspring. We have here the paradoxical situation that parents with a smaller number of young may nevertheless have a greater number of grandchildren, because mortality among well cared for and well-prepared young may be reduced even more drastically than the birth rate.

The sequence of events I have just outlined describes one of the dominating evolutionary trends in the primates, a trend that reaches its extreme in man. A broad capacity for learning is an indispensable prerequisite for the development of culture, of ethics, of religion. But the oyster proves that there are avenues to biological success other than parental care and the ability to learn.

One final point: how can we explain the harmony of living systems? Attributes of an organism are not independent variables but interdependent components of a single system. Large brain size, the ability to learn, long childhood, and many other attributes of man, all belong together; they are parts of a single harmoniously functioning system. And so it is with all animals and plants. The modern population geneticist stresses the same point. The genes of a gene pool have been brought together for harmonious cooperation, they are coadapted. This harmony and perfection of nature (to which the Greeks referred in the word *Cosmos*) has impressed philosophers from the very beginning. Yet there seems to be an unresolved conflict between this harmony of nature and the apparent randomness of evolutionary processes, beginning with mutation and comprising also much of reproduction and mortality. Opponents of the Darwinian theory of evolution have claimed that the conflict between the harmony of nature and the apparent haphazardness of evolutionary processes could *not* be resolved.

The evolutionist, however, points out that this objection is valid only if evolution is a one-step process. In reality, every evolutionary change involves two steps. The first is the production of new genetic diversity through mutation, recombination, and related processes. On this level randomness is indeed predominant. The second step, however—selection of those individuals that are to make up the breeding population of the next generation—is largely determined by genetically controlled adaptive properties. This is what natural selection means; only that which maintains or increases the harmony of the system will be selected.

The concept of natural selection, the heart of the evolutionary theory, is still widely misunderstood. Natural selection says no more and no less than that certain genotypes have a greater than average statistical chance to survive and reproduce under given conditions. Two aspects of this concept need emphasis. The first is that selection is not a theory but a straightforward fact. Thousands of experiments have proved that the probability that an individual will survive and reproduce is not a matter of accident, but a consequence of its genetic endowment. The second point is that selective superiority gives only a statistical advantage. It increases the probability of survival and reproduction, other things being equal.

Natural selection is measured in terms of the contribution a genotype makes to the genetic composition of the next generation. Reproductive success of a wild organism is controlled by the sum of the adaptive properties possessed by the individual, including his resistance to weather, his ability to escape enemies, and to find food. General superiority in these and other properties permits an individual to reach the age of reproduction.

In civilized man these two components of selective value, adaptive superiority and reproductive success, no longer coincide. The individuals with above average genetic endowment do not necessarily make an above average contribution to the gene pool of the next generation. Indeed the shiftless, improvident individual who has a child every year is sure to add more genes to the gene pool of the next generation than those who carefully plan the size of their families. Natural selection has no answer to this predicament. The separation in the modern human society of mere reproductive success from genuine adaptedness poses an extremely serious problem for man's future.

In this brief discussion of the evolution of living systems, I have been unable to do more than outline basic problems. We are beginning to understand the role of mutation, of genetic recombination, and of natural selection. The comparative study of the overwhelming multitude of diverse living systems has only begun. Because much of our environment consists of living systems, their study is of great importance. Indeed it is a prerequisite for understanding ourselves, since man also is a living thing.

Evolution, Genetics, and Anthropology

A. E. Mourant

THE BEGINNINGS OF ANTHROPOLOGY

The ability to distinguish members of other species from those of one's own is, throughout most of the animal kingdom, a vital necessity for purposes of reproduction. The power of distinguishing members of other races or communities within the species is much less widespread, and seems to be most fully developed, apart from man, in that other great social and warlike group, the Hymenoptera. Somewhat ironically, we find that among the bees the basis of distinction, and of violent adverse discrimination, is not an inherited

From Journal of the Royal Anthropological Institute *91, part 2 (1961); reprinted by permission of the author and Journal of the Royal Anthropological Institute of Great Britain and Ireland.*

or in any way permanent set of characteristics, but the ephemeral flower perfume shared at any one time by the occupants of a given hive.

Among the primates we know little of any recognition or discrimination below the species level, but we can be certain that recognition of alien species as such has always existed, and that from the beginning human beings were aware of differences between themselves and the other primates. They did not, however, necessarily become aware immediately of the differences arising between human communities as one race diverged from another, for, as with most other animal species, spatial or ecological separation was undoubtedly necessary before physical differentiation could become established. Certainly, however, from the beginning of history as recorded in writing and pictures, we find descriptions and representations of those features, both of body and dress, which characterize different races and nations, at first usually in the form of records of conquered peoples, upon monuments of victory set up by their conquerors.

For thousands of years, however, the criteria used for describing, and distinguishing between, human populations lacked precision, and little attempt was made to distinguish between inherited and acquired characteristics. Only in the last two centuries do we find any attempt at precise descriptions of racial characteristics. The science of physical anthropology can, it is true, in one sense, be traced back to the Renaissance, for it has its roots in the precise anatomical representations and descriptions of Vesalius. He, however, was not, as far as we know, interested in differentiating races, but was concerned, rather, in establishing those anatomical characteristics which all or nearly all human beings have in common.

At about the time of the Renaissance, too, the period of the great explorations began, during which most of the surface of the earth became known to, and much of it was conquered by, the peoples of Europe. Thus Europeans, within a relatively short space of time, became aware of the existence of a much greater range of human types, and incidentally of human cultures, than had ever been known to them before. Indeed, in the previous thousand years almost their only new contacts had been with invading armies from Asia.

An important step in the direction of precise differentiation of human individuals and populations was taken by Camper (1782), when he introduced the measurement of the "facial angle." With Blumenbach (1795) we are suddenly in the presence of a fully scientific investigator who, if it were possible for him to be present, would surely feel at home in a modern gathering of physical anthropologists. He proposed a classification of mankind, regarded as a single biological species, into five principal varieties, Caucasian, Mongolian, Ethiopian, American, and Malay, of which he gave qualitative but nevertheless precise anatomical specifications. He stressed, however, the variation which occurred within each variety. Cuvier (1854) reduced the varieties to the three, Caucasian, Mongolian, and Negro, which have since remained traditional.

In 1842 came one of the most important advances in the methods of anthropology, the introduction by Retzius of the concept of the "cranial index," expressing the breadth of the skull as a percentage of its length. This technical device, important in itself, became a sort of nucleus around which crystallized most of the observations made in physical anthropology during the subsequent hundred years.

EVOLUTION, NATURAL SELECTION, AND HEREDITY

In the whole of biological science, however, the middle years of the 19th century were a time not only of great advances in knowledge but of fundamental changes in views, affecting anthropology perhaps more than any other part of biology. Following the publication by Darwin in 1859 of *The Origin of Species,* he, and Huxley who took the major part in disseminating the new theory, became the unquestioned leaders of the biological world. Among their chief preoccupations were man's origin and his place in nature; in 1862 Huxley published *Man's Place in Nature* and in 1871 Darwin's *Descent of Man* appeared.

These two men, friends and close colleagues though they were, differed considerably in outlook, and this is instanced in particular by their views upon the nature of inheritable variations in living beings in general. These views had a particular bearing upon the nature of interspecific differences and upon the question, perpetually stressed by Huxley, of whether natural selection alone, acting upon a single species, could bring about a separation into two mutually infertile species.

Both men were almost certainly completely unaware of the contemporary work of Mendel who showed that, in the cases which he investigated, inheritable differences were finite and discontinuous. Darwin, though of course aware of isolated examples of discontinuous variation, appears, to the end of his life, to have regarded selection as operating essentially upon a continuous series of quantitative variations.

Huxley seems to have been much more actively interested than Darwin in the question of how hereditary variation took place, and more fully conscious of the existing lack of knowledge of these mechanisms, and of the need for further research. In 1861, four years before the publication of Mendel's classical work, he wrote to Sir Joseph Hooker asking "Why does not somebody go to work experimentally, and get at the law of variation for some one species of plant?"—a task upon which Mendel was probably even then at work. It would be possible to point to a number of statements by Huxley which show an intuitive anticipation of modern genetical theory, of which two may be quoted:

> the important fact...that the tendency to vary, in a given organism, may have nothing to do with the external conditions to which the individual organism is exposed, but may depend wholly upon internal conditions. (Huxley, 1869.)

> Hence it is conceivable, and indeed probable, that every part of the adult contains molecules, derived both from the male and from the female parent.... The primitive male and female molecules may...mould the as-

similated nutriment, each according to its own type, into innumerable new molecules. (Huxley, 1878.)

It would, however, be wrong to assume that Huxley anticipated in any complete sense the modern genetical view that the heritable basis of all variation is discontinuous. Certainly in the science of physical anthropology, which Huxley did so much to foster, and which was growing so rapidly at this time, the stress was on the precise measurement of parameters regarded as forming continuous series.

In the hundred years which followed Retzius's introduction of the cranial index, the subject matter of physical anthropology consisted almost exclusively of measurements of the various parts of the body, and observations, with more or less precise measurements, of the color of certain tissues. The total amount of information amassed was prodigious. With the shift of stress from individual to population, and the development of appropriate statistical methods by Pearson, Fisher, and others, the material served to yield a fairly complete classification of mankind, and to throw much light on prehistory.

Throughout the period which we are considering the underlying object of investigators, even if it was not always expressed, was undoubtedly to define separately, and to measure, those features of the bodily constitution which were inherited, as distinct from those acquired during the life of the individual. But in the absence of any adequate theory of the inheritance of these features the channels of information tended in the course of time to become clogged by a vast mass of rather indigestible data.

GENETICS AND NATURAL SELECTION

In 1900 two discoveries were announced which were to have a very great influence on anthropolgy. One of these, and by far the more important, was the rediscovery, independently by De Vries, by Correns, and by Tschermak, of those principles of genetics which had already been described by Mendel in 1865 and which had been not simply forgotten, but completely disregarded by the main body of biologists. The other discovery, at first sight completely unrelated, was that by Landsteiner of the human blood groups.

The essence of the Mendelian revolution was the discovery that the inherited characters, which taken together constitute the differences between individuals, are indeed separated from one another by finite differences. In sexually reproducing species, any given character results from the action of a pair of genes, one inherited from the father and one from the mother or, perhaps more commonly, of several such pairs. When the individual reproduces, a replica of one of each pair of genes is present in each of the reproductive cells and is passed on to each of the offspring. The further discoveries that the genes are located on microscopically visible structures known as chromosomes, and that the latter consist chemically of chains built up from desoxyribonucleic acid molecules, need not concern us at present.

It was not at first obvious that the new genetical theories were relevant to the evolutionary process, to the theory of natural selection, or to anthropology. The characters which were studied in the early days of genetical science appeared to many biologists to be somewhat superficial, and little connected with the great differences which interested taxonomists. In man the few known genetically segregating characters were either relatively insignificant, or pathological. It is therefore not surprising that the statistical approach of the biometricians seemed to mark a much more promising line of advance, both in explaining evolution as a whole and in classifying and explaining the differences between human individuals and populations.

To three genetical statisticians, Fisher and Haldane in Britain, and Sewall Wright in America, is due the credit for the next major development in biological thought, the explanation of natural selection in terms of genetics. The most complete treatment of the subject is found in Fisher's *The Genetical Theory of Natural Selection* (1930) which is one of the most important works on biology to appear since *The Origin of Species*. Following the work done by Huxley in establishing the validity of the theory of natural selection, Fisher took the next logically essential step and showed, in terms of the by then well-established mechanisms of heredity, how selection had operated. In genetical language, Darwin and Huxley studied phenotypes; Fisher, genes and genotypes. Fisher, indeed, showed that the "atomic" nature of heredity was implicit in the work of Darwin: granted that evolution by natural selection took place, he showed that it could happen in no other way.

There could now be no doubt that the external and measurable body characters which provided the data of physical anthropology were genetically determined; Fisher and Gray (1937) in a concise paper brought together all that was known regarding the inheritance of stature in man and interpreted it in terms of genetical theory. The inheritance of these characters, however, did not prove readily amenable to genetical analysis, and has not even now proved to be so. Thus, while the object of physical anthropology was (and is) to isolate the inherited components in the measurements, and to use them for purposes of classification and the tracing of ancestral relationships, the observational methods perforce remained exclusively those of direct measurement, and the methods of statistical analysis to which the measurements were subjected took no cognizance of genetical theory.

The field was now clear, however, for the exploitation, largely fostered by Fisher himself, of blood groups and other genetically relatively simple characters as genetical, and ultimately as anthropological, markers.

Despite Huxley's efforts to give medical students a broad background of biological knowledge, medical research at the time of his death remained divided into a number of very distinct compartments. The highly active field of bacteriology and the investigation of the response of animals and human beings to bacterial infection was scarcely seen to have any connection with the great advances in biology initiated by Darwin and Huxley. It was, however, in the course of work in this field that Landsteiner in 1900 discovered the human blood groups.

BLOOD GROUPS AND ANTHROPOLOGY

While investigating possible reactions between the red corpuscles of the blood, or red cells, of certain persons and the blood serum of others, Landsteiner showed that the red cells of any given person may carry either of two substances known as A and B, or they may carry neither of them. Subsequent work showed that the red cells of some persons carry both substances. These substances, because of the reactions described below, and of other properties subsequently elucidated, are classified biochemically as antigens. Their chemical constitution is now fairly fully known but they could then be characterized only by the use, as reagents, of certain human sera containing proteins known as antibodies, specifically related to the A and B antigens and hence known as anti-A and anti-B. When a serum containing anti-A is added to red cells carrying the A antigen, the latter combines with the antibody and the red cells are thereby caused to agglutinate, or stick in clumps. Similarly anti-B causes cells carrying the B antigen to agglutinate.

From a time soon after their first discovery, the main practical importance of the investigation of the blood groups has always lain in ensuring the compatibility of blood transfusions, millions of which are now given annually throughout the world. This has perforce led to the blood groups being studied in great detail, and they have as a result been shown to possess an interest and importance far transcending their immediate practical application.

It was clear from the beginning that the blood group of an individual was a more or less permanent attribute of his bodily constitution; it must soon have become clear that it was something inborn and in some sense inherited. The first suggestion that the blood groups were determined by Mendelian genes seems to have been made in 1908 by Epstein and Ottenberg, and in 1910 Von Dungern and Hirszfeld clearly showed that the possession of the A or B antigen was a well-defined genetical character, though the precise mode of inheritance was only determined by Bernstein in 1924. Meanwhile, in 1919, Professor and Mrs. Hirszfeld, who had been pioneers in many other aspects of blood-group study, were the first to apply them to anthropology. At the end of the First World War they were working at Salonika, a great crossroads for the movement both of troops and of refugees, and they were able to test the blood of large numbers of persons from many lands and most of the continents. They were thus able to show that, while most populations possessed all the four blood groups, the proportions in which they occurred differed widely from one population to another.

This investigation was of importance not simply as marking the discovery of one particular anthropological character, but as being the first application to anthropology of a totally new method, the study of gene distributions: since there was no necessary distinction between the individuals of one population and of another, the populations themselves became the units of study, and statistical methods, which could still perhaps be regarded as an extra embellishment in classical anthropometric work, became an essential feature of the new type of investigation.

The blood groups have certain other advantages as anthropological characters. They are fixed for life, at the moment of conception, by the genetical constitution of the individual. Also, unlike such features as the size of various parts of the body, they are unaffected by the subsequent history of the individual (apart from very rare cases, amounting to no more than a few per million of the population, who change their apparent blood group as a result of severe malignant disease). Moreover, while the visible characteristics of the body, and especially the color of the skin, have become associated in some quarters with racial prejudice, and allegations of inferiority and superiority, the blood groups have hitherto gathered no such unscientific accretions.

The medical importance of the blood groups, and the intrinsic interest of a new method of studying human populations, rapidly led to the publication of large bodies of blood-group frequency data, and in 1939 Boyd, who had himself performed large numbers of tests, was able to extract from the literature, and to compile and publish in the form of tables, the results of testing about one million individuals.

Until the year 1927 only the blood groups O, A, B, and AB were known. To these we shall now refer as belonging to the ABO system. In that year Landsteiner and Levine announced the discovery of three new blood groups, M, N, and P. The methods which they used, and which are used for the determination of all the blood groups, are technically similar, though the reagents are different, but when their mode of inheritance is examined the blood groups are found to fall into a number of genetical systems, those already named forming the ABO, MN, and P systems, the second of which has since been expanded to form the MNS system. While the groups of the different systems may resemble one another biochemically, those of one system are as distinct and separate from those of another in their inheritance as are, for instance, hair color and head shape. In a given population there may indeed be a preponderance of people with some particular combination of hair color and head shape (each admittedly more complex genetically than the blood groups) but when we study the mode of inheritance within the population, we find that these two types of character are independently inherited. Similarly a particular combination of blood groups of different systems may be common, but again a study of their inheritance will show that those of each system are independently inherited. It ought, however, perhaps to be said that the phenomenon of linkage, which occurs when the genes for two sets of characters are at different places on the same chromosome, may affect the independence of the characters when studied in individual families, but, unless the linkage is extremely close, it will not affect their independence as anthropological markers.

In 1940 the very important Rh or Rhesus blood-group system was added to the three already known, and in the succeeding years a further seven have been discovered which are of anthropological interest, in addition to a number of rare blood groups which have each been found only in a very few individuals or families throughout the world.

OTHER HUMAN GENETICAL CHARACTERS

Until about 1950, the genetical characters known in man nearly all fell into two classes, the rare congenital diseases, of little anthropological interest, and the blood groups. Already a few other genetically determined biochemical characters had been discovered, such as the ability to secrete blood-group substances in the saliva, or to perceive a bitter taste in the simple organic compound, phenylthiocarbamide. Since then, however, the number of known biochemical characters under genetical control has multiplied greatly and many of the systems involved have proved to be of considerable anthropological interest.

Without doubt the most remarkable and instructive example is that of the hemoglobins. Since their population genetics are simpler and more fully worked out than those of the blood groups, we shall consider them somewhat fully, as a possible guide to the situations which may be expected to arise in the study of the much more complex blood groups, and of the other more recently discovered biochemical factors.

By the year 1949 it had long been known that certain Negroes have red blood cells which, when examined on a microscope slide under a cover-slip, do not remain round but become crescentic or sickle shaped. It had also been established for many years that some of these persons suffer from a severe and intractable hemolytic or blood-destructive anemia, and that the condition tends to be familial. In that year Pauling, Itano, Singer, and Wells showed that the cells which tend to form sickle shapes, or sickle-cells, carry an abnormal type of hemoglobin molecule, with a higher positive electrical charge than normal adult hemoglobin, and with a lower solubility in body fluids in the unoxygenated state. In the healthy persons with sickle-cells this type is present together with normal hemoglobin while in the anemic ones it occurs by itself. It gradually became clear that, apart from cases where other abnormal genes complicate the picture, the anemic persons with sickle-cells are homozygous for a gene determining the synthesis of the abnormal sickle-cell hemoglobin, that is to say, they have received such a gene from both parents, while the healthy sicklers, who have a mixture of abnormal and normal hemoglobin, are heterozygous for the same gene, having received an abnormal gene from one parent and a normal one from the other. Since under African conditions virtually all homozygous sicklers die without producing offspring, the frequency of their abnormal gene might be expected to diminish appreciably with every generation. Nevertheless there are numerous tribes in Africa with total frequencies of sicklers, mainly heterozygous, as high as 40 percent. It was a simple matter of genetical calculation to show that, in these tribes, about 4 percent of the babies conceived, and indeed of those born alive, since the condition is not lethal *in utero,* must be homozygous sicklers, almost inevitably destined to an early death. The question therefore arose as to how such high frequencies of sicklers could exist, and presumably persist from generation to generation.

One suggested explanation was that mutation, or spontaneous change from the normal gene responsible for producing normal hemoglobin to the abnormal one causing the production of the sickle-cell variety, was taking place with sufficient frequency to balance the loss of abnormal genes through deaths from anemia. This, however, implied a frequency of change thousands of times higher than for almost any other known case of mutation, and so seemed most unlikely to be the true explanation. The only alternative appeared to be that the abnormal heterozygote, under African conditions, enjoyed a selective advantage, not only over the abnormal homozygote, but also over the normal homozygote. This is a situation well known to geneticists, and is called balanced polymorphism, in which the supply of both genes is replenished from the pool represented by the favored heterozygote, so that the balance between them tends to remain stable from one generation to another. Several workers suggested that the advantage enjoyed by the heterozygotes might be that they were more resistant than normal persons to malaria; that this was so was first clearly demonstrated by Allison (1954) who also showed that the variety of malaria involved was the malignant tertian type. The relative resistance of heterozygotes to malaria was confirmed by Raper (1956) who worked out more fully how this resistance operated. The complete solution of this primarily medical problem took many years to reach, and was achieved only because the clinical investigators had the close collaboration of biochemists, geneticists, and anthropologists. Such a situation is at the moment unique but it may become not infrequent as the conquest of the environmental diseases brings into prominence, and exposes to investigation, the hard and therapeutically intractable residue of the congenital abnormalities.

It should be mentioned that, largely as a result of the attention paid to the sickling problem, several dozen other abnormal hemoglobins are now known, a number of which are sufficiently common in particular regions of the world to serve as valuable anthropological markers. Their frequencies are probably also maintained in a state of balanced polymorphism, but the mechanisms have not been worked out. The chemical constitution of normal adult hemoglobin has now been worked out almost completely, and that of many of the abnormal varieties nearly or quite as fully. The chemical abnormalities consist in the substitution of one amino-acid residue for another in the molecule of this protein. The molecule is composed of two parts (or rather, two pairs of identical parts), and substitution in each part is controlled by a separate set of allelomorphic (or alternative) genes.

HEMOGLOBINS AND NATURAL SELECTION

In the relationship between normal and sickle-cell hemoglobins we have the clearest example yet worked out of natural selection acting upon the human species, but the fact that we are within reach of being able to measure directly the effects of the selective process implies that the frequencies of the genes concerned are labile, and they can scarcely be used as long-term anthropological markers. While, however, high frequencies of the abnormal or sickle-cell hemoglobin gene are liable to rapid change from generation to generation, low frequencies may persist for a very long time, as indicators that a modern population is descended, at least in part, from an ancestral one which possessed it and which was probably exposed to endemic infection with malignant tertian malaria. In most cases this certainly means African ancestry, but the distribution of the sickling condition in southern Asia and Europe as well as in Africa has led Lehmann to suggest that its original center of dispersion lay in southwest Asia. An alternative possibility is that mutation from the normal to the sickle-cell hemoglobin gene has taken place independently in a number of places, the new gene persisting and spreading wherever malignant tertian malaria has been endemic.

We are bound to assume the existence of selective forces favoring the spread of other hemoglobins, especially hemoglobin C in West Africa, and hemoglobin E in southeast Asia; we do not know whether these forces have operated as rapidly as that involving sickle-cell hemoglobin, but the indications are that the gene for hemoglobin E, at any rate, is a fairly stable part of the genetical picture of southeast Asia. The gene or genes for thalassaemia are found in the Mediterranean area as well as parts of Africa and Asia, and among New World populations of Mediterranean and African ancestry. It is not known whether they belong to either of the genetical systems mentioned above, which determine the production of particular abnormal types of hemoglobin, but they cause a disturbance of normal hemoglobin production broadly similar to that produced by the sickle-cell hemoglobin gene, the heterozygotes being clinically almost normal and the homozygotes suffering from a severe hemolytic anemia. Here again it is thought that the heterozygotes have an advantage over normal persons in being more resistant to malaria, but the process is less fully understood than in the case of the sickle-cell condition. Anthropologically, thalassaemia is of similar value in classifying populations to the more specific hemoglobin abnormalities.

GENETICAL CHARACTERS IN ANTHROPOLOGY

Bearing in mind the relatively simple model provided by the hemoglobins we are now in a position to consider more fully and critically the contribution to anthropology which has been made, and that which can in the future be made, by the study of the blood groups and other genetically simple biochemical characters.

All the 11 major blood-group systems have contributed to anthropological knowledge, but three of them, the original ABO system of Landsteiner and the MNSs and Rh systems, have made by far the greatest contributions. Because of their earlier discovery, their medical importance, and the ready availability of the testing reagents, far more information is available about the distribution of the ABO groups (Mourant et al., 1958) than of the others (Mourant, 1954). On the basis of blood-group frequencies as a whole the world can be divided into about six major regions differing markedly in frequencies for nearly all systems. Within each region the frequencies of the MNSs and Rh groups show highly characteristic patterns with relatively little fluctuation, whereas those of the ABO groups vary considerably even within comparatively small areas such as Great Britain. The ABO groups appear to have been subject to more intense and rapid differential processes of natural selection than those of the other systems. The comparative constancy of the frequencies of the MNSs and Rh groups may be due to the relative absence of selection, or to balance of selective effects, but the existence of an absolutely higher selection pressure on the ABO groups is in agreement with what we know more directly about the relationship of blood groups to diseases.

The best known example of association between blood groups and disease is that shown by hemolytic disease of the newborn, which is the result of blood-group incompatibility between mother and foetus, most frequently with respect to the Rh system (Levine, Katzin, and Burnham, 1941). Other systems, including the ABO system, are sometimes involved. The problem of natural selection due to this disease is interesting and important but a full discussion of it would lead us too far from our main topic. It has however been shown mathematically (Li, 1953) that it should not lead to the establishment of a balanced polymorphism such as we discussed in the case of the hemoglobins. Apart from hemolytic disease of the newborn, some half-dozen diseases have been shown to have an association with particular blood groups, groups in all cases belonging to the ABO system; the most marked example is the association between duodenal ulcer and group O. There is, however, no evidence that, in the case of any of the diseases studied, blood-group heterozygotes are relatively favored as are the hemoglobin heterozygotes by malaria. Moreover, none of the diseases proved to have a connection with blood groups has an incidence sufficiently early in life to affect appreciably the blood-group composition of the next generation. On the anthropological side too, it is (fortunately for practical applications) true to say that resemblances between populations known to be related but long separated suggest that ABO frequencies are relatively stable for periods of the order of 2000 years.

It would be unsafe, however, to accept the ABO blood groups, even for periods of under 2000 years, as completely stable population markers. One possible cause of sudden large frequency changes is epidemic disease. If the blood groups show a differential survival among sufferers from any of the diseases responsible for major epidemics, frequencies may perhaps remain stable for periods of centuries and then suffer sudden very large changes as a result of an outbreak of one of these diseases, or of a series of outbreaks. That this is a possibility is suggested by the recent work of Vogel, Pettenkofer, and Helmbold (1960), who have examined the micro-organisms responsible for plague and smallpox for the presence of antigens resembling the blood-group substances. They find an antigen like that of blood-group A in the smallpox virus, and in the plague bacillus an antigen resembling the blood-group substance H which is most abundant in group O cells. Basing their argument upon the hypothesis that an individual will have difficulty in elaborating a protective antibody to an organism antigenically resembling any of his own blood-group substances, they suggest that group-A persons are particularly susceptible to smallpox and group-O persons to plague. They compare the world distribution of the ABO blood groups and of smallpox and plague epidemics: these correspond sufficiently well to suggest the desirability of further investigation of the hypothesis that such epidemics have played a major part in determining blood-group distribution.

While, however, natural selection has almost certainly been the preponderant influence in determining blood-group frequencies in different populations, accidental fluctuations have undoubtedly affected the frequencies found in small isolated communities, and in some cases such accidentally determined frequencies may have become stabilized when, in an improved but still isolated environment, the numbers of a population have undergone a large increase. The extent to which such a process may have affected the blood-group frequencies now found in large population groups is difficult to estimate. For light upon this problem we must look on the one hand to experimental studies of animal population genetics, and on the other to such work as that initiated by Vogel, Pettenkofer, and Helmbold, and to the examination of many more small and intermediate human population groups.

It is tempting to regard the various genetical systems which have been discussed as providing us with a series of probes reaching varying distances into the past, the hemoglobins some hundreds of years, the ABO blood groups one or two thousand years, the Rh and MNSs blood groups and perhaps most of the others several thousand years. If this situation represents the truth, then we are even better provided with information than if all genetical frequencies were highly stable, for then we should have no genetical clues to events taking place within any of the major population groups since conditions became stable.

Empirically, by calling written history to witness, we can show that the temporal hierarchy of genetical systems just suggested does at least in part account for the present genetical constitution of populations. However, until far more is known than at present of the conditions determining the frequencies of the genes we are studying, we must be content to feel our way gradually from one established fact to the next. For instance, though blood-group frequencies, including ABO frequencies, are similar in populations known to be closely related, this may be the result not, as we have tended to suppose, of the absence of selective influences since separation, but of the presence of a number of strong selective forces causing gene frequencies to remain balanced at particular levels, levels determined by some condition, whether wholly external like climate, or cultural like food preferences, which the two populations, though separated, have continued to share. Alternatively, even in the absence of any continuing similarities in the external conditions responsible for natural selection, the frequencies of a particular set of allelomorphic genes may have been maintained at or near particular levels by the stabilizing influence of the gene pool as a whole controlling the operation of natural selection.

In the last 10 years many more biochemical systems under simple genetical control have been found in man. Most conveniently for practical purposes, the majority of them are expressed in some way in the blood, and so they can be investigated by using portions of specimens obtained for blood grouping. The number of known systems of this kind is rapidly increasing. Those who discover them are usually aware immediately of their possible anthropological significance and soon carry out surveys of a number of different populations, between which, as a rule, significant differences in gene frequency are found. Many of the substances involved have known physiological functions: among these are the haptoglobins and the transferrins, classes of plasma proteins involved in different stages of iron metabolism. Genetically determined variations in the control mechanisms of such important vital processes are likely to be subject to intense natural selection, and hence perhaps to be relatively short-term population markers, but the details of the mechanisms of selection are in most cases not yet known.

One system where something is known of the selective mechanism is that involving a genetically determined deficiency of the enzyme glucose-6-phosphate dehydrogenase (sometimes called G6PD). The normal biochemistry of this enzyme has long since been well established, and empirically, though the chain of biochemical events is not entirely clear, a deficiency of it is found to cause a liability to hemolytic or blood-destructive anemia following the consumption of certain drugs or of the common broad bean, *Vicia faba,* leading in the latter case to favism, a condition long familiar in Mediterranean populations. The gene involved is unique, or nearly so, among those known to give rise to human polymorphisms, in being sex-linked, or carried on the female-determining X chromosome. Thus the male, with only one X chromosome, either has the condition fully developed or not at all. Unlike some other sex-linked genes, such as those for hemophilia and color blindness, this one is readily recognizable in female heterozygotes, but there is a quantitative overlap with homozygotes. Thus surveys of gene frequency can be reliably carried out only on males. Rather surprisingly, population studies leave little doubt that this apparently harmful gene is, like those for sickle-cell hemoglobin and for thalassaemia, in some way protective against malaria. It may be that the protected persons are the female heterozygotes.

This large and growing class of known genetical systems with a biochemical expression will thus almost certainly prove to include some with gene frequencies fluctuating readily in response to changes in external conditions, but it may be expected, like the blood-group class, also to include others with gene frequencies stable over very long periods.

GENETICS, ANTHROPOMETRY, AND THE FUTURE OF PHYSICAL ANTHROPOLOGY

It may be that few new blood-group systems remain to be discovered, but biochemical systems are likely to multiply considerably in number in the near future. As all the methods of testing involved become fully applied to anthropological material, then, even if classical anthropometric methods are also fully applied, the amount of information available about the inherited features of any population will become preponderantly serological and biochemical, and remain only in relatively small degree morphological.

This does not mean, however, that it will then be permissible to neglect morphological observation, or to disregard the results of past morphological measurements. There are many weighty reasons for this. For one thing, apart from the results of ABO blood-group tests on a small number of bodies and skeletons, the only means of comparing living populations with those of the past is by means of skeletal measurements. A further reason is that the vast bulk of our existing information about living or recently living populations consists of body measurements. We must continue to make it possible to compare the peoples of the present day, and indeed of the future, with archeological material, and with living populations examined during the past century, but possibly now inextricably intermarried with others. Quite apart from these considerations, it would clearly be wrong for anthropologists to neglect just those characteristics of individuals and populations by which they are identified in everyday life.

But an understanding of the physical nature of man, and his relation to the rest of nature, demands more than a comparison of individuals or populations with one another as they exist at the time when the observations are made. Man has been evolving, however slowly, during recent millennia, and he will continue to evolve in the future. The study of the processes of natural selection and evolution is, therefore, an essential part of the investigation, not only of ancient skeletal material, but of living human populations.

Already, as we have seen, some of the serological and biochemical characters are being studied with regard to the liability of their possessors to suffer from certain diseases. The results of such studies must ultimately be interpretable, at least in part, in terms of natural selection related to features of the environment. Similarly the external characters of the body must have evolved and must, indeed, still be evolving, in response to the nature of the environment. This process of evolution may be slow, and the genetics involved almost inextricably complex, but the major morphological features of the body, being the ultimate results of the selective process, may be expected to show, and have indeed in many cases been found to show, a close relationship to certain features of the environment.

In the almost complete absence of analytical methods related, in the Mendelian sense, to the genetical content of the data, much effort has been devoted, with great effect, toward increasing the efficiency of more empirical methods of statistical analysis, that is to say, analysis in terms of phenotypes. The whole accepted edifice of physical classification of human populations depends, in fact, upon the results of such analysis.

The genetical analysis of the blood groups and biochemical characters has enabled populations to be compared much more effectively than could have been done on the basis of the observed characters (or phenotypes) alone. A knowledge of the genetics involved has also, in some cases, made possible a fairly full analysis of the mechanism by which these characters, through natural selection, become adapted to the environment. A full analysis of the modes of inheritance of the external body characters might be expected to have similar consequences for these characters. However, it is now clear that continuously varying characters such as skin color and stature are each under the control of a large number of genes, known as polygenes. Generalized methods of analysis of observations on such characters have been devised by Darlington and Mather (1949), but a full analysis in terms of individual genes is not at present in sight.

In view of the greatly increased discriminatory power which genetically based methods would almost certainly confer, much further effort is needed, but few geneticists appear to be aware of the need, and very few indeed have contributed at all substantially to the subject. In the case of stature, Fisher and Gray, as we have seen, many years ago extracted virtually all possible genetical information from the data then available; since then Tanner and Healy (Tanner, 1954; Tanner and Healy, 1956) have extended such analysis to some more recent data, but no other work of importance has been done. In the case of skin color, however, a considerable amount of work has been done recently, especially by G. A. Harrison (Harrison, 1957; Harrison and Owen, 1956–57) with promising results.

I believe that a more fundamental genetical analysis of mammalian and human morphological characters is possible than has so far been achieved, and I would commend this difficult problem to any younger geneticists who may hear or read this lecture. Such an analysis would, I hope, lead in time to much more efficient methods of dealing with the raw data of morphological anthropology. Hitherto the data themselves have proved intractable genetically: not only this, but also their sheer volume, even that of the reliable and well-standardized data alone, has discouraged any attempt at a systematic comprehensive analysis. If only methods for their analysis could be devised which were genetically sound, statistically efficient, and practically convenient, then the modern availability of electronic calculators, capable of dealing both with the complexity of the genetical situation and with the vast extent of the data, would, I predict, release from the treasure houses of the past an abounding harvest of priceless information.

Such developments are, however, not to be expected immediately, and we must now consider further the relation between the two main methods of human classification available at the present time. When blood-group observations began to be applied to anthropology there was a tendency on both sides to place emphasis on the discrepancies between the results of the new methods and those of classical anthropometry, and to claim that one method or the other was the more reliable. It is indeed not surprising that a classification based on a single genetical system, that of the ABO blood groups, failed to agree at all fully with one based on morphological characters representing the integrated effects of scores, if not hundreds, of sets of allelomorphic genes. Few physical anthropologists would now deny the classificatory value of the blood groups and biochemical characters, and most serologists and geneticists who apply their results to anthropology appreciate the importance of the morphological characters, despite the lack of any means of analyzing them genetically. The time is past, however, if it ever existed, for the two classes of information to be contrasted to the detriment of either. Morphological observations have now as great a value as they ever possessed, but they can be supplemented by information derived from a rapidly growing range of serological and biochemical investigations. Those who have attempted fully to use both methods, such as Beckman (1959) in Sweden, have found not only that there is a high degree of agreement between the classifications of populations based on the two methods, but that the most complete picture of hereditary connections between populations can be obtained only by combining all the available information of both kinds.

To Huxley more perhaps than to any other man we owe the existence, at the present time, of a fully scientific discipline of biology as a whole. To the scientific status of anthropology too, in particular, he made a very great contribution, but he did not live to see it achieve the objectiveness of, for instance, the remainder of zoology. Even at the present time anthropology still suffers both from a pseudoscientific racialism which lingers in a few quarters, and from a failure to use to the full all the methods of investigation which are now available. Only by calling upon the full resources of paleontology, anatomy, physiology, biochemistry, genetics, ecology, and psychology, that is to say, on the whole available power of biological analysis, will irrational prejudices be overthrown and a science of physical anthropology arise which is both fully objective, and adequate in its compass and its achievement to the great subject of its investigations.

REFERENCES

ALLISON, A. C. 1954. Protection offered by sickle-cell trait against subtertian malarial infection. *British Med. J.:* 290–94.

BECKMAN, L. 1959. A contribution to the physical anthropology and population genetics of Sweden. Doctorate thesis, Lund. (*Hereditas,* vol. 45.)

BERNSTEIN, F. 1924. Ergebnisse einer biostatistischen zusammenfassenden Betrachtung über die erbliche Blutstrukturen des Menschen. *Wochshr.* (Klin) 3: 1495–97.

BLUMENBACH, J. F. 1795. *Generis humani varietate nativa,* ed. tertia, Göttingen. (See *The anthropological treatises of Johann Friedrich Blumenbach,* trans. and ed. Thomas Bendyshe. London, 1865.)

BOYD, W. C. 1939. Blood groups. *Tabul. Biol.,* (Hague) 17: 113–240.

CAMPER, P. *1782. *Natuurkundige Verhandelingen.* Amsterdam.

CORRENS, C. 1900. G. Mendels Regel über das Verhalten der Nachkommenschaft der Rassenbastarde. *Ber. Deutsch. Bot. Ges.* 18: 232–39.

CUVIER, G. 1854. *The animal kingdom,* trans. W. B. Carpenter and J. O. Westwood. New ed. London.

DARLINGTON, C. D., and MATHER, K. 1949. The elements of genetics. London.

* This is the earliest work of Camper available in London, but the concept of the "facial angle" may have been introduced in one of his earlier works.

Darwin, C. R. 1859. *On the origin of species by means of natural selection, or the preservation of favoured races in the struggle for life*. London.

———. 1871. *The descent of man, and selection in relation to sex*. 2 vols. London.

Dungern, E. von, and Hirszfeld, L. 1910. Ueber Vererbung gruppenspeziflscher Strukturen des Blutes. *Zeitschr. Immun. Forsch.* 6: 284–92.

Epstein, A. A., and Ottenberg, R. 1908. Simple method of performing serum reactions. *Proc. N. Y. Path. Soc.* 8: 117–23.

Fisher, R. A. 1930. *The genetical theory of natural selection*. Oxford.

Fisher, R. A., and Gray, H. 1937. Inheritance in man: Boas's data studied by the method of analysis of variance. *Ann. Eugen.* (London) 8: 74–93.

Harris, H. 1959. *Human biochemical genetics*. Cambridge.

Harrison, G. A. 1957. The measurement and inheritance of skin colour in man. *Eugen. Rev.* 49: 73–76.

———, and Owen, J. J. T. 1956–57. The application of spectrophotometry to the study of skin colour inheritance. *Acta Genet.* 6: 481–84.

Hirszfeld, L., and Hirszfeld, Hanna. 1919. Serological differences between the blood of different races. The result of researches on the Macedonian front. *Lancet* 2: 675–79.

Huxley, T. H. 1862. *Evidence as to man's place in nature*. London.

———. 1869. The genealogy of animals. Rev. of Natürliche Schöpfungs Geschichte in *The Academy,* 1869. (Reprinted in Collected Essays, vol. 2.)

———. 1878. Evolution in biology. *Encycl. Britannica,* 9th ed., vol. 8. (Reprinted in Collected Essays, vol. 2.)

Landsteiner, K. 1900. Zur Kenntnis der antifermentativen, lytischen und agglutinierenden Wirkungen des Blutserums und der Lymphe. Zentralbl. Bakt., 27: 357–62.

———, and Levine, P. 1927*a*. A new agglutinable factor differentiating individual human bloods. *Proc. Soc. Exp. Biol.* 24: 600–602.

———. 1927*b*. Further observations on individual differences of human blood. *Proc. Soc. Exp. Biol.* 24: 941–42.

Landsteiner K., and Wiener, A. S. 1940. An agglutinable factor in human blood recognized by immune sera for rhesus blood. *Proc. Soc. Exp. Biol.* 43: 223.

Levine, P.; Katzin, E. M.; and Burnham, L. 1941. Isoimmunization in pregnancy, its possible bearing on etiology of erythroblastosis fetalis. *Journ. Amer. Med. Assoc.* 116: 825–27.

Li, C. C. 1953. Is Rh facing a crossroad? A critique of the compensation effect. *Amer. Nat.* 87: 257–61.

Mendel, G. 1865. Versuche über Pflanzen-Hybriden. *Verh. Naturf. Ver.* (Brünn) 4: 3–47. (Publ. 1866.)

Mourant, A. E. 1954. The distribution of the human blood groups. Oxford.

———; Kopeć, Ada C.; and Domaniewska-Sobczak, Kazimiera. 1958. *The ABO blood groups: Comprehensive tables and maps of world distribution.* Oxford.

Pauling, L.; Itano, H. A.; Singer, S. J.; and Wells, I. C. 1949. Sickle-cell anemia, a molecular disease. *Science* 110: 543–48.

RAPER, A. B. 1956. Sickling in relation to morbidity from malaria and other diseases. *British Med. Journ.* 1: 965–66.

RETZIUS, G. 1842. *Uber die Schädelformen der Nordbewohner.* Stockholm.

TANNER, J. M. 1954. Lack of sex linkage and dominance in genes controlling human stature. *Proc. 9th Int. Congr. Genet.,* pp. 933–34.

———, and HEALY, M. J. R. 1956. The genetics of human morphological characters. *Adv. Sci.,* (London) 13: 192–94.

TSCHERMAK, E. 1900. Uber künstliche Kreuzung bei *Pisum sativum. Ber. Deutsch. Bot. Ges.* 18: 158–68.

VOGEL, F.; PETTENKOFER, H. J.; and HELMBOLD, W. 1960. Über die Populationsgenetik der ABO-Blutgruppen. *Acta Genet. Statist. Med.* 10: 267–94.

VRIES, H. DE. 1900. Sur la loi de disjonction des hybrides. *C. R. Acad. Sci.* (Paris) 130: 845–47.

Five Steps to Man

John Napier

The naming and classification of any new human or near-human fossil is bound to promote controversy, particularly when a transitional form is involved. Officially, taxomic designations must be derived solely from the physical characteristics of those parts of the fossil that have been recovered; this precludes the introduction of certain accessory evidence, such as that of ecology and culture, which in forms transitional between the non-human and human grades is particularly crucial.

A number of other factors which provide a ready source of disagreement must also be taken into account. Firstly, fossils are representatives of populations, and populations are the units of evolution. Early human material tends to be fragmentary and therefore, in practice, the diagnosis of a new population is usually based on parts of a few individuals. Within the population there undoubtedly will have been considerable individual variation and, when only one or two individuals are known, there is, of course, no means of

From Discovery *(now incorporated in* Science Journal), *Vol. 25, (1964): 34–36; reprinted by permission of the author and publisher.*

telling whether they are typical examples of their kind or whether they represent extreme variations. Secondly, at a time of rapid evolutionary diversification, some of these variations may well overlap those of a separate population, even one which lived at the same time. *Homo habilis* appears to have occupied broadly the same niche in time and space as the near-men known to us as the Australopithecines, and because of the close ancestral relationship of the hominine and australopithecine groups (*see* Figure 1) the two forms share many physical characteristics. It would seem, however, that they differed radically in their way of life. These considerations combine to make the naming and classification of *Homo habilis* somewhat contentious.

It is no longer meaningful to think of man's evolution in terms of a series of direct ancestors—a concept which is usually expressed graphically in terms of a 'tree' and which tends to give a false impression of simplicity. Rather it is necessary to appreciate that it was populations, not individuals, that were evolving, that they were widely distributed in space and time, and that from them there emerged a population which represented a new grade of evolution. This new grade, if distinct enough, will eventually result in a new biospecies which, by definition, will be reproductively isolated from all other species. Figure 1 attempts to illustrate this approach; it shows the expanding nature of evolution and the approximate location of known fossils according to their age, and their affinities to other species. Such a scheme does not call for direct linkage between individuals and thus avoids over-indulgence in the idea of "missing links."

The ancestral apes, represented by the Pongines in the diagram, diverged approximately 20 million years ago from the stock that ultimately gave rise to man. From then on within the Hominidae (Hominids or man-like forms) two separate major groups arose: the Australopithecines are an important group of near-men known best from fossils found in South Africa. They are of great significance to the story of human evolution because, as we shall see, they provide us with a very good idea of what the ancestors of *Homo habilis* must have been like. Ultimately the Australopithecines died out leaving no known descendants.

The evidence from Olduvai—where an australopithecine *Zinjanthropus* was discovered by Dr. L. S. B. Leakey in 1959—is that these near-men were living at the same time as *Homo habilis* or true man. This co-existence has been the subject of much concern among anthropologists who have doubted that early man would have permitted another group so similar to himself, to have existed side by side with him. The situation however is entirely comparable to the successful co-existence of pygmies on the one hand, and gorillas and chimpanzees on the other, in certain tracts of the Congo Forest.

The evolution of modern man can be considered in terms of five grades: (1) Early pre-human; (2) Late pre-human; (3) Early human; (4) Late human; and (5) Modern human.

EARLY PRE-HUMAN

As might be expected the first grade of hominine evolution is still largely unknown. The two most likely contenders are, firstly, *Kenyapithecus* from

Fort Ternan in Kenya known from part of the jaw and teeth only; the provisional age of this fossil is about 12 million years. Secondly, *Ramapithecus* from Northern India. Dr. Elwyn Simons of Yale University has recently re-studied the upper jaw of this form and found it to show many hominid-like features. It seems possible that these creatures may be closely related, and together represent the earliest known stage of evolution on the human line.

LATE PRE-HUMAN

This grade is represented by the Australopithecines. They were clearly less like modern man than *Homo habilis,* and although there is some doubt about their dating they were certainly still living one million years ago. Several specimens of the pelvis are known, and they show that these creatures were very close to the human threshold in terms of walking ability. However, Dr. S. L. Washburn of the University of California has recently suggested that the Australopithecines were not capable of walking in the sense that modern man walks, but they may well have been capable of running. Strangely enough, running requires considerably less subtle adaptations of the pelvis than does walking.

Large numbers of Australopithecine remains have been found but so far there is no unequivocal evidence that they made stone tools, an important non-physical characteristic of man. The possibility remains, however, for a number of stone tools been found in the same deposits as australopithecine teeth at the Sterkfontein Extension Site in South Africa. Nevertheless many people hold the view that these tools are not the work of Australopithecines but are likely to have been made by some higher form—probably of the genus *Homo*—that is known to have existed at this time level at nearby Swartkrans. Although Australopithecines probably did not *make stone tools* they may well have *used stones as tools*—a nice distinction, but an important one. The brains of the Australopithecines were quite advanced, and their teeth were man-like in their general form but not in their size; the molars were exceptionally large, a fact which is reflected in the size of the bone buttresses and flanges on their skull and facial skeletons.

The known Australopithecines are too late in time to be ancestral to *Homo habilis* or to modern man (see Fig. 1). They are also too specialized. The use of Australopithecines as 'models' for the late pre-human grade is justified by the belief that the ancestors of the Australopithecines were also ancestors of *Homo habilis*.

EARLY HUMAN

The first importance of *Homo habilis,* the representative of this third grade, is that it appears to have crossed the threshold between human and pre-human grades to become the earliest true man. Potassium-argon dating indicates that he was living in East Africa as early as two million years ago. From the evidence of his fossil foot—which lacks only the back of the heel and toes

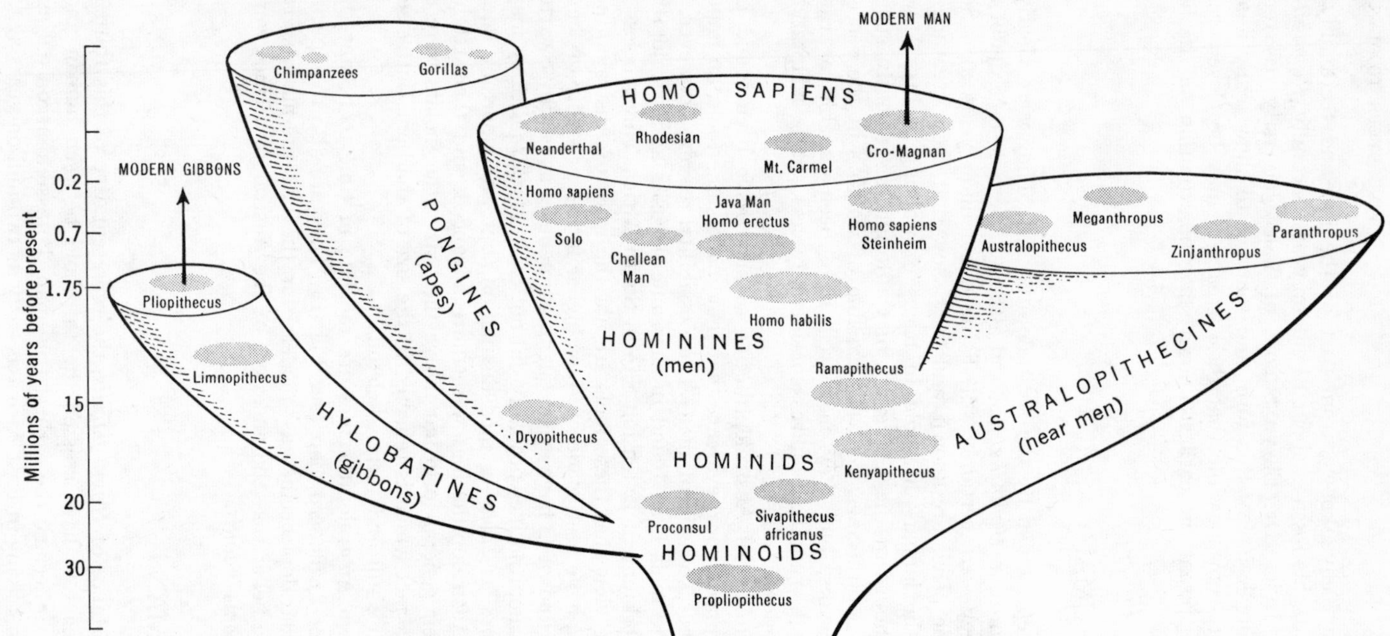

FIGURE 1. *Cone of Hominoid evolution illustrates a more sophisticated way of looking at evolution than by means of an evolutionary 'tree.' It stresses that fassil finds should be regarded as representatives of populations which were widely dispersed in time and space. It also eliminates the need to draw direct ancestral links between the different fossils. Nearness of their characteristics to those of modern man are expressed by their closeness—horizontally and vertically—to line leading to modern populations.*

and is therefore relatively easy to reconstruct—his height can be estimated to have been in the region of four feet. He was not particularly muscular, had fairly large jaws and a brain capacity greater than that of the Australopithecines, but smaller than that of Java Man (*Homo erectus*), and, of course much smaller than that of modern man. In their absolute dimensions and in their relative proportions the teeth are closer to those of modern man than to those of the Australopithecines, which usually have disproportionately large molars. The hands are decidedly not those of an ape, nor are they typically those of a modern man; they are perhaps surprisingly less "advanced" than one might expect from the study of the foot. It appears that *Homo habilis* was not capable of opposing thumb and forefinger in the characteristic precision, or pen-holding, grip of modern man, due principally, I believe, to a relatively short thumb. The hand, however, does have one notable human characteristic: the tips of the fingers and thumb were broad and stout and surmounted by flat nails. I have suggested that such a hand would be capable of making the stone tools found in Bed I at Olduvai. It seems reasonable to conclude that *Homo habilis* did, in fact, make the stone tools found on the site. The alternative possibility is that they were made by *Zinjanthropus,* the so-called Nutcracker Man, whose remains are found at the same level of the site. *Zinjanthropus* is a primitive member of the australopithecine stock and is therefore much less likely to have been adept as a toolmaker. The idea that the tools could have been made by a third, and yet undiscovered species, is unacceptable on the principle of Occam's razor.

The foot of *Homo habilis* is very close to that of modern man: it has many of his special characteristics, such as a big toe in line with the other toes, and a transverse and longitudinal arch system. However, it has not yet attained the structural perfection and—one is therefore inclined to deduce—the function of the modern foot.

Homo Habilis is known to us from a number of finds comprising parts of seven individuals extending from the bottom of Bed I at Olduvai well up into Bed II, and covering a time span of one million years. On many of these levels are found the remains of mammals, rodents, tortoises, birds and fish—the scavenging and hunting detritus of *Homo habilis*. At the bottom of Bed I were a number of large stones arranged in a semi-circular form, some piled on top of one another. Dr. Leakey and other observers regard these as the remains of a primitive shelter or windbreak.

So far, we know of *Homo habilis* only from Olduvai, but the French discovery in 1692 of part of a skull from Lake Chad in N. Africa may possibly represent another population that should be included in the early human grade.

LATE HUMAN

The fourth grade of human evolution is represented by the Java, Pekin, Ternifine, and possible Heidelberg, men collectively referred to as the species *Homo erectus*. These forms were relatively big brained, with heavy jaws and, as their name implies, were fully erect in posture. The later representatives of the species were moderately advanced toolmakers: Pekin Man constructed the classic choppers of the Choukoutien industry, but Ternifine Man from North Africa and Heidelberg Man from Germany were involved in the hand-axe industry which never spread further east than India. Pekin Man also knew the use of fire.

MODERN HUMAN

By about 250,000 years ago the earliest type of modern man (*Homo sapiens*) had come into being. He is known to us from two fragmentary skulls found at Swanscombe in Kent and Steinheim in Germany. From then on the fossil record becomes more abundant, and relationships correspondingly more complex and controversial. Towards the end of the last glaciation—about 30,000 years ago—there suddenly appeared, possibly from the East, the first representatives of modern man in the form of Cro-Magnon. With the coming of Cro-Magnons no more Neanderthalers are found and the later fossil remains become indistinguishable from those of present day skeletons.

This stratification of human evolution into grades makes it clear that *Homo habilis* represents a major step in the story of human advancement. He bridges the gap between the Australopithecines, which had not required human status, and *Homo erectus* who clearly had. The anatomical facts concerning *Homo habilis* are these:

1. He had a brain with a cranial capacity of 680 cc.
2. He had a skull which in its curvatures is more man-like than that of the Australopithecines.
3. He had a lower jaw, admittedly chinless, which contained teeth that in their relative proportions are more man-like than those of the Australopithecines.
4. He had a hand which, though not 'human' in the modern sense was functionally able and was characterized by flat tips to the fingers and thumb.
5. He had a collar-bone, which was entirely modern in its principle features.
6. He had a foot in which the big toe was arranged as in modern man, and in which the arch system of the modern human foot was present.

In addition to these diagnostic features, there are certain accessory items of evidence that are circumstantial. His fossil remains were associated with "living-floors" on which are found:

(i) Stone tools that are unequivocally artifacts;
(ii) Bones of large mammals which have been cracked open to extract the marrow, and which presumably provide evidence of scavenging;
(iii) Small mammal, reptile and fish remains that suggest a moderate amount of simple hunting;
(iv) Structures of piled stones which can best be explained at present as windbreaks or shelters.

There is thus a forcible argument for regarding *Homo habilis* as having crossed the threshold between the pre-human and human grades. Exactly what his precise relationship was to *Homo erectus* and *Homo sapiens* is still not clear—nor indeed the relationship of these two forms to each. Whatever the final answer—and it is highly unlikely that there ever will be a *final* answer—there is no doubt that the human phase of evolution passed through a number of grades of anatomical and cultural improvement. As far as our present knowledge goes these grades are exemplified by *Homo habilis—Homo erectus—Homo sapiens*.

SUPPLEMENTARY READINGS

DE CAMP, L. SPRAGUE. *The Great Monkey Trial*. New York: Doubleday, 1968.

DOBZHANSKY, T. *Mankind Evolving: the Evolution of the Human Species*. New Haven, Conn.: Yale University Press, 1962.

HOWELL, F. CLARK and BOURLIERE, F., eds. *African Ecology and Human Evolution*. Viking Fund Publications in Anthropology, No. 36, 1963.

HOWELLS, W. W., ed. *Ideas on Human Evolution: Selected Essays 1949–1961*. Cambridge, Mass.: Harvard University Press, 1962. (Reprinted 1967, New York: Atheneum.)

LASKER, G. W., ed. *The Processes of Ongoing Human Evolution*. Detroit: Wayne State University Press, 1960.

MCKERN, SHARON S. and MCKERN, THOMAS W. *Tracking Fossil Man: Adventures in Human Evolution*. New York: Praeger, 1970.

SPUHLER, J. N., ed. *The Evolution of Man's Capacity for Culture*. Detroit: Wayne State University Press, 1959.

three

GEOLOGIC TIME

The direct evidence of the course of human evolution consists of the ancient remains of the bones and teeth of man's ancestors. One of the most important considerations in the interpretation of the significance of any human fossil is its chronological position. No matter how complete or how well-preserved a fossil might be, its value to the study of the developmental history of mankind is limited until it can be placed accurately in time. Smiley's article describes the more important dating techniques and discusses the problems related to their use, while the selection by Oakley demonstrates how such techniques have altered our interpretations of the fossil evidence.

On Understanding Geochronological Time

Terah L. Smiley

INTRODUCTION

Until recently, estimates on the age of the Earth and the length of geochronological time making up the history of this planet have fluctuated between periods of time ranging from thousands of years to those amounting to billions of years. The present-day estimates are given as being in the general magnitude of 5×10^9 (5 billion) years. One can well question how these estimates have been derived, what is their total meaning, and exactly how valid we believe them to be. Also, one may question the value of knowing or the need of having accurate answers to this age problem. These questions, simple in wording and intent, require careful analysis before attempts to give answers can be made.

The topic of *geochronological time,* or geological time as it is sometimes called, under discussion here is in itself something of an enigma. In 1941, Adolph Knoph remarked in a James Arthur Foundation lecture at New York University that if he were ever asked, as a geologist, ". . . . what is the single greatest contribution of the science of geology to modern civilized thought?" the answer could be "the realization of the immense length of time. So vast is the span of time recorded in the history of the Earth, that it is generally distinguished from the more modest kinds of time by being called 'geologic time.' "

Geologic processes have been operating through this 5-billion year history, and biological processes have been in operation at least 3 billion

From Arizona Geological Society Digest *7 (1964): 1–11; reprinted by permission of the author and publisher.*

years. Mountains have been pushed high above the surrounding plains only to be worn back to their base levels through erosion and the eroded materials carried away to be deposited in basins where later mountain-building processes thrust these rocks high above their base levels to form new mountains. Certain ocean bottom levels have been thrust upward until they emerged from the sea and became continental areas, and certain continental areas have sunk beneath the oceans where they were covered with marine sediments only to later be raised once again. Ore bodies have been formed, eroded, or carried away in solution form and these materials used in the reconstitution of new ore bodies. Volcanoes have time and again raised their bombastic voices and coughed up materials from deep inside the earth. When plant and animal life did appear, the biological forms lived and died, and the material from their bodies enriched the ocean bottom ooze and the continental soils from which later forms of life could thrive. The crust of the earth has never been completely quiescent, nor is it today; rather in places it has constantly been raised, lowered, and shifted. If we had had a time-lapse rate camera focused on the Earth since its beginning, we would be able to see and study these processes in dynamic operation, similar to the way cloud formations are now photographed.

Before we can understand such a history, we must examine the basis on which our premises are built, one of the most basic of which is time itself. There is probably no English word as commonly used and as little understood as the word *time*. Interpretations of the word are as varied as the countless people who use it. To a large extent this is probably because it has never been satisfactorily defined for many fields of science and remains mainly as a concept for most of us in spite of all that has been said and written on it. If each of us were to take pencil and paper to write a personal concept of time, the probability would be small that any two of these concepts would be exactly the same. For some reason we generally refuse to come to grips with the problem of a definition and slough off any concern with it by the feeling that the concept is "too immense" or "too complex" to hold our attention in more than a cursory way.

In the theoretical books and articles on time—such as Schlegel's "Time and the physical world," Blum's "Time's arrow and evolution," Reichenbach's "The direction of time," Whitrow's "The natural philosophy of time," and Grunbaum's "Time and entropy"—the major problem involved centers around *entropy* and how the direction of time is affected by "reversible time" when working with isolated particles on the subatomic level.

The trend of modern science dictates that we must set up some common working definition of time. We must have some basis for understanding it at least to a point where we can work with results achieved by research in our own laboratories and by colleagues in other fields who are also concerned with temporal problems. We cannot advance far without this type of cooperative and understanding effort.

I believe that to be effective a definition of time should encompass biological and radioactive matter if it is to be used in such fields as geochronology, geology, and archaeology. The definition I use ignores, having little bearing on our particular problem, the Lorentz transformation equation as illustrated by the clock paradox problem and the time-invariant Clausius process. Also, it assumes that there is some "loss" of usable energy in the universe, and I'll put the word loss in parenthesis, because unless we look upon it as a perfect perpetual-motion machine, the universe has to be moving toward some increased degree of entropy. With these exceptions in mind, I would define time as *the direction and continuance taken by all matter in the universe as it moves toward higher entropy.*

This definition includes all matter ranging in size from submolecular particles to megascopic plant and animal life. The original source of this matter, or particles making up this matter, is a complex study and not our concern in this discussion. Our interest centers around the particles from the moment they became part of this planet. We must not, however, attempt to treat these particles as isolated matter else we come back to the problems bothering the theorists working with the reversible direction of time and with entropy. Using this definition of time, we should have no great difficulty fitting into the total time continuum the life history of the Earth, including the minutia making up this history, such as the dating of rocks formed during certain periods or when certain events occurred.

The geochronological time scale as we know it today is, in brief, the geologic column containing interpreted "dates" on the various divisions of the column that have been derived by applying radioactivity dating and other techniques to particular rock types, and it represents the composite work of many people through the last two centuries.

The geologic column is a descriptive outline of time-rock units, which enables students of the earth sciences to properly categorize and order historical materials in their proper position on a relative time basis. These time-rock units are practical divisions representing sediments deposited in a given area somewhere within the total corresponding time unit. In almost all cases, as will be explained later, identifications of these units are based on the remains of plants and animals that lived in that general area at that time.

In the column, for example, the *Paleozoic Era* refers to "early" life forms, the *Mesozoic Era* refers to "middle" life forms, and the *Cenozoic Era* refers to "recent or late" life forms. So few fossils have been found in pre-Paleozoic or *Precambrian* rocks that, coupled with the external similarities of the rocks, it has been virtually impossible to set up worldwide time-rock units for this vast span of time comprising approximately 85 to 90 percent of the Earth's history. Some fossils have been found, however, in these ancient rock types, such as those studied and described by Tyler and Barghoorn for the Gunflint Formation in southern Ontario that are dated at approximately 2 billion years of age and those described by Glaessener stratigraphically located deep in Precambrian rocks in southern Australia.

Cambrian rocks are distinguished, or characterized, by the first abundant records of fossil life of which trilobites are the most famous. In general, the Cambrian Period rocks contain such a diversity of types that we can be certain of a long period of Precambrian development that has not been reflected in the fossil record; most of the major phyla at least of the invertebrates were already in existence by this time. One might say that perhaps in the life forms the major development in the Cambrian was that of "hard parts" or "bony" material that could be more easily fossilized. The Ordovician Period contains abundant remains of fishlike vertebrates and more highly developed trilobites. The Silurian Period is based on the presence of reef-corals and abundant brachiopods. The Devonian contains numerous remains of fish and primitive land plants. And so the story goes, each *Era, Period,* and *Epoch* having its own characteristic forms. It must be kept in mind that, although each subdivision has its own characteristic forms, these do not represent sudden changes in life forms; rather as the fossil record is studied, described, and as additional material makes it more complete, we can see a continuous sequence of life evolving and diversifying, and finally we subdivide the total history, as based on faunal succession, on a more or less arbitrary basis.

The first written record on fossils, to my knowledge, is that reported by the Greek philosopher Anaximander in the sixth century B.C., who wrote that the peculiar forms of rocklike materials within the rocks in the Nile Valley were actually remains of fish; therefore, at one time these rocks had to have been on the bottom of the sea. Aside from rather sporadic and scanty references written during intervening centuries, it was not until the time of Nicolaus Steno in the A.D. 1600s and Linnaeus in the 1700s that serious consideration was given to fossil remains.

These "early-day" people, such as the Englishman William (Strata) Smith, studied fossil remains primarily in England and France. They learned to recognize particular groups or assemblages of fossils, and they began correlating these fossil assemblages over wider and wider areas. They found that the best material for correlation was the "guide" types, which had a limited time span but were of widespread distribution. In this correlation work, they were aided by generalizations, such as the one first formally presented by Steno in approximately 1669 and called the "Law of Superposition" in which it is stated that in an undisturbed sequence of sedimentary rocks, the youngest strata are on the top.

After considerable study, Conybeare and Phillips described in 1822 the rocks of the Carboniferous Period. They were followed in the 1830s by Sedgwick, Murchison, Lyell, and Alberti who described still other periods.

Prior to the development and use of radioactivity dating methods, numerous theories were advanced by various individuals concerning the age of the Earth and the total span of time for the geologic column. Certain people concerned themselves with measuring the increasing salt content of the oceans, and, extrapolating that data back in time to a period when the oceans were free of salt, they calculated figures on the minimum age of the Earth. Other people worked with the rates of sedimentation of various deposits, then, compiling all the data they could locate on the thickness of *all* deposits, they came forth with minimum ages on the Earth. Still other techniques were applied with so-so results.

No matter what techniques were employed to determine the time span in actual years, the "elastic" geologic column could be stretched or shrunk according to the latest estimates. This was made possible because the major division of the column was and still is, as previously stated, based on fossil life forms found imbedded in the sediments. Paleontologists paid little attention to time in finite years, and it was only when some theorist shrunk the scale to such a ridiculously low figure that even the fossils squirmed did they come forth with personal ideas on "rates" of evolution and other paleontological processes that sometimes needed to be taken with almost as much salt as the salinity of the oceans theories demanded.

Nevertheless, it was the paleontologists who developed the first sound approaches to the problem of finite years for the geologic column, although they did this by a round-about means while studying the origin and development of faunal life forms. These characteristic forms were used to correlate "time" units within the limits set by crustal disturbances and unconformities of varying importance that mark the boundaries of the *Eras*. With more refined taxonomic classification and procedures, they have learned to identify types marking the divisions of lesser importance, such as the *Periods*, the *Epochs*, the *Ages*, and the *Stages*.

Such divisions were, and are, easy to recognize where unconformities and (or) other rock "breaks" occur. In areas where no lithologic breaks are discernible, deep-seated problems arose, and still arise, on whether or not the particular rocks belong to this or that time period. Only a few of these problems have as yet been solved to everyone's satisfaction. The more minutely the uplift of mountains and crustal movements are studied and dated by radioactivity techniques, the more drawn out and complex the tectonic processes become, until at present it seems that these processes are always in operation in some degree in some locality, although certain major events may have occurred in a comparatively short span of years. Thus, crustal movements and unconformities are losing some of their importance as universal boundary markers.

The stratigraphic paleontologist has had to concern himself with problems such as those encountered in working out the biostratigraphy of an area where a particular rock unit is based on the assemblage of fossils. In this usage, time is relative because the major problems center around the relationship of one unit to another.

In February 1896, I believe it was, Henri Bacquerel, while waiting for the skies to clear in order to conduct an X-ray experiment on fluorescing substances in sunlight, left a photographic plate and a piece of uranium salt in a desk drawer. Several days later the sun was shining, and when he went to remove the plate to continue his study, he found it had been exposed to some unknown radiation. This rather fortuitous incident led to new investigations and ultimately into radioactive disintegration, nuclear fusion and fission, and to other such studies. Shortly after this incident, the Curies began their search for sources of radioactivity.

In 1909, John Holy, in his book *Radioactivity in Geology,* discussed radioactivity in rocks and the energy needed for the mountain-building processes. Thus, for the first time the "radioactive" clock gave us our very first technique for measuring in actual years the long expanses of time involved in the Earth's history. Discovery after discovery followed, and by 1931 *The Age of the Earth* was published by the National Research Council. This work was based on the lead-ratio techniques and traced an orderly succession of geologic events back over 2 billion years. With the development of mass spectrometry in the late 1930s still other and more accurate methods were made available. All these depend, however, on the concept of the statistically derived invariant rate of radioactive disintegration. Investigations into better instrumentation and new methods continue to the present time, and refinements are constantly being made in the framework of the history of the Earth.

METHODS

There are today many techniques being used to study the Earth's history and processes that have operated during this history. These various techniques and methods being used give results we can classify into three broad categories. These are:

1. Relative placement methods or those that are concerned with relating particular materials or events to other materials or events to the extent that one is previous to, contemporaneous with, or follows the other. Time cannot be considered here in terms of years or even as a theoretical unit of measurement. In this category are such methods as:

Paleontology (invertebrate and vertebrate)
Stratigraphy
Geomorphology
Palynology
Thermoluminescence
Thephrochronology
Fluorine analysis
Etc.

2. Time placement methods that include those that attempt to place definite dates in terms of calendar years on events or items, but because these methods incorporate within that temporal placement a certain statistical error, the results are given in intervals (or globs) of time rather than in points in time. All the actual age determinations used in the geochronological time scale have been derived by these methods with the exception of that covering the last several thousand years in which tree-ring "dating" can be employed. In this group are such methods as:

Radiocarbon
Potassium-argon
Lead ratio techniques
Rubidium-strontium
Laminations, including glacial and nonglacial varves
Ionium
Etc.

3. Absolute placement methods. In this category are those methods that attempt to place in terms of a single year various materials or events. The only entry in this group is:

Dendrochronology (tree-ring dating)

There is no method known that yields "dates," rather they yield such information as ratios between parent and daughter materials, or they tell us when a certain annual lamination was deposited, or when a particular ring was formed on a particular tree.

Without going into the details on how radioactive techniques such as potassium-argon are carried out, let me say that all these involve laboratory analyses of materials composed of small particles that were part of still older materials during the first part of their stay on this planet, excluding, of course, recently arrived extraterrestrial material such as meteorites and cosmic dust. We do not "date" the particles, rather we derive the elapsed time since their assemblage into a particular type of matter or the elapsed time since they were metamorphosed into their present form. The better our techniques can pinpoint the elapsed time of this assemblage or metamorphosis, the smaller will be the "glob" of time concerning this transformation. This glob represents the period of time during which these materials *could have been* assembled.

It is not possible to walk into the field and simply remove a chunk of rock from an outcrop and take it into the laboratory for dating. In the first place, we cannot take a piece of innocuous material, place it in a magical black box, close the door, twist a few dials, make a few adjustments, then turn on the power and, after lights have flashed, bells have rung, and puffs of white smoke have cleared, read off the age of the object on a dial attached to the box. As magical as some of the laboratory apparatus might seem to be, it can only do tasks which it was designed, constructed, and programmed to do. The results yielded in these analyses are so much analytical gibberish until the data are translated into understandable terms.

Our laboratory methods or techniques are designed to give to us information we can use for age determinations. What do we mean by the term *aging* of rocks and how is this aging accomplished? If you can pardon my loose usage of common expressions and terms, I might say that *aging* is the result of the wear and tear on materials caused by the operation of life processes with the passage of *time*. When the term *aging* is voiced, most of us immediately think of it in terms of "life" and "biological" "life" at that. Without going into the philosophy of life and the causes that brought it about, or bring it about, let me simplify this by stating that in an analogous way, "life" exists on a submolecular or submicroscopic level as well as on the megascopic one. By submolecular or submicroscopic level, I mean the levels on which are the molecules, the atoms, and the subatomic particles that make up the material we see when looking through an optical microscope. These materials constitute all matter in the Universe, and this matter has "life." To be certain, it is not the same life on the biological microscopic or megascopic level, and it is called *molecular* or *atomic* life to differentiate it from the biological type.

As this matter "ages" through time, it undergoes changes in its structure as energy and matter are assimilated and dispensed. Those we normally consider as biological aging processes, similar to our life processes, are on a different level from those processes on subatomic or submolecular levels. Rocks and minerals are comprised of the same type of minute particles as those in our bodies and from which our bodies derive their building materials and their energies. If we could look deeply enough into our own or other biological life, we would see that the same aging processes are in operation within the minute particles making up these biological forms. I should say perhaps, for the sake of accuracy, that our bodies are simultaneously aging on several levels, which are the submolecular, the molecular, and the megascopic levels of assemblages of matter.

Rocks are *born,* that is the particles are assembled into a particular matter, or they are metamorphosed from one type into a new type of matter through external pressures, temperatures, and the disintegration process common to radioactive isotopes. Rocks *age,* because with the passing of time, there are changes brought about in their internal structures because of various "life" processes; and rocks *die,* either through disintegration by mechanical and chemical weathering or metamorphosis into different materials.

Thus, the passage of time brings on changes in the inanimate as well as the animate material. Such common expressions as "the eternal hills" or the "everlasting rocks" may give a connotation of no change, but the various processes in operation do, with the passage of enough time, cause mountains to be worn down; even the particles making up the rocks and mountains are subject to aging and change. Our laboratory methods simply measure some of these changes, mainly radioactive decay, and from these age-determination studies we can go on to calculate *dates* in the Earth's history.

Providing the total time span of the Earth is anywhere near the estimates now being given, we have very little if any definite knowledge of the matter making up this planet during the first half of its stay. Earth scientists now consider this age to be in the general magnitude of 5 billion years; some astronomers are thinking of the age of the Universe as being in the magnitude of 8 to 10 billion years.

Most of our knowledge extends back only through the Cambrian Era, but the aging of materials taken from the oldest rocks thus far located and studied takes us back to a period approximately 3 billion years ago. These materials are undoubtedly reconstituted from earlier materials; thus, all we can say is that this age represents the beginning of the present life cycle of this particular material. As more and more studies are done, there is some possibility that still older rocks will be located, and eventually we may learn something of this earlier part of the Earth's history.

PROBLEMS

The second major division of this portion of the discussion is concerned with *problems* in age determinations, and of these I will only touch on what I consider to be a few highlights. In the Geochronology Laboratories, for example, only a small percentage of the staff's time is devoted to the so-called age determinations. Approximately 75 to 80 percent of our time is concerned with understanding the material being analyzed and interpreting the results yielded by such analyses.

All *dating* is a matter of interpretation no matter whether it is a *date* on a structure in an archaeological site, or the *date* of a glacial recession, or the *date* of a particular rock formation. In my own experience, I believe that interpretation can be strengthened and made more accurate by following three steps, which need not necessarily be undertaken in the order given here. These are: (1) to determine exactly *what is the material* being analyzed for its age, (2) the determination of the complete "life history" of the material being studied, and (3) learn the precise association between the material studied and the phenomenon being "dated."

The physical properties of the material being analyzed must be minutely examined if we are to know what we are studying. The inside rings of a thousand-year old tree will, for example, give a radiocarbon age of 1,000 years, although the tree was a live growing entity when cut for our study.

Not all materials can be so analyzed that we can obtain their age even if they seem to be of the proper type. Of these so-called "datable" materials, some yield such data and some do not. I can best compare this to what would happen if I were to walk out on the University campus and, considering all coeds to be "datable," ask the precise age of each one I met. The answers would fall into three general categories, I believe. Most of them would tell me it was none of my business how old they are. A smaller number would give me some sort of vague reply, such as that they are over 16 (and obviously under 75). Only a very few would give me a straightforward answer. Our "datable" materials are much like this; most of them ignore all that we can do to obtain clear-cut *aging* data, a few specimens give us evasive or vague information, and only a very few yield definite quantitative data.

We need to study the materials to the extent that we rather fully understand what they tell us when we make an analysis. To illustrate this point, let me again use radiocarbon work as an example. Every radiocarbon analysis coming out of the laboratory is as accurate as can be determined by modern science. In other words, every radiocarbon age determination has an extremely high degree of probability of being correct. This does not mean, however, that the application of that age determination in terms of calendar years to an archaeological or geological event can be done with any high degree of accuracy. All that any radiocarbon analysis does is to simply determine the ratio in a given amount of material between the existing nonradioactive carbon 12 and 13, and the radioactive carbon 14 isotopes, and plugging this ratio information into an equation based on the disintegration processes, we calculate the time when the material was a live substance. This ratio may have subsequently been altered or disturbed through either a natural or an artificial cause, and this cannot be determined on the basis of the laboratory analysis alone. We cannot simply assume that all such analyses are valid for the dating of a prehistoric event.

The second major problem is the determination of the complete "life history" of the material being studied. Aside from dendrochronology, all our dating techniques are based on the disintegration of radioactive materials. The analyses of these materials yield results based on the ratio between the amount of parent material still remaining in our sample and the amount of daughter products given off during disintegration. Any disurbance in this ratio leads to an "erroneous" figure as far as the true age relationship is concerned. Recognition of this problem causes us to carefully study field and laboratory conditions to determine whether or not exogenic or endogenic processes may have disturbed the natural ratio. Samples are discarded if there is much doubt that we must have contamination that cannot be overcome or for which we cannot correct.

In radiocarbon work many samples submitted for study are comprised of small bits of charcoal because there is no single piece large enough to analyze by itself. The small bits may represent many individual shrubs, trees, or other types of organic matter that may have had a long life or a short one. What are we dating? It is not *a* piece of homogeneous material, but rather we are obtaining *an average age of all the material making up the total sample*. Some of these materials may be reliable and some may not; we have no way to know exactly how much contamination may be in the sample, thus, the "date" can be erroneous.

We have found in potassium-argon work that we need to study the source locality in detail to determine the field conditions that controlled the geologic structure of the area and the exogenic and endogenic processes that may have had some effect on the sample. These latter would include nearby volcanic activity, long exposure to the atmosphere, hydrothermal conditions, and other such phenomena. We must know, as an added example, if the sample studied is an indigenous part of the parent rock or if it is a bit of residue from an older rock that was carried in during sedimentation. If we understand the complete life history of the sample, this problem will not be of extreme importance when proper steps are taken to counteract such conditions, or it will tell us that we cannot expect reliable results from the laboratory analyses.

In tree-ring dating we know that the tree was a live growing botanical entity at the time when the last seasonal growth was formed. It stands to reason that the use of the tree in the construction of a house or some other architectural or functional feature could not have occurred until after the tree died. The investigator must determine the length of time after such a terminal date before the tree was used in construction. This means that he needs to reconstruct the story of that particular specimen from the time it was a living tree until it was found in the site in question. To do this, he must determine how the tree was used, under what conditions it was used, when it was used, and, unless it is an integral part of a wall or some other architectural feature, how did the specimen come to be where it was found.

The third major problem concerns the precise association between the material studied and the event or item we want dated. Solutions to this problem are based in part on answers derived from the preceding problem concerning the life history of the sample.

We cannot assume that simply because an object or a bit of material has been found in a certain stratum that its history is exactly the same as that for the stratum. We know that certain minerals migrate from the country rock into the particular samples we are studying and that there is cross migration from the sample materials into the country rocks. The entire processes of erosion and sedimentation are concerned with the tearing down of rocks and the transportation of that material into another environment where it is used to create new types of rocks. Under these conditions, we can have older materials being incorporated into younger sediments.

We must also realize that to "date" material from a lava does not, necessarily, date the eruption of a particular volcano. We have to determine the association between the lava, in this case, and the particular volcano—they may or may not be related. In such problems there must be close coordination between the laboratory and fieldwork. Further, the researcher should test several different types of material from the same horizon to learn what has happened in the field in regard to the material being studied. Such analyses may indicate that two seemingly contemporaneous materials were actually not contemporaneous or that two apparently unrelated events might actually be the result of a common event and so on.

Each particle of material studied has its own history, but each particle has never been completely isolated from all other matter. In this same sense, no event in the Earth's history was ever a complete entity in itself; thus, we must study the total chain of related events if we are to understand the one with which we are working. The investigator must assume responsibility for these field observations, and to do this he must be cognizant of the total conditions of the particular temporal problem and its relationship to other events in the history of that specific area. "Sloppy" fieldwork is no more excusable than "sloppy" laboratory work.

The literature on earth sciences contains numerous "dates" on rocks and events. What is meant when such a "date" reads, for example, 2.3×10^9 years? Geochronologists or geologists do not have the same definition for the word date as do physicists, historians, or other scientists. The common dictionary definition of the word date is that it is a point in space-time. We must modify this definition because we cannot be nearly precise enough to pick out *a point* in space-time. As stated earlier, what comes from the various aging methods are "globs" of time during which the material we are studying could have been "born." When geologists speak of an "absolute" date they mean that this is a "date" in terms of calendar years, whereas they had been using dates based on guesswork and estimations or on the relative time relationship of one rock type to another or of one event to another. While they strive for accuracy and precision, they are not using the term "absolute" in its normal dictionary definition.

The "date" of 2.3×10^9 years, then, simply means that the material was assembled into its present form somewhere around 2 billion 300 million years ago. There is the strong tendency to forget the standard deviation that is a part of this "age." Thus, although this is a statistical calculation, we feel that this date is very precise, as far as our present-day instruments go, and its accuracy is somewhere in the proper magnitude.

In tree-ring studies, when the term *date* is used it refers to *the year* in which a particular ring was formed on a particular specimen. When this tree was cut and used to help construct a house, or put to some other use, is a different matter. All we *know* is that it could not have been so used until after the year in which the last ring was formed.

Our love for pigeonholes and our consuming desire to place each piece of data in a labeled box has led us into some false assumptions regarding the use of the units making up the divisions or the column. In probably no single locality can we be absolutely certain that the deposit represents the total time span of a single division of the time scale. All we can do is work one segment and extrapolate from that segment into the others.

Although few believe, I hope, in the catastrophic theory on the periodic extinction of whole groups of animals and plants, as first advanced by the early-day French paleontologist Cuvier, I fear that we try to read into the column such breaks as these even though none exist. Unless we have unconformities marking the boundaries, we become confused in relating materials to one time unit or another.

I want to close here by stating that in discussing these problems I am always reminded of an analogy that has been used many times but is still pertinent. You perhaps recall the scene in Carroll's story of Alice in Wonderland where she is talking to the Mad Hatter about many things, and they finally come around to the topic of time.

The Mad Hatter remarked, "I dare say you never even spoke to Time."

"Perhaps not," Alice cautiously replied, "but I know I have to beat time when I learn music."

"Ah, that accounts for it," said the Mad Hatter. "He won't stand beating. Now if you only kept on good terms with him, he'd do almost anything you like with the clock."

Any investigator working with temporal problems also has to keep on good terms with time because it is capricious and undependable unless mastered to a point where it can serve the purpose that we need for these problems. I am afraid, however, that many of us only think in terms of beating time rather than understanding it and putting it to its proper usage.

Dating the Emergence of Man

Kenneth P. Oakley

The subject of my address begs two questions: (1) What do we mean by man? and (2) What kinds of dating are both available and applicable?

Man is a member of the Mammalian Order *Primates,* which is usually divided into two main Suborders: the Prosimii, including tree shrews, tarsiers, lemurs, and lorises (e.g., bush-babies); and the Anthropoidea, including monkeys, apes, and men. Apes and men are now classified as members of one Superfamily, the Hominoidea, comprising two families, the Pongidae (apes) and Hominidae (men and their immediate antecedents). There are few if any authorities who would agree with equating "Hominidae" with "men," because it is scarcely conceivable that the earliest members of this family could have shown the basic mental attributes of man as generally understood. Ten years ago I ventured to overcome this semantic difficulty by suggesting that whereas the family Hominidae can be defined in accordance with customary zoological practice, as it is distinguished from the Pongidae by their dentition and skeletal adaptation to bipedal gait, only those later Hominidae capable of regular tool-making qualified for inclusion in the category of "man," for this behavior involves in the first instance conceptual thought and then tradition on a scale that is in effect a new kind of inheritance, marking man off from other organisms. This definition of man as the tool-making Primate was at one time criticized on the grounds that it did not fall into line with the established procedures in Systematics;

Presidential address delivered to Section H (Anthropology) on 4 September 1961, at the Norwich Meeting of the British Association. This address was subsequently published in The Advancement of Science *18, no. 75 (1962): 415–26. Reprinted by permission of the author and publisher.*

but it is now being more widely recognized that some behavioral aspects of organisms can be used legitimately in classification, just as tangible characteristics are.

Studies in the evolution of the Primates, and particularly of the Hominoidea, have been much handicapped up to now by our ignorance of the "dating" of their fossil remains. Not only is the placing of these fossils in their correct time sequence (relative dating) important for an understanding of their evolutionary relationships, but assessment of the actual amount of time separating one form from another (chronometric dating) is of equal, perhaps greater, importance. In this address I shall consider the dating of the six main points of emergence in the evolution of the Primates up to modern man:

1. The Primate threshold—the earliest Prosimii
2. The first evident Anthropoidea
3. Diversification of Hominoidea with the emergence of Hominidae
4. The earliest tool-making Hominidae
5. The earliest large-brained Hominidae
6. The earliest men of completely modern type.

The earlist known Primates were small tree-dwelling creatures no bigger than mice, fossil tree shrews, or tupaioids, sometimes described as "insectivores on the Primate threshold." They are known from Paleocene rocks in Europe and North America.

Assessing the antiquity of the earliest Primates in years opens the general question of chronometric dating of the Tertiary periods. Until recently we have depended almost entirely on the invaluable time scale worked out by Professor Arthur Holmes in 1947 on the basis of plotting maximum thicknesses of the sedimentary formations in the various periods in sequence as ordinates against a curve drawn through the few reliable dates in years obtained from uranium lead or uranium helium ratios in igneous rocks of known stratigraphical ages. This geologic time scale was recently revised by Holmes in 1959 in the light of further data, including the results of applying a new method of chronometric dating, the kalium/argon or potassium/argon method. This is based on the fact that all naturally occurring potassium contains .01 percent of a radioactive isotope potassium = 40, which on decay branches into calcium = 40 and argon = 40, and has a halflife of 1.3×10^9 years. It is much more applicable to dating Tertiary rocks than the older radioactivity methods, both on account of its shorter half-life and the fact that potassium is an element occurring in a number of fairly common minerals, both igneous and sedimentary. Estimation of the radiogenic argon from within the potassium-bearing crystals (isolated, and ground up, or in some cases in the pulverized rock as a whole), is made by means of a mass-spectrometer and is a measure of their age in years.

Dr. J. S. Evernden and Dr. G. H. Curtis at the University of California, Berkeley, have obtained a remarkably consistent series of results in applying this method, particularly to glauconite in marine sediments, and to sanidine and biotite in volcanic ashes and tuffs. Their results indicate that we now have a dating tool applicable to the segment of geologic time (the Tertiary and Quaternary eras) which is of greatest interest to the anthropologist.

Remarkably few changes were necessary in Holmes's geologic time scale in the light of all the reliable dates lately obtained by the K/A and older isotopic methods. In certain cases I believe Holmes's original scale is closer to the truth than some of the new isotopic datings might suggest, and this is particularly relevant to the antiquity of the Primates. Thus, Holmes estimated that the base of the Paleocene was at 70 million years; yet several independent age determinations have given results indicating (according to Lawrence Kulp of the Lamont Laboratory, New York), that the base of the Paleocene is at 63 million years and the base of the Lower Eocene at 58 million years. However, it should not be assumed that any of the dated Paleocene rocks are at the *base* of the Paleocene. Indeed one of the most reliably dated Tertiary rocks is uranium ore (pitchblende) of Upper Paleocene age in Colorado, with a calculated age of about 60 million years. In view of the considerable evolutionary progress occurring within the Paleocene and the great geomorphological changes indicated by the widespread Cretaceous/Eocene unconformity, 70 million years is the more acceptable dating of the base of the Paleocene, giving the minimum duration of this period of Prosimian emergence some 10 million years.

Considerable diversification occurred among the evolving prosimians during the Paleocene period, some stocks showing mainly tupaioid characteristics (e.g., the Plesiadapidae), others with more lemuroid features, and the most advanced showing many tarsioid traits.

During Lower Eocene times lemuroids and tarsioids became clearly differentiated (although none corresponded except in broadest outlines and in a few isolated traits with the lemurs and tarsiers living today). Remains of these prosimians have been found in the Blackheath Beds south of London where they were living under tropical conditions somewhat more than 50 million years ago, according to K/A estimates made on glauconite in marine deposits with this stratigraphical position in various parts of the world. Several new K/A dating based on glauconite from British and French deposits in the Eocene are as follows:

	Million years
Middle Eocene	
Lutetian: Fosse, Paris Basin	47
Lower Eocene	
Ypresian: Oldhaven Black heath Beds	57 ± 2
Landenian (Basal): Thanet Sands	58

There is good reason to infer that the Prosimii Anthropoidea threshold had been passed before the end of the Eocene period, some 40 million years ago, but so far the evidence of Eocene higher Primates is incomplete. One might have expected to find cercopithecoid monkeys at the level of emergence of Anthropoidea, but in fact the earliest undoubted fossil higher Primates are pongids in the basal Oligocene beds of the Fayum (e.g., *Apidium*). The fragmentary specimens from the Upper Eocene of Burma and China, claimed by some authorities as representing early Anthropoidea, are possibly better regarded as advanced prosimians, although anthropoid traits do predominate in the Burmese form *Amphipithecus*.

By Miocene times we have evidence that the higher Anthropoidea, counting as Hominoidea, were becoming diversified; indeed some of the pongid stocks showed the emergence of those "tesserae" or elements in the Hominoid "mosaic" which were in time to form part of the genetic pattern characteristic of the Hominidae. Thus, the Dryopithecinae found in the Miocene deposits of Europe, Asia, and Africa are pongids, but they show the molar cusp patterns which W. K. Gregory regarded as the ground plan of hominid molars. The total hominid dental pattern, with sectorial rather than bicuspid first molar and reduced canines, has not yet been found in any Miocene anthropoid.

The East African dryopithecine *Proconsul* occurs in deposits rich in potassic minerals suitable for dating by the K/A method. The deposits on Rusinga Island in Kenya, and those close to the volcano Napak in Uganda also yielding remains of *Proconsul,* have been widely accepted by palaeontologists on the basis of correlation by fossil mammalia (particularly Proboscidea), as Lower Miocene (Burdigalian), the dating of which on the revised geologic time scale is about 25 million years. In fact Burdigalian glauconite from Austria and obsidian from Oregon gave just this figure. However, Dr. Evernden told me recently (June, 1961), that in his opinion the two most reliable dates which he and his co-workers obtained from samples of biotite in the *Proconsul* beds on Rusinga Island were 22 and 15 million years, indicating that much of this important pongid material may be Middle or even Upper Miocene; but these results (unpublished) are still regarded as provisional until a longer series of samples has been run through the "K/A mill."

Proconsul was a generalized monkey-like pongid, a semi-brachiator adapted to life in the gallery forests fringing streams which led down to the lakes in Central Africa during Miocene times. It was not highly specialized, and probably close to the group of hominoids which, through adaptation to life in more open grassy country on the edges of the savannah, evolved into Hominidae. Indeed, it would not be at all unexpected if the latest of the *Proconsul* beds in East Africa, perhaps on the Upper Miocene/Lower Pliocene boundary, eventually yield incipient hominids.

The chronology of the Pliocene period is of critical importance to us because this was probably the period when the Hominidae were becoming differentiated. The much discussed fossil primate *Oreophithecus* is regarded indeed by Dr. J. Johannes Hürzeler as an early hominid, but Dr. P. M. Butler and some others place it in a separate, rather specialized radiation within the Hominoidea. It comes from the lignite of brown coal deposits of Grosseto in Tuscany. These deposits were accumulated in forestfringed lakes during Early Pontian (Vallesian) times. The Pontian stage has now been almost universally classified as Lower Pliocene, although some French palaeontologists still retain it in the Upper Miocene. So far no minerals in the *Oreopithecus* beds have been regarded as datable, but since potassium-bearing clay minerals found in a Late Cretaceous coal seam in Alberta, it is possible that mineralogical researches in the Grosseto coal beds might result in the discovery of datable material, such as authigenic illite.

A potassium-argon determination on biotite from a volcanic tuff stratigraphically on the Miocene/Pliocene boundary in Nevada has given a date of 12 million years. This falls into line with other Pliocene K/A age determinations recently published:

	Million years
Upper Pliocene	
glauconite from marine sandstone, California	5
Middle Pliocene	
glauconite from marine sandstone, Belgium	7
Lower Pliocene	
biotite from tuff, Delmontian, California	11

It is probable that the Hominidae emerged in tropical Africa during Pliocene times when very dry conditions prevailed in many regions which had been well watered during the preceding period. The oldest known unquestionable hominids are, in fact, the relatively small-brained Australopithecinae of Africa, and the larger-brained *Pithecanthropus* of Eastern Asia. Since *Australopithecus* anatomically fills the bill so well as the first stage in hominid emergence, it has seemed reasonable to regard it as antecedent to *Pithecanthropus,* but there has long been doubt as to whether any of the Australopithecinae are in fact older than the earliest pithecanthropines in Java. I see the problem as in essence a reflection of the two conflicting points of view: the traditional one that man originated in Asia, and the modern evolutionists' concept of Africa as the man's centre of origin. The solution of the problem depends largely on determining the absolute ages of the deposits yielding the fossil hominid remains in Africa and Java respectively. So long as this could only be investigated by comparing the associated fossil faunas in the two areas, the problem seemed insoluble, because of the extreme difficulty of correlating in detail by terrestrial mammalia halfway round the world and across several environmental boundaries.

Thus, some palaeontologists have regarded the earliest deposits with hominid remains in Java as Lower Pleistocene, and the earliest East and South African deposits containing fossil Australopithecinae as Middle Pleistocene; while other palaeontologists considered that the relative dating was the other way round. The subperiod in question, the end of the Lower Pleistocene and the beginning of the Middle Pleistocene, might be called the palaeontologists' battlezone. At last we are within sight of resolving this question by means of chronometric dating based on the potassium/argon method.

To appreciate the problems involved, I should recall that the Pleistocene period has generally been divided in Europe and Asia on the basis of the glaciations which affected the higher latitudes, and the broadly equivalent pluvials or wetter periods of the tropics. The beginning of the period has generally been regarded as marked by the commencement of glacial or pluvial conditions, but the definition of the period advocated in 1911 by Emile Haug, as commencing with the spread of three genera of terrestrial Mammalia, *Equus* (one-toed horse), "*Bos*" (ox), and "*Elephas*" (elephant) has now been widely accepted on the basis of the approval of the International Geological Congress of 1948.

This definition of the Pleistocene, of course, involves the inclusion of many deposits which in the older papers and textbooks were classified as Pliocene, for example, the Crags of East Anglia and the Upper Siwalik beds in Pakistan.

The Pliocene/Pleistocene boundary is of crucial importance from the point of view of dating hominid orgins, and, in spite of the adoption of the "Haug Line" in 1948, there is by no means universal agreement among palaeontologists as to where this should be drawn in some parts of the world. On account of this uncertainty it is difficult to make use of some of the K/A datings that relate to it.

The *Villafranchian* stage is now generally accepted as Lower Pleistocene, and in the Old World the appearance and spread of *Equus*, "*Bos*," and "*Elephas*" serve well to mark its base. But in North America the Blanco formation has been regarded by many palaeontologists as equivalent to the Villafranchian, and yet some of the potassium/argon dates on minerals from the Blancan deposits exceed 3 million years. It is, of course, possible that the Blanco is only in part Villafranchian and that much of it is Upper Pliocene. Even so, K/A datings on a number of unquestionably Lower Pleistocene deposits have proved to exceed one million years; for example, biotites in volcanic ashes overlying a very early glacial till of the Sierran Glaciation of California (at Sutter Buttes) have given dates averaging 1.6 million years. It would be far easier to agree on the chronometric dating of the Pliocene/Pleistocene boundary if minerals suitable for K/A determinations were available in the district near Rome, where Italian geologists in 1954 defined the base of the Calabrian, the marine equivalent of the Villafranchian (which in the type areas consists of fresh-water and terrestrial deposits). It is hoped that mineralogists will contribute to solving this problem by identifying authigenic potassic minerals in the Calabrian sediments; for example, illite again may occur.

The enlargement of the estimated duration of the Pleistocene period from little more than half a million years to over two million years is certainly in agreement with several independent indications. The widely used figure of rather more than half a million years was no more than a rough estimate for the duration of the main glacial Pleistocene (beginning with the Günz glaciation in the Alps), and received astronomical sanction through the widespread belief in the Milankovitch theory of the causes of glacial flutuation. However, as soon as the Pleistocene was defined to include the Villafranchian stage, all estimates of duration of this period, based on the assumption that it began with the Günz glaciation, were very wide of the mark. Thus, the thicknesses of sediments in the Java Geosyncline alone suggest that the Villafranchian stage was at least as long as the whole of the Post-Villafranchian (now counted by most palaeontologists as beginning with the Cromerian stage, or Günz-Mindel interglacial).

I must say that when one stands on the 600-foot marine platform, which bevels the Chiltern Hills and the North Downs, and carries deposits now classified as Villafranchian, the idea of this feature having been formed two to three million years ago seems closer to reality than the suggestion that such a considerable change in geomorphology has occurred in little more than half a million years.

I believe that spectacular results from new techniques, such as the potassium/argon method, sometimes lead us to lose sight of the wisdom of inferences drawn by earlier workers. For instance, the German geographer Ludwig Pilgrim had already estimated in 1904 on the basis of erosion, that the duration of the Quaternary period had been 1.62 million years, of which 1.29 had been dominated by glaciations.

Our new realization that the amount of time represented by the Lower Pleistocene is probably nearer two million years than half a million is of considerable importance from the point of view of hominid evolution. We may even find that the emergence of the first fully fledged Hominidae occurred within the Villafranchian rather than during the Pliocene *sensu stricto*. The amount of time now available also adequately accounts for the widespread distribution of the Hominidae by the beginning of the Middle Pleistocene.

As regards the relative ages of the earliest hominid-bearing deposits in Africa and Java we had reached an impasse until the results of applying the potassium/argon technique to this problem became available quite recently.

It has been agreed that the oldest hominid remains in South Africa are those of *Australopithecus* from the bone breccias at Taung and Sterkfontein, which were formed under very dry conditions following a period of wetter (pluvial) climate. The associated fauna at Sterkfontein, for example, has been accepted by many (but not by all) palaeontologists as Late Villafranchian. The deposits of the succeeding stages at Swartkrans and Kromdraai were formed when conditions had again become pluvial, and when the contemporaneous hominids were australopithecines of the genus *Paranthropus*, with an associated fauna now generally accepted as Middle Pleistocene.

In Java the oldest hominid remains are a mandible referred to *Meganthropus* (in fact remarkably similar to *Paranthropus*), and from the same deposits the adult cranium and mandible of *Pithecanthropus modjokertensis*. The latter is the earliest known large-brained hominid (i.e. hominine). These remains are from the Djetis beds, which contain a fauna claimed by Professor von Koenigswald to be Lower Pleistocene (Villafranchian); although both Dr. D. A. Hooijer and Dr. B Kurtén now maintain that it is not older than early Middle Pleistocene. The suceeding Trinil beds from which the type specimen of *Pithecanthropus erectus* was obtained by Dubois in 1891, contain an undoubted Middle Pleistocene fauna. Thus, the main question for us is whether the Djetis beds are older, contemporaneous, or younger than the Taung/Sterkfontein interpluvial. The present consensus of palaeontological opinion is that the Djetis beds are Cromerian (earliest phase of Middle Pleistocene), and that the Taung/Sterkfontein breccias are approximately the same age or slightly older. All these deposits contain a fauna largely Villafranchian in character, but it is possible that some Villafranchian forms persisted longer in Java than in Africa. A correlation of the Sterkfontein interpluvial with the Cromerian stage favored by some authorities is attractive in so far as it agrees well with the interpretation of the main pluvial and interpluvial in tropical Africa as corresponding with glacials and interglacial of Europe. The Cromerian deposits belong to the Günz-Mindel or so-called First Interglacial. Moreover, the travertines which were laid down under pluvial conditions preceding the Sterkfontein/Taung deposits would correspond on this scheme with the Günz and Pre-Günz glacial stages in Europe. Yet, I believe we are often led astray by the "fallacy of hard and fast lines." Correlation is rarely so clear-cut in reality as we would like it to be.

Some unexpectedly important developments in dating the earliest African hominids have occurred recently through research in East Africa and in French Equatorial Africa.

In 1959 Dr. and Mrs. L. S. B. Leakey discovered an australopithecine cranium in Bed I, Olduvai, Tanganyika, associated with an industry of Oldowan pebble-tools. The skull was described by Dr. Leakey under the new name "*Zinjanthropus*," but it is now widely recognized as representing an East African species of *Paranthropus*.

When I say that a date exceeding one million years for Olduvai Bed I would confirm its Villafranchian age, I am using as a chronometric basis the fairly large number of potassium/argon datings of deposits of Mindel glacial age in various parts of the world, which are consistently of the order of 400,000 years, so that the base of the Middle Pleistocene may be counted as slightly more than half a million years.

In a first perusal of the results which Evernden and Curtis obtained by applying the K/A technique to minerals in Olduvai Bed I, it is difficult to put one's finger on any obvious possible source of error. On the other hand, I am extremely hesitant to accept the results *in toto,* because they would imply that Bed I took three-quarters of a million years to accumulate, an incredibly slow rate of about .05 mm. per year, whereas the succeeding lake beds, although of the same general character, evidently accummulated at the average rate of 1.5 mm. per year. I am inclined to accept the date of the top of Bed I as the order of magnitude of 1 million years (Fig. 1), for this is in line with other evidence and based on determination of the radiogenic argon in two different minerals biotite and oligoclase, of which the former (giving 1.0 and 1.1) is the more reliable, but it may be wiser to maintain an attitude of reserve in regard to the results from minerals in the lower portion of the bed, which range from 1.57 to 1.89 million years.

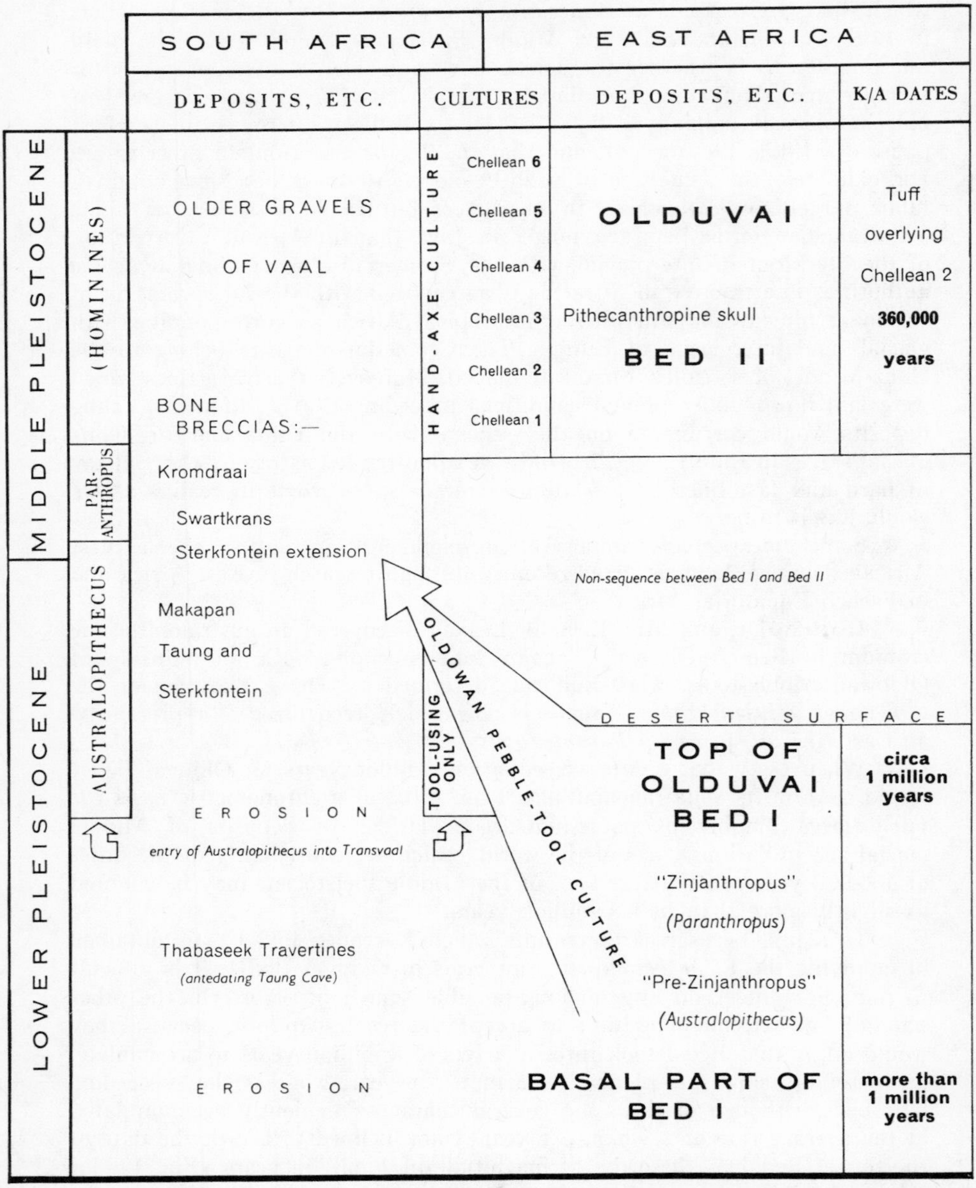

SOUTH AFRICA

EAST AFRICA

DEPOSITS, ETC.

CULTURES

DEPOSITS, ETC.

K/A DATES

MIDDLE PLEISTOCENE

(HOMININES)

OLDER GRAVELS OF VAAL

HAND-AXE CULTURE

Chellean 6

Chellean 5

Chellean 4

Chellean 3

Chellean 2

Chellean 1

OLDUVAI

Pithecanthropine skull

BED II

Tuff overlying Chellean 2 **360,000 years**

BONE BRECCIAS:—

PAR-ANTHROPUS

Kromdraai

Swartkrans

Sterkfontein extension

Non-sequence between Bed I and Bed II

LOWER PLEISTOCENE

AUSTRALOPITHECUS

Makapan

Taung and

Sterkfontein

OLDOWAN PEBBLE-TOOL CULTURE

TOOL-USING ONLY

DESERT SURFACE

TOP OF OLDUVAI BED I

circa 1 million years

EROSION

entry of Australopithecus into Transvaal

"Zinjanthropus"

(Paranthropus)

Thabaseek Travertines

(antedating Taung Cave)

"Pre-Zinjanthropus"

(Australopithecus)

EROSION

BASAL PART OF BED I

more than 1 million years

FIGURE 1. *Attempted correlation of early Hominoid deposits in South and East Africa (1961).*

The reasons for my reserve do not include any doubt that Villafranchian dates of between one and two million years are to be expected; nor do I doubt that some volcanic minerals at Olduvai are accurately datable. Indeed tuff above the Chellean 2 hand-axe level in Bed II at Olduvai has given a perfectly acceptable date of 360,000 years. Nor would it be surprising if there is a long-time gap represented by the non-sequence between Beds I and II. This major break in the sequence was already noted by E. J. Wayland in 1935, and recent studies indicate, moreover, that the top of Bed I was desertic. The main reason for my doubting whether the dates of up to 1.89 million years are correct for the lower portion of Bed I is that the mammalian fauna throughout this bed is said to be *Upper* Villafranchian. At least according to available information none of the species, which, according to Prof. Arambourg, characterize the *Lower* Villafranchian of Africa, is represented in this bed.

Dr. Evernden tells me that he will not be satisfied until four times the number of samples from Bed I have been dated by his technique. Meanwhile the problem is being investigated from another angle: Prof. W. Gentner and Dr. H. J. Lippolt of the Max-Planck Institut für Kernphysik, of Heidelberg, working in consultation with Professor von Koenigswald of Utrecht, have been applying the potassium/argon method to basalt antedating Bed I, and their results will provide a valuable cross check on the dating of pyroclastic sedimentary minerals in Bed I. In so far as there is a chance that tuffs contain traces of older generations of argon-40 (either as occlusions formed in contemporaneous crystals before their eruption, or as invisibly fine detritus from potassic basement rocks), the K/A dating of a lava originally as homogeneous and fluid as basalt is likely to be nearer the truth. [While this Address was being delivered, I received a message from Professor Gentner permitting me to announce that the age of the top layer of the underlying basalt had been determined in his laboratory as 1.3 million years.]

During the summer of 1961 news was received from Paris that an australopithecine with some traits similar to *Paranthropus* had been found by Monsieur Yves Coppens while collecting at Koro Toro, northeast of Lake Chad. It was in apparent association with Lower Villafranchian mammalia including *Elephas* (*Archidiskodon*) *africanavus* (=*planifrons*, s.l.).

As more evidence comes to light it begins to look as though there were several lines of Hominidae evolving simultaneously in Africa during Villafranchian times, perhaps diverging in adaptation to several environments. Palaeontologists are familiar with such adaptive radiation in the early stages of evolution of a new group. If this proves to be the case with the Hominidae, it would be natural enough to find *Paranthropus* earlier than *Australopithecus* in some areas and vice versa elsewhere.

As the post-cranial bones of *Paranthropus* are, according to Dr. J. R. Napier, more anthropoid (pongid) in functional organization than those of *Australopithecus,* it is possible that the former had diverged less from the forest apes, and mainly frequented woodland savannah, whereas *Aust-*

ralopithecus, more "human" in some respects, may have been able to move more freely in dry open country and was probably more carnivorous.

It can be reasonably argued that the earliest Hominidae were the Australopithecinae originating in Central Africa over two million years ago, beginning one might say as "apes" that had become pre-adapted to life on the open edges of the savannah by walking upright. One still encounters a barely conscious prejudice against believing that the Hominidae branched from a simian stock in such comparatively recent times—geologically speaking. How refreshingly free from such prejudice Darwin would have been, for he stated it

> was probable that Africa was formerly inhabited by extinct apes closely allied to the gorilla and chimpanzee; and as these two species are man's nearest allies, it is somewhat more probable that our early progenitors lived on the African continent than elsewhere.

When I look at a distribution map of gorilla and chimpanzee, and then consider the Australopithecinae and their distribution (Fig. 2), I cannot suppress the thought (perhaps reprobate in orthodox circles) that these creatures while technically Hominidae qualify admirably as Darwin's "Third Ape."

There no longer seems any reasonable doubt that the African Australopithecines were hominids, that some of them made tools according to a

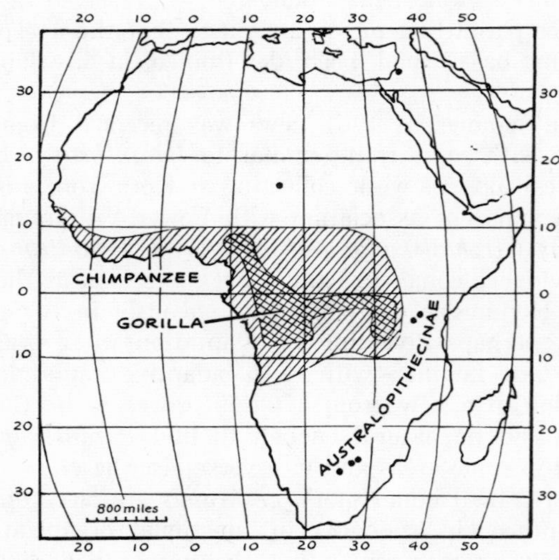

FIGURE 2. *Recent distribution of Gorilla and Chimpanzee, and the known sites of Australopithecinae (Sept. 1961).*

definite tradition, and, therefore, although small-brained, were "men" in the sense of regular tool-makers.

The evolving hominids were distinguished from the pongids or typical apes by their dentition and by their ability to walk habitually on two feet, but there must have been some threshold at which their mental attributes became "human" as generally understood. At one time it was widely held that this transition from "animal" to "man" occurred when in the course of evolution the brain had expanded to a certain volume, which was greater than that found in apes. This "cerebral Rubicon" (taking it as the mean volume within a population) has usually been placed at *circa* 900 c.c., but a few authorities, including Keith, have assessed it at 750 c.c. Some neuroanatomists, however, doubt any close correlation between brain size and mental ability; and an empirical definition of man is now favoured: man as tool-maker. Wherever we find evidence that certain hominids were regularly making tools according to a set pattern, we may infer that they were capable of conceptual thought, and of establishing a tradition. Such creatures were, I submit, "men" whatever the size of their brains. In fact, with discoveries of pebble-tools in association with Australopithecinae at four or five sites, it has become increasingly difficult without special pleading to doubt that these hominids were the makers of the tools.

The next emergence to consider is that of the large-brained hominids, the Homininae as distinct from the small-brained hominids or Australopithecinae. The oldest known Homininae are the pithecanthropines. Recently it was announced that leucite crystals from volcanic rock contemporaneous with the Trinil beds in Java had been dated by the K/A technique as slightly less than 500,000 years old. The Djetis beds with the oldest known pithecanthropines are older, but only by a few tens of millennia, so one may regard it as a reasonable assumption on the available evidence that the emergence of the Homininae did not occur before, say, 600,000 years ago, whereas the small-brained tool-making Australopithecinae existed in Africa just over one million years ago.

The dating of the Mindel glaciation is of great importance because this was the time of transition from Lower Pleistocene to Middle Pleistocene fauna, and it may well have been a critical time in connection with the full emergence of the large-brained Hominids. All the remains of members of the *Pithecanthropus* group, including those from Java, Peking, and Ternifine, are associated with a fully developed Middle Pleistocene fauna. The jaw of *Homo heidelbergensis,* possibly in advance of its Asiatic contemporaries, was found below loess of the second phase of the Mindel glaciation and was associated with a Cromerian fauna, transitional from that of Lower Pleistocene time to that of the Middle Pleistocene (thus *Elephas antiquus* is abundant in the Mauer sands although accompanied by *Rhinoceros etruscus*). This stage is now recognized as the Mindel I/Mindel II interstadial which has been named Cortonian, on the assumption (perhaps questionable) that the Corton beds are in this stratigraphical position. Phonolite tuff from Laacher See in Germany, on a horizon equated with the "Cortonian" interstadial or with the succeeding glacial stage (i.e.,

Mindel II), has been dated as about 400,000 years by the potassium/argon method, so that this may be taken as a close approximation to the dating of Heidelberg Man.

A most interesting recent development in the stratigraphic dating of fossil man has been the recognition of pollen in the Choukoutien deposits which yielded the remains of Peking Man (*Pithecanthropus pekinensis*). Dr. Vasari's study of this pollen has revealed that the contemporaneous flora was that of a cold steppe, so that although Choukoutien fauna is Cromerian in facies, its stratigraphic horizon is probably that of the Mindel II glaciation and *not* of the Cromerian interglacial as has been so widely assumed. The potassium/argon dating of the Laacher See tuff at *circa* 400,000 years thus also gives us a fair measure of the antiquity of Peking Man.

The advanced pithecanthropine skull recently discovered by the Leakeys on the Chellean III horizon in the Chelles-Acheul sequence of the Olduvai Gorge has been dated approximately by the K/A method, for the age of an immediately overlying volcanic tuff was determined by Evernden and Curist as 360,000 years old.

It now seems undoubted that the early Chelles-Acheul hand-axe makers of Africa and Europe were pithecanthropines. This was first established in the 1950's by Professor Arambourg's announcement of the discovery of the so-called *"Atlanthropus"* jaws and parietal bone in association with early Chelles-Acheul hand-axes at Ternifine in Algeria. The horizon of Ternifine Man may be a shade later than that of the Chellean Man of Olduvai, but they are both of the same order of antiquity and in the same cultural tradition.

The late Dr. A. C. Blanc provided the K/A Laboratory in Berkeley with black pumices found in river sands overlying a Chellean (Abbevillio-Acheulian) living site at Torre in Pietra near Rome. Sanidine crystals from these pumices have been dated at 430,000 years old. In the spring of this year I had an opportunity to examine this beautifully stratified series of deposits, very reminiscent of those at Swanscombe, and there seemed little doubt to me that the Chellean floor was slightly younger than the layer with black pumices. Thus, we are getting a convergence of evidence that the Chellean hand-axe makers lived nearly 400,000 years ago.

Before the end of Middle Pleistocene times, while the hand-axe culture was developing through the Acheulian stages (and while the chopper/chopping tool cultures of South-East Asia were developing in parallel), the pithecanthropines were evolving into the larger-brained hominines grouped under the genus *Homo*, that is to say into the prototypes of *Homo sapiens* and *Homo neanderthalensis*.

The chemical methods of relative dating (based on absorption of fluorine and uranium and on loss of collagen) have thrown doubt on the dating of all the skulls of *Homo sapiens* (*sensu stricto*) claimed as being of Lower or Middle Pleistocene age.

For example, the Galley Hill skeleton found in 1888 in Middle Pleistocene gravels near Swanscombe, Kent, was shown in 1948 to be a comparatively recent intrusive burial by means of the fluorine method of estimating relative antiquity, and more recently this was confirmed by other chemical tests, and finally by radiocarbon dating of its residual collagen which indicated that it was only between 3000 and 4000 years old (3310 ± 150, *fide* H. Barker). On the other hand the same *relative* dating tests confirmed the great antiquity of the Swanscombe skull, in the sense that they proved its contemporaneity with the associated Second Interglacial (Hoxnian) fauna. Dr. Karl Adam has reported that on the evidence of its stratigraphic position and associated fossil mammalia, the similar cranium from Steinheim is of Late Hoxnian age. These last two skulls demonstrate that men with brains morphologically of modern type existed before the end of Middle Pleistocene times.

The carbon-14 or radiocarbon method is limited in practice to about 70,000 years, but at this range is most valuable in connection with the chronometric dating of the later Neanderthaloid and the earliest representatives of completely modern man, *Homo sapiens sapiens.* Charcoal from an upper level of Neanderthalian culture (Mousterian) in Gorham's Cave, Gibraltar, was dated by the late Professor de Vries as 49,000 years old, so we may reasonably infer that in Western Europe Neanderthal Man was flourishing more than 50,000 years ago, in fact during the early stages of the Würm glaciation, now estimated to have begun 70,000 years ago.

The onset of the Last Glaciation was just as fluctuating as its termination: a number of Early Würm interstadials have now been recognized and dated. Their deposits have frequently been assumed to be representatives of the Last Interglacial, for example, the temperate bed at La Cotte de St. Brelade, Jersey, *circa* 47,000 years old (*fide* Professor de Waard), the Senftenburg deposit in Austria dated to 52,000 years, and the Chelford deposit in Warwickshire, *circa* 53,000 years, equivalent to that of Brørup in Denmark, which is nearly 60,000 years old.

Charcoals from a number of Levalloiso-Mousterian or Neanderthalian occupation sites in South-West Asia have been dated by the radiocarbon method, including several levels in the et-Tabun Cave on Mount Carmel and in the Shanidar Cave, Iraq. They range from > 52,000 years to about 35,000 years ago, so evidently Neanderthalers persisted in this corner of South-West Asia through the interval of time represented by the Göttweig interstadial in the loess sequence of Central Europe which appears to have lasted from > 45,000 (possibly *circa* 50,000) to *circa* 35,000 years ago. However, it is by no means certain that the changes in climate glacial/interstadial or pluvial/interpluvial, were closely contemporaneous in all areas. The oldest Neanderthal remains in the Shanidar Cave are believed to be older than 50,000 years, and therefore presumably pre-Göttweig and contemporaneous with Early Würm, but the Galilee skull associated with Micoquian hand-axes is the only known South-West Asiatic Neanderthaler now accepted as dating from the Eemian or Last Interglacial, and contemporaneous with the Ehringsdorf Neanderthalers.

The following is a selection of dating on Mousterian charcoals from

South-West Asia (made available through the courtesy of Professor H. de Waard and Dr. J. C. Vogel):

	Years b.p.
Final Levalloiso-Mousterian, el-Kebara	34,700
Upper Levalloiso-Mousterian, et-Tabun B	39,500
Lower Levalloiso-Mousterian, et-Tabun C (horizon of skeleton Tabun I)	*c.*41,000
Lower Levalloiso-Mousterian, Ras el-Kelb	>52,000

Professor H. de Waard of Groningen has informed me that wood excavated by Professor Desmond Clark on an Upper Acheulian hand axe site near Kalambo Falls in Northern Rhodesia has been dated absolutely by radiocarbon as 57,300 ± 500 years old. I suggest that the Kanjera skulls (*Homo sapiens* sub-sp.) from a Kenya Acheulian site may prove to be of the same order of antiquity, even if perhaps slightly older, for the "Kanjeran pluvial" is possibly equivalent to Early Würm in the glacial regions of Europe.

Charcoal from a dry-phase deposit containing Sangoan implements at Kalambo has been dated as between 40,000 and 45,000 years old. The anthropological interest of this latter date is its link with the fact that the cranium of *Homo rhodesiensis* from Saldanha in the Cape Province was associated with an equivalent industry (Fauresmith). The type skull of *Homo rhodesiensis* (or as some would express it, *H. sapiens rhodesiensis*) from Broken Hill, Northern Rhodesia, was on a slightly later archaeological horizon (Proto-Stillbay) referable to a pluvial stage some 30,000 years before the present, according to indications from other sites.

The Florisbad skull (*Homo sapiens helmei,* perhaps the prototype of the Bushman) was recovered from deposits of a dry or interpluvial stage in the Orange Free State, and is now estimated to be *circa* 37,000 years old on the basis of a revised radiocarbon dating of an associated layer of peat.

At Niah Cave in Sarawak a fossil human skull of modern form was found by Mr. Tom Harrisson in association with charcoal dated in Groningen as *circa* 40,000 years old, which is, at any rate, in agreement with the general conclusion that *Homo sapiens sapiens* was emerging and spreading widely during Göttweig times when the last of the Neanderthalers and Neanderthaloids were dying out, or being replaced.

In Western Europe the oldest unquestionable example of *Homo sapiens sapiens* is the Cro-Magnoid skeleton from Combe Capelle in the Dordogne; it is from the level of Lower Aurignacian culture dated as *circa* 30,000 years old on the basis of radio-carbon age determinations of Aurignacian I charcoal from La Quina in the Charente department of France.

Finally, we may summarize the dating of the six stages of Primate emergence leading to modern man as follows:

	In millions of years
Earliest Primates (Prosimii)	70
Earliest Anthropoidea	40
Incipient Hominidae	12
Oldest toolmaking Hominidae ('men')	1
Oldest hominines (large-brained men)	$\frac{1}{2}$
Oldest examples of modern man	$\frac{1}{25}$

SUPPLEMENTARY READINGS

OAKLEY, KENNETH P. *Frameworks for Dating Fossil Man.* Chicago: Aldine, 1964.

SIMPSON, G. G. *Life of the Past.* New York: Bantam Books, 1968.

four

FOSSIL MAN

The evidence of man's evolutionary past is composed of fossil skeletal material that has been excavated from the Pleistocene beds of the Old World. From the first cranial fragment picked up near Cannstadt, Germany, in 1700 to the modern organized search for fossil evidence at Olduvai Gorge in Tanzania, East Africa, our knowledge of the earliest hominids has slowly developed. The discovery, identification, and reconstruction of these ancient populations reads like a prehistoric detective story. In the following pages, Pilbeam, Simons, Bartholemew, and Birdsell demonstrate how the fossil evidence has been utilized in reconstructing man's developmental history.

Man's Earliest Ancestors

David R. Pilbeam

No longer is it a question of whether man has evolved from some pre-human primate but of when and from which primate. Our work on human evolution, like most of the relevant fossils themselves, has been concentrated on the evolution of man during the Pleistocene period, now believed to cover the past three million or so years of geological history. Although there are still doubters, it is widely accepted that we can now trace, often with some certainty, our evolution from such creatures as *Australopithecus* from the South African Early Pleistocene. They were animals standing little more than four feet tall, with apesized jaws, teeth and brains. Fossil apes are known from these times too; thus, two million years ago at least, men and apes were already distinct.

Although the pre-Pleistocene hominid story has remained something of a mystery, within the past five years it has become clear that at least one claimant deserves careful consideration: *Ramapithecus*. This is an Indian Late Miocene fossil primate, found in the 1930s. It was described then as a hominid—belonging to the same zoological family as does modern man—but was cold-shouldered by the American anthropological establishment. The reinstatement of *Ramapithecus* as an ancestor of the Pleistocene hominids is one of the most important recent developments in palaeoanthropology, for it pushes back the time of differentiation of apes and men to 14 million years ago, and perhaps much further.

Since the work of the 18th century Swedish naturalist Linnaeus, every living species of plant and animal has been described by two Latin names.

From Science Journal *3, no. 2 (February 1967): 47–53; reprinted by permission of the author and publisher.*

Modern man, for example, is known as *Homo sapiens*. All living men are thought to belong to a single species, and all are therefore regarded as members of *Homo sapiens*. A species is the largest group of organisms that interbreeds under natural conditions, producing offspring fully fertile with others of both their own and preceding generations.

Closely related species, however, are grouped in the same genus. For example, *Canis lupus,* the timber wolf, and *Canis niger,* the red wolf, are different but related species sufficiently similar to be placed in a single genus, *Canis*. The morphological similarities of the two species are due to fundamental genetic similarities.

The unit which evolves is the population, not the individual. The genetic structure of a species changes through time as the relative biological success or failure of each genetic type causes some individuals to leave more offspring, some less, than others. In fact, the species is the important unit of evolution, and before the evolutionary history of a particular group can be studied the fossils must also be divided into species ideally having the same sort of variability within groups and the same sort of gaps between groups as are found within and between modern species.

Related genera are grouped into families, just as related species are grouped into genera. I should point out here that species are thought to be related because they are physically similar, and that they are similar because they evolved from some common ancestor.

The three living great apes—the orangutan, gorilla and chimpanzee known respectively as *Pongo pygmaeus, Gorilla gorilla*, and *Pan satyrus*—are classified in one family, the Pongidae. Hence the term pongid, which can be used to describe any living great ape. Modern and fossil men are classified in another family, the Hominidae (thus the appropriate descriptive term—hominid).

Comprehensive field studies of the great apes, particularly of the chimpanzee, have developed only recently. Already, however, they have revealed the complexities of the social life of these mammals. In certain areas, chimpanzees have developed a simple tool-using culture. Occasionally they have been seen to band together for the capture and eating of red colobus monkeys, and they do share food. The great apes, far from being "brutish," as most 19th century naturalists believed, are now known to be intelligent animals, living in relatively complex groups. Of course, they must not be treated as models for the early hominids, but it is evident that complex social behaviour is possible with an "ape-sized" brain.

The great apes are certainly man's closest living relatives. To the classical evidence of dentition, comparative anatomy and embryology has been added fresh information from such diverse fields as molecular biology, parasitology and animal behaviour. All strengthen this conclusion. Yet there are many obvious differences between members of the two families. Is it possible to account for these differences in evolutionary terms? If so, when did our ancestors begin to differ from those of the apes?

The living pongids are basically forest dwelling vegetarians, living in or near the edges of tropical rain forests in Africa (the gorilla and chimpan-

HOMINIDS

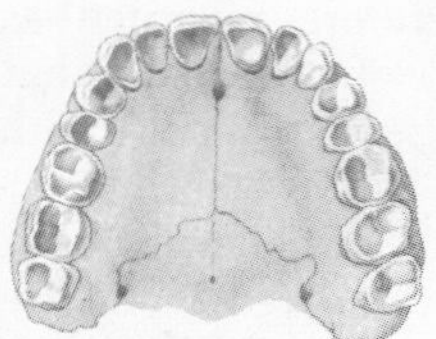

Telanthropus, Transvaal
$\frac{3}{4}$–1 million years

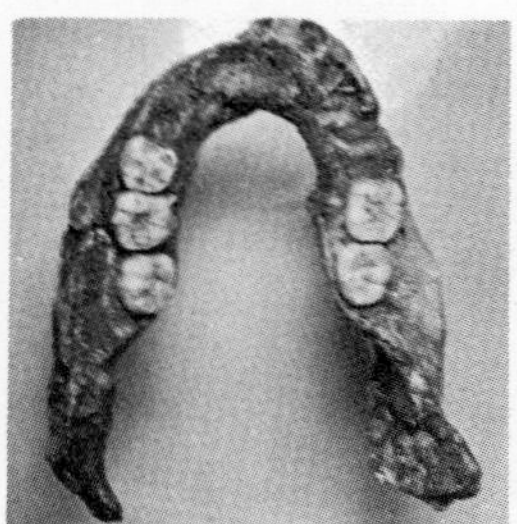

Australopithecus africanus, Transvaal
2 million years

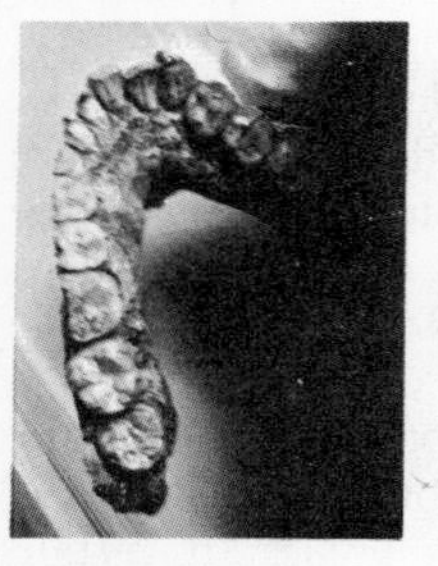

Propliopithecus, Egypt
30 million years

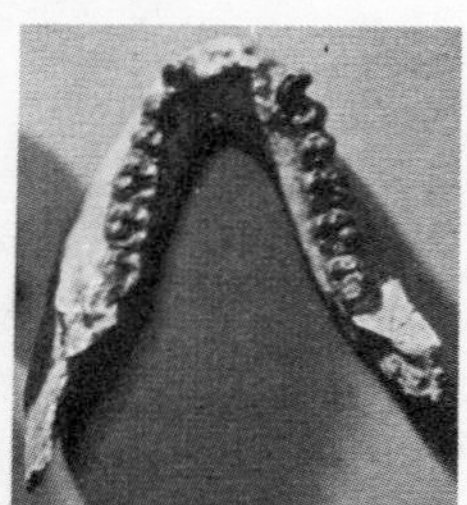

RAMAPITHECUS

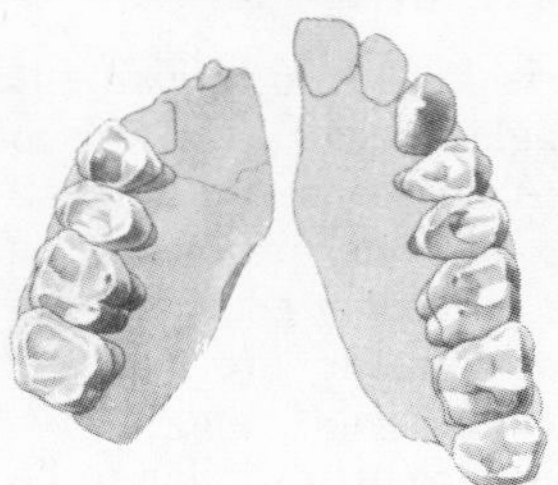

Ramapithecus, India
14 million years

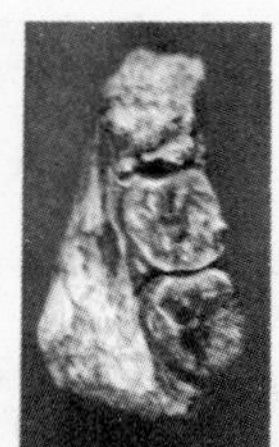

PONGIDS

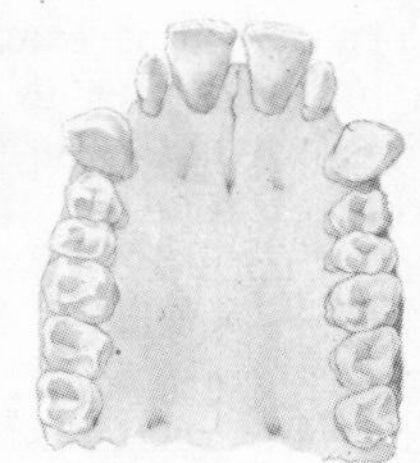

Dryopithecus (Sivapithecus), India
14 million years

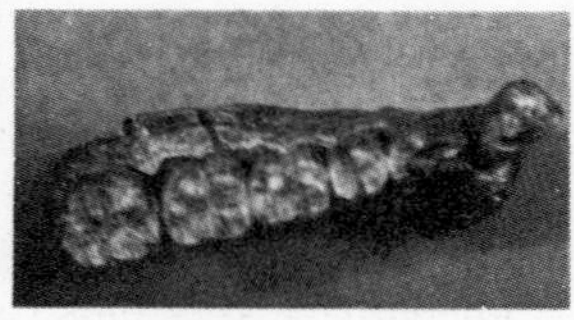

Dryopithecus (Proconsul), Uganda
19 million years

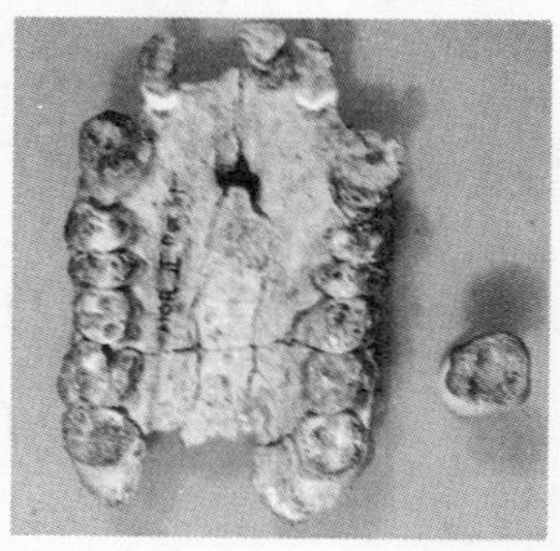

Aegyptopithecus, Egypt
30 million years

FIGURE 1. *Jaw structure is a criterion for classifying hominids and pongids and helps to place new fossils. Drawings show upper jaw of man, Ramapithecus and gorilla from two viewpoints. Photographs show typical fossil material from the same viewpoints. The dental arcade or tooth row in man and the other hominids is roughly semicircular in shape, the teeth are small and there is no gap—diastema—between them. In the gorilla and other pongids, on the other hand, the arcade is*

HOMINIDS **RAMAPITHECUS** **PONGIDS**

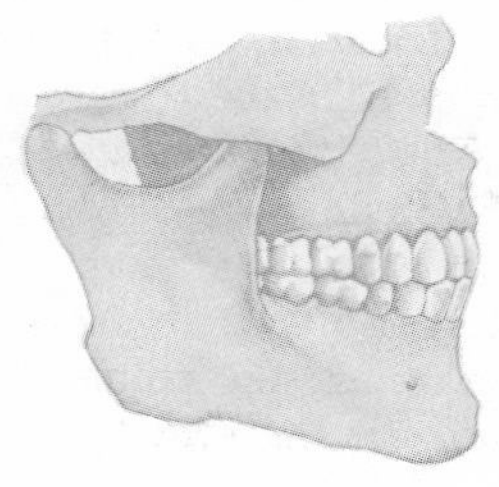

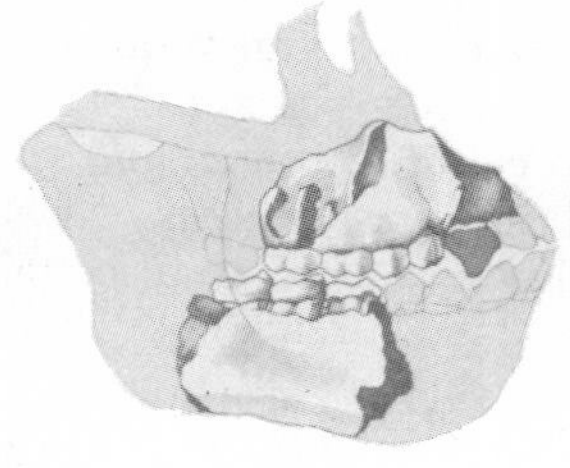

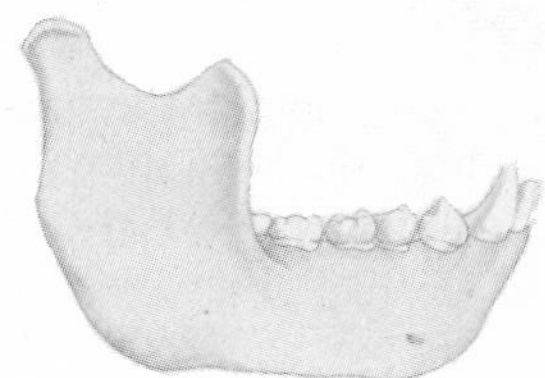

Australopithecus robustus, Transvaal
$\frac{3}{4}$–1 million years

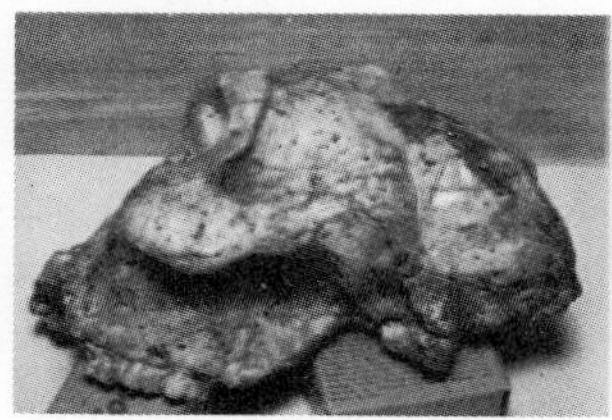

Ramapithecus, India
14 million years

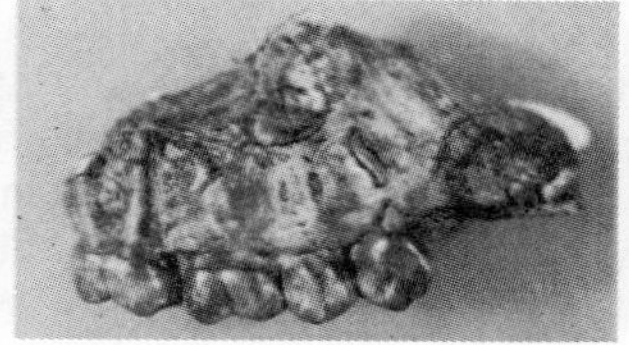

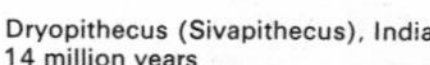

Dryopithecus (Sivapithecus), India
14 million years

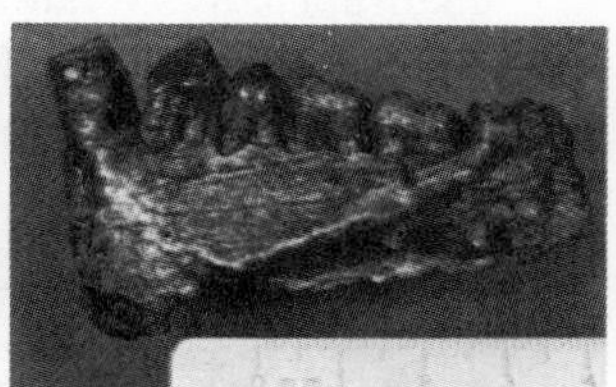

Dryopithecus (Proconsul), Uganda
19 million years

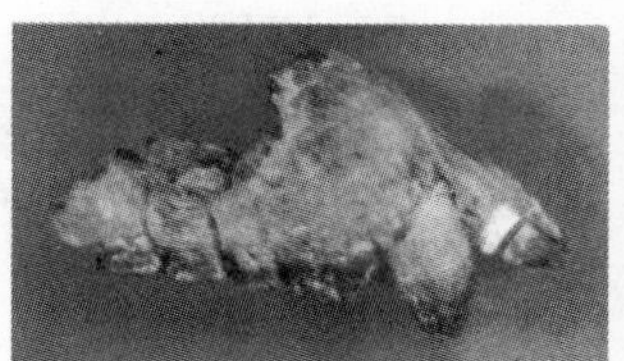

Propliopithecus, Egypt
30 million years

Aegyptopithecus, Egypt
30 million years

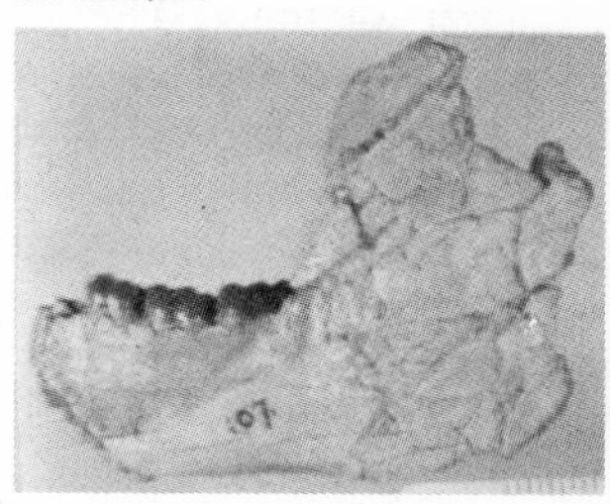

rectangular in shape, the teeth—especially the canines—are large and there is a diastema between the 2nd incisors and the canines. The rounded form of the arcade, the relatively small teeth and the lack of a diastema in Ramapithecus suggest strongly that it should be placed with the hominids even though it also possesses some pongid characters. Although the evidence is by no means conclusive Aegyptopithecus has now been placed with the pongids and Propliopithecus tentatively with the hominids.

zee) and Borneo and Sumatra (the orang-utan). The gorilla eats mostly vegetable food, the chimpanzee and orang-utan seem to prefer fruit. Powerfully built creatures, they show many adaptations to life in or near the trees. The orang is the most arboreal of the three and spends most of its time eating, sleeping, playing and relaxing in trees. Newly discovered remains of ancestral gorillas of the Miocene epoch were certainly less bulky and more arboreal than their present day descendants. This, the largest of the living apes, now spends most of its time on the ground. Like the orang, the chimpanzee nests mostly in the trees but spends much more time on the ground. Perhaps this is because the local forest is more open.

Modern man, like his Pleistocene ancestors, is almost entirely a terrestrial animal. We are erect bipeds and, except as babies, we do not walk quadrupedally. While most great apes can walk bipedally, they rarely do so and on the ground they are predominantly quadrupeds. Perhaps the most obvious character of distinction between men and apes is brain size. Human brains are three times as large as those of chimpanzees and, however one defines the term. We are certainly more intelligent. Many anthropologists believe that man owes his enormous brain to the habit of tool making, although it is more likely that an increase in the complexity of his culture has gone hand in hand with brain expansion.

Human culture must have developed from simpler social traditions, from groupings comparable in complexity with those of present day chimpanzees. We can recognize the existence of true culture in the stone artifacts of the archaeological record. However, stone tools obviously represent only a fraction of the learned behaviour—language, customs, religions and laws—that make up culture. Stone tool making, to a regular and recognizable pattern, began perhaps two or three million years ago. At that time our ancestors were small brained, like the living apes, but this does not mean that they should be called "apes" or "ape-men." They were primitive hominids. From what we can reconstruct of their behaviour, it seems that they were omnivores and hunters like later men, rather than predominantly vegetarians like the living pongids.

Tool making, and before that tool using, has had obvious influences on our anatomy. The jaws and teeth of gorillas differ in many ways from those of men. Most obviously, our teeth are smaller. Gorilla canines are large and projecting. The front lower premolar, because of its contact with the large upper canine, becomes an elongated, rather blade-like tooth. It is described as "sectorial" and with a canine makes an efficient pair of shears for cutting through tough vegetable material such as the bamboos on which gorillas feed. Man, with his modest canines, has no sectorial teeth. Like the posterior premolars, the anterior premolars have two cusps. Our incisors and canines are, in fact, much reduced in size compared with our premolars and molars. Hominid incisors and canines need not be used to dismember prey, nor to break open hard fruits and nuts. Tools can be used in their place. As ancillary teeth and fingers, tools were clearly very important in human evolution. They became not only cutters but diggers, spears and axes. In short, artifacts were used not only as tools, but as weapons too.

The canines of male pongids are larger than those of females; these teeth are important in aggressive behaviour both within and between species. In hominids, it is thought, this function of the canines has disappeared. Students of primate behaviour such as A. Kortlandt and the late K. R. L. Hall have suggested that this was the original function of tools, as important elements in display and defence in place of large canines. The use of weapons, and the adoption of a bipedal, terrestrial way of life, has wrought profound changes in our behaviour and physical make-up. These trends seem to have been well under way in the hominids of the Early Pleistocene. They used and made stone tools, and hunted their food. They were bipeds and their dentition was similar to ours in all features except size.

It has already been stressed that these early men were not "apes". The idea has taken a long time to sink into the collective anthropological consciousness but important recent work on ape behaviour has finally dispelled these doubts. Jane Goodall's brilliant field research on chimpanzees in Tanzania has shown us just how complex, in fact, is their behaviour. G. B. Schaller has done the same for the gorilla in the Congo. Research into the social structure of the advanced co-operative hunting carnivores such as wolves and Cape hunting dogs, suggests that many of the features in which we differ from non-human primates might be due to the evolution of social hunting in the hominid line. Man seems to have evolved from a primate with a social structure similar in complexity to that of the chimpanzee. But he has evolved into something much more than a mere ape, and luckily the course of his evolution is preserved in the fossil record.

In 1856 a Frenchman, Edouard Lartet, described the lower jaw of a fossil ape which had been found in beds of Middle Miocene age at St Gaudens in south western France. He called this specimen *Dryopithecus fontani*. Others of the same species have since been found in France as well as elsewhere in Europe. During the past 110 years several hundred ape fossils have been discovered in places as diverse as China, India, Russia, Spain and Kenya. All fall between the Oligocene and Pliocene epochs. The rocks from which they come can now be dated radiometrically, and it is doubtful whether many are much older than 30 million or much younger than 10 million years. Altogether, nearly 30 genera and 50 species have been created to accommodate these creatures since Lartet described the first of them. The living and fossil pongids have been placed in separate subfamilies of the Pongidae, the first in the Ponginae, the last in the Dryopithecinae—named after *Dryopithecus*.

An interest in pre-Pleistocene human origins took me in 1963 from Cambridge to the United States, to work with Professor Elwyn Simons at Yale University. Like myself, Simons had been interested for some time in the dryopithecine problem. The larger number of published names for dryopithecines led many palaeontologists to believe that higher primate evolution in the Miocene and Pliocene had been exceedingly complex. Both Simons and I were sceptical of this view and, as more names were published it became increasingly unlikely that they all represented valid species and genera.

Our first task was to study the rather extensive literature on the subject which had appeared since 1856. Soon it became clear that many fossils had been given new names for quite inadequate reasons. The first specimen described from a new species is generally designated the 'type'; this is the individual specimen which always carries the new name, as it were, attached to it. Subsequent discoveries should be compared with type specimens and, unless the new finds are sufficiently distinct and different, they should be included in existing species. Individuals within any living species differ one from another—it is even possible to find differences between opposite sides of the same jaw—and unless the variation in the fossils is likely to exceed that range of variation normal for living related species it is unwise to give the new specimen a new name.

Next we turned our attention to dryopithecine "species" from Late Miocene and Early Pliocene deposits in Asia, principally from the Siwalik Hills of north western India, but also from China. Almost all the characters which supposedly distinguished these "species" turned out to be entirely trivial—slight differences in the degree of wrinkling on the molar crowns, and in the shape and relative proportions of the various teeth. We found that we could reduce the number of Asian species to four, three of them in the genus *Dryopithecus,* but each distinct from *D. fontani*. The one Siwalik primate that was not *Dryopithecus* was the specimen mentioned in the start of this article: *Ramapithecus*.

This fossil was found in 1932 and described in 1934 by G. E. Lewis of Yale University. He considered it a hominid. Unfortunately few others shared his view. In 1961, Simons had published a new paper on *Ramapithecus,* re-examining the evidence. He concluded that this genus belonged to the Hominidae. Dating placed it in the Late Miocene, perhaps 14 million years ago, and so the antiquity of fossil man (in the broadest sense) was extended back in time by a factor of four or five.

The original *Ramapithecus* specimen consisted of a right maxilla or upper jaw, with two premolars and two molars remaining in it. The canine socket and the root of one incisor, as well as part of the socket of a second, were also preserved. Although the fragment was not very extensive, quite enough was left to demonstrate that this was not merely another ape, another dryopithecine. The small, low crowned molars and premolars, together with the small size of the canine and incisors (inferred from their diminutive root sockets), and greatly foreshortened face, distinguish this hominid from late Miocene pongids. Using the same criteria, Pleistocene hominids such as *Australopithecus* can be distinguished from living apes such as the chimpanzee.

Sorting through the Indian fossil jaws and teeth—the majority of dryopithecines are represented by fragments of this sort—we found that we were able to divide them up into man-like and ape-like forms. A second complete maxilla, first described in 1915 as *Dryopithecus* and misinterpreted since then, joined Lewis's original specimen in *Ramapithecus*. Various isolated upper teeth could also be included. So far, our re-identified hominid specimens were confined, surprisingly, to upper jaw material.

During our survey we found we had also divided the lower jaws into two groups; some ape-like and other man-like. The man-like form had been named, again by Lewis, *Bramapithecus*. Compared with *Dryopithecus, Bramapithecus* has relatively square, compact teeth, and a greatly shortened molar tooth row. In *Dryopithecus* the molars are longer and more elongated in shape, and they increase in size from front to back. As in living apes, the jaw is deep, and the whole face projects further forward than is the case in the hominids. This trend is probably associated with feeding habits, with the importance of large teeth for chewing tough vegetable foods, and for carrying and examining objects. In hominids, the use of natural objects as tools and weapons has relieved the teeth of these functions and has helped in reduction of the face. *Bramapithecus* has a shallow lower jaw, and a foreshortened face. It is man-like, so much so that it closely resembles the mandible of a Middle Pleistocene hominid from South Africa originally known as *Telanthropus capensis,* later as *Homo erectus*.

Now we had one hominid genus, *Ramapithecus,* containing only upper jaws, and another, *Bramapithecus,* based entirely on lower jaws. It dawned on us that we were dealing with the two parts of the same form! All the specimens, upper and lower jaws together, went into a single species, *Ramapithecus punjabicus*. The similarities between *R. punjabicus* and the later hominids of the Pleistocene are quite striking. The Pleistocene forms are more completely known and, of course, *Ramapithecus* is known only from jaws and teeth, so the recovery of more complete Miocene material *might* show that similarities were confined only to the facial region. However, we have to work with the cash in hand, and that is sufficient to tell us that *Ramapithecus* was different from *Dryopithecus* in anatomically, and presumably functionally, important ways. It differs in the same features that distinguish men from apes.

We next turned our attention to the African forms. In the 1920s, E. J. Wayland, Director of the Geological Survey of Uganda, forwarded to the British Museum (Natural History) in London, a series of fossils from Koru in Kenya. The pongids were described by Hopwood in 1933 under the binomen *Proconsul africanus*. Since then, several hundred additional specimens have been recovered from a number of sites in and around the Kavirondo Gulf of Lake Victoria, and also from deposits further north in Uganda. Much later Sir Wilfrid Le Gros Clark and Dr. L. S. B. Leakey diagnosed two more species of the genus, *Proconsul nyanzae* and *P. major*. *P. major* was the largest, as big as a female gorilla. *P. nyanzae* was probably chimpanzee sized and *P. africanus* somewhat smaller.

Proconsul has been recovered from sites of mainly Early Miocene date. Recently, rocks from some of these sites have been dated radiometrically to about 20 million years. The earliest Eurasian species of *Dryopithecus* are no older than 16 or 17 million years, and it is quite possible that the *Proconsul* group was broadly ancestral to these later forms.

We concluded that the structural distinctions listed as distinguishing *Proconsul* from the dryopithecines were not in fact particularly important. So the species of *Proconsul* were transferred to the genus *Dryopithecus*. We also thought that *Proconsul* species were ancestral to the chimpanzee and the gorilla. We were not prepared to commit ourselves, however, as to exactly which species was ancestral to which living ape. Many workers had assumed that the chimpanzee and the gorilla have only recently become separated. This view was often linked to theories that the hominids themselves had differentiated only during the Pliocene. But here we recognized ancestral chimpanzees and gorillas, already distinct in the Early Miocene. Also, these forms were relatively unspecialized dentally and skeletally. They had not apparently evolved those great ape locomotor and feeding specializations associated (it is said) with habitual forest dwelling, and with fruit and shoot eating.

The dryopithecine "complex" had thus been reduced to fewer than a dozen species in one genus. Since returning to Cambridge, I have continued multivariate statistical analyses of the dryopithecines. It now appears possible that one of the Asian species of *Dryopithecus* (*Sivapithecus*), is ancestral to the orang-utan.

In 1962, Leakey described a new fossil primate from a Late Miocene formation at Fort Ternan in Kenya. The find consisted of right and left upper jaws, and an associated lower molar. He called it *Kenyapithecus wickeri.* Examining casts, photographs and the originals, we could find no characters of sufficient difference from *Ramapithecus* to warrant placing it in a new genus. In fact, the two forms were so similar that we were unable to put them even in separate species. The upper canine, which is unknown in the Indian *Ramapithecus,* was small; it was shaped rather like that of a small female *Dryopithecus* but in size was similar to that of man.

Thus in the Late Miocene of India, East Africa, and possibly Europe, too, there lived a primate so similar dentally and facially to Pleistocene man that it was difficult to find characters to distinguish it from *Australopithecus* or *Homo erectus* (a primitive species of *Homo*).

It was said when *Ramapithecus* was first described, and it will undoubtedly be said now, that *Ramapithecus* is not really a hominid, but a man-like ape. Of course, it might be. It might, too, be a hominid-like monkey, or lemur, or horse, or elephant, or whatever you like. I have listed these alternatives in descending order of plausibility, in order to stress that our assignment of *Ramapithecus* to the Hominidae is made because it is the most plausible hypothesis, the best way to account for its physical appearance. We have assumed that the similarities, in almost all known parts, to later hominids were due to the fact that *Ramapithecus punjabicus,* or something very similar, was ancestral to *Australopithecus* and *Homo.* In short, the similarities are homologies, not parallelistic developments. We are proposing the simplest explanation and using the procedure of naming as a way of making evolutionary hypotheses.

More than 30 years ago, a German anthropologist, Paul Alsberg, wrote an essay on the first *Australopithecus* specimen from Taung in Botswana. He argued that the appearance of *Australopithecus* (or indeed of any Pleistocene fossil hominid), with small anterior teeth, reduced canines and a fore-shortened face, indicated that it was a tool user. Since then many workers have emphasized that *Australopithecus* must have been continuously dependent on tools for survival. Raymond Dart, the describer of the first

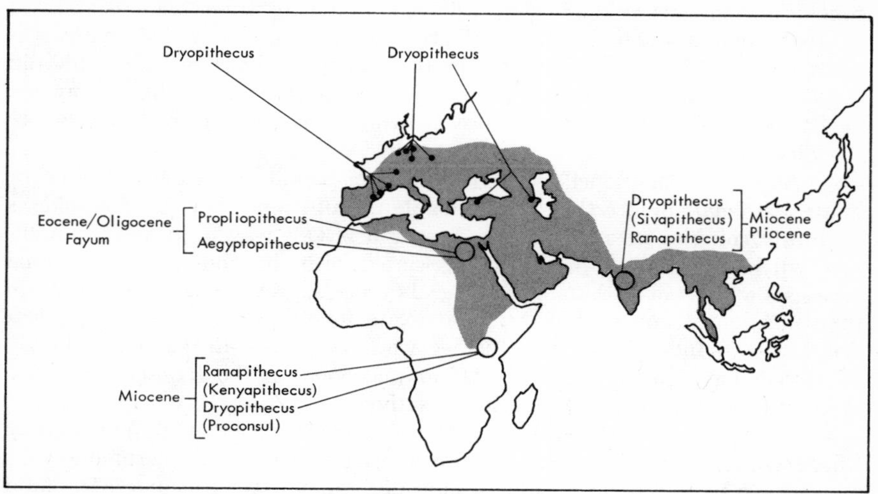

FIGURE 2. *Geographical distribution of early hominids and pongids is inferred from scattered fossils remains. The earliest ancestors of both groups are thought to be represented by* Propliopithecus *(possibly hominid) and* Aegyptopithecus *(pongid), remains of which were found in the Egyptian Fayum by Elwyn Simons. These are of Eocene/Oligocene age—about 30 to 53 million years old. Later fossils have been found in Miocene deposits in East Africa and India though whereas the hominids, represented by* Ramapithecus, *appear to have been relatively restricted the pongids, represented by* Dryopithecus, *were much more widespread and have been found at several sites in Europe and Asia Minor, although further collecting may reveal the presence of* Ramapithecus *in these areas also.*

Australopithecus skull, believes that here was a hunter who used stone and wood implements and made bone tools. It is now fairly well established, that Early Pleistocene man was a tolerably successful hunter.

I have already mentioned that *Ramapithecus* showed the same dental and facial specializations as *Australopithecus*. It is difficult to avoid the conclusion that just as these specifically hominid adaptations were established by the end of the Miocene, 14 million years ago, so too would many specifically hominid behavioural traits be developing at that time. Not only did the separation of men and apes occur further back in time than many believed, but basic hominid features seem to have been established long before the Pleistocene.

As I have mentioned, regular stone tool making began two million or more years ago. Before that, the probable use of implements by hominids is obviously going to be very difficult to establish. One way to attack the problem will be by analysis of faunas associated with the hominids. Do animal bones show signs of bashing or cutting? Is there any evidence of selectivity in the collection of bones which might indicate food preferences? For clarification, these points must await further work, although Leakey has already suggested that some of the associated animal bones at the *Ramapithecus* site in Kenya shows evidence of predatory activities.

Björn Kurtén has recently pointed out how deficient Old World Early Pliocene faunas were in the sort of medium-sized, fast-running carnivores that might have been competitors for a hunting hominid. He concludes, "...and it would seem that the treeless plain of Pontian [Early Pliocene] times may have held fewer terrors to a fast-moving, quick-witted early hominid than we might be disposed to believe. To an armed band most of the smaller carnivores would be no menace, while the large forms, although invincible as such, could be avoided by decoy and flight".

To the sociability, intelligence, and manipulative abilities of our primate ancestors were added the co-operative hunting activities of the social carnivore, producing a unique and potentially formidable new type of animal—the earliest hominid. The evolution of this new breed was well under way 14 million years ago. There we can, almost, end our story.

Five years ago, Elwyn Simons began field work in the Egyptian Fayum, a region of Eocene and Oligocene sandstones exposed in the desert to the south west of Cairo. The Fayum was once a region of tropical forests and rivers, and in Oligocene times, more than 30 million years ago, the area teemed with all kinds of animals. Among them were primitive apes.

The Fayum had been searched for fossils by American and German expeditions in the early years of this century, and a number of new genera and species of primates were recovered. Only one need concern us here, *Propliopithecus haeckeli*.

Propliopithecus has been described as many things in its time: a fossil gibbon, an early great ape, the ancestor of both men and apes, or of men, apes and gibbons. For a number of reasons, *Propliopithecus* is no longer regarded as a gibbon. It has many similarities, though, to fossil and living apes and men but, as one would expect, it is much smaller than either. Its

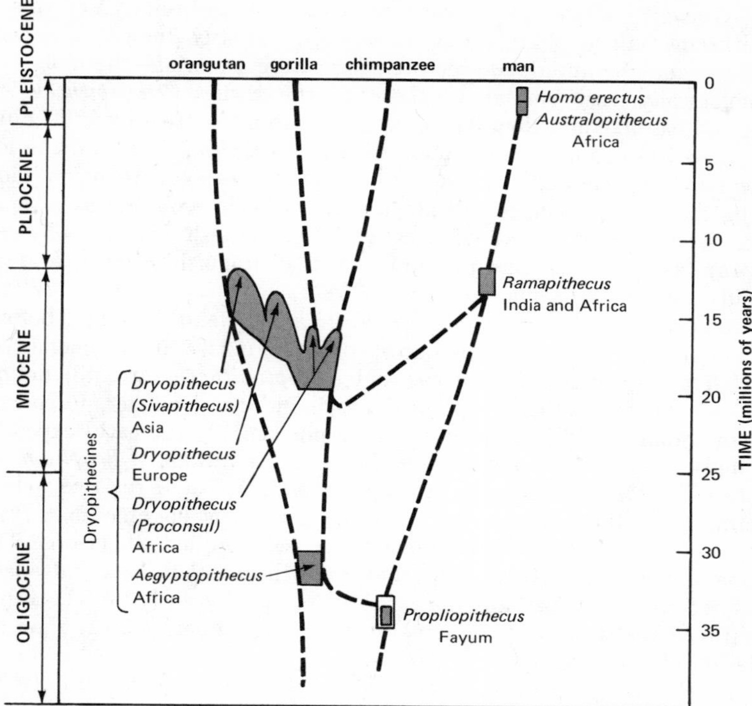

FIGURE 3. *Distribution time of hominids and pongids shows how discontinuous our knowledge really is. The evolutionary pathway to man may have involved creatures like* Ramapithecus *and* Propliopithecus, *and the present day great apes may have evolved through the Dryopithecines. Certainly the differences between* Aegpytopithecus *and* Propliopithecus *are similar in character to those which are used to separate* Dryopithecus, *a pongid, from* Ramapithecus, *a hominid. Nevertheless much more material is needed—especially from the time of 20–30 million years ago—before their evolution can be defined.*

lower jaw—all that is known—measures only about two inches from front to back. However, the morphological features of the teeth, and the shape and proportions of the jaw bone, recall those of the Higher Primates.

The molars and premolars are similar to those of *Dryopithecus* (and these are basically similar, in morphology, to those of later hominids and pongids). The molars are squarish though, and show no size increase from front to back. Also, the front and rear premolars are similar in size; the front premolar is not a sectorial tooth, and this implies that the upper canine was not large. The lower canine was relatively small.

In his field work, Simons not only found further specimens of *Propliopithecus,* but recovered the remains of a creature—later named *Aegypto-*

pithecus zeuxis—which was a very primitive dryopithecine. Yet this is a dryopithecine half as old again as the oldest previously known! The canines were large and the anterior lower premolars were sectorial—the molars were morphologically very similar to those of the earliest *Dryopithecus* from Africa and Europe, and they increased in size from front to back. The upper teeth showed the same sort of similarities to *Dryopithecus* as did the lower. So, here in the Oligocene, perhaps 30 million years ago, we have evidence showing that the great apes had already begun their evolution as a separate lineage. Now, the sort of differences which distinguish *Propliopithecus* and *Aegyptopithecus* are similar to those which distinguish *Ramapithecus,* the hominid, and *Dryopithecus,* the pongid.

Before I actually write that *Propliopithecus* was a hominid, before we commit ourselves to such a small scrap of bone, it is well to remember that the *relative* ages of *Propliopithecus* and *Aegyptopithecus* are still unknown. We do not know whether *Propliopithecus* is older or younger, for adequate field notes that would help in dating were not kept by the early expeditions. We simply cannot say if *Aegyptopithecus* is just a variant of *Propliopithecus,* or if *Propliopithecus* is ancestral to *Aegyptopithecus,* or if the two were contemporaries. If they did live at the same time it is possible that *Propliopithecus* was the earliest known hominid. A few heretics, St. George Mivart was one and Frederic Wood Jones another, believed that men and apes differentiated long ago, perhaps during the Eocene. Recently, W. L. Edwards has outlined the theoretical reasons for accepting an early rather than a late separation of man and ape.

To sum it up: we now know the mid-Tertiary ancestors of the living apes, and we have started to collect information about our own remote ancestors. Yet there is still a long way to go, for we have only the first few links in what must be a complete chain. If we are to reconstruct the ecology and behaviour of our evolutionary grandfathers (and granduncles) we need as much fossil material as possible.

We can feel satisfaction in rethinking some of the important aspects of our subject, for a little speculation, even premature speculation, is often preferable to no speculation at all.

Some Fallacies in the Study of Hominid Phylogeny

Elwyn L. Simons

The century-long search for documentation of the fossil record of man's ancestry, which was particularly stimulated by publication of Darwin's *Origin of Species* in 1859, has by now brought in relatively abundant evidence concerning the major stages of man's lineage during the Pleistocene epoch. Accelerated discovery during the past few years confirms the view that the mainstream of human evolution in Pleistocene times evidently passed through a species of *Australopithecus* and then through *Homo erectus* and men of Neanderthaloid type to the modern varieties of *Homo sapiens*. These comparatively new findings have shifted fundamental research somewhat away from the *Australopithecus-Homo sapiens* lineage, which most students consider a plausible sequence, toward the problem of the nature and distribution of pre-*Australopithecus* hominids and hominoids. It is in this area that the new discoveries of the major stages in human phylogeny will come. Generally speaking, study of the Pleistocene section of human phylogeny has been carried out by anatomists and anthropologists, while the Miocene-Pliocene portion of the story has been investigated mainly by paleontologists. There have been, and perhaps there will continue to be, good reasons for this dichotomy. The study of Tertiary Mammals (including non-human Primates) requires a more extensive background in stratigraphy, in field methods, and particularly in comparative osteology and mammalian taxonomy than is often possessed by students of man. Another factor has slowed progress in this area —the idea, expressed by some vertebrate paleontologists, that the evolution of higher Primates, and of man in particular, is too controversial and confused a subject to be worth much serious attention. If this view remains common among those best equipped to interpret fossil species, such lack of interest will only prolong the controversy.

In spite of the fact that there are almost no members of the Dryopithecinae of Miocene-Pliocene age for which reasonably comprehensive osteological remains are known, the actual number of specimens of this period that have been discovered is considerable (about 550), and the geographic range of the specimens is extensive. Moreover, advances in geochronometric dating techniques (potassium-argon analysis in particular) now, or shortly, will enable us to make a far more accurate temporal arrangement of man's pre-Pleistocene relatives than we have had. Many of these relatives fall taxonomically within the pongid subfamily Dryopithecinae. Although the fossil record for most dryopithecines is scanty, restudy of this osteologically limited material has now become imperative, because it is adequate to clarify the evolutionary succession of pongids and hominids.

I wish to state initially that I have carefully examined the view that *Proconsul,* from the East African Miocene, should be placed in a different subfamily from Eurasian dryopithecines and have found it unconvincing. Actually, there is hardly any morphological basis for separating Dryopithecinae (*Dryopithecus, Proconsul, Sivapithecus,* and related genera) from Ponginae (*Pongo, Pan, Gorilla*). Through the proper application of modern taxonomic principles, even without recovery of specimens more complete than those we now have, much more can be said about evolutionary relationships among the so-called dryopithecines than has been said to date. Dobzhansky recently summed up the pertinence of good taxonomy as it applies to fossil man. His point is equally relevant to the taxonomy of earlier hominoids.

> Does it really matter what Latin name one bestows on a fossil? Unfortunately it does. It flatters the discoverer's ego to have found a new hominid genus, or at least a new species, rather than a mere new race. But generic and specific names are not just arbitrary labels; they imply a biological status. Living men constitute a single species: *Homo sapiens.* Now, *Homo sapiens* can be descended from only one ancestral species living at any given time in the past. To be sure, some plant species arise from the hybridization of two ancestral species, followed by a doubling of the complement of chromosomes, but it is most unlikely that mankind could have arisen by such a process. It follows, then, that if two or several hominid species lived at a given time in the past, only one of them can possibly be our ancestor. All other species must be assumed to have died out without leaving descendants.

Undoubtedly a much more lucid picture of the Tertiary antecedents of man could be drawn on the basis of existing evidence were it not for the questionable nomenclatural practices of past years. Clearly, and regrettably, the taxonomic significance of the new systematics has been slower in gaining wide acceptance among anthropologists and paleontologists than among most biologists studying modern taxa. Of course, paleontologists have recognized for many years that the type individual of a fossil species is merely a specimen acquired through chance circumstances of fossilization and discovery from a population of variable organisms of which it may not even be a typical member. Types of fossil origin are thus chosen primarily as namebearers for postulated species groups. Apparently it was less generally understood, until comparatively recently, that when one makes a specimen the type of a new species, or of a new genus and species, there is an obligation laid on the proposer of the new taxon to present a good deal of morphological or other evidence of probable genetic separation from any previously described species. This point applies particularly to Hominoidea, in which there is greater variability in dental pattern and relative tooth size than there is in many other mammal groups. Distinctions in dentition in a hominid specimen, sufficient to warrant designation of the specimen as the type for a new species, must be at least as great as the distinctions that occur between species of the closest living relatives of the fossil form.

SPECIATION

In order to understand what fossil species were and are, it is necessary to comprehend the processes of speciation and to be familiar with modern methods of species discrimination among living animals. Thus, in the case of the dryopithecines, in order to distinguish two fossil species of a given genus, one should be able to demonstrate that forms which are roughly contemporaneous show characters that fall outside the extreme range of morphological variability to be noted in comparable parts of all subspecies of present-day pongids, such as *Pan troglodytes* or *Gorilla gorilla*. High physical and dental variability in given species of man and apes has long been known, but it is clear that this has not been taken into account by the majority of past and recent describers of fossil hominoids. Beginning with Mayr in 1950, or slightly earlier, several experienced taxonomists have drawn attention to the extreme oversplitting of the known varieties of Pleistocene hominids. Since the late 19th century this erroneous approach to taxonomy has produced approximately 30 genera and almost countless species. At the other extreme from this taxonomic prolixity stand such workers as Mayr and Dobzhansky, who, drawing on their knowledge of modern speciation, have adduced evidence for a single line of but a few species, successive through time, in this particular lineage. To alter their view it would only be necessary to demonstrate the occurrence of two distinguishable species of hominids in a single zone of one site, but, despite much discussion of possible contemporaneity, in my opinion such contemporaneity has not been satisfactorily established. There is fair morphological evidence that there were two species of *Australopithecus* (*A. africanus* and *A. robustus*), but their synchronous existence has not been confirmed by finds of both at the same level in one site. Although the concept of monophyletic hominid evolution during the Pleistocene is now widely accepted, certain fallacies continue to affect thinking on probable pre-Pleistocene forms in this subfamily.

In the discussion that follows I attempt to outline and to clarify some of these fallacies. Changes in the taxonomy of fossil hominoids are suggested, on the basis of my direct observation of relevant original materials in America, Europe, East Africa, and India during the past ten years. Among those acquainted with the traditional atmosphere of controversy that has surrounded the question of hominid origins there is often some reluctance to set forth an up-to-date survey of the implications of recent research on the subject. Clearly, all the points made here cannot be extensively supported by documentary evidence in this brief review. Nevertheless, it seems advisable to set some of the newer conclusions before the public at this stage.

OVERSPLITTING OF FOSSIL SPECIES

Apart from the widespread temptation to be the author of a new species or genus, there are three primary causes of the oversubdivision of many extinct taxa (in the case under consideration, fossil Pongidae and Hominidae). These are, (i) uncertainties resulting from incompleteness of the available fossils; (ii) doubts concerning the identity and relative age of species (whether two or more given "types" are time-successive or contemporaneous); and (iii) questions relative to the possible, or probable, existence in the past of ecologic barriers that could perhaps have brought about speciation between populations widely separated geographically.

In view of these and other sources of uncertainty, taxonomists of fossil Primates have generally sidestepped the question reference of new finds to previously established species, maintaining that it is unwise to assign later discoveries to species named earlier when finds are not strictly comparable or when they consist only of fragments of the whole skeleton; they frequently describe as separate species specimens which appear to come from clearly different time horizons; and they usually draw specific or generic distinctions when materials are recovered from sites that are widely separated geographically, particularly if these sites are on different continents. With continued advances in the dating of past faunas by geochemical means, and with advances in paleogeography, it becomes increasingly possible to improve procedures and practices in the taxonomy of extinct Primates, and to resolve many of the above-mentioned problems.

Generic and specific distinctions of imperfectly known forms

In the past it has sometimes happened that a taxonomist proposing a new species or genus of fossil vertebrate has maintained that, although no characteristics that would, of themselves, warrant separation of the new fossil specimen (B) from a previously known type (A) could be observed, the recovery of more complete osteological data would show the forms concerned to be different. This sort of anticipation is poor scientific practice, and such an argument should never be used in an effort to distinguish a new taxon unless (i) there is clear evidence of a marked separation in time between the previously described species A and the putative "new" form B, or (ii) there is definite geological evidence of geographic or ecologic separation—for example, evidence of a seaway or a desert—which would greatly reduce or eliminate the possibility of morphologically similar specimens A and B being members of one widespread, variable, but interbreeding, population. Some students would not grant even these two exceptions but believe that morphological distinctions must be demonstrated. Generally, some small distinction occurs as a result of individual variation and can be misused as evidence of species difference. Therefore it is best to rely mainly on differences which can be shown to be probable indicators of distinctly adapted, and consequently different, species.

Abundant data on Recent and late Tertiary mammals show that many of the larger species were, and are, distributed in more than one continent, particularly throughout Holarctica. Moreover, the belief that there were fairly close faunal ties between Africa and Eurasia during Miocene-Recent times has been confirmed by the recovery and description, during the past three years, of new samples of continental vertebrates of this period from Kenya, Tanganyika, and the Congo. Several of the mammals in these localities show close morphological similarity to Eurasian forms, and while many African species of the period do not show extra-African ties, the types which the two land masses have in common do show that increased intercommunication was possible. The fact that some stocks did not range outside Africa cannot offset the clear evidence that many of the same genera and even of the same species occurred in both Eurasia and Africa at this time.

Taxonomic uncertainty deriving from temporal differences

Many hominoid species were proposed in the past mainly on the strength of a posited time separation from a nearly identical but presumably earlier (or later) "species." Most of the "species" designated on this basis should be reinvestigated in an effort to determine their true temporal position and taxonomic affinites. A "new look" is needed because of recent improvements in the potassium-argon method of dating, and in other geochemical dating methods which should ultimately enable students of past species to discuss them in terms of an absolue time scale. Like other kinds of scientific evidence, dates obtained by the potassium-argon method can of course be misapplied. For instance, it must be demonstrated that dated sediments come from (or bracket) the same zones as the faunas they are supposed to date. There are other well-known sources of error in geochemical dating, but in my experience the strongest criticisms of this method come from persons relatively unacquainted with the analytical techniques involved.

One example of the application of geochemical dating techniques to the study of fossil hominoids will suffice to show what wide application such information may have. Simons has proposed that, on morphological grounds, the primitive gibbon-like genera *Pliopithecus* and *Limnopithecus* can no longer be considered distinguishable. Newly recovered materials of *Pliopithecus* [subgenus *Epipliopithecus*] from Miocene Vindobonian deposits of

Europe are closely similar, both in dentition and in postcranial structure, to "*Limnopithecus*" from the Rusinga Island beds of Kenya, East Africa. The fauna associated with this East Africa primate was regarded, at the time of Hopwood's proposal that a genus "*Limnopithecus*" be established, as being of earliest Miocene age and, therefore, older than the European *Pliopithecus* materials. In his fullest discussion of the generic characteristics of "*Limnopithecus*," Hopwood was able to list only a few slight features of distinction between the tooth rows, then known, of *Pliopithecus* and of "*Limnopithecus*." These are dental variations of a degree which have repeatedly been shown to occur even within members of one small population of such living pongids as *Pongo pygmaeus* and *Gorilla gorilla*. Hopwood further bolstered establishment of his new genus by remarking that additional bases for distinguishing the genera concerned "are the various ages of the deposits in which they are found and their widely separated localities." But he did comment, "apart from convenience neither reason [for placing the African species in a new genus] is particularly sound. . . ." The point I stress here is that taxonomic separations such as Hopwood proposed are not "convenient," for they create complexity where it does not exist.

Recently, Evernden and his associates have reported a date of 14.9 ± 1.5 million years obtained by the potassium-argon technique from biotite samples of tufaceous sediments in the Rusinga Island series. Admittedly this is only a single datum, but if this sample is truly satisfactory for dating by the potassium-argon method, and if it does come from the same horizons as the "*Proconsul* fauna," it shows that the fauna which contains "*Limnopithecus*" *legetet* and "*L.*" *macinnesi* could be contemporary with the European Vindobonian materials. Nevertheless, more dating of this fauna will be necessary before we have proof that it is as young as this. If this younger age becomes established, species of "*Limnopithecus*" may well fall entirely within the known temporal distribution of European members of *Pliopithecus*. Evernden and his co-workers also state that the evidences from relative faunal dating suggest a middle or late, rather than an early, Miocene age for the Rusinga fossils. In my opinion this view is supported by close similarities between three other Rusinga primate species (which I discuss later) and forms which occur in the Siwalik deposits of India, of probable middle or late Miocene age.

Finally, it should be stressed that Hopwood did exhibit considerable foresight in recognizing the basic unsoundness of attempting to reinforce a taxonomic separation by the argument of possible (but not proved) temporal difference. The foregoing example, and others which could be noted, show the danger of using the temporal argument when separating closely similar fossil specimens taxonomically. Moreover, it has been demonstrated that many extent mammalian genera have time ranges greater than the entire Miocene epoch, as estimated at present. Numerous instances of genera with long time ranges could be adduced. For instance, the perissodactyl genera *Tapirus* and *Dicerorhinus* in all probability extend back to the early Miocene or late Oligocene, about 25×10^6 years ago; members of some genera of carnivores (*Ursus, Bassariscus, Lutra, Felis,* and others) have all been described from deposits of late Miocene or early Pliocene age (10 to 15 $\times$ 10^6 years ago). Of course, we do not know that any hominoid genera survived as long as the genera in these categories, but most hominoid genera probably endured for at least 3 to 7 million years without much change of form. Consequently, even if it were known that European and East African *Pliopithecus* differed in absolute age by 4 or 5 million years, taxonomic separation at the generic level could not safely be based on this fact alone.

Migration, paleogeography, and past restrictions of species ranges

One of the most widespread assumptions in the study of the antecedents of man is that at some early period (Miocene, Pliocene, or "Villafranchian," depending on the author concerned) the species ancestral to *Homo sapiens* was restricted to a comparatively small geographic area. This restriction is taken by many scientists to account for the supposed "failure" to find pre-Pleistocene human forerunners. Such an assumption may be referred to as the "Garden of Eden illusion." Insofar as this widespread view is held as a scientific theory by some persons interested in the evolutionary history of man, it appears to be based on analogy with the restricted ranges of various recent mammal species, particularly, in this case, of higher Primates with limited distributions, such as orangutan (*Pongo pygmaeus*) or mountain gorilla (*Gorilla g. beringei*).

PLACE OF MAN'S ORIGIN

Some people believe that the place of hominid or human origin has not been discovered; conjectures, by others, as to its location have followed shifting vogues. Thus, when the first materials of *"Meganthropus"* were recovered in Java from levels lower stratigraphically than those at which *"Pithecanthropus"* remains were recovered, many students favored the view that differentiation of the ancestral stock of mankind occurred in Southeast Asia. Later, with the realization that *Australopithecus* finds from the Transvaal were hominid remains, a case was made for initial hominid differentiation in South Africa. Now, new additions to our knowledge of early Hominidae, made in East Africa by Leakey and his associates, have shifted attention northward to that quadrant of the African continent.

It should be obvious that the oldest *known* localities of occurrence of human tools, or of given species of higher Primates, are probably not the first places where these technical developments or species arose. In order to report with confidence the exact regions of origin of the human species and of earliest cultural tiems, we would need 100 times the archeological and paleontological evidence that we now have, with absolute dates for all sites.

There are a number of possible reasons for the persistence of the "Garden of Eden" concept among scientists, but here I mention only a few of the misconceptions through which this point of view appears to have been initiated and sustained. Students who believe that ancestral species occurred in restricted areas may have in mind four well-known kinds of diffusion from local centers: (i) spreading of cultural items from specific places of invention; (ii) wandering of tribes, both historic and prehistoric, over great distances; (iii) spreading of advantageous gene mutations from individuals or local populations outward throughout an entire species population; and (iv) intercontinental faunal migrations across land bridges at various times in the past.

All these, and other, similar concepts, while pertinent in their own right, do not in my opinion validate the illusion that, through time, each species, as a unit, wanders widely from one region to another. Such a picture is particularly inaccurate in the case of Late Tertiary land-mammal species, such as species among the dryopithecines, whose main area of distribution was the tropical and warm-temperate portion of the Old World. Of course, given sufficient time, species ranges, particularly among the large Mammalia, do expand and contract, and do occasionally shift from one continent to another in response to environmental change. Nevertheless, movement of subpopulations is much greater than the range shifts of an entire species. Even within an evolving species lineage, time-successive species apparently do not appear from one of several populations of the antecedent species; in general, all populations of a single species tend to evolve together, the species changing as a whole because, as the environment changes, newly advantageous genes originating in various sections of the group spread through the species. Of course, if these streams of gene flow are broken for sufficiently long periods, speciation will ultimately occur. A single species, however, *is* a single species just because gene flow throughout all its members is (or recently has been) taking place.

RANGE OF LARGE MAMMAL SPECIES

Now, in applying these ideas to the evolution of large mammals in the Miocene-Recent period, primarily to mammals of the tropical and warm-temperate regions of Palearctica, certain points extremely relevant to the interpretation of dryopithecine evolution emerge. The first of these is illustrated in Figure 1 which shows a hypothetical model of the range of a large mammal species-series at three periods in the earth's history. The diagram is given as an abstraction because limitations in the distribution of sites yielding fossil land mammals (limitations that result from erosion of sediments or from non-deposition) are such that exact species ranges for past forms cannot now be drawn (and probably never can be). Nevertheless, this is the sort of distribution which recovered fossils indicate was characteristic, during the period with which we are concerned, of certain species of groups such as elephants, hyenas, the big cats, and ruminants. In this context it should be pointed out that the early supposition that many surviving species of large mammals have diminished ranges owing primarily to climatic fluctuations during the Pleistocene and to the activity of human hunters has, by now,

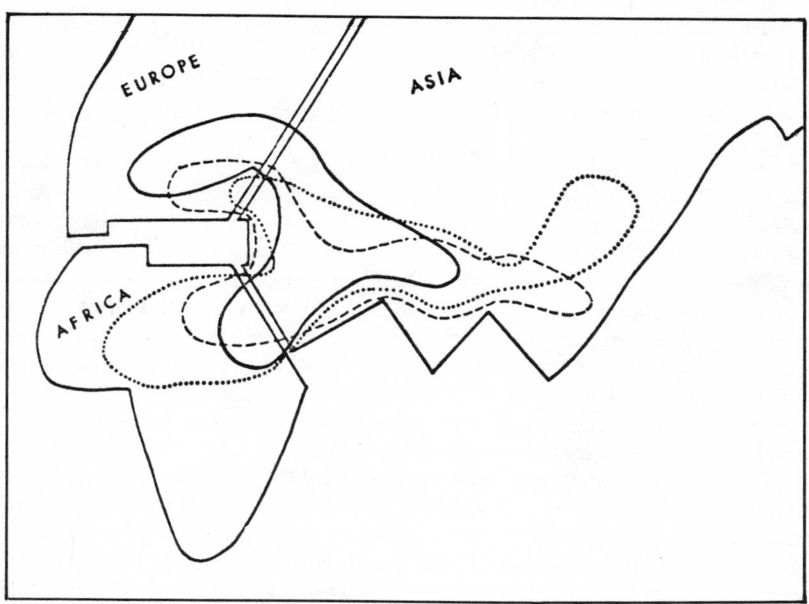

FIGURE 1. *Three species ranges, successive through time, of a hypothetical lineage of a large mammal, as they might have appeared in (dashed lines) the late Miocene, (dotted lines) the early Pliocene, and (solid lines) the late Pliocene*

been abundantly confirmed. Two examples, taken from dozens, illustrate this point. The lion, *Felis leo,* is now extinct in Eurasia except for a few small surviving populations in India. However, 15,000 to 20,000 years ago, *Felis leo* occurred widely in Europe and the Near East and was, presumably, then abundant in the Indian subcontinent and perhaps even further east. Ewer has reported fossil remains closely resembling *Felis tigris* (but from a mammal slightly larger than the largest of modern tigers) from Olduvai Gorge in Tanganyika. Today, of course, the tiger exists only in Asia.

In the sort of species succession through time that is diagrammed in Figure 1, it is not possible to say where the paleontological "species" came from—the population during, for example, the late Pliocene did not come *from* any one place and, strictly speaking, does not have a known place of origin. As nearly as can at present be determined, from the literature and from direct study of the relevant fossils in East Africa and in India in Miocene-Pliocene times, Eurasia and Africa had over 35 genera of land mammals in common. These included insectivores, anthracotheres, rodents, ruminants, monkeys, apes, hyracoids, hyenas, felids, mastodonts, deinotheres, and several other groups of mammals. Members of over 15 additional mammalian genera that now occur in Africa but have not yet been found in fossil sites on that continent have been found in Pliocene deposits of the Indian Siwalik Hills.

This total figure of half-a-hundred genera stands in spite of the early tendency to separate, at the generic level, African mammals from allied forms found elsewhere, just because they are of African provenance. Nevertheless, there are some distinct differences in African and Eurasian faunas of Miocene and Pliocene times.

Although numerous groups do appear to have been prevented from crossing between the two areas, there is now evidence that certain mammal species had no difficulty in getting across whatever partial ecological barriers may have existed between the two regions in Pliocene times. One of these is the proboscidean species *Trilophodon angustidens,* which has been found as far east as Baluchistan, occurs in the Kenya Miocene, and has recently been reported by Hooijer from the Congo. There are enough such occurrences to indicate to me that there was reasonably free faunal interchange between these two major regions of the Old World at some time in the Miocene. I see no reason why certain species of dryopithecines or early hominids, or both, could not have participated in this interchange.

Nevertheless, one may ask whether higher Primates ever had range distributions as extensive as those of such later Tertiary Mammalia as I have mentioned. Clearly, the range distribution of most present-day great apes is a restricted or relief distribution, but the fossil record of the pongids for the Miocene through the Villafranchian, as it now stands, is ample indication that certain varieties of these animals had much wider range distributions formerly than they have now. This also appears to be true for many animals of the later Pleistocene. For instance, *Pongo pygmaeus,* not restricted to the islands of Borneo and Sumatra, was then present in South China, and if the Siwalik Pliocene fossils reported by Pilgrim are truly ancestors of this species, it probably had, at an earlier date, an extended range through the Malay Peninsula and Burma into India. Probable antecedents of the gibbons (*Pliopithecus*) are known from several scattered localities throughout Europe and northern and eastern Africa; at one time they must have been distributed (in suitable habitats) between these areas and the present range of members of this genus, in Southeast Asia. Evidently the ranges of modern species of great apes have dwindled greatly as a result of environmental changes in the relatively recent past. Among such changes was shrinking of the type of forest cover that was necessary for their existence. In certain populations, such as those of *Pongo* in South Asia, extermination or restriction of isolated enclaves on offshore islands surely came about as a result of hunting by human beings.

One of the varieties of primates least affected by these types of constriction are the present-day species of the genus *Macaca.* Distribution of members of this genus (Fig. 2) illustrates the extremes of geographic range which members of a single stock of a prehominoid grade of partly arboreal primates have been able to achieve. It need not be assumed that man's ancestors had limited species range until they became terrestrial bipeds. In late-Pliocene and Villafranchian times, *Macaca* was nearly twice as widespread geographically as it is today. An acceptable evolutionary interpretation of this distribution would be that the ancestors of present-day *Macaca* reached the present extremes of their range (Japan, Gibraltar, and so on)

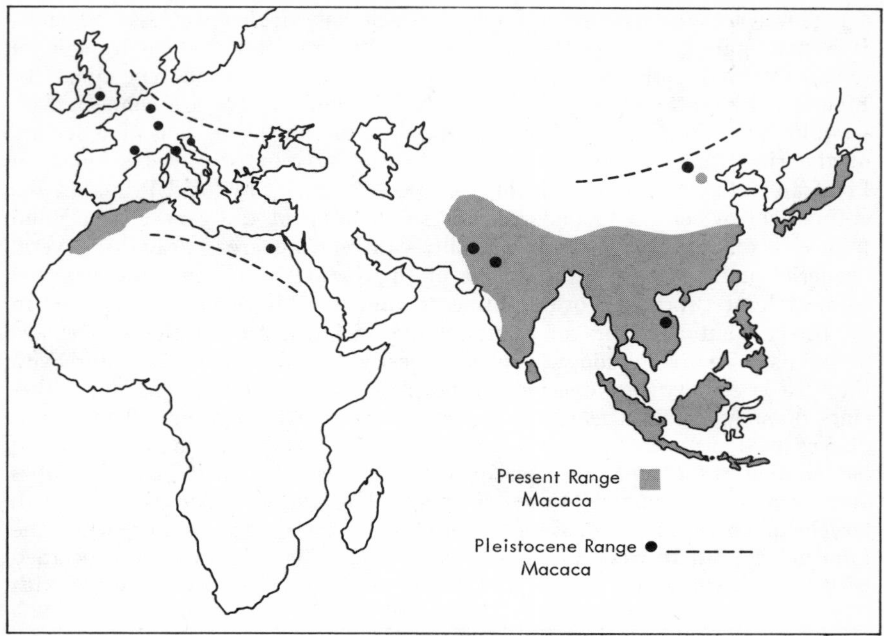

FIGURE 2. *Recent and fossil distribution of the species of* Macaca.

when continental shelves were exposed during one of the Pleistocene glaciations, and that the far-flung present-day populations are descendants of perhaps no more than one widespread species that existed 1 to 3 million years ago. Of course, this species could have been already differentiating into genetically diverse populations (subspecies), with only moderate gene exchange between them, before and while the total range of the species was approaching its greatest extent. But it seems more probable that such species distinctions as exist in *Macaca* came about through relatively recent cessation of gene flow between various populations within the entire genus range. This would be particularly the case for populations isolated on islands since the last glaciation, or separated by late disappearance of suitable habitat, as between the western population of North Africa and its eastern allies. Members of *Macaca* appear to have been able to achieve such broad distribution mainly because its species have been ecologically plastic. Some varieties, such as the Japanese monkey, have remained relatively arboreal, while others, like the Barbary ape of Gibraltar, are almost entirely terrestrial. Conceivably, from the late Miocene on, the earliest hominids were at least as capable of extending their range as the species of *Macaca* evidently were at a somewhat later date.

Thus, it can no longer be argued with confidence that the reason no pre-Pleistocene forerunners of man have been discovered is that these prehominids lived only in a limited geographical area of the Old World, and in a region (perhaps of tropical forests) which has yielded no fossil remains. It is now quite clear that the early hominoids as we know them from fossil remains ranged widely in the Old World in Miocene and Pliocene times. In Figure 3 the scattered occurrences of the hominoid genera are connected by straight lines, forming rough approximations to range diagrams. Particulars of the sites and species upon which Figure 3 is based can be found in Piveteau. In spite of three contrary factors—the rarity of fossil Primates, the enthusiasm of certain taxonomists for subdividing at the generic level, and failure to discover fossil-bearing localities in relevant areas—each of several "generic" units among Anthropoidea of this period have now been reported from at least two Old World continents, and some have been discovered in all three. That ancestors of man are not included among these extensive materials is, in my opinion, no longer an easily defended viewpoint. Moreover, the idea is equally controverted on morphological grounds. Some dryopithecines do show hominid features. The argument that human antecedents lived during pre-Pleistocene times in a restricted area which remains undiscovered has another rather unlikely consequence. This assumption implies that apes and even some monkeys (*Dryopithecus, Pliopithecus, Macaca*), although largely or partly arboreal, were able to spread their range widely, while the forerunners of man were somehow unable to do this. We are here concerned with a stock which, by the early Pliocene, was probably experimenting with

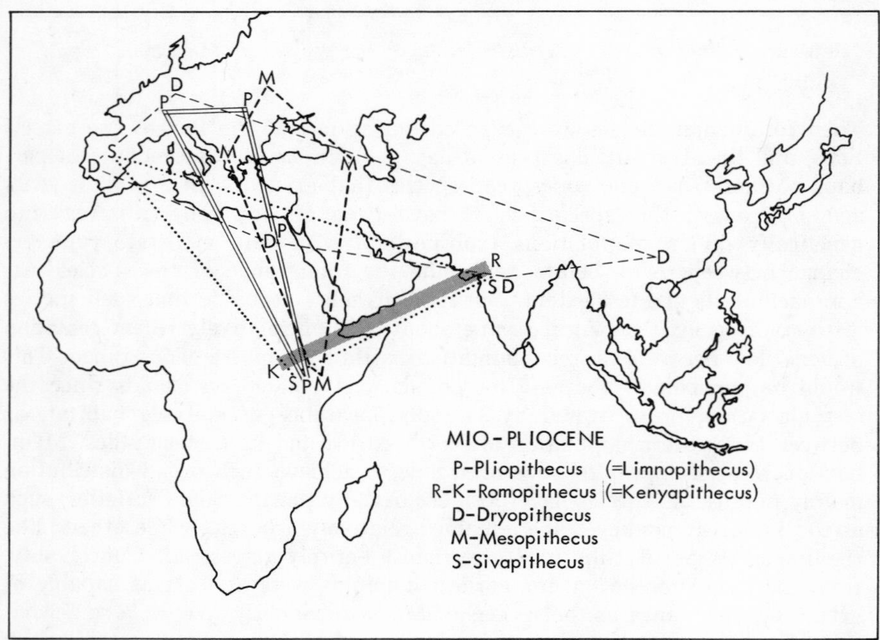

FIGURE 3. *Occurrence and range distribution of some Miocene-Pliocene* Hominoidea.

terrestrial living and bipedal locomotion. If, at this time, man's predecessors were not able to distribute themselves as readily as their contemporaries among the monkeys and apes could, then it becomes necessary to conclude that man's evolutionary emergence from his pre-human past was truly explosive. This conclusion becomes all the more necessary if we assume that our supposedly poorly distributed antecedents suddenly outdistanced their more "primitive" contemporaries in the matter of species-range extension.

SPECIES DISTINCTIONS

It should be noted that, although the particular specimens assigned by one or more competent authorities to the genera indicated in Figure 3 are adequately known for purposes of generic placement, students cannot tell definitely whether the specimens assigned to a genus were members of the same or of different species. The common practice has been to regard European, Asian, and African finds of later Tertiary fossil Mammalia as belonging to different species, presumably in part because of the tacit assumption that ecologic barriers would, in nearly all cases, have prevented members of a species from reaching all three areas. Nevertheless, since these fossil forms are known primarily from fragmentary dentitions, it remains as difficult to prove that members of populations discovered in different continents represent distinct species as to demonstrate that they are members of the same species. Consequently, it will not be possible to test the validity of species distinctions among many such extinct mammals until much greater numbers of fossils of particular groups are known. In the case of these fossil "apes," for instance, when enough material has been recovered, statistical methods may be used in making species distinctions.

In connection with Figure 3, it should also be pointed out that leading taxonomists of fossils differ as to the generic assignment of some of the species represented. For instance, after initial assignment of certain Spanish dryopithecine remains to the genus *Sivapithecus* (an assignment followed here), this material was later referred elsewhere. On the other hand, Lewis believes that materials currently assignd to *Dryopithecus* from the Miocene of Czechoslovakia should be placed in the genus *Sivapithecus*.

Consequently, I doubt that it has been established that *Sivapithecus* does not occur in Europe. Conversely, Figure 3 does not indicate a range extension of *Pliopithecus* into Southeast Asia, but it seems entirely possible that the very fragmentary type of *"Hylopithecus"* from the Siwalik "series" may represent a primitive gibbon, perhaps assignable to *Pliopithecus*. With reference to this specimen, it seems instructive to quote what must be one of the most amazing passages in the history of bad taxonomic practice. This remark occurs as a conclusion to the description of the type species of *"Hylopithecus"*: "In preference to leaving the tooth now described without a generic name and so increasing the difficulty of reference I am giving it the name of *Hylopithecus,* although I am conscious that my material is quite insufficient for diagnosis."

ORIGIN OF THE HOMINIDAE

In 1910 Pilgrim was ready to state that Hominidae are descended from *Sivapithecus*. Later, in 1922, W. K. Gregory observed "that man is a late Tertiary offshoot of the *Dryopithecus-Sivapithecus* group. . . ." Discoveries of hominoids during the half century which have elapsed since Pilgrim's writing have reinforced his viewpoint. Entirely apart from morphological considerations, such conclusions gain strength in the light of the taxonomic procedures and zoogeographic examples that I have discussed. It is curious that, in spite of numerous suitably cautious demonstrations in paleontological papers that the origins of man lay among the dryopithecines, it is still widely held by experts that next to nothing of definite value is known about the pre-Pleistocene forerunners of man. One is reminded of a possibly apocryphal comment said to have been made in 1860 by the wife of the Bishop of Worcester. On learning from her husband that T. H. Huxley had then recently argued that man had ape-like ancestors, she observed: "Descended from apes! My dear, let us hope that it is not true, but if it is let us pray that it will not become generally known." Although the fact of human evolution is no longer doubted, the phyletic sequence before the Pleistocene has never been elucidated during the more than 100 years which separate us from the pronouncements of T. H. Huxley.

Briefly, the following relevant facts as to the origin of the family of man are known. Fossil "apes" of the *Dryopithecus-Sivapithecus* type have now been recovered from deposits distributed throughout a vast area of warm-climate regions of the Old World, including sites in Spain, France, central Europe, Turkey, Georgia, the U.S.S.R., Egypt, Kenya, Uganda, Pakistan, India, and China. Without undertaking a taxonomic revision of these forms at this juncture, but assuming for the moment that all these occurrences do in fact pertain to dryopithecines, I must point out that far too many genera have been proposed for them. Some of the genera which have been named are *Ankarapithecus, Austriacopithecus, Bramapithecus, Griphopithecus, Dryopithecus, Hylopithecus, Indopithecus, Kenyapithecus, Neopithecus, Paidopithex, Proconsul, Paleosimia, Ramapithecus, Rhenopithecus, Sivapithecus, Sugrivapithecus,* and *Udabnopithecus*.

Such a large number of distinct genera implies an extensive adaptive radiation of sudden appearance in the early or middle Miocene, but in the case of the dryopithecines this diversification probably occurred more on paper than in reality. Direct study of nearly all of the original specimens of these Primates suggests to me that the dryopithecines should probably be assigned to only three or four distinct genera, perhaps even fewer.

Species of four of these "genera" (*Dryopithecus, Sivapithecus, Proconsul,* and *Ramapithecus*) are now fairly well known. To date, however, no student has adequately dealt with the possibility that not even all of these genera may be separable from each other. This is an important issue, for it now appears that the direct hominid lineage passed through members of at least two of these taxa.

Starting with the more *Australopithecus*-like of these forms and working backward through time, we can now draw some fairly clear inferences about the evolutionary appearance of Hominidae. *Ramapithecus brevirostris,* of probable early Pliocene (Pontian) age, from the Nagri zone of the Siwalik Hills of India, has long been known to possess several characters in the upper dentition and maxilla which significantly approach the dental conformation of Pleistocene species of tool-making man. Briefly, these characters, which distinguish the forms from typical pongids and suggest hominid ties, are a parabolic (not U-shaped) dental arcade, an arched palate, a canine fossa, low-crowned cheek teeth, small incisors and canines, a low degree of prognathism, and a short face. Separately, almost all of these features can be found among pongids, but their occurrence in combination in *R. brevirostris* is a strong indication of hominid ties. Recently, Leakey has described a new East African primate specimen, *"Kenyapithecus wickeri,"* probably from about the same period or a little earlier, which is exactly like. *R. brevirostris* in these and other features. In fact, in my opinion, not one *significant* character of difference exists between the two specimens (both are maxillae). This being so, the new form from Kenya should be assigned tentatively to *R. brevirostris,* at least until such a time as further material provides a basis for demonstrating that the two are different species. The conclusion that these two specimens are at least of the same genus has recently been supported by Frisch, who has also studied them directly. Perhaps the most extraordinary thing about Leakey's Fort Ternan, Kenya, specimen is its extreme similarity to the type specimen of *R. brevirostris*—an important and very significant fact that "generic" splitting only obscures. Greater differences than are to be noted here typically occur among members of a single-family social group within nearly all species of present-day hominoids. These two specimens indicate to me a considerable probability that is early Pliocene or latest Miocene times, or both, a single species of progressive (?) dryopithecine ranged all the way from northern India to East Africa, and perhaps farther. Personal examination of the specimens concerned also indicates that a third individual of this species, from the Nagri zone of the Siwalik Hills, in the Haritalyangar area, is represented by Pilgrim's specimen No. D185—the right maxilla of *"Dryopithecus punjabicus"*—in the Indian Museum, Calcutta. This specimen agrees with the other two in significant details of dental morphology, and in the possession of a much-reduced rostrum and an extremely short canine root (alveolus). These three specimens of *Ramapithecus* strongly reinforce each other in indicating a valid species group. Moreover, all three specimens come from a stratigraphic level higher than that at which most of the more generalized dryopithecine remains are found.

The transitional nature of these specimens of itself raises the question of arbitrariness in separating the families Pongidae and Hominidae—a problem which has also been posed recently in connection with another event, the discovery of close biochemical similarities between man and the apes, in particular the African apes. Nevertheless, there do seem to be fairly good reasons for continuing to view the Pongidae and the Hominidae as distinct enough to be considered separate families. What I want to stress is the fact that the transitional nature of the *Ramapithecus* materials is such that they cannot be placed with finality in either group. Personally I do not see that it very much matters whether members of this genus be regarded as advanced pongids or as primitive hominids, but perhaps considerations of morphology slightly favor placement among the hominids. There is certainly no need to produce a new, higher category for such links—an alternative which has sometimes been resorted to in the past when a fossil taxon was determined to be roughly intermediate between two others.

TWO SERIES OF DRYOPITHECINES

To date, the most extensive series of dryopithecines come from two main areas, the Rusinga Island and Fort Ternan beds of Kenya and the Siwalik Hills of India and Pakistan. A primary difficulty in understanding the actual significance of these two series of Primates arises from the fact that the Indian dryopithecines were studied and described primarily in the period between 1910 and 1937, while the dryopithecines of Kenya have been dealt with mainly since 1951. No one has ever published the results of extensive comparative study of the two sets of materials. Lewis, in the most recent taxonomic treatment of the Siwalik "apes," in 1937, reduced the number of genera to four (*Bramapithecus, Ramapithecus, Sivapithecus, Sugrivapithecus*), with ten contained species. Members of the first two of these genera he regarded as more manlike than members of the other two; *Sivapithecus* and *Sugrivapithecus* he regarded as being closer to the present-day great apes. Unfortunately, there was a lack of associations between upper and lower dentitions in the Siwalik material, and knowledge of some of these genera—such as *Bramapithecus,* known only from jaw fragments containing the last two molars—was very limited. There were no whole or nearly complete dentitions in which to study the range of variability. This situation has now changed, because of the recovery in Africa (1948–1962) of relatively complete portions of skulls, maxillae, and mandibles of several individual dryopithecines, together with postcranial bones and, in some cases, associated upper and lower jaws. Comparison of these two series of data indicate the following problems.

(1) In both the Kenyan and the Indian sites (in the lower part of the section, in particular) is found a large form with large snout, protruding incisors, slicing anterior premolars, and rather high-crowned teeth. In the East African material the lingual molar cingula are more pronounced, but otherwise, characters of dentition, snout, and jaw do not differ significantly. Mainly, these Miocene varieties have been called *Sivapithecus indicus* (Siwaliks), and *Proconsul major* (Rusinga). May it not be that these two sets of fossils represent a single species that ranged fairly widely, and perhaps over a long period, but which in known populations (even from far-flung portions of its range) is not particularly variable? This large-snouted type of ape is temporally distributed from early or middle Miocene (Rusinga; Chinji, in the Siwaliks) to latest Miocene or early Pliocene (Fort Ternan; Nagri, in the Siwaliks), as is evidenced by a very large upper canine re-

covered at Fort Ternan, at the same level as *"Kenyapithecus,"* reported by Leakey; perhaps by other teeth found at Fort Ternan, that have not been described; and by several discoveries in the Nagri Zone. Differences in the molar-crown patterns of the two populations are about as great within each area as between the two groups. A few successive species may be indicated by this material, or only a single species may be involved. This species could well be ancestral to the gorilla and chimpanzee. Ancestors of the African apes certainly need not always have been restricted to that continent.

(2) A second primate form common to the Kenya and Indian areas in the Miocene is represented by the *Sivapithecus africanus* material (Kenya) and the "species" *Sivapithecus sivalensis* (India). In this group the teeth, particularly the canines, are relatively smaller than in *"S." indicus,* and lingual cingula on upper molars apparently occur less frequently. The possibility remains high that other East African and Siwalik species, of the 15 accepted as valid in the more recent literature, will fall into synonymy with these two species as new data are recovered, or as a result of a fuller comparative study now in progress. The main distinction in dentition (and almost the only difference in known parts) between some *Sivapithecus* and modern *Pongo* is the higher degree of crenulation of the crowns of cheek teeth in *Pongo*. Several specimens of Indian *Sivapithecus* show rather crenulate molar crowns, and this may be assumed to indicate something about the origin of the orangutan. Such crenulations are particularly developed in the upper molar described by Pilgrim as *"Paleosimia,"* which may be a valid genus. In view of these crenulate teeth, it appears probable that a species that differentiated toward the Bornean great ape is represented in the Siwalik material, but this form has not been fully distinguished in taxonomic work to date. The probability that *Proconsul* cannot be separated generically from *Dryopithecus* is worth mentioning here. Both these genera, if indeed they are two rather than one, appear to be restricted to the Miocene. *Sivapithecus* apparently crosses the Mio-Pliocene boundary but is not easily separated from *Ramapithecus,* a conclusion indicated by Leakey's report on the East African materials and by my own studies on the Indian dryopithecines.

CONCLUSION

In concluding it seems advisable to make several observations as to the current state of knowledge of the origins of advanced hominoids.

The fossil hominoids of the Miocene of Kenya do not now appear to belong to the early part of that epoch, as had been previously believed, but may be of middle or, less probably, late Miocene age. Similarities between hominoids of the Miocene in India and Kenya, together with resemblances in other members of the two faunas, suggest that the Chinji Zone of the Siwaliks may be middle or late Miocene, as originally suggested by several early workers. At this time the "radiation" which produced the great apes of today and man seems barely to have begun. The possible occurrence of *Dryopithecus* in early Miocene equivalents of Egypt requires further investigation. There is now nearly universal agreement among those most competent to judge that *Oreopithecus* does not stand in the ancestral line of later pongids and hominids, although it is related to them. In view of these conclusions, the origins of man and of the great apes of Africa and Borneo are seen to lie directly among the dryopithecines. This conclusion supports the extensive discussions of Gregory as to the significance for human phylogeny of the *Dryopithecus* molar pattern and LeGros Clark's analysis of the morphological evidences favoring the occurrence of secondary canine reduction in the ancestry of Hominidae.

There is now adequate fossil evidence to indicate, (i) that, from about middle Miocene times, a few widely distributed species of the larger hominoids were present in both Eurasia and Africa and that successive differentiation of these species, through time, has occurred, with little branching or radiation; (ii) that the primary center of speciation among these animals was outside of Europe; (iii) that some dryopithecines in known parts entirely close the slight morphological gap between Hominidae and Pongidae; and (iv) that, if reports as to localities of *Australopithecus* by several serious students be accepted, the data now show that this earliest generally accepted antecedent of man was widely distributed in tropical regions of the Old World in the early Pleistocene (Fig. 4). Present archeological evidence does suggest that the use of tools may have occurred first in Africa, but this is not the same as to suppose that the initial species of man differentiated there, unless man be defined solely as a tool-manufacturing primate. To date, the latter supposition is an inference primarily supported by negative evidence—namely, the scanty recovery of australopithecines and of pebble

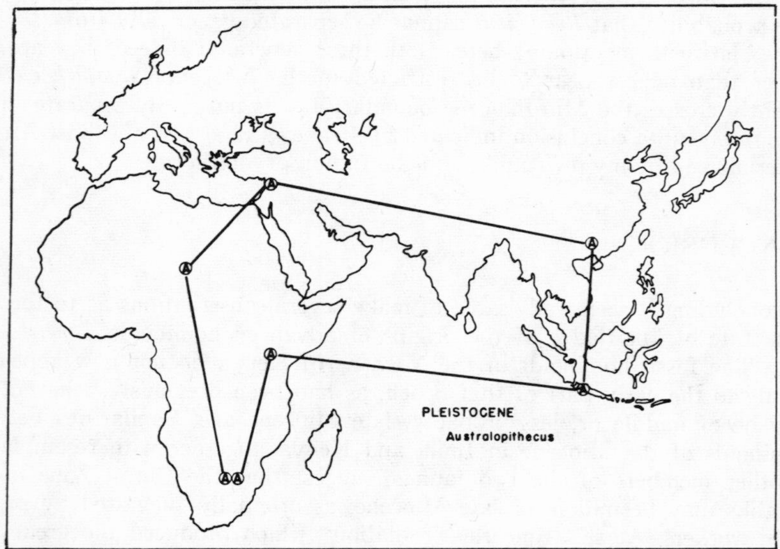

FIGURE 4. *Reported range of* Australopithecus *species.*

tools in Southeast Asia and China. It must be remembered that one creditable occurrence is all that is needed to demonstrate the early presence of *Australopithecus* in the East. Such an occurrence apparently has now been confirmed by von Koenigswald, through his description of about a dozen teeth, assigned by him to a new genus, *"Hemianthropus,"* in materials recovered from Chinese drugstores. In my opinion these teeth are from members of the Australopithecinae assignable to the subgenus *Paranthropus,* but Woo suggests that some of these teeth could belong to *Gigantopithecus.*

Ecology and the Protohominids

G. A. Bartholemew / J. B. Birdsell

Although the word ecology is used in both the biological and the social sciences, attempts to bring the biologist and students of human society together by analogical reasoning are beset with traps for the unwary. The biological world lies primarily within genetic and physiological limits, while that of the social sciences lies within cultural limits. However, whatever else man is, he is first an animal and hence subject, although usually indirectly, to environmental and biological factors.

It is generally agreed that the ecological generalizations and points of view which have proved helpful in interpreting the natural history of most mammals can be applied virtually intact to all primates except man. It should, therefore, be possible to extrapolate upward from ecological data on other mammals, and suggest the biological attributes of the protohominids and to extrapolate downward from ethnological data on hunting and collecting peoples and suggest the minimal cultural attributes of the protohominids.

We propose, first, to discuss in general terms some aspects of mammalian ecology which appears to be applicable to the protohominids; second, to apply these ideas to the available data on the australopithecines; and third, to discuss the application of a few ecological ideas to preagricultural humans. A history of the development of ecology and suggestions for its

From American Anthropologist *55 (1953): 481–498; reprinted by permission of the authors and the publisher.*

applications to anthropology, which has recently been published by Marston Bates (1953), provides basic historical orientation and perspective for such an effort.

Protohominids and tools

In retrospect, the vast sweep of evolution appears to lead inevitably to the appearance of man, but a rational interpretation of the evidence refutes this. During the Cenozoic there have been three separate mammalian evolutionary complexes, one in Australia, one in South America, and one in Eurasia, Africa, and North America. Of these complexes, only the last has produced organisms of the hominid level. Further, since the major orders of mammals were already distinct in the Eocene, each has had a separate genetic history for approximately 70,000,000 years, and only one, primates, has produced an organism at the hominid level of organization.

Since a number of mammalian orders have shown a strong independent evolutionary trend toward a large brain size, this trend is by no means peculiar to the order primates. This striking parallelism is presumably related to the fact that large brain size favors varied behavior and learning as supplements to genetically fixed responses. Why then did not the primates, like the other mammals, reach an apparent evolutionary dead end in the Pliocene? The familiar and reasonable ideas concerning the importance of arboreal life in setting the stage for the appearance of man, i.e., dependence on vision, grasping hands, and the lack of restrictive skeletal adaptations, need not be labored here, but the importance of bipedalism can profitably be reexamined.

The primates comprise the only major order of mammals which is characteristically arboreal. There can be no doubt that this arboreal heritage has been of vital importance in human evolution, but the critical stage in the transition from ape to protohominid involves the assumption of a unique terrestial mode of life. A number of cercopithecids have successfully invaded the terrestial habitat, but these all show quadrupedal adaptations. This level of adaptation, while obviously effective, if one may judge by the fossil record and by present abundance, appears to represent a stable, long-surviving, adaptive equilibrium.

The terrestrial adaptations of the hominid line represent a step into a new and previously unexploited mode of life in which the critical feature was bipedalism. Among mammals changes of this magnitude have occurred only rarely since the middle Cenozoic. Aside from the saltatorial rodents such as the jerboas and kangaroo rats, all placental terrestrial mammals other than man use both hind and front legs for locomotion. The extreme rarity of bipedalism among mammals suggests that it is inefficient except under very special circumstances. Even modern man's unique vertical bipedal locomotion, when compared to that of quadrupedal mammals, is relatively ineffective, and this implies that a significant nonlocomotor advantage must have resulted from even the partial freeing of the forelimbs. This advantage was the use of the hands for efficient manipulation of adventitious tools such as rocks, sticks, or bones. Of course, the terrestrial or semi-terrestrial living primates have their hands free when they are not moving, but only man has his locomotion essentially unimpeded while carrying or using a tool. Man has been characterized as the "tool-using animal," but this implies a degree of uniqueness to man's use of tools which is unrealistic. Not only do other primates use tools—the use of sticks and rocks by chimpanzees and baboons is generally familiar—but such unlikely animals as the sea otter and one of the Galapagos finches routinely use rocks or sticks to obtain food. Indeed, the natural history literature is replete with instances of the use of tools by animals, and there really is no clear-cut boundary between web-spinning, nest-building, and stick-wielding on the one hand, and tool use at the simplest human level on the other. However, in contrast to all other mammals, the large arboreal primates are, in a sense, tool users in their locomotion. As they move through the maze of the tree tops, their use of branches anticipates the use of tools in that they routinely employ levers and angular momentum. The grasping hands on which the locomotion and feeding of primates depends, are of course obviously preadapted for tool use.

Rather than to say that man is unique in being the "tool-using" animal, it is more accurate to say that man is the only mammal which is continuously dependent on tools for survival. This dependence on the learned use of tools indicates a movement into a previously unexploited dimension of behavior, and this movement accompanied the advent of bipedalism. With the assumption of erect posture regular use of tools became obligatory; the ability occasionally to use tools must have preceded this in time.

Protohominids and body size

The conditions of terrestrial life for a bipedal tool-using mammal virtually demanded that the protohominids be big mammals, i.e., at least in the 50- to 100-pound range, for large size of itself offers important biological advantages. In the case of the protohominids two such advantages at once suggest themselves: First, large size would remove them from the category of potential prey for all carnivorous birds, reptiles, and all mammals except the big cats and the pack-hunting dogs; second, it would allow them to utilize without restrictive anatomical specialization and with simple instrumentation, virtually the entire range of food size utilized by all other terrestrial mammals.

Sociality

Social behavior is inextricably interwoven with ecology, and although it is not possible to review the subject in detail here, certain aspects of it are basic to the development of later ideas.

The transitional protohominids must have been social to the extent of forming relatively stable family groups. Even in the absence of direct evidence, such a statement can be made with complete confidence from knowledge of the other members of the suborder Anthropoidea. First, there is the absence of seasonal sexual periodism in man and the great apes. Thus, sexual ties form a bond of sustained and continuing attraction which provides a biological basis for the long-surviving family unit. As has frequently been pointed out this is a central element in human sociality. Second, there is a long period of growth and maturation. The long childhood of man and the great apes is not a mere function of size—the blue whale, the largest mammal that has ever lived, grows to sexual maturity and to a length of 70 or more feet in two years—but it is related to the unique dependence for survival on learning in the higher primates. The acquisition of competence for independent life demands several years of parental care in the chimpanzee and a decade or more in man. Hence, survival requires a mother-offspring relation which is sustained through many years and, like sexual attraction, is not just a seasonal interlude as in other social mammals. Since these factors shape the social behavior of both the great apes and man, they must have shaped the social life of the protohominids.

Other cohesive forces, by analogy with living primates, must have supplied integration to the social organization of the protohominids. Important among these must have been dominance-subordinance relationships. The concept of social dominance has proved to be a touchstone to the understanding of the social behavior of vertebrates. It is a key factor in the social behavior of mammals as diverse as deer, seals, and primates.

In every case in which it has been studied in mammals, dominance is established at least in part on the basis of aggressive behavior, of which a large component is either directly or indirectly dependent on reproductive physiology. In mammals the male sex hormones stimulate aggressive behavior and contribute to greater body size, while the female sex hormones inhibit the former and do not contribute to the latter. Consequently, males tend to be dominant over females in most situations. In the higher primates, as in many other social mammals, sexual dimorphism in size reinforces the greater aggressiveness of the male and insures his superior social status in situations where force is involved. In most social mammals, gregariousness overcomes the disruptive effect of dominance-subordinance relations and maintains the social unit. In primates dominance is not an exclusively disruptive force, since the dominant animal may protect the subordinate animal which looks to it for protection as well as leadership.

In nonprimate social mammals, the resolution of the forces produced by dominance and gregariousness typically produces a seasonal breeding unit which consist of a dominant male and a harem of females and which usually excludes the young of previous years.

The social unit in nonhuman primates is variable, and too few detailed field studies have been published to allow extrapolation from living anthropoids to the protohominids. In modern hunting and collecting groups of man the smallest unit is the biological family including immature offspring, and in many cultures the most important functionay group is the extended family, or band. In the case of man, even at the simplest level, social dominance is not based exclusively on successful aggressive behavior. The distance between nonprimate mammals and man is too broad to be spanned by the bracketing technique previously used, but the semi-permanent biological family, including offspring, must have been a basic unit among the protohominids. Integration on any more extensive scale must have depended upon the degree of cultural attainment. It should be observed however, that fairly large groups have been reported for living nonhominid anthropoids.

Territoriality

No aspect of the social behavior of wild vertebrates has attracted more attention than territoriality, a concept which includes the entire complex pattern of behavior associated with the defense of an area. The display of ownership of places and objects is very highly developed among human beings, but this behavior pattern is not peculiar to modern man. It is almost universally present in terrestrial vertebrates, either on a permanent or seasonal basis. The large literature on the subject with regard to birds has been reviewed by Margaret M. Nice (1941). Its status in mammals has been discussed by W. H. Burt (1943), and its relation to vertebrate populations has been examined by P. A. Errington (1946).

Territoriality springs from the necessity for finding and maintaining environmental conditions suitable for survival and reproduction. The techniques of territory maintenance, the precise factors immediately responsible for it, and the immediate significance of it vary from species to species.

The maintenance of territories either by individuals or by social groups has profound effects on distribution. Birds and mammals tend to be neither continuously distributed nor irregularly grouped, but to be spaced at more or less regular intervals through ecologically suitable habitat. This spacing is determined by conflicts between pairs of individuals or between interacting groups of animals. Thus, territorial boundaries are learned and vary in time and space. If anthropologists were willing, this might almost be considered protocultural behavior at a subhuman level; in any event, it emphasizes the continuity of human behavior with that of other vertebrates.

As a result of the centrifugal effects of aggressive behavior, territory maintanance forces animals to disperse into adjacent areas. It distributes the individual organisms or social units of a species throughout the entire accessible area of suitable habitat. Should the population increase, local population density does not continue to build up indefinitely. Instead territorial defense forces individuals out into marginal situations, and thus the resources of the optimal habitat are not exhausted. Most of the displaced individuals do not survive, but some may find unexploited areas of suitable habitat and thus extend the range of the species. The result is that a population tends to be maintained at or below the optimum density in the preferred habitat, and the excess individuals are forced to marginal areas to which they must adapt or die.

Thus, territoriality is one of the primary factors which determine the density of population. It organizes a local population into a well-spaced array that allows adequate living conditions for all successful individuals. It limits the breeding population which can exist in suitable habitats and thus helps to prevent increase beyond the long-term carrying capacity of the range. This dispersive effect of territoriality can hardly help but be an important causal factor both in migration and in the spread of genes through a population. Hence, it must contribute importantly to rate of evolutionary change.

The question of the importance of territoriality to the biology of protohominids at once presents itself. Clarence R. Carpenter (1934) has demonstrated that howler monkeys and gibbons maintain territory by group action. It is clear that territoriality exists in all complex human societies, and it is clearly established that group territoriality is also important at the simplest levels of human culture. It is, therefore, reasonable to assume that protohominids similarly possessed a well-developed territoriality, presumably on the basis of the family or extended family.

Population equilibrium

One of the most critical ecological factors which can be determined about an animal is the density of its population. The number of variables which contribute to the determination of population density is enormous; a complete analysis for even the best known of living wild mammals is difficult, perhaps impossible. Nevertheless, the framework within which such an analysis can be made is known, for the factors involved in population dynamics have been studied intensively in recent years.

Since organisms are transient biochemical systems which require continuous expenditure of energy for their maintenance, the struggle for existence becomes, in one sense at least, a struggle for the free energy available for doing physiological work. This fact offers a point of view from which to approach the problem of estimating the population of protohominids, or any other mammal.

There exists a series of nutrient or trophic levels that expresses the energy relations which tie together the various organisms of the terrestial environment. The primary trophic level is that of the green plants, for only they can use radiant energy to synthesize significant quantities of organic material. The trophic level of the herbivores includes all animals directly dependent on plants for food. The next higher trophic level, that of the meat-eaters, which may be primary carnivores (eaters of herbivores), secondary carnivores (eaters of other carnivores), and so on. The final trophic level, the eaters of dead organic material, eventually returns materials to the inorganic state depleted of biologically available energy.

Materials which are used as building blocks and sources of energy by organisms cycle continuously through these trophic levels, and at each level there is an endless competition for them. There are a number of obvious corollaries which follow from these relationships. An important one is that nutrition plays a primary role in determining the major functional adaptations of animals. Life demands a continuous expenditure of energy, and this energy is available only through nutrition. These energy relations involve a sustained long-term pressure sufficiently constant to maintain and give direction to the major evolutionary trends apparent in the adaptive changes of the sort shown by hoofed mammals and the carnivorous mammals. As George Gaylord Simpson (1944) and others have pointed out, these nutritive adaptations have for the most part led not only to greater efficiency but also to more and more specialization, with a consequent reduction in potentiality for new major nutritive adaptations. Thus, adaptations toward increased efficiency in food getting, or toward avoidance of becoming food for other organisms, are largely restrictive from the standpoint of future evolutionary change.

The total weight of biological materials produced by one trophic level must necessarily be less than that of the level below it on which it depends, and greater than that of the level above, which it supports. Each nutritive level must in the long run live on the interest, not the capital, of the trophic level below it. From this there follows a maxim which allows of no exception. On a long-term basis the mean population of a species is in equilibrium with the trophic levels both above it and below it, as well as with the total limiting effects of the inorganic environment. This means that the birth rate must be great enough to balance the death rate from disease (a nutritive phenomenon from the standpoint of the disease-causing organism), predation, and accident. Consequently, birth rate is a factor subject to natural selection, and all natural populations represent approximate equilibria between biotic potentials and total resistance of the biological and physical environments. Short-lived mammals of high fecundity, such as rabbits and mice, are sometimes characterized by drastic short-term fluctuations in population size, the causes for which are still subject to active controversy. However, in this paper we shall ignore the problem of population cycles, for drastic cyclic fluctuations have rarely been observed in large tropical mammals with low reproductive potentials.

It has been generally appreciated since the time of Darwin that animals, despite their capacity to increase in numbers, tend to maintain a population which fluctuates around some equilibrium figure. This idea is of such a basic nature that it forms a foundation for the concept of natural selection which now appears to be an omnipresent evolutionary force. The factors involved in the maintenance of these equilibria are complex and variable. Since, as pointed out above, an animal population cannot possibly permanently exceed its food resources, these fix an upper limit. The determination of the actual equilibrium figure is a subtle problem which must be solved independently for each population. A thoughtful analysis of the factors limiting population in a non-hominid primate under natural conditions is presented by N. E. Collias and C. Southwick (1952) in their study of howling monkeys. For a population to maintain itself above that lower critical level which means inevitable extinction, many factors (which may vary independently) must be simultaneously satisfied. Such things as a suitable habitat, which will include adequate food resources, water, and home sites, and climatic conditions, that do not exceed the tolerance of the group, must be present.

Since biological factors vary with time, values for population equilibria are not to be measured at a given point in time. They fluctuate about a balance which is determined, not by the mean condition, but by the extremes. Indeed, one of the most firmly established ecological generalizations is Liebig's law of the minimum, which states that a biological reaction at any level is controlled not by the factors which are present in excess, but by that essential factor which is present in minimal quantity. Since, as was previously pointed out, population density is the most critical single ecological datum, anthropologists studying the simpler cultures characterized by few storage techniques would do well to search for those critical limiting factors which do determine density. Such limiting factors are not necessarily either obvious or conspicuous at all points in time, and even when they occur their expression may be subtle or apparently indirect. A semi-arid area may have many fruitful years in succession, but a single drought year occurring once in a human generation may restrict the population to an otherwise inexplicably low density. For example, the Papago Indians of the lower Colorado River were forced in drought years to revert to a desert hunting and collecting economy for survival. Thus, their population density appears in part to have been strongly affected by the preagricultural carrying capacity of this area. In some cases the size of a population will be determined not by the availability of an abundance of food during ten months of the year but by a regular seasonal scarcity in the remaining two months.

The reproductive potential of animals is such that under favorable conditions, such as having available a previously unexploited habitat, the size of a population can increase at an essentially logarithmic rate. This capacity for rapid increase makes possible the recovery of populations following drastic population reduction. In a stable population, on the other hand, the reproductive potential is expressed only as a one-to-one replacement of adult individuals.

Anothropologists are properly impressed with the complexity of learned behavior in human groups, but may fail to appreciate its significance among other mammals. Even on the nonhuman level, population density may be controlled by behavioral factors, either genetic or learned. Territoriality and dominance relations, which are dependent on learned behavior, contribute to the determination of group relations and population density. Under certain circumstances behavioral factors may be more important than nutritive factors in determining population density. For example, recent work has shown that the Norway rat under controlled experimental conditions, in which food is present in excess at all times, reaches a population equilibrium that is determined by strictly behavioral factors related to territoriality and competition for suitable homesites. Thus, experimental work confirms extensive field observations on a variety of vertebrates. Since learned behavior operates as an important factor determining density in all terrestial mammals which have been studied, and in modern man, it must have been an important factor in determining the population density of the protohominids. The importance of learned behavior increases directly with its complexity, and in man at cultural levels above the hunting and collecting stage of economy it becomes increasingly difficult to identify the ecological factors affecting population size.

ECOLOGY AND THE AUSTRALOPITHECINES

The dating of the australopithecines has proved troublesome, and final decision is now possible. Raymond Dart (1948) and Robert Broom (1950) have suggested that these protohominids lived during a period extending the Villafranchian into the middle Pleistocene. This time span overlaps the datings of early man in other parts of the world, and implies a collateral relationship with more evolved hominids. Another view has recently been given by Teilhard de Chardin (1952), who places the australopithecines in Villafranchian time, and thus removes them from contemporaneity with known African hominids. Abbé Breuil (1948) seems to reflect a similar point of view. In the former case the australopithecines would been competing in their closing phase with more advanced forms of man, and hence would have been decreasing in numbers and range. In the latter instance the australopithecines would apparently have been the sole occupants of the protohominid niche over wide areas in South Africa, with the resultant possibility of having an expanding population and range. For purposes of an ecological discussion it is necessary to assume one dating or the other; it is not important to decide whether the australopithecines were in fact ancestral to more advanced hominid types, but it is important to determine whether they were the sole occupants of the hominid niche in South Africa.

As Teilhard de Chardin (1952) points out, the australopithecine-bearing breccias and the human industry-bearing deposits have never been found conformably associated in the same site. This assumes, as did de Chardin, that *Telanthropus* is but a variant of the australopithecine type. Therefore, for purposes of discussion, we shall assume that the australopithecines are Villafranchian in date and hence earlier than the makers of the pebble-cultures of South Africa. By analogy with the ecology of other animals it would be surprising if man and the australopithecines had remained contemporaries in the same area over very long periods of time, for closely related forms with similar requirements rarely occupy the same area simultaneously.

Use of tools

Neither the archeological nor morphological evidence concerning australopithecines suggests an alternative to the assumption, which we made earlier, that protohominids were dependent on the use of tools for survival. It is generally agreed that the australopithecines were bipedal. Referring to our previous discussion, this strongly implies that the australopithecines routinely utilized adventitious or perhaps even slightly modified tools. Dart's evidence for the use of ungulate humeri as clubs offers empirical support for this theoretical position. Unmodified rocks used as tools can rarely be identified except by context. Familiar evidence from both archeology and ethnology shows that at the simplest level, rough tools commonly are discarded after initial use. Hence, a lack of recognizable stone tools in the breccias does not indicate that these were not used. Time alone precludes the survival of wooden implements such as clubs and digging sticks, although their use by australopithecines is certainly to be expected, for even the living great apes use sticks spontaneously.

The dentition of the partly carnivorous australopithecines (see section on food size) is unformly characterized by reduced canines and incisors, and by nonsectorial premolars and molars. These dental characteristics are unique to them among all the large carnivorous mammals. The absence of teeth adapted for stabbing or shearing clearly implies the killing of game by weapons and butchering by simple tools. This observation would hold true even if the assignment of carnivorous habits to australopithecines were based only upon the abundant evidence that baboons were an important item in their diet. It is not dependent on the controversial question of their killing large hoofed mammals.

The dentition of australopithecines offers further evidence concerning their dependence on tools. As pointed out previously intrasexual combat is characteristic of the males of virtually all strongly dimorphic mammals. Australopithecines are dimorphic, but they do not have the large piercing canines so characteristic of most of the larger living primates. This striking reduction of canines strongly implies that even in intrasexual (and intraspecific) combat, the australopithecines placed primary dependence on tools.

Scale of food size

It should be possible on theoretical grounds to fix the approximate upper and lower size limits of the food which could economically be handled by the australopithecines with nothing more elaborate than a crude stick for digging and a limb bone for a club. Their capabilities would allow the utilization of the following animal foods: virtually all terrestrial reptiles and the smaller aquatic ones; eggs and nesting birds; some fish; fresh-water mollusks and crustaceans; insects; all of the smaller mammals including some burrowing forms, and larger mammals up to and including baboons. It is difficult, perhaps impossible, to determine whether the remains of the large giraffids and bovids reported from the bone breccias, represent kills by australopithecines or their scavenging from the kills of the large cats. Since few meat eaters are loath to scavenge, and the implementation which would allow the australopithecines to kill such large animals is not apparent, we suggest that scavenging from the kills of the larger carnivores may have been systematically carried out.

Like most present-day hunting and collecting peoples, the australopithecines probably used plants as their major source of food. Without imputing to the australopithecines any cultural capabilities beyond the use of a simple stick for digging, at least the following types of vegetable food would be available to them: berries, fruits, nuts, buds and shoots, shallow-growing roots and tubers, and fruiting bodies of fungi. Some of the very small vegetable foods exploited by modern human groups were probably not extensively used. Effective utilization of grass seeds and other hard-shelled small seeds require specialized gathering implements and containers, and processing by grinding or cooking.

Such activities imply technologies which cannot be assigned *a priori* to the australopithecines, and for which there is no archeological indication until much later times. In this connection it may be noted that the evidence for the use of fire by *Australopithecus prometheus,* though impressive, is still regarded by some as controversial. In summary, it seems reasonable to treat the australopithecines as generalized carnivorous animals for which the freeing of hands and the the use of simple implements enormously broadened the scale of food size to include a surprisingly large proportion of the total food resources of the terrestrial environment.

Social behavior

The biological bases for the family and social organization at the protohominid level which have already been discussed should apply to the australopithecines. Group organization beyond the family level is not indicated by the archeological context of the finds, because the rather large number of individuals recorded from Swartkrans and Sterkfontein might result from sampling of family-sized groups over many generations. However, there is at least one line of archeological evidence which suggests social organization beyond the simple family level. Since baboons travel in large aggregations and were a significant item of australopithecine diet, it would seem likely that the latter hunted in bands. A single australopithecine, even armed with a club, would not be a serious threat to a band of baboons. Such group hunting does not necessarily imply a high level of communication, such as speech, or permanence of organization, for it is characteristic of a number of nonprimate carnivorous vertebrates—many canids, some fish-eating birds, and killer-whales. Broom (1950) has shown that the australopithecines were characterized by sexual dimorphism, a widespread trait in the primates, including man. In social mammals, sexual dimorphism is almost invariably a product of the sexual selection associated with competition between males for females. Characteristically this sexual selection produces males which are larger, and more aggressive than females, and which have specialized structures for offense and defense. Although these dimorphic characters are a product of competition between males, they usually result in the males assuming the role of group defender. We propose that the sexual dimorphism of the australopithecine males may have favored a secondarily derived function related to aggressive behavior, namely the hunting of large prey, including perhaps other australopithecines. Thus, it may be that a sexual division of labor such as is present in all known hunting peoples was foreshadowed at this early level of hominid evolution.

The primates which first began to exploit a bipedal tool-using mode of life were establishing a level of adaptedness of enormous potentiality which had previously been inaccessible. They were entering a period of rapid change leading to a new kind of adaptedness. In the terminology of Simpson (1944) they were a group undergoing quantum evolution. It is to be expected that, like other similarly rapidly evolving groups, they would be represented in the fossil record not by a uniform long-persistent type, but by a variable group of related forms. The australopithecines, which probably occupy a stage near the end of a step in quantum evolution, fit this theoretical prescription nicely. The various australopithecine forms which have been named can be considered representatives of a highly polymorphic assemblage. Their polymorphism is consistent with the idea of a rapidly evolving and radiating group and thus favors the probability of the Villafranchian dating.

It is reasonable to assume that most of the recovered australopithecine fossils date from a period prior to the time they faced competition from more highly evolved hominid types. When, as they inevitably must have, the australopithecines came in contact with culturally advanced hominids, they must have been subject to rapid replacement in terms of geological time.

DISCUSSION

A paper such as this necessarily can be of only temporary utility. We feel that its principal contribution lies in raising questions, the answering of which may require orientation toward new points of view, the collection of new kinds of data, and perhaps the use of new techniques.

Students of animal ecology have developed a number of points of view which could be profitably applied to the study of preagricultural man. Two are particularly attractive. The first of these is that the basic problem of human behavior, like the behavior of other animals, is the obtaining of food, for the human body requires a continuous input of energy both for maintenance and for propagation. The second point of view involves the idea that population density normally is a complexly maintained equilibrium, dependent upon environmental as well as behavioral (and in the case of man, cultural) forces.

Anthropologists and archeologists to date have shown great ingenuity in utilizing the meager data for paleolithic and mesolithic man to establish tentative chronologies and outline cultural relationships. However, at the simplest level, the significance of material culture lies neither in the establishment of chronology nor as a measure of relationships, but as an indicator of efficiency in obtaining food. The lack of data concerning the food-getting effectiveness of the various items of material culture primarily results from preoccupation with typology rather than function. Even the best of typological labels tend to restrict functional interpretations and to ignore the role of varied behavior and human ingenuity in extending an implement's utility. Furthermore, functional interpretations can be determined only by studies of living peoples, and the ethnologist has not yet generally been stimulated to the realization of the basic importance of such data.

It is of interest that some food-getting devices which we presume to have been available to the australopithecines remain important today in the economy of hunting and gathering peoples. But there is little systematic quantitative information concerning the proportion of food obtained through the use of the hands alone, or that added by the use of the simple digging stick, club, or wooden spear. Nor at a more culturally sophisticated level is there quantitative data available to measure the increase in efficiency made possible by the invention of such devices as the spear-thrower and the bow and arrow. In making such analyses it would be useful to distinguish between the contributions of the relatively limited variety of primary tools and the more varied secondary tools. For example, the ecological significance of the first-axes of the lower and middle Pleistocene varies enormously depending upon whether they are to be interpreted as primary tools used to make wooden implements, such as clubs, digging sticks and spears, or whether they are regarded in the unlikely light of hand-held striking implements.

As pointed out previously, all animal populations, including human populations, depend on radiant energy stored chemically by photosynthesis. Animals compete endlessly between themselves for the one per cent of incident solar energy which plants are able to capture. The competitive success of an individual animal can be determined from its metabolism, and the success of a population can be expressed quantitatively as the product of population density times individual metabolism.

If one can obtain even approximate figures for (1) the production of organic material by plants, (2) population densities and, (3) metabolism, one can evaluate from one point of view the biological success of different organisms. One can compare lions and elephants, earthworms and mice, humans and all other organisms, or more pertinent to anthropologists, one can compare simple cultures existing in either similar or different environmental situations. Since human beings comprise a single species, intergroup comparisons can be made on the basis of weight per unit area. An instructive analysis of this sort for small North American mammals has been made by C. O. Mohr (1947).

To our knowledge this quantitative approach to human ecology has not been exploited by anthropologists; indeed, few attempts have been made by zoologists. O. P. Pearson (1948) has gathered figures which allow a comparison of Indians of northeastern United States with other animals common in the same area. Indians had less metabolic impact that deer, about the same impact as long-tailed shrews. E. S. Deevey, Jr. (1951), presents calculations which show the amazing trophic impact of the present human population of the world. Both these efforts are frankly exploratory and depend on approximations, but they point up an approach which merits consideration by anthropologists. If one could obtain for given areas even crude figures for human population density and for the production of organic material by the flora, he could compare the nutritive efficiencies of rainforest and grassland cultures, or the efficiency of Great Basin Indians and Australian Aborigines even though the two peoples live in arid regions of a very different character. Similarly, one could obtain quantitative estimates for the effects of rivers, lakes, sea shore, and particularly vegetation types (i.e., oak woodland) on the capacity of an area to support human populations at a simple cultural level.

As discussed earlier, natural populations tend to fluctuate about some equilibrium figure. This fact has long been recognized by biologists, but to date, despite the perspectives which it supplies, it has not significantly influenced that approach of most anthropologists. From a short-term point of view, populations are in only approximate equilibrium, but viewed from the time scale of the Pleistocene, slowly expanding populations of man can be considered as being essentially in equilibrium. It appears to us that the idea that the populations of early man were in approximate equilibrium with the environment can supply a point of view from which to interpret the dynamics of technologically simple human populations. It should greatly facilitate qualitative exploration of such considerations as spatial variation of population density; growth or decline in numbers; rates of movement as influenced by migration and gene flow; and, shifts of populations into new climatic situations which demand new modes of life and may involve biological as well as cultural changes in adaptedness. As such qualitative interpretations are refined it may be possible to develop models which depict these processes semi-quantitatively and thus allow crude predictions.

Population density is a key to these dynamic processes, for either directly or indirectly it controls all of the others. As discussed in the sections on territoriality and population equilibrium, the density of early human populations, while immediately determined by a complex of variables in which behavior plays a central role, was ultimately controlled by the environment. Even in the most favorable environments the equilibrium density attained by natural populations is somewhat below the maximum which the environment can support. The factors restricting density are behavioral in an immediate sense and involve such things as aggressive behavior and territoriality. These behavioral factors must have brought dispersive forces to bear on Pleistocene man just as they do on other mammals. The existence of such dispersive forces suggests that the evolving australopithecines must have spread with great rapidity (i.e., almost instantaneously in terms of geological time) throughout the continental tropics and subtropics of the old world. Such an expansion would leave no suitable and accessible areas unoccupied. Consequently all subsequently evolved hominids in these regions must have expanded at the expense of already established populations. The replacement of the australopithecines by somewhat more advanced but related hominids may have followed the usual mammalian pattern of the gradual expansion of the more efficient form, and the slow reduction of the numbers of the less efficient. In many instances, however, population change must have resulted from gradual genetic penetration, and much of human evolution in the Pleistocene could easily have been powerfully affected by introgressive hybridization. In this regard it should be remembered that anatomical differences do not necessarily indicate genetic incompatability between groups, and that there is no evidence of reluctance to hybridize even between widely different human types. If rapid and dramatic group replacement did occur it must have been a rare event occurring in special circumstances.

Although mammals are less affected by climate in a direct physical sense than are most organisms, physiological differences among mammals adapted to different climatic conditions have been clearly demonstrated. Distributionally the primates are an order characteristic of the tropics or subtropics. Modern man himself appears to be unable to invade the higher latitudes without fairly elaborate cultural accoutrements. It may, therefore, be concluded that during the Pliocene, the evolving protohominids occupied only the tropics, subtropics, and perhaps the fringes of the temperate zones. The only place in which human populations could have expanded into a vacuum was at the margins of the then habitable areas. Thus, changing cultural, and possibly changing biological, adaptedness would have allowed hominid expansion from the tropics into the temperate regions and ultimately into the arctic regions of the Old World. Aside from the initial continental expansion of the Old World protohominids, man expanded into major vacuums in populating Australasia, the New World, and much later, Micronesia and Polynesia. Once entered, these areas must have become filled rapidly, so that subsequent immigrants were faced for the most part with the problem of replacing established populations. Migrations, although spectacular, were probably of less importance in the Pleistocene than the processes discussed previously, which proceed normally without local catastrophic environmental change.

The anthropologists' lack of concern with the idea of population equilibrium in the simpler and more static human cultures is explicable in historical terms. Anthropologists, reacting to the claim by some anthropogeographers that extreme environmental determinism was operative on man, soon demonstrated that details of culture were not controlled directly by the environment. This broad denial overlooked man's nutritive dependence upon the environment, and long inhibited quantitative investigation of the relationship between man's population density and environmental factors.

The present interpretation of the mechanism of evolution is based upon natural selection which demands that populations be in a state of approximate equilibrium at a given time. To unravel the evolution of Pleistocene man, inevitably hampered as one is with inadequate data, one must necessarily use the idea of a population in equilibrium with the carrying capacity of the environment.

Most ecologists agree that no data are more crucial than those bearing upon population size, structure, and density. Anthropologists, even though generally unconcerned with population equilibria, in some instances have been aware of the concept (Krzywicki 1934; Steward 1938; and Evans-Pritchard 1940). But in general the importance of an ecological approach has not been appreciated. Some archeologists have hoped to reconstruct preagricultural population figures from studying the temporal and spatial distribution of sites, but the inescapable sampling errors in this approach render it unreliable. We suggest that an analysis of the energy relationships and the efficiency of the techniques for obtaining food offer a promising approach.

For several years it has been apparent that an ecological approach is imperative for all studies in population genetics, including those pertaining to man. It also offers a potentially useful point of view to the physical anthropologist, the ethnologist, and the archeologist, and it should provide an important integrative bridge between the various fields of anthropology.

SUMMARY

An attempt is made to apply ecological concepts which are widely used by vertebrate zoologists to protohominids in general and to australopithecines in particular.

Various aspects of the biology of protohominids are considered: tool use, bipedalism, body size, scale of food size, sociality, territoriality, population density and equilibria, dispersion, and nutrition.

Energy relations to the environment and population equilibria are discussed with regard to human preagricultural populations.

REFERENCES

BATES, M. 1953. Human ecology. In *Anthropology today: An encyclopedic inventory,* ed. A. Kroeber. Chicago: Univ. of Chicago Press.

BREUIL, ABBE HENRI. 1948. Ancient raised beaches and prehistoric civilizations in South Africa. *S. Afric. J. Sci.* 44: 61–74.

BROOM, R. 1950. The genera and species of the South African ape-man. *Am. J. Phys, Anthro.* n.s. 8: 1–13.

BURT, W. H. 1943. Territoriality and home range concepts as applied to mammals. *J. Mammalogy* 24: 346–52.

CARPENTER, C. R. 1934. A field study of the behavior and social relations of howling monkeys. *Comp. Psych. Mono.* 10: 1–168.

COLLIAS, N. E., and SOUTHWICK, C. 1952. A field study of population density and social organization in howling monkeys. *Proc. Am. Phil. Soc.* 96: 143–56.

DART, R. A. 1948. A (?) promethean *Australopithecus* from Makapansgat Valley. *Nature* 162: 375–76.

DE CHARDIN, P. T. 1952. On the zoological position and evolutionary significance of australopithecines. *Trans. N. Y. Acad. Sci.* Ser. 2, 14: 208–10.

DEEVEY, E. S., JR. 1951. Recent textbooks of human ecology. *Ecology* 32: 347–51.

ERRINGTON, P. A. 1946. Predation and vertebrate populations. *Quart. Rev. Biol.* 21: 144–77, 221–45.

EVANS-PRITCHARD, E. E. 1940. *The Nuer: A description of the modes of livelihood and political institutions of a Nilotic people.* London: Oxford Univ. Press.

KRZYWICKI, L. 1934. *Primitive society and its vital statistics.* London: Macmillan.

MOHR, C. O. 1947. Table of equivalent populations of North American small mammals. *Am. Midland Natur.* 37: 223–49.

NICE, MARGARET M. 1941. The role of territory in bird life. *Am. Midland Natur.* 26: 441–87.

PEARSON, O. P. 1948. Metabolism and bioenergetics. *Sci. Month.* 66: 131–34.

SIMPSON, G. G. 1944. *Tempo and mode in evolution.* New York: Columbia Univ. Press.

STEWARD, J. H. 1938. *Basin-plateau aboriginal sociopolitical groups.* Washington, D.C.: Government Printing Office.

SUPPLEMENTARY READINGS

BRACE, C. L. The fate of the "Classic" Neanderthals: a consideration of hominid catastrophism. *Current Anthropology* 5 (1964): 3–53.

CLARK, W. E. LEGROS. *Man-Apes or Ape-Men?* New York: Holt, Rinehart & Winston, 1967.

HOWELL, F. CLARK. *Early Man* (from Life Nature Library). New York: Time, Inc., 1965.

WEINER, J. S. *The Piltdown Forgery*. London and New York: Oxford University Press, 1955.

five

CULTURAL PREHISTORY

The reconstruction of man's evolutionary development, based on his biological remains, represents only part of the story. Man's ability to use and make tools was an essential requisite to his physical form. This ability increased his adaptive potential and ultimately gave him almost unlimited control over his environment. This relationship between tools and human evolution is thoroughly discussed by both Washburn and Oakley. Compared to the long and complicated picture that has characterized the biological and cultural history of man in Europe, Asia, and Africa, the American continents played a relatively late role. Yet the evidence we have has left us with a number of intriguing problems. Roberts's article remains one of the best summaries available of our knowledge and speculations in this area.

Tools and Human Evolution

S. L. Washburn

A series of recent discoveries has linked prehuman primates of half a million years ago with stone tools. For some years investigators had been uncovering tools of the simplest kind from ancient deposits in Africa. At first they assumed that these tools constituted evidence of the existence of large-brained, fully bipedal men. Now the tools have been found in association with much more primitive creatures, the not fully bipedal, small-brained near-men, or man-apes. Prior to these finds the prevailing view held that man evolved nearly to his present structural state and then discovered tools and the new ways of life that they made possible. Now it appears that man-apes—creatures able to run but not yet walk on two legs, and with brains no larger than those of apes now living—had already learned to make and to use tools. It follows that the structure of modern man must be the result of the change in the terms of natural selection that came with the tool-using way of life.

The earliest stone tools are chips or simple pebbles, usually from river gravels. Many of them have not been shaped at all, and they can be identified as tools only because they appear in concentrations, along with a few worked pieces, in caves or other locations where no such stones naturally occur. The huge advantage that a stone tool gives to its user must be tried to be appreciated. Held in the hand, it can be used for pounding, digging, or scraping. Flesh and bone can be cut with a flaked chip, and what would be a mild blow with the fist becomes lethal with a rock in the hand. Stone tools can be employed, moreover, to make tools of other materials.

From Scientific American, *203, no. 3 (1960): 62–75; reprinted with the permission of the author and publisher.*

Naturally occurring sticks are nearly all rotten, too large, or of inconvenient shape; some tool for fabrication is essential for the efficient use of wood. The utility of a mere pebble seems so limited to the user of modern tools that it is not easy to comprehend the vast difference that separates the tool-user from the ape which relies on hands and teeth alone. Ground-living monkeys dig out roots for food, and if they could use a stone or a stick, they might easily double their food supply. It was the success of the simplest tools that started the whole trend of human evolution and led to the civilizations of today.

From the short-term point of view, human structure makes human behavior possible. From the evolutionary point of view, behavior and structure form an interacting complex, with each change in one affecting the other. Man began when populations of apes, about a million years ago, started the bipedal, tool-using way of life that gave rise to the man-apes of the genus *Australopithecus*. Most of the obvious differences that distinguish man from ape came after the use of tools.

The primary evidence for the new view of human evolution is teeth, bones, and tools. But our ancestors were not fossils; they were striving creatures, full of rage, dominancee, and the will to live. What evolved was the pattern of life of intelligent, exploratory, playful, vigorous primates; the evolving reality was a succession of social systems based upon the motor abilities, emotions, and intelligence of their members. Selection produced new systems of child care, maturation, and sex, just as it did alterations in the skull and the teeth. Tools, hunting, fire, complex social life, speech, the human way, and the brain evolved together to produce ancient man of the genus *Homo* about half a million years ago. Then the brain evolved under the pressures of more complex social life until the species *Homo sapiens* appeared perhaps as recently as 50,000 years ago.

With the advent of *Homo sapiens* the tempo of technical-social evolution quickened. Some of the early types of tool had lasted for hundreds of thousands of years and were essentially the same throughout vast areas of the African and Eurasian land masses. Now the tool forms multiplied and became regionally diversified. Man invented the bow, boats, clothing; conquered the Arctic; invaded the New World; domesticated plants and animals; discovered metals, writing, and civilization. Today, in the midst of the latest tool-making revolution, man has achieved the capacity to adapt his environment to his need and impulse, and his numbers have begun to crowd the planet.

This article is concerned with the beginnings of the process by which, as Theodosius Dobzhansky says, biological evolution has transcended itself. From the rapidly accumulating evidence it is now possible to speculate with some confidence on the manner in which the way of life made possible by tools changed the pressures of natural selection and so changed the structure of man.

Tools have been found, along with the bones of their makers, at Sterkfontein, Swartkrans, and Kromdraai in South Africa and at Olduvai in Tanganyika. Many of the tools from Sterkfontein are merely unworked river pebbles, but someone has to carry them from the gravels some miles away and bring them to the deposit in which they are found. Nothing like them occurs naturally in the local limestone caves. Of course the association of the stone tools with man-ape bones in one or two localities does not prove that these animals made the tools. It has been argued that a more advanced form of man, already present, was the toolmaker. This argument has a familiar ring to students of human evolution. Peking man was thought too primitive to be a toolmaker; when the first manlike pelvis was found with man-ape bones, some argued that it must have fallen into the deposit because it was too human to be associated with the skull. In every case, however, the repeated discovery of the same unanticipated association has ultimately settled the controversy.

This is why the discovery by L. S. B. and Mary Leakey in the summer of 1959 is so important. In Olduvai Gorge in Tanganyika they came upon traces of an old living site, and found stone tools in clear association with the largest man-ape skull known. With the stone tools were a hammer stone and waste flakes from the manufacture of the tools. The deposit also contained the bones of rats, mice, frogs, and some bones of juvenile pig and antelope, showing that even the largest and latest of the man-apes could kill only the smallest animals and must have been largely vegetarian. The Leakeys' discovery confirms the association of the man-ape with pebble tools, and adds the evidence of manufacture to that of mere association. Moreover, the stratigraphic evidence at Olduvai now for the first time securely dates the man-apes, placing them in the lower Pleistocene, earlier than 500,000 years ago and earlier than the first skeletal and cultural evidence for the existence of the genus Homo. Before the discovery at Olduvai these points had been in doubt.

The man-apes themselves are known from several skulls and a large number of teeth and jaws, but only fragments of the rest of the skeleton have been preserved. There were two kinds of man-ape, a small early one that may have weighed 50 or 60 pounds and a later and larger one that weighed at least twice as much. The differences in size and form between the two types are quite comparable to the differences between the contemporary pygmy chimpanzee and the common chimpanzee.

Pelvic remains from both forms of man-ape show that these animals were bipedal. From a comparison of the pelvis of ape, man-ape, and man it can be seen that the upper part of the pelvis is much wider and shorter in man than in the ape, and that the pelvis of the man-ape corresponds closely, though not precisely, to that of modern man. The long upper pelvis of the ape is characteristic of most mammals, and it is the highly specialized, short, wide bone in man that makes possible the human kind of bipedal locomotion. Although the man-ape pelvis is apelike in its lower part, it approaches that of man in just those features that distinguish man from all other animals. More work must be done before this combination of features is fully understood. My belief is that bipedal running, made possible by the changes in the upper pelvis, came before efficient bipedal walking, made possible by the changes in the lower pelvis. In the man-ape, therefore, the adaptation to bipedal locomotion is not yet complete. Here, then, is a phase of human evolution characterized by forms that are mostly bipedal, small-brained, plains-living, toolmaking hunters of small animals.

The capacity for bipedal walking is primarily an adaptation for covering long distances. Even the arboreal chimpanzee can run faster than a man, and any monkey can easily outdistance him. A man, on the other hand, can walk for many miles, and this is essential for efficient hunting. According to skeletal evidence, fully developed walkers first appeared in the ancient men who inhabited the Old World from 500,000 years ago to the middle of the last glaciation. These men were competent hunters, as is shown by the bones of the large animals they killed. But they also used fire and made complicated tools according to clearly defined traditions. Along with the change in the structure of the pelvis, the brain had doubled in size since the time of the man-apes.

The fossil record thus substantiates the suggestion, first made by Charles Darwin, that tool use is both the cause and the effect of bipedal locomotion. Some very limited bipedalism left the hands sufficiently free from locomotor functions so that stones or sticks could be carried, played with, and used. The advantage that these objects gave to their users led both to more bipedalism and to more efficient tool use. English lacks any neat expression for this sort of situation, forcing us to speak of cause and effect as if they were separated, whereas in natural selection cause and effect are interrelated. Selection is based on successful behavior, and in the man-apes the beginnings of the human way of life depended on both inherited locomotor capacity and on the learned skills of tool-using. The success of the new way of life based on the use of tools changed the selection pressures on many parts of the body, notably the teeth, hands, and brain, as well as on the pelvis. But it must be remembered that selection was for the whole way of life.

In all the apes and monkeys the males have large canine teeth. The long upper canine cuts against the first lower premolar, and the lower canine passes in front of the upper canine. This is an efficient fighting mechanism, backed by very large jaw muscles. I have seen male baboons drive off cheetahs and dogs, and according to reliable reports male baboons have even put leopards to flight. The females have small canines, and they hurry away with the young under the very conditions in which the males turn to fight. All the evidence from living monkeys and apes suggests that the male's large canines are of the greatest importance to the survival of the group, and that they are particularly important in ground-living forms that may not be able to climb to safety in the trees. The small, early man-apes lived in open plains country, and yet none of them had large canine teeth. It would appear that the protection of the group must have shifted from teeth to tools early in the evolution of the man-apes, and long before the appearance of the forms that have been found in association with stone tools. The tools of Sterkfontein and Olduvai represent not the beginnings of tool use, but a choice of material and knowledge in manufacture which, as is shown by the small canines of the man-apes that deposited them there, derived from a long history of tool use.

Reduction in the canine teeth is not a simple matter, but involves changes in the muscles, face, jaws, and other parts of the skull. Selection builds powerful neck muscles in animals that fight with their canines, and adapts the skull to the action of these muscles. Fighting is not a matter of teeth alone, but also of seizing, shaking, and hurling an enemy's body with the jaws, head, and neck. Reduction in the canines is therefore accompanied by a shortening in the jaws, reduction in the ridges of bone over the eyes, and a decrease in the shelf of bone in the neck area. The reason that the skulls of the females and young of the apes look more like man-apes than those of adult males is that, along with small canines, they have smaller muscles and all the numerous structural features that go along with them. The skull of the man-ape is that of an ape that has lost the structure for effective fighting with its teeth. Moreover, the man-ape has transferred to its hands the functions of seizing and pulling, and this has been attended by reduction of its incisors. Small canines and incisors are biological symbols of a changed way of life; their primitive functions are replaced by hand and tool.

The history of the grinding teeth—the molars—is different from that of the seizing and fighting teeth. Large size in any anatomical structure must be maintained by positive selection; the selection pressure changed first on the canine teeth and, much later, on the molars. In the man-apes the molars were very large, larger than in either ape or man. They were heavily worn, possibly because food dug from the ground with the aid of tools was very abrasive. With the men of the Middle Pleistocene, molars of human size appear along with complicated tools, hunting, and fire.

The disappearance of brow ridges and the refinement of the human face may involve still another factor. One of the essential conditions for the organization of men in co-operative societies was the suppression of rage and of the uncontrolled drive to first place in the hierarchy of dominance. Recently it has been shown that domestic animals, chosen over the generations for willingness to adjust and for lack of rage, have relatively small adrenal glands, as Curt P. Richter of Johns Hopkins University has shown. But the breeders who selected for this hormonal, physiological, temperamental type also picked, without realizing it, animals with small brow ridges and small faces. The skull structure of the wild rat bears the same relation to that of the tame rat as does the skull of Neanderthal man to that of *Homo sapiens*. The same is true for the cat, dog, pig, horse, and cow; in each case the wild form has the larger face and muscular ridges. In the later stages of human evolution, it appears, the self-domestication of man has been exerting the same effects upon temperament, glands, and skull that are seen in the domestic animals.

Of course, from man-ape to man the brain-containing part of the skull has also increased greatly in size. This change is directly due to the increase in the size of the brain: as the brain grows, so grow the bones that cover it. Since there is this close correlation between brain size and bony brain-case, the brain size of the fossils can be estimated. On the scale of brain size the man-apes are scarcely distinguishable from the living apes, although their brains may have been larger with respect to body size. The brain seems to have evolved rapidly, doubling in size between man-ape and man. It then appears to have increased much more slowly; there is no substantial change in gross size during the last 100,000 years. One must remember, however, that size alone is a very crude indicator, and that brains of equal size may vary greatly in function. My belief is that although the brain of *Homo sapiens* is no larger than that of Neanderthal man, the indirect evidence strongly suggests that the first *Homo sapiens* was a much more intelligent creature.

The great increase in brain size is important because many functions of the brain seem to depend on the number of cells, and the number increases with volume. But certain parts of the brain have increased in size much more than others. As functional maps of the cortex of the brain show, the human sensory-motor cortex is not just an enlargement of that of an ape. The areas for the hand, especially the thumb, in man are tremendously enlarged, and this is an integral part of the structural base that makes the skillful use of the hand possible. The selection pressures that favored a large thumb also favored a large cortical area to receive sensations from the thumb and to control its motor activity. Evolution favored the development of a sensitive, powerful, skillful thumb, and in all these ways—as well as in structure—a human thumb differs from that of an ape.

The same is true for other cortical areas. Much of the cortex in a monkey is still engaged in the motor and sensory functions. In man it is the areas adjacent to the primary centers that are most expanded. These areas are concerned with skills, memory, foresight, and language; that is, with the mental faculties that make human social life possible. This is easiest to illustrate in the field of language. Many apes and monkeys can make a wide variety of sounds. These sounds do not, however, develop into language. Some workers have devoted great efforts, with minimum results, to trying to teach chimpanzees to talk. The reason is that there is little in the brain to teach. A human child learns to speak with the greatest ease, but the storage of thousands of words takes a great deal of cortex. Even the simplest language must have given great advantage to those first men who had it. One is tempted to think that language may have appeared together with the fine tools, fire, and complex hunting of the largebrained men of the Middle Pleistocene, but there is no direct proof of this.

The main point is that the kind of animal that can learn to adjust to complex, human, technical society is a very different creature from a tree-living ape, and the differences between the two are rooted in the evolutionary process. The reason that the human brain makes the human way of life possible is that it is the result of that way of life. Great masses of the tissue in the human brain are devoted to memory, planning, language, and skills, because these are the abilities favored by the human way of life.

The emergence of man's large brain occassioned a profound change in the plan of human reproduction. The human mother-child relationship is unique among the primates as is the use of tools. In all the apes and monkeys the baby clings to the mother; to be able to do so, the baby must be born with its central nervous system in an advanced state of development. But the brain of the fetus must be small enough so that birth may take place. In man adaptation to bipedal locomotion decreased the size of the bony birth-canal at the same time that the exigencies of tool use selected for larger brains. This obstetrical dilemma was solved by delivery of the fetus at a much earlier stage of development. But this was possible only because the mother, already bipedal and with hands free of locomotor necessities, could hold the helpless, immature infant. That small-brained man-ape probably developed in the uterus as much as the ape does; the human type of mother-child relation must have evolved by the time of the large-brained, fully bipedal humans of the Middle Pleistocene. Bipedalism, tool use, and selection for large brains thus slowed human development and invoked far greater maternal responsibility. The slow-moving mother, carrying the baby, could not hunt, and the combination of the woman's obligation to care for slow-developing babies and the man's occupation of hunting imposed a fundamental pattern on the social organization of the human species.

As Marshall D. Sahlins suggests, human society was heavily conditioned at the outset by still other significant aspects of man's sexual adaptation. In the monkeys and apes year-round sexual activity supplies the social bond that unites the primate horde. But sex in these species is still subject to physiological—especially glandular—controls. In man these controls are gone, and are replaced by a bewildering variety of social customs. In no other primate does a family exist that controls sexual activity by custom, that takes care of slow-growing young, and in which—as in the case of primitive human societies—the male and female provide different foods for the family members.

All theses family functions are ultimately related to tools, hunting, and the enlargement of the brain. Complex and technical society evolved from the sporadic tool-using of an ape, through the simple pebble tools of the man-ape and the complex toolmaking traditions of ancient men to the hugely complicated culture of modern man. Each behavioral stage was both cause and effect of biological change in bones and brain. These concomitant changes can be seen in the scanty fossil record and can be inferred from the study of the living forms.

Surely as more fossils are found these ideas will be tested. New techniques of investigation, from planned experiments in the behavior of lower primates to more refined methods of dating, will extract wholly new information from the past. It is my belief that, as these events come to pass, tool use will be found to have been a major factor, beginning with the initial differentiation of man and ape. In ourselves we see a structure, physiology and behavior that is the result of the fact that some populations of apes started to use tools a million years ago. The pebble tools constituted man's principal technical adaptation for a period at least 50 times as long as recorded history. As we contemplate man's present eminence, it is well to remember that, from the point of view of evolution, the events of the last 50,000 years occupy but a moment in time. Ancient man endured at least 10 times as long and the man-apes for an even longer time.

Skill as a Human Possession

Kenneth P. Oakley

I. EVOLUTION OF SKILL IN PRIMATES

To trace the origin and development of skilled behavior in man, it is necessary to consider the history of the primates. The earliest were the *Prosimii*. These evolved from tiny insectivores similar to those found in Cretaceous rocks in Mongolia. By the middle Eocene, when sub-tropical conditions were widespread, there were prosimians in almost all parts of the world. In many ways they resembled their modern survivors, the tree-shrews, lemurs, and tarsier. Like them, they probably lived mainly on insects and fruit. In common with other primitive mammals they had five movable digits on each limb. These were well adapted to climbing trees and grasping branches. Among the more advanced types the first digit acquired unusual mobility, so that it could be opposed to the others. This both enhanced grasping power and facilitated the catching of small insects and the plucking of fruits with the forelimbs. Thus the forelimbs began to assume many functions which in four-footed animals are usually performed by jaws and teeth. In other words, hands were being born out of habit.

Ground-dwelling mammals explore their environment and test the objects they encounter by smell; but as soon as any of them leave the ground and take to climbing, flying, or swimming other senses become more important. Being small and defenseless, the ancestors of the primates probably took to an arboreal life for security and for new sources of food. But life in the trees made its own demands; it put a premium on increased

From History of Technology, *ed. Charles Singer et al. (Oxford: The Clarendon Press, 1954), vol. 1, pp. 6–13, 15–16, 18–34; reprinted by permission of the author and the publisher, The Clarendon Press, Oxford.*

acuity of sight, touch, and hearing—particularly sight, which rapidly displaced smell as the master sense. Many early prosimians were probably, like the tarsier, nocturnal feeders: a habit dependent on special powers of vision.

In very primitive prosimians, the eyes are at the side of the head, divided by a snout. In due course the eyes shifted to a forward-facing position, so that both could be focused on the same near point; the brain thus perceived a stereoscopic picture, that is, one having depth and solidity. The spectral tarsier (*Tarsius*), surviving in the Indo-Malay archipelago, is a "living fossil" representing this stage in the evolution of the higher primates. Its eyes are enormous, and their field of vision is not divided by a snout.

Certain Eocene prosimians were ancestral to the higher primates (monkeys, apes, and men). They exhibited an increase in size, more particularly in brainsize. The portion of the brain associated with coordination of impressions of the senses other than smell—namely, the greater part of the cortex of the cerebrum—is relatively much more extensive and also more highly organized in structure in monkeys than in the prosimians. In the evolution of apes and men the cerebral cortex continued to increase in size, with the result that it became infolded, forming a complex pattern of convolutions and fissures.

Comparing the exploratory behavior of a typically terrestrial animal with that of a monkey, the enormous difference in their powers of sensory appreciation becomes obvious. A dog or an earth-bound insectivore, such as a hedgehog, tests an unusual object by sniffing it; a monkey fingers it while examining it visually. As a primary result of adaptation to life in the trees, the hand in the higher primates became not only a grasping organ but an important sense organ. The development of close cerebral co-ordination between touch and sight made possible the skilled manual activities of man.

Among early primates, concomitance of acute vision and prehensile powers gave a scope for intelligence, which was, however, limited in relation to manipulative skill by the restrictions of arboreal life. There is no reason to suppose that forest monkeys of today are any more intelligent than their Oligocene ancestors of 40 million years ago. The only further openings for development of intelligence were through abandonment of arboreal habits and adaptation to life on the ground, with retention of the nimbly prehensile hands of arboreal creatures. Prosimians at the end of the Oligocene evolved in three directions. One line, the New World monkeys, acquired extreme agility in the trees by developing prehensile tails. A second line, the Old World monkeys, mostly restricted to forests, retained the tail but only as a balancer—or even lost it. A few species became ground-dwellers, but were limited by undue specialization of the feet.

The third line included the ancestors of apes and men. The early members were probably not very different from *Proconsul,* which lived in East Africa early in the Miocene. They were unspecialized, monkey-like creatures, no doubt capable of tree-life and occasionally of swinging by their arms from bough to bough (brachiation), but also able to run along the ground, and even to rear up and scuttle on two legs. Subsequent evolution in this group proceeded along two divergent lines. In one line, leading to the specialized forest-bound apes of today, brachiation became firmly established as the main mode of locomotion. The arms lengthened, and the hands were specialized for hooking on branches. The other line, leading to man, had the advantage of remaining relatively unspecialized. Our monkey-like ancestors were probably used to tree-life, but in regions where woodland was interspersed by grassland they had to move in the open, and they acquired the habit of walking on two legs. This set the hands free to carry young and to collect food. These early *Hominidae,* which were probably clearly differentiated from the apes or *Pongidae* before the end of the Miocene, developed two interrelated specializations: first, the pelvic girdle was modified for the upright gait, and secondly, the foot lost prehensile power and became a rigid supporting organ. The legs now outgrew the arms in length. The hand retained its primitive simplicity and prehensile power but, freed from its locomotive functions, became progressively more skilled as a manipulative organ.

II. MAN AS THE TOOL-MAKING PRIMATE

Differentiation between anthropoid apes on the one hand and fully evolved men on the other is readily made on the basis of comparative anatomy, but the question of how to distinguish "men" from their immediate forerunners, which would have been smaller-brained and rather apelike, is still open to discussion. There was an evolutionary tendency among most primates to increase in body-size, and for their brains to increase at least in proportion. In the later stages of the evolution of man there was enlargement of the brain unrelated to any increase in bodysize. Yet, even so, brain-size is an unreliable criterion of humanity, and it is now recognized that a functional criterion, as for example, ability to make tools, is at least equally valid. We may consider some of the chief factors which led to man's becoming a tool-maker.

It has been said that "Man's place in nature is largely writ upon the hand." Any evidence bearing on the evolution of the human hand would be extremely interesting. Unfortunately the fossil evidence on this point is very meager, but it is not probable that the origin of tool-making was related to any advancement in the functional anatomy of the hand. Regarded anatomically, the prehensile hands of the less specialized monkeys would be capable of making tools if directed by an adequate brain. In many ways our own hands are more primitive than those of the anthropoid apes, our closest living relatives. The reason is plain: the hands of the apes are specialized for brachiation, but our forerunners, while developing specialized feet, retained the pliant generalized hands characteristic of the small tree-dwelling creatures, the distant ancestors of apes and men. In fact, the pentadactyl or five-fingered hand of man is so generalized that one would have to seek among the first mammals, or even go back to the reptiles from which they were derived, to find such primitive simplicity.

In its musculature, the hand of man is in fact closer to that of an Old World monkey than to that of any of the great apes. No ape can extend all its fingers flat on the ground and at the same time extend its wrist, for if the wrist is extended flexion on the fingers is inevitable. Consequently, when apes walk on all fours they support themselves on their knuckles, but men and monkeys can walk on their palms. There is no sign in the hand of man of any of the muscular specializations connected with brachiation, but there is evidence that our ancestors were climbers.

It is a common fallacy to suppose that monkeys cannot oppose the thumb to the other digits. Most Old World monkeys do this in catching insects. It is true that apes and men have developed a greater power of rotating the thumb, which facilitates its opposition to the other digits. In man, the thumb is relatively longer and more powerful than in apes and monkeys. Even so, Wood Jones writes: "We shall look in vain if we seek for movements that a man can do and a monkey cannot, but we shall find much if we look for purposive actions that a man does do and a monkey does not." In other words, manual skill reflects a fine central nervous mechanism rather than a specially delicate distal muscular apparatus. Men with coarse hands are sometimes capable of much finer craftsmanship than those with refined hands; moreover the remarkable skills developed by those whose hands have been maimed, or even lost, is testimony for our conclusion that so-called manual dexterity is mainly of cerebral origin. One must, however, bear in mind that any anatomical structure can evolve in relation to the whole organism.

Man owes much of his skill to his visual powers, and yet apes and many monkeys have eyes capable of refined stereoscopic and color vision. Man is, however, psychologically distinguished by his capacity for close visual attention, and for prolonged co-ordination of eye and hand. These are reflections of cerebral rather than ocular functions. Convergence of the eyes upon hand-work is largely dependent on conscious concentration—in other words, it is under the control of the cortical motor areas, which act in response to co-ordinated impulses from the eyes. It has been reported that chimpanzees can learn to use their hands under the direction of their eyes for long enough to thread a needle, but in general the attention that an ape can give to manipulating an object is very fleeting. Furthermore, the erect posture of man, and the fact that his skill is poised above the top of the spine instead of being slung in a forwardly projecting manner as in apes, make it easier for him to pay close attention to any point over a wide field of vision.

There is evidence suggesting that some early *Hominidae,* beginning to walk upright on open ground but possessing brains no larger than typical apes, may have been anatomically well enough equipped to use tools. What is in doubt is when and why in their evolutionary career the *Hominidae* became tool-makers. It is probable that at first they were, like many of the lower creatures that we have discussed, occasional urers of ready-to-hand tools and weapons.

Tools (including weapons) may be regarded as detachable additions to the body, supplementing mainly the functions of hands and teeth. So long as our early Tertiary ancestors led an arboreal life, their prehensile hands were fully occupied in climbing and feeding. They had neither need nor opportunity to use external objects as functional extensions of the limbs. But when they began to walk or sit on open ground, their hands were free to handle objects, first perhaps out of idle curiosity, later to some purpose. Baboons, which are ground-dwellers, sometimes use pebbles to kill scorpions —a favorite food—and if followed they will sometimes scamper up a hillside and dislodge stones or roll boulders down the slope to deter their pursuers. Observations on captive anthropoid apes have shown that emancipation from arboreal life offers wider scope for their latent intelligence. Chimpanzees make use of sticks for various purposes when captivity forces them to spend most of their time on the ground.

Though they have less concentration in solving problems, some monkeys are as quick-witted as apes. From the results of one intelligence test, a capuchin monkey was rated as high as a chimpanzee. This is probably exceptional, but it is worth bearing in mind as we attempt to trace the origins of human behavior, because the evidence of fossils and of a study of comparative anatomy both suggest that the *Hominidae* arose from monkey-like ancestors. If they were like monkeys of today, they would have been intensely active in body and mind, restlessly inquisitive, and quick in perception and plan. Judging by the experimental tendencies in the behavior of monkeys, the early *Hominidae* may well have begun to leave the forests out of sheer restless activity and curiosity. Recent behavior tests showed that even in rats the instinct to explore exists as a measurable urge.

The earliest *Hominidae* are believed to have existed in Miocene times. In so far as they were adapted to life on the ground, they would have been capable of using improvised tools and weapons, as do baboons and chimpanzees when circumstances demand. Such a need would arise more often in the open, where life was more precarious than in the forest. All this would have reacted favorably on the evolution of the brain, for those individuals with a well co-ordinated cortex were obviously most likely to survive. The *Hominidae* may have remained for millions of years at the stage of occasional tool-using. . . .

. . . Because there is a tendency to be . . . impressed by the occasional manufacture of tools by apes . . . the difference in level of mentality implied between these and the earliest efforts of man may be overlooked. Even the crudest Paleolithic artifacts indicate considerable forethought. The range of types of tool in the earliest Stone Age industries shows that almost at the dawn of culture tools were being made to make other tools. Using a hammerstone to make a hand-axe, and striking a stone flake to use in shaping a wooden spear, are activities which epitomize the mental characteristics of man—as most logically defined.

The capacity for foresight in man arises from efficient utilization of the records of the individual's past experience; that is, it reflects an improvement is cortical function. This is worth considering further. The nerve-cells in the cerebral cortex can be compared to the [tubes] of an electronic computor. They are organized to receive information from the sense-organs and, by a process compared to the calculating mechanisms of a computor, to solve problems and direct suitable bodily activity through the motor cells and nerves controlling muscles. The calculations made by the cortical cells are based not only on information received in the present, but on the patterns of activity left by past experience, that is to say on memory. The co-ordination of past and present information, leading to reasoning and voluntary action, is largely the function of the so-called "association areas" of the cortex.

The difference in size between the brains of ape and man is mainly due to the expansion in the human brain of those cortical parts concerned with the integration through which conceptual thought becomes possible. The most distinctive anatomical feature in the human brain is the large size of the frontal and temporal lobes. There is reason to suppose that these are particularly connected with the higher mental faculties. The human brain is also distinguished by an increase in the importance of the area containing motor cells. These are concentrated in a band extending from the top or crown to half-way down the side of each cerebral hemisphere, thus including the hind part of the frontal lobe, adjacent to the front margin of the parietal lobe which receives sensations of touch. . . .

However skilled behavior in man be viewed, the conclusion that it is dependent on a large and efficiently organized cerebrum is unavoidable. Even those movements which have been so deeply impressed by training or practice as to be habitual, such as walking or knitting, are impaired or lost if one side of the motor area becomes damaged, as by cerebral hemorrhage. Acts based on reflexes in the lower part of the brain or spinal cord, like the movements of flight in birds, or the discharge of urine in man, are unaffected by such damage.

It is evident that the powers of conceptual thought on the one hand, and of skilled behavior on the other, are closely related. Owing to the interconnections between the motor area and the higher association areas, the movements initiated in the human brain are those which the individual can see and feel himself doing. In the association areas some patterns of past activity are stored and, on being revived as memory, serve as the origin of ideas, and therefore of consciously planned conduct.

Since the skills of man depend so much on education, it is evident that language has greatly facilitated such activities as systematic tool-making. Oral tradition, in effect a new kind of inheritance, is sometimes regarded as more distinctive of man than tool-making. Apes have a language of the emotions, but the trick of giving names to things as well as to feelings implies conceptual thought. Moreover, it is extraordinarily difficult, if not impossible, to think effectively, to plan, or to invent, without the use of words or equivalent symbols. Most of our constructive thinking is done in unsounded words. The mental processes of our ancestors, before the invention of language, must have been similar to those of the uneducated born-deaf, who think in terms of events as a whole, not in terms of one thing at a time which has a name or comparable symbol. Helen Keller, deaf, dumb, and blind since infancy, has described how at seven she suddenly realized that "everything had a name." This discovery had a tremendous effect on her mind, for it opened the way to communication with other human beings. Verbal language is a technical aid, a tool which had to be invented. Through its introduction man acquired the power of logical thought.

When things have been given names—or symbols of some sort, for language does not necessarily demand speech—the mind can isolate and regroup them instead of thinking of them only as parts of a continuous sequence of events, as in a dream or silent film. The ability to tap memories, and at the same time to isolate and rearrange the ideas they present, is the prerequisite of invention and planning.

It is reasonable to infer that the brains of such *Hominidae* as were capable of making tools involving foresight would have been functionally advanced enough for speech, but that does not mean that the earliest toolmakers did in fact speak. Speech had to be invented. No one could deny that the brain of Helen Keller was advanced enought for verbal language long before she was seven. There are indications that speech, as we know it, though not necessarily language, was invented only at a comparatively late stage in cultural development. The invention was not delayed by any imperfection of the vocal apparatus; the larynges and tongue and lip muscles of apes are capable of articulating words. Chimpanzees have been taught to articulate such words as *papa, cup*. There is much in favor of the view that man's earliest means of communicating ideas was by gestures with the hands, and there is some evidence that these generate, in sympathy, unconscious movements of the mouth. Sympathetic action of hand and mouth has been observed in chimpanzees and children. It has been suggested that an increasing preoccupation of the hands with the making and use of tools could have led to the change from manual to oral gesturing as a means of communicating. The earliest words to be invented probably represented actions; the naming of objects would have come later.

It is no longer thought that speech is connected with the development in man of a special center in the cerebral cortex. Speech depends on the functioning of various cortical mechanisms which were already established in lower primates. Speech and its associated activities are disturbed by any injury within a broad zone extending along the side of the dominant (usually the left) cerebral hemisphere from just in front of the visual area, by the auditory area, to just below the motor area. If the injury is near the visual cortex, the patient will see printed words without realizing what they mean; if near the auditory area, he will hear words without understanding them; and if below the motor area the patient will suffer from aphasia or inability to articulate words. Injury at corresponding points in the opposite hemisphere rarely causes any disturbance of speech.

Owing to the fact that the nerve-fibers cross over in their way from the cortex to the stem of the brain, the left side of the brain controls movements on the right side of the body, and vice versa. The fact that, in most individuals, language-associations are built up in the part of the cortex which controls the right hand is probably connected with their being right-handed

—another indication of the close connection between manual activity and speech. Both may be considered as forms of tool-making.

III. ORIGINS OF TOOL-MAKING

We may now return to the origins of regular tool-making. Perhaps within the Pliocene, certainly by the dawn of the Pleistocene, that is about a million years ago, the typically human level of cerebral development had been reached. Stone artifacts of standardardized types have been found in Lower Pleistocene deposits in various parts of Africa, and in deposits only slightly more recent in Asia and western Europe. They show that tool-making was no longer merely occasional, but served permanent needs of these earliest men.

The apes of today are forest creatures subsisting on fruits, leaves, shoots, and insects, but all races of man include a substantial proportion of flesh in their diet. Early Paleolithic men were hunters. Meat-eating appears to be as old as man. In so far as the early *Hominidae* were adapted to a mixed environment, partly wooded, partly open, their diet would inevitably have been more varied than that of forest-bound primates.

It seems probable on the analogy of baboons that any hominids living in open country like the African savanna, as some of them did, would take to flesh-eating when the struggle for existence was intensified by excessive drought. Baboons, almost the only monkeys completely adapted to life away from woodlands, prey on poultry and occasionally on lambs and other animals of similar size, using their powerful canine teeth as offensive weapons. This habit becomes more prevalent when conditions of existence are hard. A recent report on the habits of baboons in Zululand states that they often join in organized hunts. Usually, led by a veteran of the troop, they surround a small antelope or other victim and, at a given signal, close in on it and tear it to pieces. After the affair is over only the skull and limb-bones are left.

In men, the canine teeth are much smaller than in baboons or in the apes, and are level with the other teeth. It has been suggested that reduction of these teeth in the evolution of man occurred as and when their functions were taken over by the hands, and by weapons and tools. In the fossil *Australopithecinae* of South Africa, probably slightly modified descendants of our Pliocene ancestors, the canines are small and level with the other teeth, even in the earliest stages of wear, and even in males. These hominids may have been tool-users, but there is no evidence that they were tool-makers. Thus it appears that the canine teeth were already reduced in the *Hominidae* at an evolutionary stage below that of tool-making. The Australopithecines lived in open country, probably hiding in caves and rock-crannies for protection. Whether the smallness of their canines was related to the use of hand weapons or not, the Australopithecines and the proto-men of Pliocene times would have needed means to defend themselves when foraging in the open. Walking on two legs with hands free, they may well have used stones as missiles, and sticks or animal long-bones as clubs.

In times of drought, then, our precursors would readily have taken to eating flesh. Although they lacked teeth suited to carnivorous habits, they were no doubt at least as ingenious as baboons in killing small animals. Life in the open set a premium not only on cunning but on co-operation. In view of the mentality and social life of other primates it is likely that the proto-men hunted in hordes, and killed medium-sized mammals by cornering them and using improvised hand-weapons.

Direct evidence of the Pliocene *Hominidae* and their habits is still lacking, but there is reason to suppose that they were not very different from the Australopithecines, now regarded as a side-branch of the family which survived locally into Early Pleistocene times. There are indications that some at least were carniverous. The scattered fragments of animal bones, egg shells, and crab shells found with *Australopithecus* in the cave deposits at Taungs, Bechuanaland, had all the appearance of food refuse. In the *Australopithecus* level in one of the Makapan caves, Transvaal, quantities of antelope limb-bones were found, some apparently smashed as if to extract the marrow, but there were no undoubted tools.

By the time that the *Hominidae* had evolved into tool-makers they were evidently largely carnivorous; quantities of meat-bones were associated with the remains of Pekin man (*Pithecanthropus pekinensis*). It is easy to see how tool-making might arise out of the adoption of carnivorous habits. Though they may have killed game easily enough, the proto-men must often have had difficulty in removing skin and fur, and in dividing the flesh. Without strong canines, sharp pieces of stone would provide the solution. Here surely was the origin of the tradition of tool-making. Where no naturally sharp pieces of stone lay ready to hand, more intelligent individuals saw that the solution was to break pebbles and produce fresh sharp edges. Perhaps accidental breakages in using pebbles as missiles had been observed. Once this tradition had begun, the manifold uses of chipped stones became obvious.

Dentally, and from the alimentary point of view, we should be vegetarians. We lack the teeth of true carnivores, and we have the long gut associated with herbivorous diet. Furthermore, our nearest living relations, the anthropoid apes, are herbivores, and consume only small quantities of animal protein. Man's change of habit from herbivore to semicarnivore gave a new potential. To store a given amount of energy, a carnivore needs a smaller quantity of food than a herbivore. Its way of life is accordingly very different, from the point of view of the economy of energy. Instead of eating almost continuously, like their fruit-and-plant-eating ancestors, the earliest men must have spent most of their daytime in hunting. This activity increased interdependence and encouraged social grouping. New skills and aptitudes were thus developed, through which man was able not only to survive climatic changes, but even to create his own environment. The evolution of new bodily equipment in response to environmental change normally requires hundreds of thousands, if not millions, of years; but by inventing extra-bodily equipment—such as tools, weapons, shelter, clothing—which could be discarded or changed as circumstances dictated, man became the most adaptable of all creatures.

With fire, weather-proof shelters, and skins or other clothing at his command, man became free to spread into every climatic zone. These cultural activities depended on tool-making, but were made possible through man's power, not only of conceptual thought, but of communicating inventive ideas and thus of building traditions. Where tradition is limited, culture ceases to evolve and may degenerate. Of this there are many examples.

IV. EVOLUTION OF HUMAN SKILL

Having inquired into the factors of the origin and development of human skills, we find three questions to be considered: (i) Can stages in the evolution of human skill be recognized? (ii) If so, is there evidence that they are correlated with stages of physical evolution? (iii) Does skill vary with species or racial type?

It is possible to distinguish six main levels of culture on the basis of the use and making of tools, and to correlate them broadly with known types of *Hominidae*:

(*a*) Occasional use of improvised tools and weapons. "Eolithic." *Australopithecus* and Pliocene hominids?

(*b*) Occasional tool-making. Dawn of Early or Lower Paleolithic. Earliest species of *Pithecanthropus?* and of *Homo?*

(*c*) Regular tool-making, but little or no standardization. Lower Paleolithic. *Pithecanthropus* (e.g. of Pekin), and some early precursors of *Homo sapiens* (e.g. of Fontéchevade in the Charente).

(*d*) Regular tool-making, with marked standardization, but little specialization. Lower Paleolithic. Early precursors of *Homo sapiens* (e.g. of Kanam in Kenya, and Swanscombe, Kent).

(*e*) Manufacture of specialized tools and weapons:
- (1) Elementary. Middle Paleolithic. *Homo neanderthalensis* and some early *Homo sapiens*.
- (2) Composite. Upper or Late Paleolithic and Mesolithic. *Homo sapiens* (e.g. Cro-Magnons).

(f) Use of mechanical principles (machine tools). Modern *Homo sapiens*. Characteristic of Neolithic and Metal Ages, but foreshadowed in some Upper Paleolithic and Mesolithic practices.

Though man's Pliocene ancestors were not tool-makers, they were tool-users. Direct proof is difficult to obtain, but it is supported by evidence from the Australopithecine sites in South Africa. None has yielded any undoubted tools or weapons, but at Taungs there were baboon skulls which seemed to have been artificially pierced. It is also suggested that occasional river pebbles in the dolomite fissure deposit at Sterkfontein, containing remains of an Australopithecine, had been carried to the site by that creature.

Even when tool-making became widespread among the first men, it was probably for long only an occasional practice, since improvised implements and weapons often served well enough. Improvisation has played an important part in human culture at all periods. Some modern Australian aborigines carve wooden implements with naturally sharp pieces of stone. Thus a man of the Pitjendadjara tribe will take an unflaked piece of stone to chop a slab of wood from a tree-trunk, and with another unflaked stone deftly work the wood into a highly finished spear-thrower. This example of primitive craftsmanship may remind us that we cannot estimate exactly the skill of the earliest men from the crude stone tools which are almost the only evidence of their culture, for much of their equipment may have been of wood and other perishable materials. Identification of the first stone tools is almost impossible, for not only were they usually pieces of naturally fractured stone, but man's first attempts to improve their shape would have been indistinguishable from the accidental chippings produced by natural agencies. For this reason, none of the so-called eoliths can be accepted unreservedly as human work. Except for their occurrence in a cave deposit with hearths and human remains, few of the stone artifacts of Pekin man would have been recognized as human work.

There were no recognizable tools with the remains of the oldest known fossil man, the species *Pithecanthropus robustus* found in lake-clays at Sangiran in Java; or with the later *P. erectus* from river gravel at Trinil, Java; or with the species of *Homo* in river sands at Mauer near Heidelberg. This is not surprising when one considers that their dwelling-sites are unknown, and that in any case some human groups may have long remained at the stage of occasional tool-making.

Though not the oldest industry, that in the cave deposits at Choukoutien in China, with remains of *Pithecanthropus pekinensis,* is among the most primitive known. Thousands of artificially broken pieces of stone, of kinds foreign to the site, were found in all the occupation layers. Few are recognizable implements. It appears that Pekin man collected stones from a nearby river-bed and from neighboring cliffs, and brought them to the cave in order to work them into implements when required. He broke up the lumps by using a stone slab or large bone as an anvil and striking them with a hammerstone. Usually he found it most convenient to use the resulting flakes, though sometimes the residual cores proved more useful (Fig. 1a, b). Occasionally, flakes were crudely trimmed into points or scrapers. Rough choppers were made by removing a few flakes from the surfaces of oval boulders. The rarity of definable tools in the Choukoutien deposits indicates that though Pekin man was a regular and systematic tool-maker, he made little attempt at standardization; in fact many of his implements were evidently of the occasional type.

For some purposes he used broken bones as implements (Fig. 1c). The crudity of his industry is partly accounted for by the poor quality of veinquartz, the only raw material easily available to him, but this is not the whole explanation, for the precursors of *Homo sapiens* in Africa made shapely hand-axes from equally intractable stone. In the higher occupation layers at Choukoutien there was a noticeable increase in the percentage of

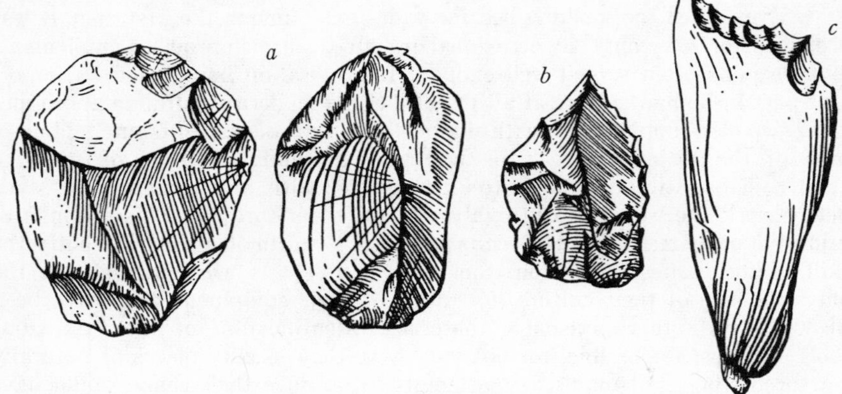

FIGURE 1. *Tools of Pekin man. (a) Quartz chopper tool. (b) Pointed flake of quartz. (c) Broken animal bone chipped for use as tool. (Adapted by Jacquelyn Hetrick.)*

tools chipped in more readily flaked stone (chert). Therefore the later stages of the industry appear more highly evolved, not through any advance in manual dexterity, but because of greater care in securing suitable raw material. Chert was already known to Pekin man at the time of his first occupation of the caves, but was presumably less accessible. Its more frequent use in the upper layers seem to indicate the development of a tradition leading to increased persistence and forethought.

All we know of the hand of Pekin man is a wrist-bone. It shows no feature which distinguishes it from that of modern man. An analysis of the better-defined tools from Choukoutien has shown that the majority were chipped by right-handed persons. Monkeys and some other animals show individual preference for the use of one hand or paw, but the acquisition of greater skill in the one hand is a human trait linked with the dominance of one side of the brain, and doubtless connected with the habitual use of tools. Ninety-five per cent of modern adult human beings are right-handed, but left-handedness was commoner in early times, as it still is among untrained infants. Our word dexterity is from the Latin root *dexter* (Greek *dexios*), which means "on the right (hand)."

Pekin man had considerable skill as a hunter, for his own remains are associated with quatities of bones of butchered animals, chiefly deer, but also bison, horse, rhinoceros, elephant, bear, hyena, and tiger. The killing of some of these must have involved the use of pits or traps. Throughout the long period of their occupation of the caves—probably seasonal—the Choukoutien hunters regularly used fire. The discovery of how to make fire was man's greatest step forward in gaining freedom from the dominance of environment.

The earliest known Stone Age industries in Africa are probably older than those of Choukoutien. They are represented chiefly by pebbles flaked to produce a cutting or chopping edge. These pebble-tools approach a standard form (Fig. 2), and are usually accompanied by rough flakes which may themselves have been occasionally used as tools. . . .

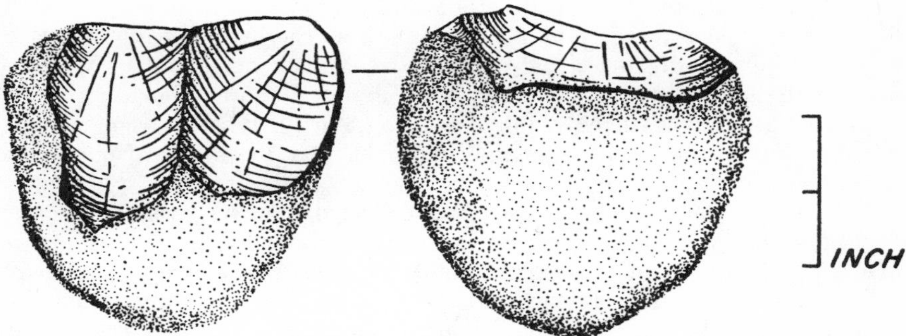

FIGURE 2. *Quartzite pebble-tool from southern Rhodesia. Lower Paleolithic. (Adapted by Jacquelyn Hetrick.)*

At Olduvai, in Tanganyika, it has been shown that pebble-tool culture evolved into the Chelleo-Acheulian culture, which was distinguished by the hand-axes widespread throughout Africa and parts of west Europe and south Asia during much of the Pleistocene. Hand-axes (Fig. 3, left) were made by flaking a pebble or stone slab round the edges from both sides, so as to produce a pointed tongue-shaped tool with a sharp margin. These were the first standardized implements; they served a great variety of purposes. They were not hafted, nor (apart from the forms known as cleavers—see Fig. 3, right) were they axes in the true sense. They were probably used mainly as hunters' knives, but may have served also for

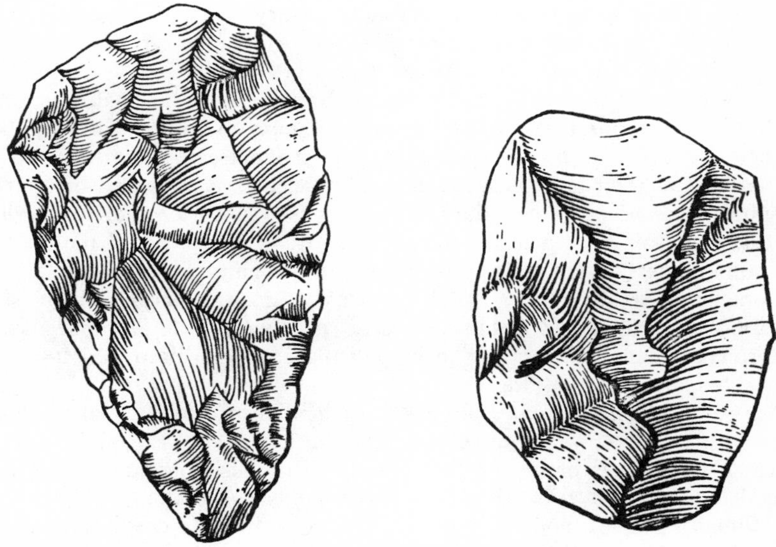

FIGURE 3. *Acheulian flint hand-axe from Wolvercote, Oxfordshire (left). Acheulian cleaver in quartzite from Madras, India (right). (Adapted by Jacquelyn Hetrick.)*

cutting wood or for digging up grubs and roots. Acheulian peoples used flake-tools to some extent, but the hand-axe was the predominant tool of a cultural tradition which not only spread over nearly one-fifth of the land-area of the globe, but persisted for more than a hundred thousand years. The hand-axe peoples lived mainly in open country, ranging from the hot African deserts to the cool grasslands and open wooded valleys of northwest Europe.

Chellean and Acheulian implements collected from successively younger deposits in any one region show on the whole a gradual refinement of workmanship, but the comparative uniformity of industries of this group over so vast an area is most remarkable. Many Acheulian hand-axes from the Cape, Kenya, Madras, and London are indistinguishable from each other as regards form, whether made of flint, sandstone, quartz, or lava.

Men who made tools of standard type must have formed in their minds images of the ends to which they labored. Human culture (and by culture we mean here all that a society practices and produces) is the outcome of this capacity for conceptual thought. The leading factors in its development are tradition coupled with invention. The primitive hunter made an implement in a particular fashion largely because as a child he had watched another at work. The standard hand-axe was not conceived by any one individual *ab initio,* but was the end-product of exceptional individuals in successive generations, not only copying but occasionally improving on the products of their predecessors. As a result of co-operative hunting, migrations, and trade, the traditions of different groups of Paleolithic hunters sometimes became blended.

The development of speech must have greatly facilitated these processes. The extreme slowness of cultural evolution during the Lower Paleolithic may have been related to the rudimentary form of language. It has been suggested that the hand-axe people were still communicating by gesture and gabble, and had not yet achieved true word-making.

We have no reason to infer that all Early Paleolithic men had brains qualitatively inferior to those of the average man of today. The simplicity of their culture can be accounted for by the extreme sparseness of the population and their lack of accumulated knowledge. A supposed hallmark of the mind of *Homo sapiens* is the artistic impulse—but archeological evidence suggests that this trait manifested itself almost at the dawn of tool-making. Crystals of quartz were collected by Pekin man many miles from his home, and one may presume that, partly at least, this was because their shape and appearance appealed to him. Some of the finer Acheulian hand-axes are masterpieces of artistic craftsmanship, displaying perfection which exceeds bare technical necessity (Fig. 9).

The only undoubted skull of an Acheulian hand-axe maker is that found in gravel at Swanscombe, near Dartford in Kent, England, in 1935–36. In so far as it is preserved, it is barely distinguishable from some skulls of modern *Homo sapiens,* though it is probably more than 100,000 years old, Human skulls of modern type were also found with Acheulian hand-axes at Kanjera in Kenya, though their contemporaneity is more open to doubt.

Like their more brutish contemporaries in China, the hand-axe people

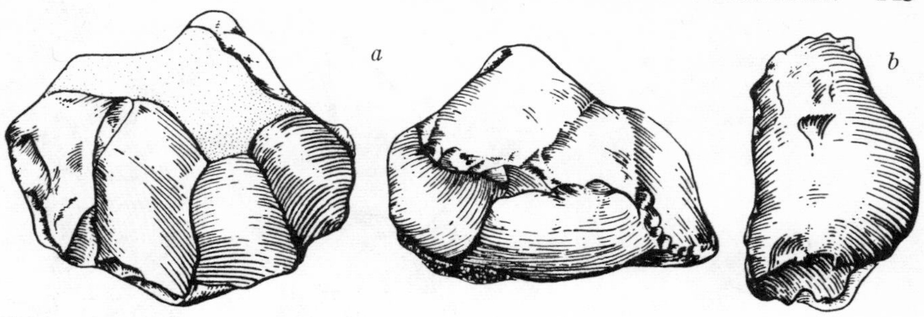

FIGURE 4. *Clactonian flint artifacts. (a) Core. (b) Flake-tool. Swanscombe, Kent. (Adapted by Jacquelyn Hetrick.)*

were well advanced in hunting skill. Lake-side dwelling sites of Acheulian man, in both Kenya and Spain, revealed quantities of broken bones of fast-moving animals such as gazelle and zebra, as well as of elephant and other big game. There is evidence of the use of fire by Acheulian hunters at only a few localities, in the Transvaal (Makapan), Spain, and Palestine.

Early stone industries are sometimes classified according to whether most of the tools were made by trimming a block of stone to the required shape (core-tool), or by detaching a flake from the pebble or block and using that (flake-tool). Acheulian hand-axes are classed as core-tools. Probably, however, in the basic stone-working tradition both cores and flakes were used with little discrimination. The Choukoutien industry was not far removed from that stage, and in parts of Africa and Europe there were groups of people who for long retained or reverted to it. The Clactonian of Europe (Fig. 4), and the industries of the type of that of Hope Fountain in southern Africa, are examples of such primitive Paleolithic cultures, which existed alongside the more advanced Chelleo-Acheulian. Skulls of Late Clactonian man recently found at Fontéchevade, in the Charente, appear to be similar to the Swanscombe type (primitive *Homo sapiens*).

The evidence indicates that man originated in Africa but spread fairly rapidly into Asia and Europe, carrying a basic stone-working tradition out of which various specialized cultures evolved. In Africa the core hand-axe culture developed; in eastern Asia another core-culture, distinguished by standardized chopping tools (Fig. 5); and in western Asia and Europe, flake-cultures. There was considerable overlapping of these traditions, with consequent hybridization of cultures in some regions.

It would be wrong to give the impression that there was no specialization of tools in Lower Paleolithic times. The hammerstone or anvil for flaking, the flake for cutting skins, the crude chopping-tool for splitting bones or wood, were primary specializations in the most primitive known industries. But the use of a single standardized tool-type for a variety of different purposes was a leading feature of Lower Paleolithic culture. The pointed hand-axe is an extreme example of an all-purpose tool, for it served equally well for piercing, cutting, and scraping. With the advent of what is generally known as the Middle Paleolithic stage of culture, specialized types of tool were devised to perform each of these functions, and

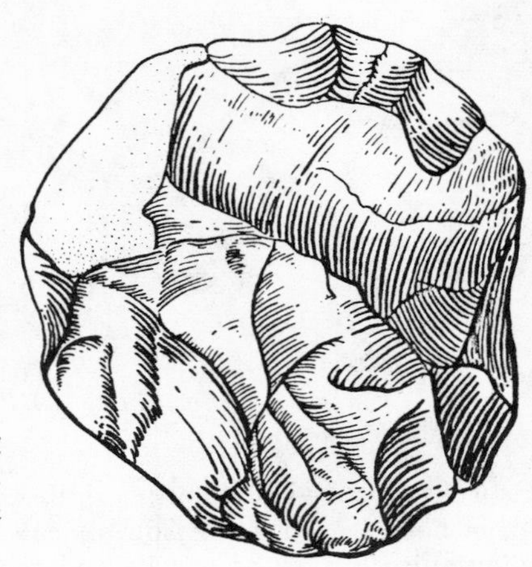

FIGURE 5. *East Asiatic chopper-tool in silicified tuff. Java. Lower Paleolithic. (Adapted by Jacquelyn Hetrick.)*

specialization then became a conspicuous feature of culture. For example, it became the fashion among some later hand-axe people, and also among some of the flake-tool people, to prepare blocks of stone in such a way that a flake of accurately determined form could be struck. The preparatory flaking aimed at so shaping the block that the flake eventually detached was immediately serviceable as an implement, without further trimming. This was the specialized tortoise-core technique used by many different groups of hunters in Africa, Asia, and Europe, including the Neanderthalers. Cultures in which this technique was extensively employed are generally termed Levalloisian.

The typical Levallois tool struck from a tortoise-core combines the plano-convex form of some hand-axes with the straight cutting-edge of the ordinary flake, and was thus very well suited for use as a skinningknife. The tortoise-core technique is innteresting for the evolution of skill, because its manufacture implies much more forethought than that of any of the tools characteristic of Lower Paleolithic culture. An unstruck tortoise-core so closely resembles a high domed plano-convex hand-axe that one way in which the technique was discovered might have been through the accidental breaking of such a tool. The Levalloisian or tortoise-core technique long continued in use with various modifications, particularly in Africa.

It has been convenient to use the term "tool" to include weapons. During Lower Paleolithic times these were simple missiles such as pebbles or all-wood spears, and presumably also pits and traps. The frontal bone of a hyena skull at Choukoutien had been smashed by a missile boulder. The oldest known actual weapon (and, incidentally, the oldest surviving piece of woodwork) is the pointed end of a yew-wood spear associated with the typical Clactonian industry in the water-logged Elephant Bed at Clacton-on-Sea in Essex, England. It has been shaped by the use of flint flakes. Judging from the practice of modern Australian aborigines, many of the so-called scrapers from Lower Paleolithic sites were probably used for working wood rather than for dressing skins as was formerly supposed. A complete spear of yew-wood, with fire-hardened tip, within the skeleton of an elephant and associated with a Levalloisian flint industry, was found at Lehringen, about 30 kilometers southeast of Bremen, Germany.

The typical Neanderthalers, or *Homo neanderthalensis,* formed a specialized offshoot of mankind, the earliest members of which (for instance at Ehringsdorf, Germany) were barely distinguishable from the precursors of *Homo sapiens.* They were essentially a European and west Asian group. Their culture, known as Mousterian, had Clactonian roots and followed a flake-tool tradition, but was locally influenced by the Acheulian. The early Neanderthalers lived under the warm conditions that prevailed in Europe during the third interglacial period, and their mode of life was similar to that of the Acheulians. The later or typical Mousterian culture developed under the wet or tundra conditions associated with the fourth glaciation. The Neanderthalers adapted themselves to the severe climate by using caves as dwellings wherever possible, and probably by wearing animal pelts as rough cloaks in severe weather, as do the modern inhabitants of Tierra del Fuego.

In material equipment the Neanderthalers showed little more inventiveness than the Lower Paleolithic peoples. They do not appear to have mastered the craft of working bone, but like Pekin man they sometimes used broken long bones of animals as tools. They selected dense bones for chopping-blocks and pressure-flakers (Fig. 6c), and broke fibulae of bear for use as skin-sleekers. Mousterian industries consist principally of stone flake-tools, struck either in the simple Clactonian fashion, or by the Levalloisian technique, but with edges finely retouched by pressure-flaking to make them more durable. They include three main standard types, (*a*) triangular points with both edges retouched (Fig. 6a); (*b*) D-shaped side-scrapers (Fig. 6b); (*c*) small heart-shaped hand-axes. The flake-tools were predominant. The Neanderthalers used spears of wood. A Neanderthal skeleton

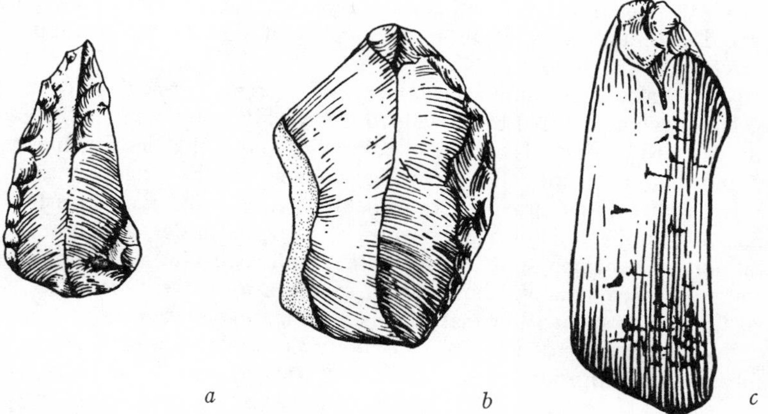

FIGURE 6. *Mousterian artifacts. (a) Flake point and (b) sidescraper in flint, from Le Moustier, Dordogne. (c) Bone compressor from La Quina, Charente. (Adapted by Jacquelyn Hetrick.)*

at Mount Carmel had a clean-cut hole, extending through the head of one thigh bone into the pelvis, which was the work of a wooden spear point. Some of the more advanced Neanderthalers appear to have used hafted narrow flint points as detachable spearheads. Occasionally they applied the principle of hafting to scrapers. Thus their equipment was more specialized than that of their predecessors, though still very elementary. They were fearless and proficient hunters, for they slew mammoth, rhinoceros, and bear. Their weapons included missile stones, but it is doubtful if they were slung or used in the form of a bolas. The abundance of limb-bones of game animals, and the rarity of ribs and vertebrae, in the Neanderthal cave-dwellings show that they did not drag whole carcasses to the cave, but cut them up and carried away portions. They made extensive use of fire, and cooked their meat.

Judging from the few arm and hand bones known, Neanderthal men were usually right-handed. Their fingers were relatively shorter and thicker than those of modern man, but the joints allowed easy movement. Their implements, although simple, were often exquisitely finished, particularly in the Upper Mousterian, indicating considerable dexterity, and pride in exercise of skill. At Sergeac, in the Dordogne, they made a few tools in rock-crystal of gem-stone quality, indicating some artistic sense.

In most parts of Europe, Middle Paleolithic culture gave place with almost dramatic suddenness to the Upper Paleolithic, distinguished by a wide range of new specialized tools and weapons, and by various new techniques. These rapid cultural advances were associated with the emergence of highly successful types of *Homo sapiens,* notably the Cro-Magnons. They spread from southwest Asia during the second half of the last glacial period, and entirely supplanted the Neanderthalers, whose disappearance may be likened to the reduction in the number of aborigines in contact with European culture. The Cro-Magnons and related groups were not only much more inventive than their predecessors, but exhibited remarkable aesthetic sense and displayed artistic skills scarcely excelled in any later period. This rapid evolution of culture may have been due to the invention of a system of verbal symbolism.

Upper Paleolithic industries show an increased mastery over materials. New techniques had been evolved for working flint and similar stone, such as the production of narrow blades with parallel sides by means of punch and hammer, and the surfacing as well as the edge-trimming of flakes by indirect percussion or pressure (e.g. Solutrean spearheads). Artifacts of complicated form were wrought in bone, antler, and ivory by a combination of sawing, splitting, grinding, and polishing. By now, tools were not only used to make implements in the sense of end-products, such as meat knivers or spears, but many tools were made which were tool-making tools. This is good evidence that the hunter-craftsman was showing considerably greater foresight, and no longer worked merely to satisfy immediate ends. Thus, numerous specialized types of flint chiseling-tools (burins) were devised mainly for working bone, antler, ivory, and probably wood into other tools (Fig. 7a–e).

It may be noted that many of the tools and weapons of the Upper

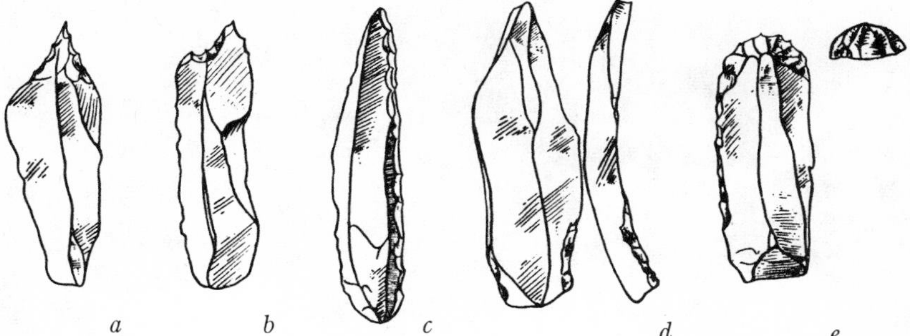

FIGURE 7. *Upper Paleolithic blade tools in flint. (a) Solutrean piercer or "hand drill," Dordogne. (b) Magdalenian concave end-scraper or "spoke shave," Dordogne. (c) Gravettian knife-point, Dordogne. (d) Magdalenian burin, Dordogne. (e) End-scraper, Vale of Clwyd, Wales. (Adapted by Jacquelyn Hetrick.)*

Paleolithic peoples were composite (Fig. 8). Missile and thrusting spears were regularly provided with hafted heads of bone, antler, or flint, and some of the flint blade-tools were set in bone or wooden handles. One important factor in the efficiency of a tool or weapon is the means of giving its working edge or point the desired motion through the material to be worked or penetrated. Originally all tools were grasped in the hand; the first step towards a mechanical device was hafting. In Upper Paleolithic times, men were beginning to apply mechanical principles to the movement of tools and weapons. Spears were launched with throwers which, working on the lever principle, increase the effective propelling power of a man's arm. The bow was invented late in this period, probably in north Africa. It was the first means of concentrating muscular energy for the propulsion of an arrow, but it was soon discovered that it also provided a means of twirling a stick, and this led to the invention of the rotary drill.

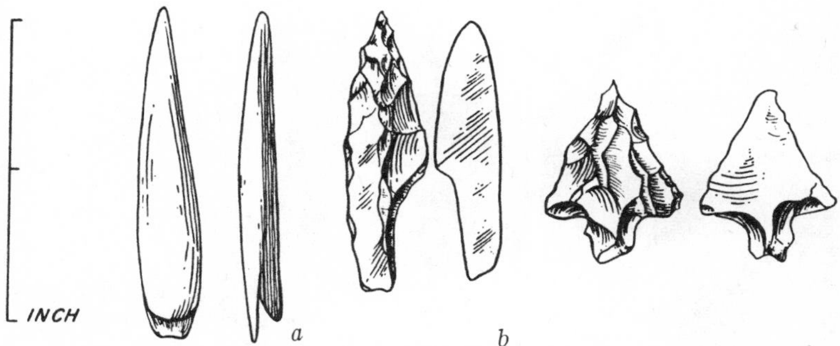

FIGURE 8. *Upper Paleolithic hafted weapon-tips. (a) Aurignacian split-base bone point, Dordogne. (b) Solutrean shouldered "willow-leaf" point showing pressure-flaking, Dordogne. (c) Aterian arrowhead, Morocco. (Adapted by Jacquelyn Hetrick.)*

FIGURE 9. *(Photographs courtesy of the Robert H. Lowie Museum of Anthropology, University of California, Berkeley.)*

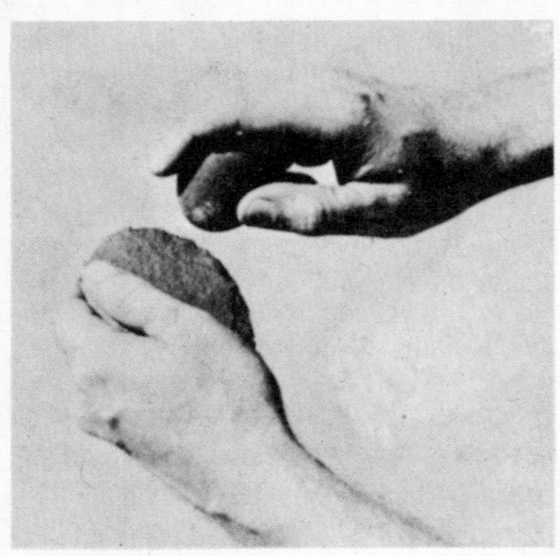

(Above) Percussion-flaking with small hammer stone.

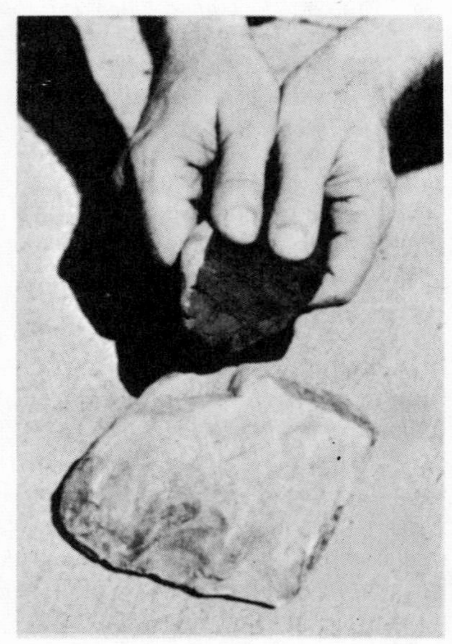

(Right) Anvil technique in which artifact is struck against fixed anvil to remove flake from upper surface.

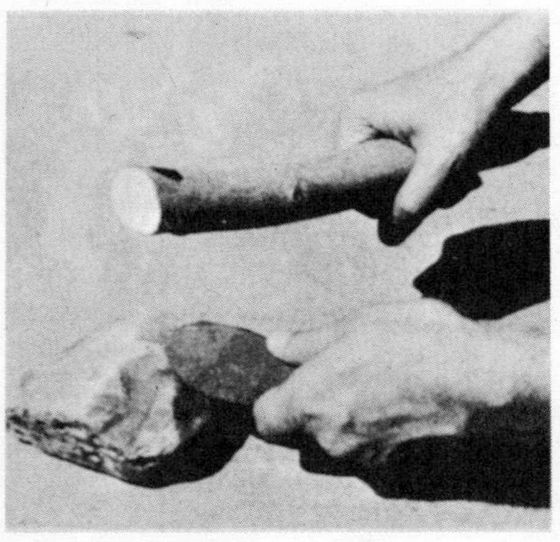

(Left) Indirect percussion on anvil. Artifact edge is placed on a fixed point of anvil and held by its other end. Baton strikes center of artifact causing flake to detach from upper surface above point of contact with anvil.

(Right) Pressure-flaking chert with deer antler. Point of antler is placed near edge of artifact and pressed downward and away from worker to remove a small flake from the desired place on undersurface of artifact. Pad of leather or cloth is necessary to prevent cutting hands.

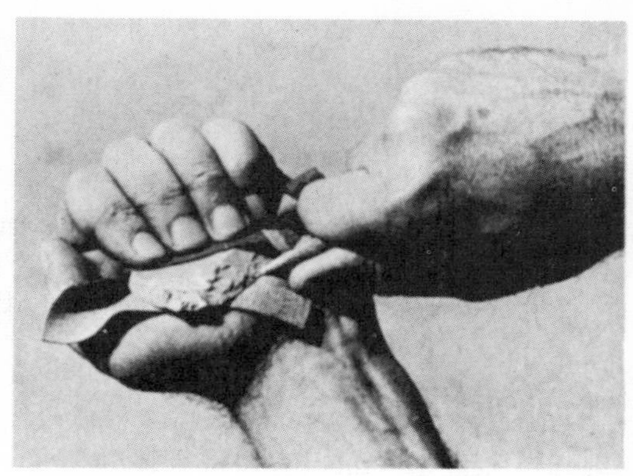

(Left) Pecking groove in grantite stone with a smaller fine-grained stone. Repeated blows crush bits of the surface to produce the groove shown. The groove will be used to lash hammer to a wood handle.

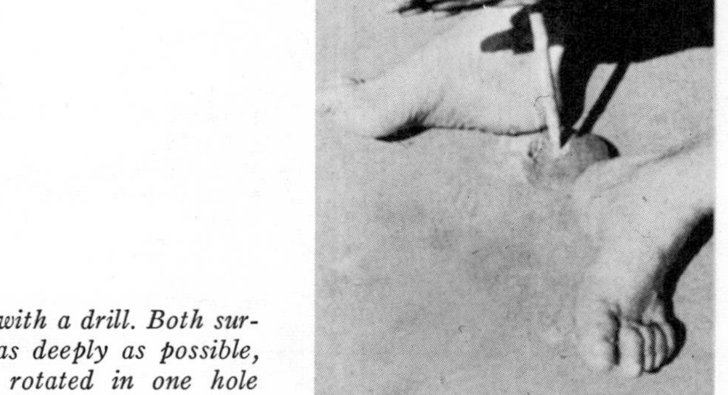

(Right) Boring a hole with a drill. Both surfaces are first pecked as deeply as possible, and then the stick is rotated in one hole using wet sand as abrasive.

Bone and ivory bodkins, bone needles with eyes, belt-fasteners, and, rarely, even buttons have been found in Upper Paleolithic sites. Carved representations of clothed figures show that these hunters wore sewn skin garments with fitting sleeves and trousers. These greatly increased their efficiency in the very cold winters that they had to endure.

Thus men were making their own environments in various ways. In the limestone hills of western Europe, the Upper Paleolithic tribes made their winter homes in shallow caves or rock-shelters. They were principally hunters of reindeer and horse. In the summer, they followed the migrating herds and used tents or huts as dwellings. In eastern Europe, they specialized in hunting mammoth, and adapted themselves to life on the open steppe by constructing permanent communal huts deeply sunk in the ground. The cave-art of the western tribes shows that some of these hunters had remarkable powers of observation and visual memory. Most of the drawings and paintings were done in the dark innermost recesses of caverns, usually by the light of open stone lamps. The acuity of vision and co-ordination of hand and eye which late Paleolithic tribal artists possessed is illustrated by the fineness of some of their tools and engravings.

In spite of their artistic and other skilled achievements, the Upper Paleolithic people of Europe and Asia were economically no more than food-collecting savages. Their varied culture, probably reflecting an increase in population and a certain amount of leisure within each group, was possible only because game was abundant.

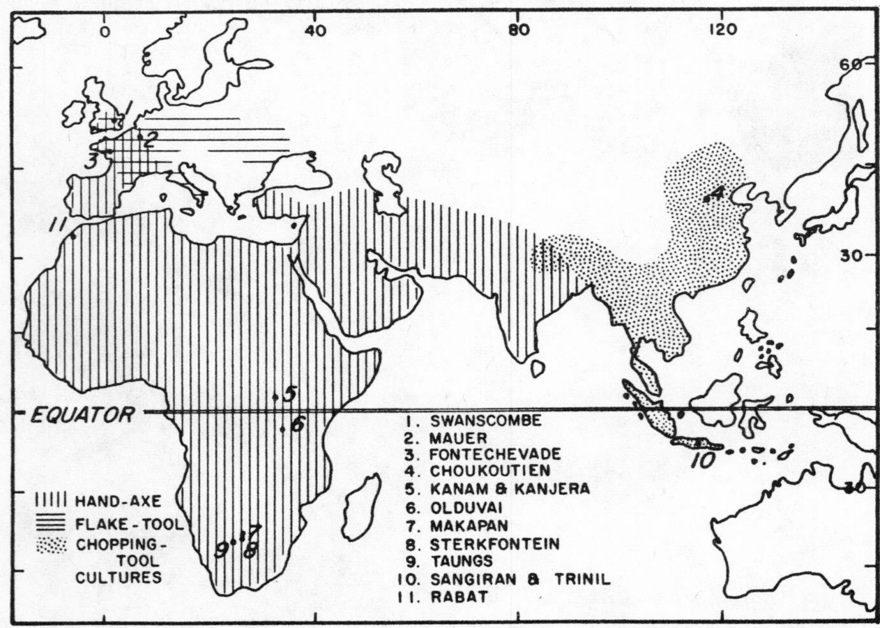

FIGURE 10. *Distribution of Lower Paleolithic industries and sites of early hominids. (Adapted by Jacquelyn Hetrick.)*

By various inventions, men now came to adapt their mode of life to the new environments consequent on the climatic changes which brought the last glaciation to an end. In this Mesolithic phase, life remained at the level of bare subsistence until certain groups in the Middle East began the revolutionary practice of cultivating plants and domesticating animals as sources of food and raw materials. With food-production, man passed from the hunting stage and was on the way to civilization. He ceased to be a rare species. Larger, settled communities could be supported, and it was no longer necessary for all their members to be occupied in gathering or producing food, with the consequence that a great variety of new skilled crafts could develop. . . .

Earliest Men in America

F. H. H. Roberts, Jr.

Since the days of Columbus and the beginning of colonization in the Americas there has been an ever-growing interest in the aborigines, their place of origin, their physical relationships, and the length of time that they have inhabited the New World.

Throughout the years many theories have been advanced about them and speculations have led from one extreme to another. Some scholars have identified the American Indians with the Lost Tribes of Israel, others have suggested that they were descendants of the Carthaginians, the Phoenicians, or other Old World peoples. There is a small minority which argues that there was an independent racial development in the Western Hemisphere, but lack of evidence for human precursors and the absence of primitive types of man are opposed to that idea. Even though they appear to comprise several physical types, striking similarities between the New World peoples and eastern Asiatics, as well as certain cultural resemblances and some possible linguistic relationships, are now generally believed to indicate an Old World genesis with subsequent migration. There probably was no single

This article was prepared for the International Commission for a History of the Scientific and Cultural Development of Mankind and was originally published in the Journal of World History, *Vol. I, no. 2 (1953), 255–77. Reprinted by permission of the author and the International Commission for a History of the Scientific and Cultural Development of Mankind.*

mass movement, rather a continuing series of migrations by small groups over a long period of time, although the spread eventually may have accelerated and larger bodies of people have been involved. Opinions differ with respect to the routes followed. Many have reached the conclusion that the northern ones were the most likely, with the earliest of the movements from northeastern Asia to Alaska being in the Bering Strait region. The avenues followed, once the people had reached North America, would be governed in no small degree by climatic conditions and the time when the migrations occurred. Data pertaining to the latter are gradually accumulating and at least the broad outlines of the picture are beginning to appear. From early Colonial days to the present occasional finds have been made which tend to indicate a reasonable antiquity. At first there was overemphasis of the significance and age of such discoveries. Later they were greatly underrated, and in many cases what undoubtedly was sound evidence was either ignored or thrown away. During the last twenty-five years, however, the study of the subject has progressed satisfactorily, and it is now generally accepted by scholars that there were some early Americans, the term "early" being used in the sense of its relation to modern aborigines and not in its Old World meaning. To differentiate the older from the later peoples, the name Paleo-Indian is used for the former. The choice of designation may not have been entirely appropriate but it has served the purpose.

There are several kinds of evidence for an early occupation. Stone implements are found in association with the bones of extinct species of animals and invertebrates, or with species no longer living in that particular region. Artifacts occur in conjunction with pollens and plant remains differing from the existing flora. Tools, hearths, and human skeletons are present in deposits that can be correlated with geologic phenomena, and former habitation areas are located on old terraces and along the shores of lakes that dried up long ago. The materials thus far found can hardly be classed as cultures, although such has been done in a few cases, because they are insufficient for a well-defined picture of the group or groups concerned. In many instances there are no human bones which can be correlated with the other remains. At best they consist of a definite lithic industry or a complex of implements with an indication of a few cultural traits and frequently are recognizable only by the presence of one or two characteristic types of artifacts. However, there appear to have been two basic patterns. One was predominantly a hunting economy, with gathering a secondary feature, while the other was primarily gathering with hunting and fishing playing a minor role. This, no doubt, is attributable in some degree to environment but other factors seem to have been involved, and just what they were is not clear from present knowledge.

1. FLUTED BLADE INDUSTRY

The best known and most widely distributed of the North American materials attributable to an early horizon are those in which the artifact assemblage contains projectile points or blades which are characterized by facial fluting. Longitudinal channels on each face extend from the base towards the tip and produce lateral ridges paralleling the edge of the blade. The length of the channels varies from face to face and from blade to blade, but the feature is readily recognizable and is one that thus far has been noted only in North America. The first examples of the type found *in situ* came from a fossil bison quarry near the town of Folsom, New Mexico, and were called by that name. Subsequently all fluted blades were designated Folsom and there was much loose talk and writing about Folsom Man and the Folsom Culture. As more discoveries were made it became apparent that there were regional differences in the forms of the fluted blades and that perhaps some of the variations might have chronological significance. Also, it was observed that the artifact assemblage was not always consistent. This led to the conclusion that there was a basic industry of which fluted blades were the main criterion, but that there were regional centers and local developments which could not be included in a single category. Now, instead of calling all such finds Folsom, more specific names are given.

Most of the fluted blades and occasional traces of associated implement assemblages are found in the eastern part of North America, although a few examples are known from Alaska, some have been reported from northern California, southeastern California, southwestern Nevada, and one example was recently reported from the State of Durango, Mexico. The main area of distribution, however, extends from Alberta and Saskatchewan in Canada on the north to southern New Mexico and southeastern Arizona on the south, and from the eastern slopes of the Rocky Mountains on the west to an eastern boundary which cuts across the western portions of the Dakotas, Nebraska, Kansas, Oklahoma, and into Texas where it turns eastward to the Mississippi River and thence northeastward along the Ohio River to western Pennsylvania and north to the southern shores of Lakes Erie and Ontario. The chief concentration of material appears to be in the western plains, although smaller centers are indicated at the junctures of the Missouri and Ohio Rivers with the Mississippi, in Ohio, western Pennsylvania, western New York, Vermont, Virginia, northern North Carolina, Tennessee, and Georgia. The best information about the significance of the fluted blades and associated materials has come from sites in New Mexico, Colorado, and Texas. This is particularly true with respect to their age and the reason for the difference between the two main forms of the blades. One series shows excellent workmanship with fine secondary chipping along the edges, while the other tends to be larger, less carefully made and does not have the peripheral retouch.

The original site near Folsom, New Mexico, was of definite importance because it established beyond question the fact that man-made objects could be found in association with the bones of extinct species of animals and in deposits of some geologic age. It was the first discovery of that nature which was accepted by most scholars as being authentic and paved the way for the investigations of subsequent years. At that location nineteen fluted points, the kind with fine secondary chipping along the edges, were found in association with the bones of about twenty-three large bisons which were identified as being an extinct species and to which the name of

Bison taylori was given. *Bison taylori* may be a variety of *Bison antiquus* or perhaps actually that species. Folsom clearly was the scene of a kill and there was no question about the contemporaneity of the animals and the men who made the artifacts. The bones and the fluted points were in a stratum of dark clay containing gravel lenses and small concretions of lime. The deposit undoubtedly had been left by an old bog or water hole. Extending above that layer were several feet of sediments consisting of highly restratified earth that some geologists have identified as belonging to the close of the Pleistocene period and others have attributed to the early Recent. There is general agreement, however, that their age closely approximates the transition between the end of the Pleistocene and the beginning of the Recent. There was little to indicate what the tool complex associated with such points might be because the only other artifacts found consisted of a portion of a nondescript flake knife, and one example of a generalized type of scraper. Considerable additional information about that aspect of the problem was obtained subsequently from two other locations where there was a whole series of implements in association with similar points or blades.

At the Lindenmeier site in northern Colorado the same kind of fluted point, now generally called Folsom fluted, with secondary rechipping occurred in an occupation level together with several types of planoconvex end and side scrapers; scrapers with concave edges, often called spokeshave scrapers; a number of different forms of cutting edges; large blades; drills, flakes with small, sharp graver points, frequently more than one on each flake, that may have been used for scratching lines or designs on bone (these are not to be confused with the European burin but are an American form sometimes erroneously classified with the drills); rough choppers; hand hammers; shaftsmoothers and rubbing stones of sandstone; small tabular-shaped pieces of sandstone which were used as palettes for the mixing of paint, nodules of hematite and red and yellow ochers that provided the pigment. There are no polished stone tools. Most of the implements are flake-type, only the large scrapers, choppers, and hammers were made from cores. The flaked artifacts show that either percussion or percussion-and-pressure techniques were used in their manufacture. Bone artifacts in the assemblage consist of awls and punches; pointed fragments that may have served as spearheads; small, slender, needle-like specimens with eyes that may actually have functioned in sewing or may have been parts of a necklace; tubular beads with scratched ornamentation; tabular pieces of the game-counter type with simple incised decorations; and ornamented scraps from larger objects of unknown purpose. All of this material was found in association with bones of *Bison taylori* and the large American camel, species long since extinct. Included, however, were bones from deer, pronghorn, wolf, fox, and rabbit, species still living in parts of the area. As there has been little or no change in these mammals from late Pleistocene times to the present, their presence is not significant from the standpoint of age. There was evidence for the mammoth at the Lindenmeier site, but not in direct association with implements, although it came from the same horizon as the other assemblages.

The Lindenmeier site is located on the bottom of a vestigial valley that has taken on the appearance of a terrace as the result of the wearing away of the ridges that formerly bordered its southern edge. The bone and implement assemblages occur in the bottom of or just below a dark-soil layer that was formed during a wet cycle. Numerous layers of geologic debris extending above it show that there were several periods of erosion and aggradation, alternating arid and humid eras, between the abandonment of the location by the Paleo-Indians and the present. By determining the relationship between the occupation level and the terraces of the main drainage systems of the region, and by correlating those terraces with traces of glacial stages in the mountains on the west, it was possible to demonstrate that the period of the occupation was in late Wisconsin times, during the closing stages of Wisconsin 3 or the Mankato.

The other location where fluted points with fine secondary rechipping, Folsom fluted, were found with other types of implements is in eastern New Mexico, about 170 miles south of Folsom, between the towns of Clovis and Portales in an area known as the Black-Water Draw. Several sites there produced a variety of scrapers and blades accompanying the points. Again they were in association with bones from the same extinct bison and were in deposits identified as late Pleistocene. The sites in question, however, contain much additional material and are extremely significant in helping to explain the difference beeween the finely chipped fluted blades and the larger less carefully made ones. In the various Black-Water Draw locations examples of the latter occur in a stratum below that containing the kind found at Folsom and are in association with mammoth, native horse, and bison bones. Native camel bones are present although there is some question whether that animal was hunted. Several species of turtles are also represented, and there are bones from various small mammals. It is obvious from the evidence that the larger points, called Clovis fluted, primarily were intended for killing larger animals and that they probably represent an early stage in the development of the type. This does not necessarily mean, however, that similar specimens found elsewhere under differing conditions are older than the form found at Folsom. The large crude types may have continued to be made for a long time in other parts of the country after the smaller, finer variety was developed. Other finds of similar large points in association with mammonth skeletons have been made at Dent, Colorado; near Miami and Abilene, Texas; and at Naco, Arizona, not far from the Mexican border. One or two other cases have been reported but there is some question at to their authenticity. There have been other discoveries of implements associated with mammoth but the blades were of a totally different type. In addition to the large fluted blades at the Black-Water Draw sites, bone artifacts which may have been projectile points, and hammer stones were found in the same level. As a matter of fact, there is some indication bone points may have preceded those of stone not only in that district but in other parts of North America as well. An upper layer in the sites, overlying those with both types of fluted points, contained several different kinds of blades which have a bearing on a number of implement assemblages or complexes. Since they do not pertain to the present series they will be discussed in a later section of this paper. It is significant, however, that they are stratigraphically the most recent of the Black-Water Draw materials.

Black-Water Draw consists of a series of dry basins. Bluish-gray deposits in their bottoms indicate that they were at one time more or less permanently filled with water. Excavations have shown that the lake beds rest disconformably on caliche, a white and greenish calcareous clay, or its corresponding gravels. Rising above the latter are a layer of speckled white sand, the upper part of which contains some diatoms; a layer of bluish-gray diatomaceous earth, which also contains mollusks; a layer of brown to gray silt and sand; a layer of dark-colored, wind-blown sand; and a layer of light-colored, surface wind-blown sand. The speckled sand stratum has been interpreted as recording the transition from a dry era to a relatively moist one as recorded by the diatomaceous earth. The lack of diatoms in the lower part of the speckled sand is believed to show that in the beginning the lake was temporary, later becoming permanent and slightly brackish. There seems to have been some interruption in the growth of the lake because in places there is a disconformity between the speckled sand and the layer above. The bluish-gray silt is clearly a lake deposit, although it is likely that the water occasionally receded from portions of the shore and made it possible for hunters to gather there, build their fires and leave the artifacts and animal bones which are now the concern of archeologists. The brown to gray silt and sand is actually a continuation of the bluish-gray stratum, but progressive coarsening of the material and an increase in the percentage of saline diatoms demonstrate a decrease in moisture and that the lakes were drying up. Their final disappearance is shown by the layers of wind-blown sand. The speckled sand stratum is the one which contains the mammoth, camel, and horse, and large fluted blades, the bluish-gray one is that of the small fluted blades and *Bison taylori,* while the brown-gray layer is the source of the other types of blades. In general it may be said that the main body of the deposits records the last definitely moist or pluvial age in the region. It undoubtedly was the same pluvial as that which produced the ancient Lake Estancia farther west. The heavier precipitation at that time probably resulted when the Azores high pressure area moved northward with the retreat of the Wisconsin ice sheet. A late Pleistocene age is also indicated by the correlation of the Black-Water Draw lake beds with clay deposits in Texas which have been identified as belonging to Wisconsin glacial times. In that respect there is good agreement with the evidence from the Lindenmeier site.

At two localities in Texas, one near Lubbock and the other near Lipscomb, a considerable number of the Folsom fluted were found in association with bones from *Bison taylori*. At the Lubbock site the situation was quite similar to that in the Black-Water Draw in that the bones and artifacts came from a diatomaceous earth stratum in the bed of a filled lake. The formation has been referred to the same age horizon and is believed to correlate with the same phenomena. There was only the one level at Lubbock but it is significant, so far as the main problem is concerned, in that material from it has been dated by the radiocarbon method. That feature will be considered later, however, in connection with other radiocarbon dates for Paleo-Indian sites. At the Lipscomb site the manifestations were that a herd of large bison had been trapped in a natural depression, perhaps during a heavy snow storm, and that hunters had taken full advantage of the situation to slaughter many of the animals. Others may have perished naturally as a number of the skeletons were complete and showed no traces of butchering. There was nothing from which to judge the geologic age of the site, but the animals were again *Bison taylori*.

Augmenting data were also obtained from two caves. One is located in the Sandia Mountains east of Albuquerque, New Mexico, and the other is in the Guadalupe Mountains in the southeastern corner of the state. At Sandia cave Folsom fluted points were contained in a layer lying beneath a crust of calcium carbonate that entirely covered and sealed in the deposits beneath it. The points were found in a stratum of cave debris which had been consolidated into breccia. There were numerous other artifacts similar to those found at the Lindenmeier and Black-Water Draw sites and a few blades of which the type affiliations are not wholly clear. Associated with the implements were bones from bison, camel, horse, mammoth, ground sloth, and wolf. The bison was a somewhat smaller animal than *Bison taylori* but appears to be an extinct species. The presence of horse, mammoth, and ground sloth is of interest because that is the only site thus far reported where those animals apparently belong in a Folsom fluted blade horizon. As previously noted, such an association is not uncommon in strata where Clovis fluted specimens are found but it is not expected in Folsom fluted levels. In Sandia Cave there also was other evidence of an early occupation. It does not pertain to the fluted blade industry, however, and will be considered later. The cave in the Guadalupe Mountains contained relatively late materials belonging to one of the widespread Pre-Columbian southwestern culture patterns. Two and one-half feet below those remains, lying close to charcoal and ashes from a fire, were a Clovis fluted point, bones from an extinct species of bison, and from an animal of the musk-ox family which is now found only in much colder climates than that of southern New Mexico. Other faunal material, although not directly associated with the remains of the fire and the Clovis fluted blade, also indicate a much cooler climate and add weight to the late Pleistocene dating of the other assemblages.

In the eastern United States are two sites in which the fluted blade industry is well-represented and several others where its former presence is indicated. None has produced any geologic evidence of age but the implement assemblages do suggest relationship to the general widespread pattern. In Dinwiddie County, Virginia, on the Williamson farm about five miles east of Dinwiddie, fluted blades, plano-convex scrapers, rough flake knives, and considerable chipper's debris are scattered along a flat-topped ridge for a distance of about one mile. The area where they occur varies in width from a few hundred feet to about two hundred yards. Nothing has been found *in situ* thus far, and the likelihood of doing so is not promising because the location has been cultivated since earliest Colonial times. There are no animal bones with the lithic specimens, and there is nothing to provide a geologic correlation. Consequently, there is no clue to the possible age of the site. The general character of the artifacts, however, and the fact that the stone from which they were made, while mainly of local derivations, differs completely from that used by more recent Indians in that area suggests that they may have reasonable antiquity. The artifact assemblage definitely is that of a hunting complex. The points are interesting in that they more closely resemble the Clovis fluted in style and workmanship but are nearer in size to the Folsom fluted. It would seem that they had some relationship with the western forms and possibly were derived from them, although some are inclined to believe that such was not the case. They do exhibit certain local characteristics. An analogous situation is to be noted for the Shoop Site northeast of Harrisburg, near Enterline, in southeastern Pennsylvania. At that location fluted blades occur in association with end and side scrapers, flake knives, biface knives, burin-like tools, a few flakes with small graver points similar to those in the western assemblages, and utilized spalls. The number of artifact forms is much smaller than in western sites and in that respect is quite similar to the Williamson site in Virginia. The specimens were all surface collected, test excavations revealed no depth to the deposits, and there is no evidence upon which to base an estimate of age beyond the type of the artifacts and the weathering of the stone from which they were made. It is interesting to note that, as was mentioned for the Williamson site, the implements were not made from stone such as was commonly used by later groups. As a matter of fact, most of the lithic material from the Shoop site originated elsewhere, the bulk of it probably being from western New York state. In that connection it should be pointed out that at the Williamson site in Virginia there were small quantities of nonlocal stones, the most abundant being from sources in extreme southeastern Pennsylvania. Farther south on the Yadkin River in North Carolina fluted points and implements similar to those from the Shoop and Williamson sites are reported from a narrow terrace which is the highest habitable spot in that particular district. Most of the artifacts were made from a local stone which did not work well, and the fluted blades are rough and atypical. The site has not been thoroughly investigated as yet but there is every indication that it is related to the other two. Furthermore, in the nonlocal stones is a good representation of the material which predominates at the Williamson site. Because of the similarities and apparent relationships between the three sites and the materials from them, they have been considered as representing a single phase and are designated the Enterline Industry. The matter of the differences in lithic materials is interpreted as showing that peoples moving rapidly southward from the western New York area took their implements, possibly rough blanks also, with them and did little chipping at the Shoop site. Some of them may have roamed toward the southeast and finding suitable stone there made tools which were carried with them as they swung back in a southwesterly direction and eventually arrived at the Williamson location. There they tarried and finding a good source of local material proceeded to manufacture points and other implements. Subsequently they drifted on into North Carolina carrying some of their implements with them, but after settling on the Yadkin began to use the stone from deposits there. On the basis of typology and certain techniques in the manufacture of the implements the Enterline Industry has been suggested as representing the oldest of the fluted blade series. Such a conclusion, however, is open to question and at present many do not agree with it, although they recognize that the Enterline Industry does represent a variant of one of the early horizons in North America. It may not have been an outgrowth of the fluted blade industry as known on the western plains but may have stemmed from the same basic tradition which was carried by a group which crossed Canada and migrated southeastward through Ontario to New York and thence into Pennsylvania, Virginia, and North Carolina.

2. OTHER COMPLEXES

Mention has already been made of additional materials in the Sandia Cave, New Mexico. Besides the stratum containing Folsom fluted blades there was a lower artifact bearing layer separated from that above by a deposit of yellow ocher containing neither artifacts nor animal bones. This ocher rested on a layer of cave breccia similar to that of the Folsom fluted level. From the breccia came a series of stone projectile points, knives, scrapers, fragments from large blades, and a number of grooved stone balls, possibly bolas such as were used in South America in later times. Associated with the implements were bones of the native horse, camel, and extinct bison, mammoth, and mastodon. Some of the bones and artifacts were mixed with ashes and charcoal in hearths on the original floor of the cave. The distinctive implements in the assemblage were the projectile points. They are an easily recognized type because the blades are lanceolate in shape and have one side notch at the base. Such forms are not common in North America and except for those in Sandia Cave have been reported only as scattered and isolated finds, most of them in the southern plains area, although one example has been noted from the Columbia River basin in Oregon and one from southern Ontario. The form is suggestive of the well-known points from the Solutrean Industry in the Old World, although it probably was not related to or derived from them. The worksmanship of the Sandia specimens certainly is not comparable to that of the Solutrean. It has not been possible to show any direct physical connection between the deposits in the cave and those of known geologic age outside, but the nature of the breccia in the Folsom fluted and Sandia layers, coupled with that of the yellow ocher stratum, indicates that all were laid down during a much wetter period than any known for the region in recent times. The faunal material represents that of a cooler climate, and as cool moist conditions sufficient to produce comparable phenomena have not occurred in that area since the pluvial following the maximum of the Wisconsin glaciation, the occupation of the cave is believed to have been at that time. The chief interest in the older Sandia assemblages, however, is in the evidence for hunting culture in the region prior to that of the Folsom fluted group. Whether or not the older Sandia level is contemporaneous with or perhaps older than that of the Clovis fluted is still not known.

Mention was made of the fact that an upper layer in the Black-Water Draw sites in New Mexico contained types of blades or projectile points which do not belong in the fluted category. A number of the forms fall into a group which originally was called Yuma from the county in eastern Colorado where the first examples were found. Subsequently it was learned that there were numerous variations in the group and that more specific designations were required. At the Black-Water Draw specimens of the Plainview, Eden Yuma, and Scottsbluff Yuma type points were taken from the stratum overlying the Folsom and Clovis fluted forms. They were associated with large numbers of bison bones and were accompanied by rather nondescript flake scrapers. Thus far the bison has not been identified as to species. The main importance of the evidence there is that it demonstrates that the types are subsequent to the fluted examples. Other sites have indicated that such might have been the case but did not show it as clearly. It is possible that some of the points had a late contemporaneity with Folsom fluted and then continued in use after that form was no longer made. The Plainview points, which resemble Clovis fluted forms but have only basal thinning produced by removing several small short flakes running lengthwise of the blade instead of a pronounced groove been found *in situ* at several locations. The type site is near Plainview in the high plains of northwestern Texas. The remains of approximately one hundred bison much larger than the modern animal and provisionally identified as *Bison taylori* were found there. Associated with the bones were the projectile points, scrapers, and blades which probably were used as knives. The deposits in which they were found tentatively have been assigned to the late Pleistocene but it seems more likely that the age probably is early Post-Pleistocene. At the Red Smoke site on Lime Creek in western Nebraska a Plainview assemblage is present in the upper levels of a terrace which has been correlated with the Mankato substage of the Wisconsin glaciation. This would indicate a late Pleistocene age for that locality and it may well be that the hunters making that type of projectile point were in that portion of the Great Plains for some time before drifting on south to the Texas–New Mexico area. Two of the Plainview points were found at the Lindenmeier site lying on top of the dark soil layer containing the Folsom fluted assemblage, and from the geologic dating there late Pleistocene would not appear to be out of order.

The situation with respect to the Eden and Scottsbluff Yuma types is not as satisfactory as that for the Plainview. There are indications that the two forms were partially contemporaneous with the Plainview and that they probably continued to be made for a longer period, in fact outlived it. On the other hand, one or two bits of evidence also suggest that the Scottsbluff may have had its beginning prior to the Plainview. The Eden point is long and narrow with horizontal parallel flaking extending across the face of the blade and has a marked median ride which produces a diamond-shaped cross section. There is a slight stemming at the base and the edges of the stem are smoothed. Examples of this type have been found *in situ* at the Finley site in the Eden Valley, Wyoming. They were in an assemblage consisting of stone knives, Scottsbluff points, and bison bones which have tentatively been referred to as *Bison occidentalis* Lucas. The lack of skulls and horn cores makes the identification uncertain. The deposit in which the materials occur has been placed in the period following the maximum of the Mankato, but prior to the onset of the arid and warmer climate of middle Post-Pleistocene times. Hence it would seem that the age probably is early Post-Pleistocene. Eden type points also were found at the Horner site near Cody, Wyoming. The assemblage there was similar to that at the Finley site, except that the Scottsbluff points were missing and that there was a greater variety of knives and scrapers. Geologically the age appears to be approximately the same. The presence of Scottsbluff forms at the Finley site shows that they were, a least in part, contemporaneous with the Eden.

The Scottsbluff type usually has horizontal parallel flaking across the face of the blade, is rather wide in comparison to the length, and is relatively flat and without marked median ridges. The stem indentations are rather more marked than in the case of the Eden. The type site for the form is near Scottsbluff, Nebraska, and the assemblage there consisted of points, knife blades, and scrapers in association with fossil bison. The latter has been referred to as *Bison occidentalis* Lucas. The deposit in which the materials were found was originally identified as post-Kansan and pre-Wisconsin. There has been considerable scepticism over that dating, however, and it seems more likely that the age should be late Pleistocene, if not actually early Post-Pleistocene. Similar points found at other locations in Nebraska rather clearly indicate the latter. But that the form may be basically old is suggested by a recent discovery in Mexico where a point or blade that could be considered as representing the prototype of the Scottsbluff was in association with remains of Imperial mammoth and other artifacts of a nondescript nature. The mammoth skeleton was partly articulated, and the artifacts were among the bones in such a fashion as to warrant the conclusion that hunters had been butchering the animal. The deposits in which the material occurred have been correlated with a post-pluvial beach of ancient Lake Texcoco which is believed to be late Pleistocene age. That the Scottsbluff form was widely distributed is indicated by specimens found in Alaska, Alberta, Saskatchewan, Montana, various Wyoming and Colorado localities, and Texas. In general, however, it should be said that most straitigraphic evidence has been that it was a later form than the blades of the fluted industry.

In southwestern New Mexico, also recently reported from the Rio Grande drainage in the central part of that state, southeastern Arizona, and extending across the international border into northern Mexico, erosion has exposed concentrations of artifacts, hearths, and other traces of human occupation. These manifestations have been called the Cochise Culture. From geological evidence, the typological characteristics of the artifacts, and the accompanying fossil material, the remains have been grouped into three stages or sequent phases. The oldest is found in sand-gravel deposits that also contain bones from the mammoth, native horse, camel, bison, and extinct wolf, pronghorn, and coyote. Hickory charcoal, a form of word no longer growing in the area is present in the assemblage. The sand-gravel layer is believed to represent floodplain deposits from a permanent stream, and as such a feature would require much moister conditions than now prevail in the region, the same being true for the growth of hickory, the last pluvial seems to be the period indicated. In combination with the extinct animal forms such a condition would imply a terminal Pleistocene or early Post-Pleistocene for the artifacts. The latter are mainly grinding or hammering stones, only a few knives and scrapers have been found, and there are no projectile points. The economy appears basically to have been food-gathering rather than hunting. The two later stages fall definitely within Post-Pleistocene times, the second possibly not beginning until the start of the late Post-Pleistocene stage. The second continues the tradition of a predominance of food-grinding implements, although it has a few projectile points which are not considered an integral part of the complex. The third stage is characterized by many projectile points as well as an abundance of grinding stones and bespeaks a combined hunting and foodgathering subsistence. The later stages are of interest because they have cross-ties with other remains.

At Bat Cave in the southwestern end of the Plains of San Augustin in south central New Mexico there are three levels in the deposits. Points similar to those noted in the second stage of the Cochise occur in the upper fourth of the middle and lower half of the upper layer in association with points of a type that is widely distributed over southern New Mexico, Arizona, and northern Mexico. Above them were points similar to those found farther west in Pinto Basin in southeastern California and others like those in the third stage of the Cochise. The grinding tools, rough scrapers, and knives throughout are quite similar to those of the second and third stages of the Cochise and show no changes from top to bottom. The middle layer in the cave deposits is considered as dating from middle Post-Pleistocene times, and the first artifacts did not appear until late in the period. The top level is believed to have started with the beginning of late Post-Pleistocene. Strictly speaking, Bat Cave does not belong in the Paleo-Indian category but it is important because of the associations of materials belonging to a somewhat later horizon and also because of the light that it throws on the problem of the development of maize or Indian corn. A series of shelled cobs, loose kernels, various fragments of husks, leaf sheaths, and tassels was recovered from the accumulated refuse constituting the top layer. A distinct evolutionary sequence is shown from the bottom to the top. The bottom level maize is a primitive variety that is both a pod corn and a pop corn, while that at the top was an essentially modern form. Since the primitive maize was not introduced into that area from Mexico until late

Post-Pleistocene times, the evolutionary process leading to modern maize apparently required only a few thousand years instead of the many millennia formerly postulated.

Westward from the Cochise area in southern Arizona is Ventana Cave located in the Castle Mountains. It probably is one of the most important archeological sites ever found in the southwestern United States because of the depth of its deposits and the long sequence of cultural materials found there. In the bottom level were stone implements accompanying bones from the extinct horse, ground sloth, tapir, jaguar, and wolf. The artifacts were projectile points, choppers, scrappers, and graver points. The complex was quite similar to that noted for the fluted blade industry but in this case the blades or points were not fluted. The assemblage of artifacts and bones was in a lime-cemented layer of volcanic debris which, with other indications of water action, presents strong evidence for a wet cycle in that part of the arid Southwest. Furthermore, the faunal remains are interpreted as indicating more moisture than at present and there was a savannah type of habitat, an open grassland crossed by permanent, shaded streams, rather than the characteristic desert with intermittent drainage as known in recent years. The wet period necessary to produce such phenomena is believed to be that coincident with the Wisconsin 3 glaciation. Since the artifacts were found almost in the top of the beds which indicate the humid period, they must date after the climax of the period but could still be considered as late Pleistocene. Some think that the pluvial lagged somewhat in areas that far south and for that reason consider the Ventana Complex as falling in the beginning phase of early Post-Pleistocene. On the basis of archeological evidence the Ventana assemblage is believed to be somewhat older than the first stage of the Cochise.

The top of the bed containing the Ventana materials gave evidence of considerable erosion and the overlying deposits which are largely of a midden nature rest disconformably on it. There is nothing to indicate the length of the time interval represented by the break in continuity. The upper midden consisted of two zones. The one resting on top of the Ventana layer was moist, probably the result of seepage from a spring, while the upper one was dry. The deepest part of the moist zone yielded artifacts like those of the second stage of the Cochise and projectile points similar to those found in the Pinto and Mohave basins in California. In the upper part of the moist zone were artifacts correlating with the third stage of the Cochise. The dry zone contained potsherds and other culturel material left by peoples living in the area from about the beginning of the Christian era until as late as A.D. 1400. The faunal remains throughout the two upper zones are all of modern species. The age of the moist zone has been correlated with the beginning of the late Post-Pleistocene stage. The main significance of the materials in the two upper zones is that it shows an almost unbroken sequence of remains during that period and also helps to crossdate the later Cochise stages and the Lower Colorado River Basin and southern California remains farther west.

The Pinto and Mohave basins in the desert area in southeastern

California are formations attributed to the pluvial of late Pleistocene times. Assemblages of implements consisting of projectile points, choppers, a large variety of scrapers, flake knives, gravers, drills, leaf-like blades, and oval blades are found along their old shore lines, occasionally in association with bones from extinct animals. From this it has been suggested that the implements must have been contemporaneous with the ancient lakes. The material is mainly from the surface, however, and in view of the relationships with Ventana Cave and the Cochise probably should be regarded as Post-Pleistocene. A related complex, called San Dieguito, occurs as far as the west coast in southern California and is thought to be of approximately the same age. Along the lower Colorado River and in neighboring desert regions are scattered artifacts, primarily simple choppers and flakes, which are said to pre-date the Pinto basin and related forms. The complex has not been clearly defined as yet and is not widely accepted. Recent announcement of the occurrence near La Jolla of artifacts attributable to third interglacial man in southern California is supported by such debatable evidence that it has not been given serious consideraton. As a matter of fact, present concensus is that the oldest traces of man in California date toward the end of the early Post-Pleistocene stage. Associated with the artifacts of the Pinto Basin and San Dieguito complexes are projectile points similar, although somewhat smaller, to those found in Gypsum Cave, Nevada. Like Ventana Cave, Gypsum Cave contained several cultural horizons in its deposits. In upper levels was evidence of occupancy by the modern Paiutes, by earlier Pueblo peoples of pre-Columbian times and below them, separated by a sterile layer of considerable thickness, where deposits in which artifacts were found in association with dung and bones of the giant sloth, bones from three species of extinct camels, an extinct wolf, and the native horse. There has been some question about the contemporaneity of the men who occupied the cave and the horse but the fact that projectile points similar to those collected there, long triangular-shaped blades with square shoulders merging into a stem that tapers into a rounded or pointed base, are also found in open sites in western Nevada in conjunction with horse and camel bones seem to validate the occurrence. The man-made objects and extinct animal remains were found in deposits correlated with the beginning of the period of aridity following the pluvial which was responsible for the last great rise in the level of ancient Lake Lohantan in Nevada. This would place the first occupation of the cave in the early Post-Pleistocene. Other caves in Nevada, particularly in the Humboldt Valley, give evidence of inhabitation in later times than the first at Gypsum Cave. Their age is toward the end of the early Post-Pleistocene. A better understanding of the sequence of developments and relationships in the aboriginal industries of the Great Basin and its southern peripheries will be forthcoming when the material recently obtained from Danger Cave, near Wendover, Utah, has been studied and reported upon. At that location there were midden deposits ranging from 11 to 14 feet in depth resting on an old beach of glacial Lake Stansbury. The strata in the midden record a series of frequently recurring occupations and the artifacts definitely belong in the Pinto Basin–Gypsum Cave–Cochise tradition. The first occupation of Danger Cave was shortly after the water had receded below the level of the cave floor. The beach level is that of the 110 foot level and is considerably later than that of the maximum reached during the Wisconsin glaciation. It apparently dates from about the end of the early Post-Pleistocene and is in agreement with the age noted for some of the other complexes.

In the extreme northern part of the Great Basin in south-central Oregon there are a number of sites where traces of the Paleo-Indian have been found. The materials were either beneath layers of pumice from the Mt. Mazama or the later Newberry eruptions, the terminal activity of each of those volcanoes. Extensive studies have shown that the Mt. Mazama eruption, which created Crater Lake, took place late in the early Post-Pleistocene. At the Wickiup Dam site on the Deschutes River, two stone knives were recovered from a stratum of glacial outwash, some distance below the pumice layer, and there is little doubt but that they must have been deposited in terminal Pleistocene or beginning Post-Pleistocene times. In one of the Paisley Caves, No. 3, which actually was a shelter on the high beach level of ancient Lake Summer, fragments of crudely shaped points and scrapers were present in a stratum separated from the Mt. Mazama pumice by several sterile layers. The artifacts were in an assemblage of bones from aquatic birds, bison, fox, wolf, bear, mountain sheep, camel, and horse. The two latter, of course, being extinct forms. The occupation appears to have been not long after the shrinking lake exposed the shelter floor and has been referred to the latter part of the last pluvial. The Fort Rock Cave contained, in the deposits beneath the pumice layer, which is attributed to Mt. Newberry, numerous stone scrapers and points, bone tools, fragments from wooden implements, numerous sandals made from shredded sagebrush bark, and some basketry fragments. The Newberry eruption is considered to have taken place after that of Mt. Mazama but, in view of the fact that the artifacts are quite comparable to the Paisley Cave materials, must be of about the same age. As a matter of fact, they probably are considerably older than the pumice. At Lower Klamath Lake on the Oregon-northeastern California line artifacts have been noted in association with extinct fauna, including the mammoth, in a deposit identified as probably late early Post-Pleistocene. Other sites in the same area show an occupation beginning with the onset of the Post-Pleistocene period. The latter correlates with the start of the upper zones in Ventana Cave and the second stage of the Cochise. It is significant to note that none of the northern Great Basin materials suggest relationship to the fluted industries of the plains or the various Yuma forms. They unquestionably follow a separate line of development.

3.

There are numerous other sites and cultural remains in the United States and Canada which supplement and corroborate the evidence in preceding pages, but space will not permit their consideration. However, a site on Cape Denbigh on the North Bering Sea coast of Alaska should be mentioned. At that location a complex of implements was found in a stratum that stratigraphically is older than previously defined coastal cultures of the area. Deposits containing the latter are separated from the older level by a sterile layer of laminated sandy loam representing an interval of unknown duration. Geologically the bottom level gives evidence of deposition at a time when the climate was colder than that of the present but its age has not been determined. The implement complex shows the closest similarities to Old World industries of any thus far discovered in the Americas. It includes finely rechipped lamellar flakes, tiny blades made from such flakes, and the polyhedral cores from which they were removed; burins comparable to the major types of the Aurignacian and the modified forms made throughout the Mesolithic and the silver-like spalls resulting from the sharpening of the burins; flake knives; keeled scrapers; plano-convex blades, probably end hafted; side scrapers and end scrapes; several variations of Yuma type blades; and one fluted point more suggestive of the Enterline Industry than any of the other fluted blade forms. The small representation of fluted and Yuma speciment suggests that they were not an integral part of the complex. In fact they may well be vestiges of an earlier period. If they are removed from the assemblage and the various burins are disregarded, the remaining artifacts constitute a series strikingly similar to that of the third stage in the Gobi Desert Mesolithic described by N. C. Nelson. That there was any close relationship between the Cape Denbigh peoples and the Paleo-Indians of the Plains and Great Basin areas to the south seems unlikely at this time, although future evidence may require some modification of that idea. They did, however, have a bearing on the development of subsequent Eskimo cultures.

Evidence for the Paleo-Indian in Mexico is rather meager because until recently little attention was paid to the older type of remains. Discovery of the mammoth with associated artifacts in the Valley of Mexico has already been mentioned. Other implements are reported from deposits which have been identified as late Pleistocene or have been assigned to early Post-Pleistocene. The much debated Tepexpan man is purported to have come from the same deposits as the mammoth and some of the artifacts and has been regarded as belonging to the late Pleistocene. The largest series of implements antedating the better known ceramic horizons is that of the so-called Chalco Industry which occurs in and above beach gravels and on hill slopes in strata referred to terminal early Post-Pleistocene or beginning middle Post-Pleistocene. At all events it appears that there was a Paleo-Indian in the Valley of Mexico at approximately the same time as in regions farther north. The only suggestion of an early man in Central America is in Nicaragua where barefooted human beings and several kinds of animals left imprints in a layer of volcanic mud which subsequently was covered by other volcanic debris and numerous successive mud flows and soil zones. The mud flows have long since turned to stone and resting on top of these deposits, 10 feet above the tracks, are archeological remains correlated with the earliest ceramic horizon in Guatemala and El Salvador. Hence it seems that the tracks represent considerable antiquity, although their geologic age is still undetermined.

In South America there have been numerous discoveries that have been interpreted as evidence for an early occupation. There is considerable disagreement over their actual significance because of difficulties in identifying and correlating deposits in many portions of the continent, because of the apparent longer survival of animal forms now extinct with a lessening of the significance of faunal associations, and because of a tendency to rely too much on the typology of implements in making age determinations. That many of the finds do have importance, however, is indicated by materials from caves in southern Patagonia where stone and bone implements were found in association with horse and giant sloth bones in deposits correlated with phenomena pertaining to the retreat of the last advance of the Pleistocene ice sheet in that area with attendant land rises, changes in river levels, and lake shrinkages. That people were present there in the early Post-Pleistocene seems unquestionable and to reach Patagonia they must have traversed South America, migration by boat at that time probably not being possible. Consequently it is reasonable to assume a Paleo-Indian population for that continent.

4.

Human remains attributable to the Paleo-Indian have not been described. Thus far no skeletons have been found which can be correlated with the better known implement complexes. Burials have come from deposits which have been referred to the late Pleistocene or early Post-Pleistocene in both continents. In no case, however, have the bones been other than *Homo sapiens*. The physical features tend to follow a general pattern in that the oldest are characterized by dolychocephalic crania with no artificial deformation, and are followed by mesocephalic and brachycephalic forms with a progressive increase in the practice of cranial deformation. The brachycephalic group for the most part exhibits more Mongoloid traits than the others. Occasional primitive features may be noted in individual skeletons but they are not sufficient to suggest other than modern man.

Present evidence is that the earliest occupants of the Americas did not antedate the climax of the Wisconsin glaciation, although large portions of North America undoubtedly were still covered by remnants of that Ice sheet when the first immigrants arrived. Little is known about the early peoples beyond the fact that they were hunters and food gatherers, made certain types of bone and stone implements, and hunted some species of animals now extinct. No form of habitation beyond rock shelters or occupied caves has thus far been found which can be attributed to them. The time of their arrival in the New World is uncertain. During the last stage of the Pleistocene the great central plain in Alaska and the lowlands bordering Bering Sea and the Arctic Coast were not glaciated, and shortly after the climax of the Wisconsin there was an open corridor along the eastern slopes of the Rocky Mountains leading from Alaska to the northern plains. On various occasions a land bridge connected Alaska with Asia, from time to time there were ice bridges, and there no doubt were periods when the strip of water at Bering Strait was narrower than it has been in recent years. Knowledge of glaciation in Siberia is limited, but passage from central Asia would have been possible at the time of the open corridor. Consequently, movement from Asia, probably crossing just north of the Strait proper, and eastward to the MacKenzie River were wholly feasible. As a matter of fact, the migrants could have reached Alaska before the opening of the corridor and as soon as it was available have followed up the MacKenzie and into the northern plains. That they did so is indicated by the fact that the earliest traces of their presence are in late Pleistocene deposits. When they had moved as far south as the Missouri River in western Montana, some of them may well have turned and continued along its valley upstream to the passes leading to the Snake River plain and the northern Great Basin, reaching that area at about the time other groups arrived in Wyoming and the western Dakotas. Subsequently another route opened by way of the upper Yukon and its tributaries and thence down the Liard and Peace River valleys to the plains. Later still another avenue south along the Fraser River, between the Rockies and the Coast Range, leading to the Great Basin became available. There is a possibility that there was some migration along the southern coast of Alaska, but it must have been later and the evidence for it is not convincing as yet. That full advantage was taken of the several inland paths is demonstrated by the finding of artifacts, camp sites, and associated bones from extinct species of animals along their courses. Some of the groups from the Great Basin no doubt moved on southward through California and Nevada into north-western Mexico and along the strip of coast west of the Sierra Madre Occidental. A few apparently turned eastward across southern Arizona and eventually drifted back northward a short distance in the Rio Grande Valley. From the northern plains the diffusion was along the eastern edge of the mountains with some groups spreading out to the more southerly reaches of the Mississippi River and on to the eastern part of the country, while others continued on southward and thence along the plateau between the Sierra Madre Occidental and the Sierra Madre Oriental. Somewhat later others probably passed across southern Canada in moving east. As yet there is no evidence of contact between the peoples going southeast of the mountains and the backwash from the western group in the Rio Grande Valley. Descendants from both groups eventually must have passed through the Central American funnel and into South America where some may have diffused along the Venezuelan Andes to the plains of the Orinoco, while others traveled along the Andes to southern Bolivia where they spread southeastward across the Gran Chaco into Brazil, south of the Amazonian Forest, and on southward into Argentina. Small groups may have crossed the range moving westward into the coastal belt south of the Atacama Desert.

The question of dates for the various occurrences discussed in preceding pages is somewhat difficult to answer. Estimates based on geologic evidence are that the maximum of the final stage of the Wisconsin glaciation was reached about 25,000 years ago, that the final recession of the ice sheets started about 20,000 years ago, and that the corridor along the eastern slopes of the Rockies opened between 15,000 and 18,000 years ago. There appears to have been a similar opening 35,000 to 40,000 years ago, but there is nothing thus far to indicate that use was made of it by man. The beginning of Post-Pleistocene times is placed at approximately 9000 years ago. Using the same criteria, and age of the Lindenmeier site was given as 10,000 to 25,000, the Black-Wated Draw as 10,000 to 13,000, the oldest Cochise at a little over 10,000 Gypsum Cave is approximately 10,000, the bottom level at Ventana Cave about 10,000 and the fall of the Mt. Mazama pumice between 4,000 and 7,000 years ago.

The recently developed and still debated radiocarbon (C-14) method of age determination has provided a number of dates which are interesting even though they may not be accepted as final. Material suitable for dating by that method is not available from all of the Paleo-Indian sites and many of them still can be placed only in a relative chronology. The Mankato substage of the Wisconsin has consistently shown an average of 11,400 years before the present which is somewhat less than half of the estimated geologic age. The Folsom fluted blade deposit at Lubbock, Texas, is reported as 9,883 ± 350 years before the present which is the only fluted blade industry date available as yet. From stratigraphic evidence the Clovis fluted blade complex obviously is older and the geologic estimate of 10,000 to 13,000 years does not appear too greatly out of line although it is somewhat at odds with the radiocarbon date for the Mankato. Gypsum Cave in Nevada gave dates of 10,455 ± 340 for a level 6 feet 4 inches below the top of the deposits and an average of 8,527 ± 250 for a level 2 feet 6 inches below the top. The latter probably is the date for the oldest cultural material. Sandals from the Fork Rock Cave in Oregon tested 9,053 ± 350, and a piece of wood from a tree killed by the Mt. Mazama eruption tested 6,453 ± 250 years. The first stage of the Cochise yielded dates of 7,756 ± 370 and 6,210 ± 450, the second stage 4,508 ± 680 to 4,006 ± 270, and the third stage 2,463 ± 310. The site in Wyoming which contained both Eden and Scottsbluff Yuma points dated 6,876 ± 250. The oldest date for Bat Cave was 5,931 ± 310 years before the present. The Humboldt Valley caves provided specimens which tested 7,038 ± 350, 5,737 ± 250 and 2,482 ± 260 years. California thus far has produced a date of only 4,052 ± 160, but beads made from shells which must have come from the west coast were found at the 7,000 years level in one of the Nevada caves which is good evidence for an earlier occupation in California. The oldest date for archeological material in Alaska thus far is 5,993 ± 280. The Patagonian Cave containing artifacts in association with extinct horse and giant sloth has a radiocarbon age of 8,639 ± 450 years before the present, which is quite in line with those for North America.

In closing it should be pointed out that the early industries in the Americas in the main suggest a late Paleolithic-early Neolithic tradition without marked similarities to Old World forms. The only Mesolithic is found in a limited area in Alaska. There is widely scattered evidence for occupation from late Pleistocene through the early Post-Pleistocene but, with one or two questionable exceptions, there is nothing to show that people were present during the warm-dry middle Post-Pleistocene. From the beginning of the late Post-Pleistocene to the present there is an unbroken record of an aboriginal population. Whether the apparent gap is real or only because archeologists have failed to look for sites falling in that period is still to be determined. An interesting phase of the whole American problem and one which as yet has received virtually no attention is that pertaining to the events in Asia which may have induced or at least stimulated the migrations to the New World.

SUPPLEMENTARY READINGS

Bordes, Francois. *The Old Stone Age*. New York, Toronto: McGraw-Hill, 1968.

Braidwood, Robert J. *Prehistoric Men*. Glenview, Ill.: Scott, Foresman, 1967.

Butzer, Karl W. *Environment and Archeology*. Chicago: Aldine Publishing, 1964.

Clark, G. *World Prehistory: an Outline*. Cambridge: University Press, 1961.

Jennings, Jesse D., and Norbeck, Edward eds. *Prehistoric Man in the New World*. Chicago: University of Chicago Press for Rice University, 1964.

MacGowan, K. and Hester, J. A. *Early Man in the New World*. Garden City, N. Y.: Doubleday, 1962.

six

LIVING PRIMATES

Our closest relatives in the animal kingdom are the lower primates, monkeys, and apes. Although we have a tendency to ignore this relationship, much can be learned about our physical and cultural origins by studying these creatures in their native habitat and in the research laboratory. Washburn, Jay, and Lancaster demonstrate the kind of knowledge to be gained from primate research, while Napier emphasizes the importance and scope of such studies.

Field Studies of Old World Monkeys and Apes

Sherwood L. Washburn / Phyllis C. Jay / Jane B. Lancaster

For many years there has been interest in the evolutionary roots of human behavior, and discussions of human evolution frequently include theories on the origin of human customs. In view of the old and widespread interest in the behavior of our nearest relatives, it is surprising how little systematic information was collected until very recently. At the time (1929) Yerkes and Yerkes collected data for their book on the great apes, no one had devoted even one continuous month to the systematic study of the behavior of an undisturbed, free-ranging nonhuman primate. Apparently scientists believed that the behavior of monkeys and apes was so stereotyped and simple that travelers' tales or the casual observations of hunters formed a reliable basis for scientific conclusions and social theorizing. As a part of the program of the Yale Laboratories of Comparative Psychology, Yerkes encouraged a series of field studies of the chimpanzee, the mountain gorilla, and the howling monkey. These first studies proved so difficult that Yerkes could write, in the introduction to Carpenter's study, "His is the first reasonably reliable working analysis of the constitution of social groups in the infrahuman primates, and of the relations between the sexes and between mature and immature individuals for monkey or ape." Zuckerman, quite independently, had realized the importance of field observations and had combined some field work with physiology and the older literature to produce two very influential volumes. From this beginning, only Carpenter continued to make field studies of behavior, and his study of the gibbon is the first successful study of

From Science *150 (17 December 1965): 1541–47. Copyright 1965 by the American Association for the Advancement of Science; reprinted by permission of the authors and publisher.*

the naturalistic behavior of a member of the family Pongidae. Hooton summarized what was then known about the primates, particularly stressing the importance of behavior and the work of Carpenter and Zuckerman.

The war stopped field work, and no major studies were undertaken for some 15 years. Then, in the 1950s, investigators in Japan, England, France, Switzerland, and the United States independently started studies on the behavior of a wide variety of free-ranging primates. For the history of science it would be interesting to examine the reasons for this burst of parallel activity. Field studies were undertaken at more or less the same time, and publications start in the late 1950s and accelerate rapidly in the 1960s. This trend is still continuing and is well shown by the pattern of frequency of citations in a recent review by Hall. The review cites the papers of Bingham, Carpenter, Köhler, Nissen, Yerkes, and Zuckerman, but there are no references to additional field studies in the period 1941–1951, and most of the references are to papers appearing in 1960 or later.

The increased interest in primates, and particularly in the behavior of free-ranging primates, has given rise to several symposiums, and results of the new studies have been published almost as soon as they have been completed. Data from the recent field studies are included in volumes edited by Buettner-Janusch, Washburn, Napier and Barnicot, and, especially, DeVore. The volume edited by DeVore is devoted entirely to recent field studies and their evaluation. It includes accounts of the behavior of five kinds of monkeys, of chimpanzees, and of gorillas. Each chapter is by the person who did the field work, and in addition there are eight general chapters. Two new journals also are devoted to primates. *Primates,* published by the Japan Monkey Centre, is now in its 5th year, and *Folia Primatologica* has completed volume 3. Carpenter's field studies and general papers have been reprinted so that they are now easily available. Southwick has published a collection of readings in primate social behavior, and Eimerl and DeVore contributed a volume on the primates to the Life Nature Library. Field studies have recently been reviewed by Jay, and proceedings of a symposium organized and edited by Altmann should appear shortly. This abundance of published material makes it hard to believe that only 2 years ago a course on primate social behavior was difficult to teach because of the lack of easily available, suitable reading material.

Obviously, with so much new data a complete review is impossible. Here we wish to direct attention to the nature of the recent field studies and to a few of their major contributions. Perhaps their greatest contribution is a demonstration that close, accurate observation for hundreds of hours is possible. Prior to Schaller's field work, reported in 1963, it was by no means clear that this kind of observation of gorillas would be possible; previous investigators had conducted very fragmentary observations, and Emlen and Schaller deserve great credit for the planning and execution of their study. A field study of the chimpanzee that seemed adequate in the 1930s now seems totally inadequate, when compared to Goodall's results. Today a field study is planned to yield something of the order of 1000 hours of observations, and the observer is expected to be close to the animals and to recognize individuals. A few years ago observations of this length and quality were thought unnecessary, if not impossible.

The importance of studies in which groups are visited repeatedly and animals are recognized individually may be illustrated by the problems they make it possible to study. For example, during one season of the year chimpanzees "fish" for termites by breaking off sticks or stiff grasses and sticking the prepared implement into a termite hole, and this whole complex of nest examination, tool preparation, and fishing is learned by the young chimpanzee. It can be seen at only one time of the year and can be appreciated only by an observer whose presence no longer disturbs the animals. Habituation to the observer is a slow and difficult process. Goodall reports that after 8 months of observations she could approach to no closer than 50 meters of the chimpanzees and then only when they were in thick cover or up a tree; by 14 months she was able to get within 10 to 15 meters of them. The problem of tool use in nonhuman primates has been reviewed by Hall, but the essential point here is that the amount of throwing and object manipulation in the monkeys (Cercopithecidae) was greatly exaggerated in travelers' tales, which were uncritically accepted, and it took years of observation in a favorable locality to reveal the complexity of this kind of behavior in the chimpanzee.

PREDATION

Another example of the value of continued observations is in the study of deliberate hunting by baboons. In three seasons of field work and more than 1500 hours of observation DeVore had seen baboons catch and eat small mammals, but apparently almost by chance, when the baboon virtually stepped on something like a newborn antelope and then killed it. But in 1965 DeVore saw repeated incidents of baboons surrounding, hunting, and killing small mammals.

The whole matter of predation on primates has been difficult to study. Rare events, such as an attack by an eagle may be very important in the survival of primates, but such attacks are seldom observed, because the presence of the human observer disturbs either the predator or the prey. We think that the present de-emphasis of the importance of predation on primates arises from these difficulties of observation and from the fact that even today most studies of free-ranging primates are made in areas where predators have been reduced or eliminated by man. Most predators are active at night, and there is still no adequate study of the nocturnal behavior of any monkey or ape. Predation probably can best be measured by studying the predators rather than the prey.

Recognition of individual animals is necessary for the study of many problems, from the first stages of the analysis of a social system to observations of social continuity or constancy of group membership; such observations are exceedingly difficult under most field conditions. For example, understanding of the dominance system implies repeated recognition of a number of animals under sufficiently various conditions so that the patterns of interaction become clear. Again, to be sure that a group has lost or gained a member, the observer must know the whole composition of the group.

Long-continued observations have proved to be important in many unexpected ways. For example, rhesus monkeys have been observed in several of their many very different habitats, and it has been found that young rhesus play more in cities than in some kinds of forest and play in the forest more at some seasons that at others. These differences are due in part to the amount of time which must be spent in getting food; the same forest troop may play more when fruits are available and hunger may be rapidly satified than at times of the year when the diet is composed of tiny seeds which take a long time to pick. Extracting the small seeds of sheesham pods during the months when rhesus troops spend most of their time in the sheesham trees takes many hours of the day. What might easily have been described in a short-term study as a species-specific difference of considerable magnitude turns out to be the result of seasonal and local variations in food source. It is essential to sample behavior in several habitats to gain an understanding of the flexibility of the built-in behavior patterns of a species, flexibility which precludes the need for development of new forms of genetically determined behavior to cope successfully with different habitats.

The long-term study in which many groups of a species are observed in different, contrasting localities, and in which at least some groups are known so well that most of the individuals can be recognized, will correct many false notions and will make valid generalizations possible. Although so far there have been only a few major investigations of this sort, some important generalizations seem possible.

ENVIRONMENT AND SOCIAL BEHAVIOR

Nowhere is the extent to which the behavior of a species is adaptable and responsive to local conditions more apparent than among groups of rhesus living in India. Rhesus occur naturally in such diverse environments as cities, roadsides, cultivated fields, and many types of forest ranging to altitudes of over 2400 meters. Contact with man varies in these habitats from constant and close to rare and incidental.

Where rhesus groups are subjected to pressures of trapping, harassment, and high incidence of infectious disease, groups are tense and aggression is high. These pressures are found in areas where there is most contact and interaction with man, such as in cities and at places of pilgrimage. The animals are in generally poor physical condition, and numerous old and new wounds are evidence of a high rate of intragroup fighting. Tension among groups occupying adjacent areas of land is similarly high where there is insufficient space for normal movement and behavior, and where there may be intense competition for a limited supply of food and water. This is in sharp contrast to those groups living away from man where normal spacing among groups can be effected by the means evolved by the species. In the latter environments, such as forests, the rhesus are in excellent physical condition and what aggressive behavior occurs functions to maintain stable social groups and relationships among the members of the group; wounds are substantially fewer, and disease appears to be rare.

These has been considerable controversy in discussions of the relationships among social groups of the same species as to whether or not the geographical area occupied by a group should be called a territory or a home range. The point we wish to emphasize is that, within one species, populations living in different habitats may act quite differently toward neighboring groups. Populations may be capable of a wide variety of behavior patterns ranging from exclusive occupation of an area which may be defended against neighboring groups to a peaceful coexistence with conspecifics in which wide overlap in home ranges is tolerated. Because local populations of a species may maintain their ranges in different ways it is necessary to investigate all variations in group spacing in diverse habitats before attempting to describe characteristic behavior patterns for any species.

Not unexpectedly, population and group composition reflect these differences in habitat and stress. Groups living on the Gangetic plains, where trapping, harassment, and disease are important factors, are smaller, and the proportion of young members is also significantly smaller. The long-term effects of pressures on different rhesus populations in northern and central India are now being investigated by a team of anthropologists of the National Center for Primate Biology.

A city presents a very different set of challenges to a rhesus group than does a forest. Often there are no trees to sleep in; living space must be shared with man and his domestic animals. Food is not available in the form common to other habitats, and monkeys may have to depend on their skill in stealing food from man. Often the food has been prepared by man for his own consumption, or it consists of fruits and vegetables pilfered from houses, shops, and streets. Garbage is picked through and edible portions are consumed. It is essential that the monkeys learn to differentiate between those humans who represent a real threat to their safety and those who are safe to approach. They must react quickly and learn to manipulate doors, gates, and other elements of the physical environment unique to their urban habitat. This is a tremendously different setting from that in which most rhesus live. City rhesus are more manipulative, more active, and often more aggressive than are forest rhesus. Clearly, the same species develops quite different learned habits in different environments.

ANNUAL REPRODUCTIVE CYCLE

The belief, which has been widely maintained, that there is no breeding season in monkeys and apes gave rise to the theory that the persistence throughout the year of groups, or highly organized troops, was due to continuous sexual attraction. The evidence for a breeding season has been reviewed by Lancaster and Lee who found that in many species of monkeys there is a well-marked breeding season. For example, Mizuhara has presented data on 545 births of Japanese macaques of Takasakiyama. There were on the average approximately 90 births per year over six consecutive years. The average length of the birth season was 125 days, but it varied from 95 to 176 days. The majority of the births occurred in June and July. Copulations were most frequent in November to March and were not observed during the birth season, and in spite of this the highly organized group continues as a social unit throughout the year.

The birth season has been studied in other groups of Japanese macaques, and in general the situation is similar. There is no doubt that both mating and birth seasons are highly restricted in the Japanese macaque. The birth season is spring and summer, but its onset and duration vary considerably. If observations were limited and combined for the whole species, as they were in early studies, the birth season would appear to be much longer than in fact it is for an individual group, and it is the events within the local group, not averages of events for the species, that bear upon the role of sexual attraction in holding primate society together.

Under very different climatic conditions, in India, rhesus macaques also have a birth season, but copulations were observed in all months of the year, although probably not with equal frequency. Among rhesus on a small island off Puerto Rico births occur from January to June, and copulations are restricted to July–January. These data confirm the point that a birth season will be more sharply defined in a local group than in a species as a whole. There is a mating season among rhesus introduced on the island, but only a peak of mating in the same species in their native India. It is clear that survey data drawn from many groups over a wide area must be used with caution when the aim is to interpret the behavior of a single group. Since the birth season is an adaptation to local conditions, there is no reason to expect it to be the same over the entire geographical distribution of a species, and under laboratory conditions rhesus macaques breed throughout the year.

No data comparable to those for the macaques exist for other primates, and, since accurate determination of mating and birth seasons requires that reasonable numbers of animals be observed in all months of the year and that groups be observed in different localities, really adequate data exist for only the Japanese macaque. However, Lancaster and Lee were able to assemble data on 14 species of monkeys and apes. They found that probably the most common situation is a birth peak, a time of year at which births tend to be concentrated, rather than sharply limited mating and birth seasons. This is highly adaptive for widely distributed species, for it allows the majority of births to occur at the optimum time for each locality while maintaining a widely variable basic pattern. The birth season may be a more effective adaptation to extreme climatic conditions. There may be a birth peak in the chimpanzee, and there may be none in the mountain gorilla, but, since we have no more data than are necessary to clarify the reproductive pattern in a single species of macaque, we can conclude only that, while birth seasons are not present in either gorillas or chimpanzees, a peak is possible in chimpanzees, at least for those living near Lake Tanganyika.

Prior to the recent investigations there was a great deal of information on primate reproduction, and yet as late as 1960 it was still possible to maintain that there were no breeding seasons in primates and that this was the basis of primate society. Until recently the question of seasonality was raised without reference to a birth season as distinguished from a birth peak, or to a limited mating season as distinguished from matings throughout the year with a high frequency in a particular period.

FREQUENCY OF MATING

Obviously many more studies are needed, and one of the intriguing problems is the role of potency. Not only does the frequency of mating vary through the year, but also there appear to be enormous differences in potency between species that are reproducing at a normal rate. In nearly 500 hours of observation of gorillas, Schaller saw only two matings, fewer than might be seen in a troop of baboons in almost any single morning. The redtail monkey (*Cercopithecus ascanius*) mates rarely, but the closely related vervet (*Cercopithecus aethiops*) does so frequently. To a considerable extent the observed differences are correlated with structure, such as size of testes, and all these species seem to be reproducing at an adequate and normal rate. There is no evidence that langurs (*Presbytis entellus*) are less successful breeders than rhesus, but the langurs copulate less frequently.

Now that more adequate data are becoming available, the social functions of sexual behavior should be reinvestigated. The dismissal of the theory that sexual attraction is *the* basis of primate society should open the way for a more careful study of the multiple functions of sexual behavior. The great differences among the primate species should provide data to prove or disprove new theories. In passing it might be noted that the human mating system without estrous cycles in the female and without marked seasonal variations is unique.

SYSTEMS OF MATING

Mating systems, like the presence or absence of seasonality in breeding and the frequency of copulation, are extremely variable in monkeys and apes. Eventually the relation of these variations to species adaptations will be understandable; at present it is most important to note that monkeys do not necessarily live either in harems or in promiscuous hordes as was once assumed. Restrictive mating patterns such as the stable and exclusive pairbond formed between adult gibbons and the harem system of the Hamadryas baboon are comparatively rare. The most common mating pattern of monkeys and apes is promiscuity more or less influenced by dominance relationships. In species in which dominance relations are not constantly at issue, such as langurs, chimpanzees, or bonnet macaques, matings appear to be relatively promiscuous and are often based on the personal inclination of the estrous female. When dominance relationships are constantly at issue, as in baboons, Japanese macaques, and rhesus macaques, sex often becomes one of the prerogatives of dominant rank. In such species dominant males tend to do a larger share of the mating than do more subordinate animals, but it is only in unusual situations that subordinate animals are barred from the mating system altogether. Mating systems probably support the general adaptation of the species to its environment. In most baboons and macaques the tendency for a few males to do much of the mating may be partly a by-product of natural selection for a hierarchy of adult males which dominates the troop so that in a dangerous terrestrial habitat external dangers will be met in an orderly way. Selection is not only for a male which can impregnate many females but it may also have favored a dominance-oriented social organization in which sexual activity has become one of the expressions of that dominance.

DOMINANCE RELATIONSHIPS

Long-term field studies of monkeys and apes in their natural habitats have emphasized that social relationships within a group are patterned and organized in very complex ways. There is no single "monkey pattern" or "ape pattern"; rather, there is great variability, both among different species and among different populations of the same species, in the organization and expression of social relationships. A difference in the relative dominance of individuals is one of the most common modes of social organization in monkey and ape societies. Dominance is not synonymous with aggression, and the way dominance is expressed varies greatly between species. In the gorilla, for example, dominance is most often expressed by extremely attenuated gestures and signals; a gentle nudge from the dominant male is more than enough to elicit submissive response from a subordinate, whereas, in baboons, chases, fights, and biting can be daily occurrences. In many primates there is a tendency for the major age-sex classes to be ranked in a dominance order; for example, in baboons, macaques, and gorillas, adult males as a class are usually dominant over adult females, and females are dominant over young. This may not always be true, for in several species of macaques some females may outrank some adult males, although groups dominated by a female (such as the Minoo-B troop of Japanese macaques) are extremely rare. Dominance relationships may be quite unstructured, as in the chimpanzee, where dominance is expressed in interactions between individuals but where these relationships are not organized into any sort of hierarchy. A much more common situation is one in which dominance relations, among males at least, are organized into linear hierarchies that are quite stable over time, as in baboons, langurs, and macaques. Sometimes these dominance hierarchies are complicated by alliances among several males who back each other up very effectively or even by an alliance between a male and a female. Although dominance varies widely among monkeys and apes both in its form and function, it is certainly one of the most important axes of social organization to be found in primate societies.

GENEALOGICAL RELATIONSHIPS

Recognition of individual animals and repeated studies of the same groups have opened the way to the appreciation of other long-continuing social relationships in monkeys and apes which cannot be interpreted in terms of dominance alone. Long-term studies of free-ranging animals have been made on only two species of nonhuman primates, Japanese macaques, which have been studied since 1950 by members of the Japan Monkey Center, and Indian rhesus macaques living free on Cayo Santiago, Puerto Rico, the island colony established by Carpenter in 1938. In these studies, when the genealogy of the animals has been known, it has been obvious that genetic relationships play a major role in determining the course and nature of social interactions. It becomes clear that bonds between mother and infant may persist into adult life to form a nucleus from which many other social bonds ramify. When the genealogy of individual animals is known, members of commonly observed subgroupings, such as a cluster of four of five animals grooming or resting together, are likely to be uterine kin. For example, members of a subgroup composed of several adult animals, both male and female, as well as juveniles and infants, may all be offspring of the same female. The relations continue to be very important in adult life not only in relaxed affectional relationships but also in dominance interactions. Sade saw a female rhesus monkey divert the attack of a dominant male from her adult son and saw another adult female protect her juvenile half-sisters (paternity is not determinable in most monkey societies). There is a very high frequency of grooming between related animals, and many animals never seek grooming partners outside of their own genealogies.

It should be stressed that there is no information leading us to believe that these animals are either recognizing genetic relationships or responding to any sort of abstract concept of family. Rather these social relationships are determined by the necessarily close association of mother with newborn infant, which is extended through time and generations and which ramifies into close associations among siblings. We believe that this pattern of enduring social relations between a mother and her offspring will be found in other species of primates. Because of their dramatic character, the importance of dominance and aggression has been greatly exaggerated compared to that of continuing, positive, affectional relations between related animals as expressed by their sitting or feeding together, touching, and grooming. Much of this behavior can be observed easily in the field, but the extent to which it is in fact an expression of social genealogies has been demonstrated only in the studies cited above.

Positive, affectional relations are not limited to relatives. Male Japanese macaques may take care of young by forming special protective relationships with particular infants, but whether these males have any special relationship to the infants as either father or brother is uncertain, and the mating system is such that paternity cannot be known either to the observer or to the monkeys. MacRoberts has recorded a very high frequency of care of infants by males in the Gibraltar macaque. In addition, he has demonstrated that these positive protective relations are very beneficial to the juvenile. Two juveniles which had no such close relationship were forced to be peripheral, were at a great disadvantage in feeding, and were groomed much less than other juveniles in the group.

The status of the adult can be conferred on closely associated young (frequently an offspring when the adult is female), and for this reason the young of dominant animals are more likely to be dominant. This inheritance of rank has been discussed by Imanishi for the Japanese macaque and by Koford for the rhesus. Sons of very dominant females seem to have a great advantage over other males both because their mothers are able to back them up successfully in social interactions and because they stay with their mothers near the other dominant animals at the center of the group. They may never go through the stage of being socially and physically peripheral to the group which is typical for young males of these species. A male cannot simply "inherit" high rank; he must also win this position through his own abilities, but his chances of so doing are greatly increased if he has had these early experiences of associating with and being supported by very dominant animals.

There could hardly be a greater contrast than that between the emerging picture of an orderly society, based heavily on affectionate or cooperative social actions and structured by stable dominance relationships, and the old notion of an unruly horde of monkeys dominated by a tyrant. The 19th-century social evolutionists attributed less order to the societies of primitive man than is now known to exist in the societies of monkeys and apes living today.

COMMUNICATION

Research on the communication systems of monkeys and apes through 1962 has been most ably summarized and interpreted by Marler. Most of the data represent work by field observers who were primarily intersted in social structure, and the signals, and their meanings, used to implement and facilitate social interactions were more or less taken for granted. Only in the last year or so have communication systems themselves been the object of careful study and analysis. Marler has emphasized both the extraordinary complexity of the communication systems of primates and the heavy dependence of these systems on composite signals. Most frequently it is not a single signal that passes between two animals but a signal complex composed of auditory, visual, tactile, and, more rarely, olfactory signals.

Communication in some monkey species is based on a system of intergrading signals, whereas in others much more use is made of highly discrete signals. For example, most sounds of the vervet monkey are of the discrete type, there being some 36 different sounds that are comparatively distinct both to the human ear and when analyzed by a sound spectrograph. In contrast, Rowell and Hinde have analyzed the sounds of the rhesus monkey and found that of 13 harsh noises, 9 belonged to a single intergrading subsystem expressing agonistic emotions.

As more and more study is done on primates it will probably be shown that their communication systems tend to be of mixed form in that both graded and discrete signals are used depending on the relative efficiency of one or the other form in serving a specific function. In concert this use of both discrete and intergrading signals and of composites from several sensory modes produces a rich potential for the expression of very slight but significant changes in the intensity and nature of mood in the signaling animal. Marler has emphasized that, except for calls warning of danger, the communication system is little applied to events outside the group. Communication systems in monkeys and apes are highly evolved in their capacity to express motivation of individuals and to facilitate social relationships. Without this ability to express mood, monkeys and apes would not be able to engage in the subtle and complicated social interactions that are a major feature of their adaptations.

SOCIAL LEARNING

Harlow and Harlow's experiments show the importance of learning in the development of social life; however, monkeys and apes are so constituted that, except in the laboratory, social learning is inevitable. They adapt by their social life, and the group provides the context of affection, protection, and stability in which learning occurs. No one factor can explain the importance of social behavior, because society is a major adaptive mechanism with many functions, but one of the most important of these functions is the provision of a rich and protected social context in which young mature. Field observations, although mainly observations of the results of learning rather than of the process itself, provide necessary clues as to the nature of the integration of relevant developmental and social factors. These factors can then be estimated and defined for subsequent intensive controlled research in a laboratory or colony.

It has become clear that, although learning has great importance in the normal development of nearly all phases of primate behavior, it is not a generalized ability; animals are able to learn some things with great ease and other things only with the greatest difficulty. Learning is part of the adaptive pattern of a species and can be understood only when it is seen as the process of acquiring skills and attitudes that are of evolutionary significance to a species when living in the environment to which it is adapted.

There are important biological limitations which vary from species to species and which do not reflect differences in intelligence so much as differences in specializations. For example, Goodall has observed young chimpanzees learning to fish for termites both by their observation of older chimpanzees and by practice. It takes time for the chimpanzee to become proficient with these tools, and many mistakes are made. Chimpanzees are not the only primates that like termites, and Goodall has observed baboons sitting near chimpanzees watching and waiting while the latter are getting termites. The baboons are just as eager as the chimpanzees to eat termites but are unable to learn how to fish for termites for themselves.

It is likely that there are important variables among groups of a single species that make it possible for the acquisition of new patterns of behavior or the expression of basic learned species patterns to vary from group to group and from one habitat to another. For example, the nature of the integration and operation of a social unit vary in the extent to which it depends on the personalities of individuals in the group—this is another dimension of our understanding of how social behavior may affect species survival. Particularly aggressive adult males can make the behavior of their groups relative to that of adjacent groups with less assertive males substantially different. For example, a group with very aggressive males can control a larger geographic area than is occupied by a group with much less aggressive males. The tenor of life within a group may be tenser or more relaxed depending on personalities of adults in the group.

Imprinting has traditionally been distinguished from other learning processes by the fact that in imprinting the young animal will learn to follow, to be social, without an external or immediate reward. However, among monkeys and apes, simply being with other animals is a reward, and learning is reinforced by the affectional, attentive, supportive social context of the group. Butler was the first to use the sight of another monkey as a reward in psychological experiments. The field worker sees sick and practically disabled animals making great efforts to stay with their group. Among ground-living forms, animals that have lost or broken limbs or are so sick that they collapse as soon as the group stops moving, all walk along as the troop moves. Instances of wounded rhesus macaques' moving into langur groups after the rhesus have left or been forced out of their own group have been recorded. Clearly, it is essential for the young monkey or ape to mature in a social setting in which it learns appropriate skills and relationships during early years and in which it continues to learn during adulthood. "Where the individual primate is, in temporary isolation, learning a task without reference to any other member of its species, the learning is not normal."

FUTURE PRIMATE STUDIES

At present many long-term studies are in process and major films are being edited (Goodall on chimpanzee and DeVore on baboon). There will be about twice as may major accounts available in 2 years as there are now. Since it is now clear that detailed descriptive studies of undisturbed free-ranging primates can be made, and since available data show that there are substantial differences in the behavior of the different species, more species should be investigated. So far studies have concentrated for the most part on the larger ground-living forms which are easier to study. There is no study of *Cercocebus,* little on *Colobus,* and nothing on the numerous langurs (*Presbytis*) of southeast Asia. New World monkeys have been investigated very little, and there are numerous genera that have not been the subjects of a major field study. Also, since local variation is important, forms such as the chimpanzee and gorilla should be studied in more and contrasting localities.

Once the general characteristics of the behaviors of several species are known, then interest can shift to topics such as detailed ecology, birth, infant behavior, peer groups, affectionate behaviors, sex, or dominance, to mention only a few. The behavior of a whole species is a large problem, and description has to be at a very general level when the goal is a first general statement. A problem-oriented study permits choice of species and elaboration of techniques. A further advantage of the problem-oriented approach is that it allows the close coordination of the field work with experimental work in the laboratory. Fortunately, no division has developed between those doing the field work and those involved in the experimental analysis of behavior. Many scientists have done both controlled experiments and field studies. The interplay between naturalistic observation and controlled experiment is the essential key to the understanding of behavior. The character of the natural adaptation of the species and the dimensions of the society can be determined only in the field. Many topics, such as geographic range, food, predation, group size, aggression, and the like, can be seen only under field conditions. But the mechanisms of the observed behavior can be determined only in the laboratory, and this is the more complicated task. The relation of a field study to scientific understanding is like the relation of the observation that a man walks or runs to the whole analysis of locomotion. The field worker lists what the animals eat, but this gives no understanding of nutrition. The kinds of interactions may be charted in the field, but their interpretation requires the laboratory. Field workers saw hours devoted to play, but it was Harlow's experiments that showed how essential this activity was to the development of behavior. As the field studies develop it is to be hoped that they will maintain a close relation to controlled experiment. It is most fortunate that the present studies are being carried on by anthropologists, psychologists, and zoologists. An understanding of behavior is most likely to come from the bringing together of the methods and interests of many sciences, and we hope that the field studies remain a part of general behavioral science and do not become independent as workers and problems become more and more numerous.

Even now, in their preliminary state, the field studies can offer some conclusions that might be pondered by students in the multiplicity of departments now dividing up the study of human behavior. Behavior is profoundly influenced by the biology of the species, and problems of perception, emotion, aggression, and many others cannot be divorced from the biology of the actors in the social system. Early learning is important, and an understanding of the preschool years is essential to an understanding of behavior. Play is tremendously important, and a species that wastes the emotions and energies of its young by divorcing play from education has forfeited its evolutionary heritage—the biological motivation of learning. Social behavior is relatively simple compared to the biological mechanisms that make the behavior possible. Ultimately a science of human behavior must include both biological and social factors, and there is no more reason to separate the study of human behavior into many compartments than there would be to separate the field studies from the intellectual enrichment coming from the laboratory.

Prospects in Primate Biology

John R. Napier

PREFACE

In recent years the great increase in studies in physical anthropology as well as the paleontology at the more recent periods of geologic time has focused scholarly attention on man's relative and potential ancestors to a new level of intensity. Partially, this has been the result of the effect of the evolutionary theories postulated since 1930 by Huxley, Dobzhansky, and others. As Mayr (1963, *Animal Species and Evolution*, p. 637) has stated:

> It was hopeless to try making sense of hominid phylogeny as long as the fossil remains of man's ancestors were considered anatomical "types." . . . The study of the geographic variation of animals and a new insight into the process of speciation have introduced into the study of fossil man new concepts [and] —a great simplification of the general picture.

An understanding of man's rapid mental evolution in the past million years, based presumably on the refinements of speech and tool making, has led biologists and anthropologists into a major field of study—the social organization and behavior of primates. Primate biology gives every indication of being one of the most vigorous and rewarding areas of research although still in its formative stages. One of the charming idiosyncracies of this field of study is that it is interdisciplinary, that is, it is the proper concern of

From Proceedings of the United States National Museum *125, no. 3662 (1968): 1–27; reprinted by permission of the author and publisher, the Smithsonian Institution Press.*

"so-called" biologists, "so-called" anthropologists, and "so-called" paleontologists. Such an unorthodox area for research can obviously best be performed in unorthodox places, perhaps one reason why Hooton's hope (cited by Napier) that primate biology would become established as a separate teaching division in universities has not been realized. Universities as a whole are largely losing their ability to be innovative, thus putting more pressure on smaller institutions like private laboratories or museums to maintain their fundamental reasons for being. I once characterized the Smithsonian Institution as populated by specialists who were inheritors of a tradition of the "unfashionable in pursuit of the unconventional." The urgent need for studies such as those outlined in this paper is underscored by Dr. Napier's concise account of the rapidly diminishing status of many of the primate species. Conservation is by no means a subject to be ignored by scientists. Environmental studies make conservationists out of the most realistic among us. Primate biology thus becomes one of the most urgent of all interdisciplinary concerns of science today.

S. Dillon Ripley, Secretary
Smithsonian Institution

Primate biology as a scientific endeavor is unique inasmuch as it provides a mirror into which man may look to discern the nature of his own species.

Nonhuman primates, occupying an intermediate position between other mammals and man, serve as a constant reminder of the continuity of mammalian life. Thomas Henry Huxley in 1876 expressed the essence of this special primate role:

> Perhaps no order of mammals presents us with so extraordinary a series of gradations as this—leading us insensibly from the crown and summit of the animal creation down to creatures from which there is but a step, as it seems, to the lowest, smallest and least intelligent of placental mammals.

The significance of this relationship between man and the nonhuman primates is—to translate and paraphrase the late Earnest Hooton's happy plagiarism of the poet Terence—that "anything to do with primates is something to do with man." It is inherently probable, therefore, that any basic concept developed in the fields of primate physiology, psychology, or therapeutics, for example, can be applied also to man. This tenet now widely appreciated provides the rationale for the extensive use of primates as experimental subjects in medical and sociological research.

Not so widely appreciated, however, is the urgency of providing rearguard suport for the flying columns of applied primate research.

Perhaps at this point it should be emphasized that there are two main types of primate research that, broadly speaking, can be classified as applied/project-oriented or academic/subject-oriented. Project-oriented research is research *with* primates using them as other laboratory animals are used in order to test the efficacy of a technique that cannot be so tested in man.

Subject-oriented research is research *on* primates that leads to a further understanding of their biology and, by the nature of their relationship to man, to the development of hypotheses that can be tested subsequently in a human context. Subject-oriented research, thus, tends to produce results that are seldom of immediate applicability to areas of human health and welfare; they are usually at least one stage removed from medical or sociological usefulness.

The work of Landsteiner and Wiener (1940) on the *Rhesus-antigen,* which was later shown by Levine et al. (1941) to be identical with the blood-factor involved in cases of human erythroblastosis foetalis, provides a good example of the value of a "once-removed" type of applicability.

As an example of subject-oriented research, Haddow's (1952) field study on *Cercopithecus ascanius schmidti* may be recalled. This basic research project not only contributed to our knowledge of the ecology and behavior of the redtail guenon, but also it provided the essential background to Haddow's later work on the epidemiology of sylvan yellow fever. The work of Harlow and his associates (1958–1965), of Mason (1965), and Hinde (1966, 1967) on the affectional systems of monkeys and apes already has had profound repercussions in the areas of child health and development and social psychology. In the field of sociology and social anthropology the zoological perspective (particularly in primate field studies) is leading already to a better understanding of human behavior and human social systems (Tiger and Fox, 1966; Morris, 1967). Subject-oriented research also is often anticipatory as discussed by Riopelle (in press), who recalls, inter alia, that W. S. Hunter developed the delayed-response test in 1913 long before it became useful as a means of measuring function in the frontal lobes in man.

Subject-oriented research requires not only a specific training in primatology (at least at graduate level) but a continuing exposure to an academic environment where peer-contact has the salutary effect of promoting self-criticism and of stimulating intradisciplinary, subject-oriented thinking. Project-oriented research, on the other hand, given good primatological advice at its inception, need not be done in a primate-oriented environment; it can be carried out wherever appropriate laboratory facilities and experienced animal handlers are available.

It is easy to understand why, in a period of political or economic crisis with a premium on pragmatism, the "once-removed" aspect of subject-oriented research does not usually attract much in the way of sympathy or support. This attitude, however, is invoking expediency at the risk of self-immolation. It is precisely in such times that a long-term view is necessary. In a recent article, Leaf (1968) stated: "Emphasis only on applied research in medicine would quickly exhaust the present level of understanding and yield only inadequate solutions to major health problems." In particular reference to primate biology, the need for subject-oriented research is pressing, for seldom in the history of scientific endeavor has any new edifice been erected with so little regard for the nature of the bedrock. In a letter to *Science,* Moor-Jankowski (1965) pointed out that the paucity of subject-oriented research in primatology has been due not so much to the lack of support (by funding agencies) as to the lack of competent scientists. This deficiency can be traced to the fact that university training for this fruitful field of research is virtually nonexistent.

The hope expressed by Hooton (1954) that primate biology would become established as a separate teaching division in the universities has not been realized. This is not to say that the subject is not being taught at all—far from it. Primatology always has constituted an important aspect of degree courses in anthropology and is taught in most university departments. Principally, however, the emphasis is placed on primate evolution—and a somewhat anthropocentric approach to evolution, at that. Only rarely, for example, are primate anatomy, genetics, behavior, and serology covered in any detail. Primate systematics and classification seldom, if ever, form a part of the curriculum. Perhaps the complete absence from scientific literature of a student textbook on primatology is the best pointer to the present deplorable state of affaris.

It would seem to be a matter of fundamental importance that in countries where primate research is active and ongoing that there should be centers where teaching and training programs in primatology can be carried out and where future staffing needs of research institutes and primate breeding centers can be catered to.

Considering the enormous national investment in primate research, it seems quixotic, to say the least, not to insure that centers of research are also centers of education. Basic research and education programs are inseparable. The establishment of graduate and undergraduate education programs will bring about a rapid accumulation of the baseline data so urgently needed by research scientists today.

It is not possible to anticipate in detail the direction that future research will take, but, without a shadow of doubt, it will become heavily committed in the areas of child development, and mental, social, and environmental health and behavior. In these fields the experimental animal must be a primate. Information, firmly rooted in biology, will be needed about the behavioral parameters of primates under varying conditions: firstly, in the field in the framework of ecology; and secondly, in artificial environments ranging from the near-normal conditions of the field-cage to the wholly artificial conditions of the laboratory. These studies of naturalistic and "semi-naturalistic" behavior are subject-oriented just as certainly as are the more traditional academic disciplines of anatomy, taxonomy, and phylogeny.

PRIMATE BIOLOGY TODAY

The last ten years have seen the coming of age of two subjects concerned with the science of man—human biology and primate biology. Although they can scarcely be considered new disciplines, they reflect a new attitude of mind and provide fresh ways of looking at old problems.

The approach to both is naturalistic. The animal, whether man or nonhuman primate, is studied primarily as a living creature in the context of its normal environment; it is regarded as a member of a natural population, not as an individual; and it is regarded as an expression of the phenotypic variation of the species rather than as the archetype of the race. These principles require new and liberal perspectives in study methods. Human walking, for instance, one of the more simple components of human behavior, cannot be investigated merely by studying the osteology of the limbs, nor can it be explained solely in terms of the biomechanical functions of the relevant muscle groups. Walking also is concerned with the environment of men who walk and with their physiological needs in a variety of different habitats; it is concerned with the effects of culture on the periodicity of this human activity and the historical conditions that led to its evolution.

To study primate behavior entails a consideration of anatomy, physiology, biochemistry, ecology, ergonomics, paleontology, anthropology, and genetics. With a multidisciplinary approach of this sort, primate biologists cannot affort to be specialists. While inevitably possessing special knowledge in particular fields, they require a general awareness of all relevant fields. In this context "awareness" can be interpreted as an attitude of mind that, in turn, can only evolve from a training that is designed to develop it. There is much to be said for the training of the specialist with his rigorously channelled expertise, providing that his future employment asks no more of him than this; but there is a real place in twentieth-century science for the multidisciplinary scientist.

The interrelationship of primate and human biology is intricate and important both pragmatically and philosophically. They stand in much the recent innovation of primate phylogeny with a relatively brief history as mining engineering and petrology, as sociology and social anthropology. The first of each pair is concerned primarily with the present, and the second is involved principally with the past. Primate biology, though not a historical subject per se, stands in historical relationship to human biology. Man is a recent innovation of primate phylogeny with a relatively brief history as *man* but an extremely ancient one as a *primate*. Chimpanzees and gorillas are the living descendants of the same group from which man's remote ancestors were drawn millions of years ago. In this regard they serve as genetic models for man. Their value for biomedical research depends on this close blood relationship. Other primates—the baboons, for instance, which, like man, are recent innovations—are too phylogenetically remote to serve as genetic models. Baboons and macaques occupy a broadly ecological niche today as the primate precursors of man occupied some fifteen million years ago. The study of these animals, which can be regarded as ecological models, might, therefore, be expected to provide valuable clues for the development of hypotheses concerning the roots of the human social organization. It is no coincidence that baboons, macaques, and chimpanzees are the most widely used of all nonhuman primates in biomedical and sociological research.

The past of organisms is one of the determinants of their future, and the most fruitful place to look for man's past is not only in ancient and inaccessible rocks but also in the structure and behavior of living primates.

At Oxford, England, in 1864 Disraeli said: "The question is this: is man an ape or an angel? My Lord, I am on the side of the angels." A hundred years later we are no longer interested in the answer to Disraeli's rhetorical question. We do not regard it as being particularly important. Man and apes are part of one zoological order, the Primates, an order that also includes the monkeys and the lemurs, and the close relationship of these forms to man is no longer a matter of dispute or concern. The essential conformity of man and the primates in morphology, physiology, serology, and behavior is beyond question, and the problem now facing primate biologists is the clarification of the relationships within the order, with extension of knowledge in depth and breadth to include as much information on structure, genetics, behavior, and ecology for as many different species of primates as possible.

Professor Sir Wilfrid Le Gros Clark in an address to anthropologists in 1959 discussed the evolution of a new discipline. He observed that all branches of science in their neonatal stages passed through a collecting and cataloging phase. As far as primate biology is concerned, these preliminaries must be regarded as an essential stocktaking exercise during which the language and methodology of the subject must develop and the basic facts of primate biology are collected, synthesized, and disseminated. Primate biology is still, strictly speaking, in this phase. We still need to find out what it is all about, what we know, what we don't know, what is relevant, and what is totally irrelevant. Primate biology needs a plan, a blueprint from which to build a significant and durable structure.

DIMINISHING PRIMATE STOCKS

High on the priorities list of a primate research program should be studies directed toward the understanding of the *captive* primate. Before the end of this century there will be only a few natural populations of primates, living undisturbed lives, left in Africa, Asia, or Latin America. The majority of nonhuman primates will be captive in one sense or another. They may be under close restraint in medical laboratories, in zoos, in breeding ranches in the tropics, in free-ranging colonies in temperate zones, on isolated islands, or in reservations and game parks, but captive, nevertheless. This gloomy prognosis is the inevitable result of extrapolation from three unrelated trends: firstly, the ever increasing deforestation that results from agricultural development in tropical countries; secondly, the widespread native habit of killing monkeys for food, particularly in West Africa, where they constitute a vital source of animal protein; and thirdly, the exorbitant rate of consumption of primates by research scientists. Importation of monkeys into the United States during F.Y. 1966 has been estimated to have exceeded 100,000 individuals; the vast majority, it can be assumed, ended up in biomedical research laboratories. This rate of consumption could lead rapidly to extinction of certain populations in the wild: monkeys simply do not breed at this rate. Rhesus monkeys and the common langur (*Presbytis entellus*) already are showing signs of depletion in certain regions of Asia. Southwick, Beg, and

Siddiqi (1961), who carried out a population study of rhesus monkeys in 1959–1960 in the Uttar Pradesh province of India, observed a marked shortage of juveniles in many troops.

The golden tamarin (*Leontideus rosalia*) is said to be near extinction in Brazil although the blame in this instance cannot be laid at the door of the scientist. In Sierra Leone it has been estimated that, for every young chimpanzee exported for research or for zoos, between four and six mothers have to be killed. Since each of these mothers might be expected to produce up to ten offspring in a lifetime, the potential loss to the wild population for *every* young chimpanzee captured is between forty and sixty individuals. Estimations of this sort can never be particularly reliable, but even the loss of a single breeding female for every infant captured could eventually have a severe effect on population numbers.

There are clearly several ways of approaching the problem of diminishing primate stocks. Firstly, there is the matter of conservation. This is an admirable concept, and, indeed, conservationists can chalk up a number of important successes for which the whole world should be grateful, but unless the aims of conservation are anticipatory rather than retrospective, the problem of the primates will not be solved by such measures. The only possible procedure for the orangutans of Borneo (it seems inevitable that the Sumatran race is past saving) is to establish protected colonies on suitable islands. The real problem for the future are monkeys such as the patas, the vervet, the baboon, and the macaque, all of which, though plentiful now, may not always remain so. On the basis of present trends, it is difficult to see how natural populations of these animals can survive beyond the end of the century. It is the *potentially* vanishing species that should be the principal targets of conservationists, not populations that are already doomed.

Information is urgently needed on the population numbers of free-ranging primates, particularly the most popular laboratory animals, in order to guide future policies on importation of primates and the establishment of breeding colonies at home. We have little or no precise knowledge of current wild population numbers or of population dynamics in the countries of origin of these animals. Rumors abound, but factual information is lacking.

CHOICE OF PRIMATES IN MEDICAL RESEARCH

Although the literature in recent years on the care of primates in medical research laboratories has grown astronomically, relatively little consideration has been given to the selection of primates specifically appropriate to particular types of research investigations.

The choice of a nonhuman primate is largely a hit-or-miss affair and will continue to be so until the biological properties of all species have been fully investigated. Reference to recent publications (e.g., Montagna, 1967), to the symposium volumes edited by Vagtborg (1965) and Fiennes (1966), respectively, and to the textbooks of Ruch (1959) and Fiennes (1967) would reveal a great deal of information on the proved and potential usefulness of particular species for particular problems. A comprehensive account of the research potential of the 197 species of primates is beyond the scope of the present article.

Choice of a suitable primate for a specific project, therefore, must depend on hearsay, on the published reports of other workers, or, in the last instance, on trial and error. Finally, selection will be influenced by pragmatic considerations that relate to available space, available resources, and available primate species. There are no hard and fast principles by which suitable animals may be selected except that of phylogeny, which, at best, can act only as a general guide.

The phylogenetic article of faith is simply stated: The experimental results that are most likely to be meaningful in a human context are those carried out on animals that have the closest genetic relationship (and, therefore, phylogenetic proximity) to man.

The phylogeny of the primates is shown diagramatically in Figure 1, wherein primate families and their component genera have been arranged in terms of their relative closeness to man.

PROSIMIANS. The Prosimians comprise six families, which are arranged as follows: Tupaiidae, Lorisidae, Daubentoniidae, Indriidae, Lemuridae, and Tarsiidae (Napier and Napier, 1967). The use of prosimians as laboratory animals has been discussed recently by Manley (1966), Montagna (1967), and Hill (in press).

Treeshrews (Tupaiidae) are not unequivocally primates. Opinions differ strongly at the present time as to whether they should be so regarded. The attitude taken by the author is that, whether technically they are primates or not, they are thought to be so close to the phyletic root of the order (at a time when all primates were insectivores, so to speak) that they should be retained in the Primates, if only as a permanent reminder of the generalized mammalian origins of the stock. Treeshrews have not been used widely as laboratory animals except in strictly physiological experiments, but with the new information emerging on breeding behavior (Martin, 1966), they may well attract more attention.

Among the Lorisidae, galagos are potentially the most useful. Their relatively short gestation period (*Galago crassicaudatus:* 130–135 days; *G. senegalensis:* 144–146 days) and the not uncommon occurrence of twin births mark them as possibles. A number of primate centers and research laboratories are breeding these animals successfully. The melanistic race, *G. c. argentatus,* is tougher and heavier than the brownish *G. c. crassicaudatus* and may prove to be more hardy in captivity; it is possible that it may be a good subject for an open-air colony situation.

The Lemuridae are the only other family of the Prosimian radiation that are likely to be available for laboratory work; the remaining families are too rare and too delicate to be considered. Lemurs, specially the robust ring-tail (*L. catta*), have been bred successfully in quite large numbers in laboratories and zoos in recent years as also, to a lesser extent, have the black lemur (*L. macaco*) and the brown lemur (*L. fulvus*); however, it is certain that scientists who have a special reason for employing these animals

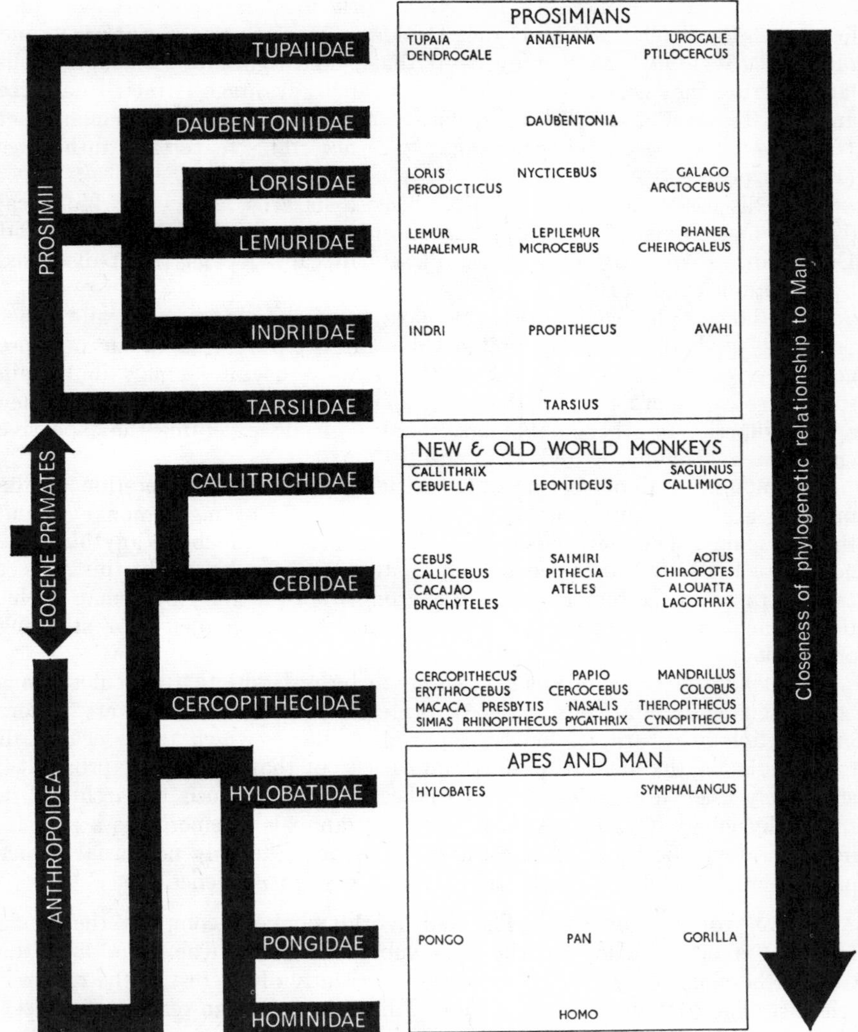

FIGURE 1.

in research will have to depend wholly on their own breeding stocks in the future as all Madagascan prosimians are rigorously protected. The value of prosimians as laboratory animals is largely unknown, but, generally speaking, their usefulness lies in the field of basic research. This is exemplified by the ongoing studies of Montagna and his colleagues on cutaneous anatomy and physiology. As substitutes for higher primates in the fields of cancer research, immunology, and pharmaceutics, they leave much to be desired.

NEW WORLD MONKEYS. The New World monkeys comprise two families, the Callitrichidae[1] and the Cebidae. Marmosets (*Callithrix*) and tamarins (*Saguinus*) have enjoyed—if that is the right word—a high popularity during the last five years. Their principal advantage is their small size and the free availability, in particular, of *Saguinus*. The common marmoset (*C. jacchus*) is becoming increasingly rare according to certain authorities (Hill, in press).

A discussion of the suitability, disease hazards, and basic biological data of marmosets and tamarins has been summarized by Deinhardt and Deinhardt (1966); breeding of marmosets in captivity has been discussed by Hampton et al. (1966).

Although phylogenetically the most remote from man of all higher primates—and, therefore, of limited value in procedures that hinge on close genetic proximity to man—marmosets are most useful animals in certain specific research projects. In the study of viral hepatitis, for example, they appear superior to other nonhuman primates, always excepting the expensive chimpanzee (Deinhardt and Deinhardt, 1966).

Among the Cebidae, the only species that merit consideration at the moment are the squirrel monkeys, the douroucoulis or night monkeys, and the capuchins. The shortness of this list reflects as much as anything the neglect of the New World genera by primate biologists. No doubt this neglect can be traced to the remoteness of this group from the story of human evolution, which in the past constituted the principal raison d'être for studying primatology.

Cebus, the capuchin, which is said to be resistant to tuberculosis, has been discussed by Stare et al. (1963), principally in relation to dietary factors in the etiology of atherosclerosis. Squirrel monkeys, which fulfill nearly all the criteria for the ideal laboratory animal except that of phyletic proximity, are widely used in neuroanatomical studies in arteriosclerosis research and in space physiology. One of the most surprising animals to emerge as a promising laboratory species is *Aotus* (the douroucouli), the only nocturnal higher primate and one of the most primitive monkeys in existence.

OLD WORLD MONKEYS. The Old World monkeys comprise the single family Cercopithecidae; of the two subfamilies, the Colobinae and the Cercopithercinae, only the last named are presently of interest to the research scientist. The contribution of the Cercopithecinae to human research has been discussed by Jolly (1966).

Macaca mulatta, the rhesus monkey, the "monkey" of medical literature, is too well known to merit discussion here; its use in the identification of the Rh blood factor and in the development of poliomyelitis vaccine is common knwoledge. The breeding record of the rhesus macaque, its toughness, availability, and cheapness make it the best all-round research animal. Certain other macaque species as the crab-eater, the pig-tail, the stump-tail,

[1] The spelling of Callitrichidae is that originally used by Thomas (1903). The termination appears to be formed in accordance with Appendix D, Table 2, of the "International Code of Zoological Nomenclature" (1964), and, therefore, there is no case for amending Thomas' spelling.

the bonnet, and the Japanese macaque all breed well in captivity. The last mentioned promises to be especially valuable as a species that can be bred freely in open-air compounds, even in high latitudes.

The closely related Celebes black "ape" (*Cynopithecus niger*) is another primate that seems to breed well in captivity. As a bonus, Celebes apes are, for Old World primates, quite friendly animals. One might guess that imported stocks of *Cynopithecus* are never likely to be adequate for extensive research usage due to the restricted range of the species. Their future usefulness will have to depend largely on domestic breeding programs.

Baboons have grown in popularity in recent years and are becoming biologically very well documented (Vagtborg, 1965). They are of particular value in surgical procedures (Moor-Jankowski, 1967). Baboons have been used extensively in studying the etiology of atherosclerosis and other cardiovascular diseases of man at Sukhumi in the U.S.S.R., for instance, and at the Southwest Foundation, San Antonio, Texas.

The leaf-eating section of the Cercopithecidae, the Colobinae of southeast Asia (*Presbytis, Nasalis,* etc.) and Africa (*Colobus*) are so specialized in their diet and, relatively speaking, so little known biologically that they have no place in medical laboratories at the present time. A possible exception to this generalization is the Hanuman or entellus langur (*P. entellus*), which is hardier than most other species and more ground adapted (Jay, 1965).

The remaining Old World monkeys to which reference should be made have been grouped by some taxonomists (Jolly, 1965) into a tribe, the Cercopithecini, that includes the following genera and subgenera: *Cercopithecus, Cercopithecus* (*Miopithecus*), *Cercopithecus* (*Allenopithecus*), and *Erythrocebus*. This tribe is not generally regarded as important in biomedical research, but there are at least three species that are worthy of note—the talapoin, the savannah monkey,[2] and the patas. The talapoin is untried as a laboratory animal but is theoretically desirable in view of its small size and the possession of a sexual swelling in females. Savannah monkeys have been used fairly extensively, notably in the culture of poliomyelitis vaccine. Patas monkeys are used quite widely in Britain today; the fully adult male patas monkey, however, equals a male baboon in size.

Some slight success in breeding talapoins in the laboratory has been reported (Hill, 1966*a*). There is little information on breeding of patas monkeys beyond the fact that between 1959 and 1963 twenty-four births were recorded in world zoos (Napier and Napier, 1967). Goswell and Gartlan (1965) have recorded a single instance of a laboratory birth. Savannah monkeys and their allies, on the other hand, breed moderately freely. It seems logical to anticipate that other members of the genus *Cercopithecus,* such as *C. ascanius schmidti* (the red tail), would be of value in research once they are better known biologically.

APES. It is hardly necessary to discuss the apes in the context of human research. While it is obviously highly desirable on phylogenetic grounds that chimpanzees should be used for many aspects of biomedical

[2] Common names of the three geographical species of the savannah monkey (*C. aethiops* group) are the grivet, the vervet, and green monkey.

research, their expensiveness and relative rarity should preclude their use other than in very exceptional circumstances wherein no alternatives exist. This does not prevent chimpanzees from being employed in experimental work that does not result in the sacrifice of the animal. It is perhaps in the fields of functional morphology and growth and aging studies that these animals can contribute most to human understanding.

Gorillas and orangutans have no place in the medical laboratory owing to their extreme rarity although, as in the case of chimpanzees, they can contribute to many aspects of human biology. The only remaining ape species to be considered is the gibbon. Being the most active of all primates, they require considerable space in order to remain healthy through the performance of a normal locomotor repertoire. Their unique—in an Old World primate sense—social behavior patterns make them unsuitable as breeding animals.

The scientist faced with a research problem must choose the animal most suited to his requirements. Perhaps the most serious question that he must ask himself is: Need primates be used at all for this particular experiment? Would not a white rat, a guinea pig, or a rabbit do just as well? The conservation of wildlife is a serious scientific, economic, and social problem and not simply a hobby for elderly ladies. Primates are rare animals, and it should be a matter for profound thought before the decision is made to remove an animal from the wild. Medically useful primates must be bred in captivity in sufficient numbers so that the cause of scientific conservation is not imperilled by the extravagant demands of a sister science.

PRIMATE BIOLOGY AT THE SMITHSONIAN

This recently inaugurated primatology program has a single, clear purpose: To foster the development of primate biology as a scientific endeavor on an international scale. It is to be hoped that this new program will play a central and a catalytic role in the rapidly expanding field of primatology by encouraging basic research, particularly in systematics, and promoting educational programs in the universities, particularly those closely associated with centers of primate research.

The Primate Biology Program is planned as an international facility having, in the first instance, two offices, one in Washington, D.C., at the Smithsonian Institution, and one, in London, England, with close affiliations to the University of London. For geographical and other practical reasons it is likely that the program emphasis will differ somewhat between the two centers; for instance, the magnificent collections, the preparation and storage facilities of the U.S. National Museum, and the proximity of other major museum collections would favor Washington as the locus of systematics research. On the other hand, the close association of the London office with the University of London will facilitate the development of this center as a locus of undergraduate teaching. Graduate training programs would be located in both centers; however, it is not envisaged that the various projects will be divided between the two centers so much as shared between them. Each will contribute to the total program as its native talents and material resources dictate. A regular exchange of students and professional staff between London and Washington will do much to foster the principle of unity.

The following section constitutes a working plan that embodies a research and education program of considerable magnitude and breadth. It is not anticipated that all the projects will develop simultaneously; indeed, it may be several years before some of them can be initiated.

Research program

Certain aspects of primate biology such as systematics and nomenclature, anatomy and physiology, evolution, zoogeography and population dynamics, free-ranging behavior and ecology, and base-line data on the ecology of captivity are in urgent need of development. These problems are the basic requirements of research workers who, in the design stage of their experiments, must ask themselves a series of questions (the particular fields of study that might be expected to supply the answer are shown in parenthesis):

Q. 1. Which is the most suitable primate for my purpose? (Anatomy, physiology, psychology. Evolution. Systematics and nomenclature.)

Q. 2. Where can I obtain a regular supply of this species? (Zoogeography. Population dynamics.)

Q. 3. How can I best maintain these animals in captivity? (Free-ranging behavior and ecology. Base-line data on captivity ecology.)

It is in such fields of inquiry as these that the Smithsonian Primate Biology Program will concentrate its efforts.

PRIMATE SYSTEMATICS. Problems in primate systematics are many and great and constitute a major handicap in the rapid development of research programs employing nonhuman primates as experimental animals. The interpretation of results in fields of physiology, pharmacology, psychopathology and neuropsychiatry, comparative psychology and ethology often depends on a precise knowledge of the systematic status of the subject animal. With imperfect identification, the contributions of previous research workers cannot be utilized, experiments cannot be repeated, and hypotheses—dependent on the precise knowledge of relationships—cannot be developed or tested.

A revision of primate systematics is long overdue for many groups and should rank high in the priorities of any program. Research in primate taxonomy should start with revision of genera. It is difficult to talk about species within a genus without knowing the exact limits of variations among genera themselves. Genera in most urgent need of revision, other than those already being examined, are found in most of the prosimians, many of the Cebidae, certain Cercopithecidae (particularly *Cercopithecus* and *Cercocebus*), and all the Colobinae. Only after restudying such genera can classifica-

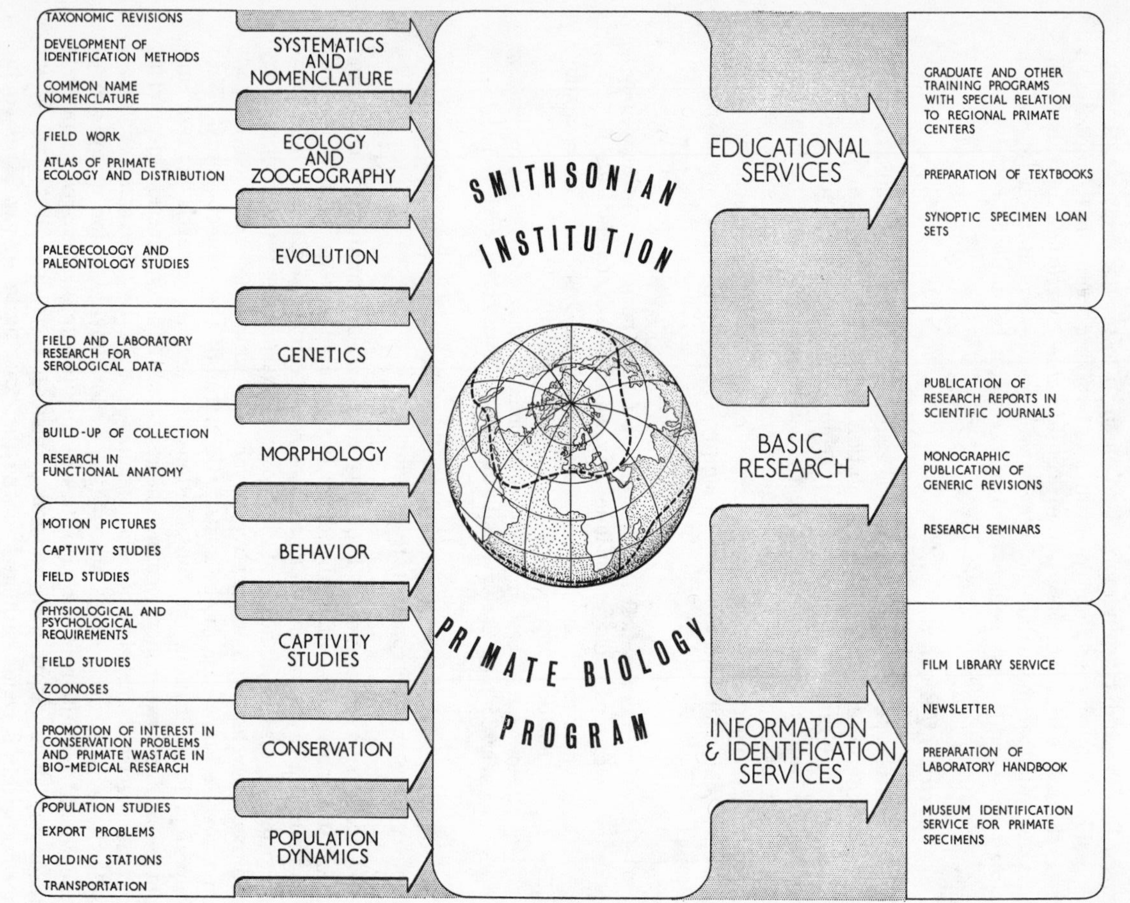

TAXONOMIC REVISIONS
DEVELOPMENT OF IDENTIFICATION METHODS
COMMON NAME NOMENCLATURE
SYSTEMATICS AND NOMENCLATURE
FIELD WORK
ATLAS OF PRIMATE ECOLOGY AND DISTRIBUTION
ECOLOGY AND ZOOGEOGRAPHY
PALEOECOLOGY AND PALEONTOLOGY STUDIES
EVOLUTION
FIELD AND LABORATORY RESEARCH FOR SEROLOGICAL DATA
GENETICS
BUILD-UP OF COLLECTION
RESEARCH IN FUNCTIONAL ANATOMY
MORPHOLOGY
MOTION PICTURES
CAPTIVITY STUDIES
FIELD STUDIES
BEHAVIOR
PHYSIOLOGICAL AND PSYCHOLOGICAL REQUIREMENTS
FIELD STUDIES
ZOONOSES
CAPTIVITY STUDIES
PROMOTION OF INTEREST IN CONSERVATION PROBLEMS AND PRIMATE WASTAGE IN BIO-MEDICAL RESEARCH
CONSERVATION
POPULATION STUDIES
EXPORT PROBLEMS
HOLDING STATIONS
TRANSPORTATION
POPULATION DYNAMICS
SMITHSONIAN INSTITUTION
PRIMATE BIOLOGY PROGRAM
EDUCATIONAL SERVICES
GRADUATE AND OTHER TRAINING PROGRAMS WITH SPECIAL RELATION TO REGIONAL PRIMATE CENTERS
PREPARATION OF TEXTBOOKS
SYNOPTIC SPECIMEN LOAN SETS
BASIC RESEARCH
PUBLICATION OF RESEARCH REPORTS IN SCIENTIFIC JOURNALS
MONOGRAPHIC PUBLICATION OF GENERIC REVISIONS
RESEARCH SEMINARS
INFORMATION & IDENTIFICATION SERVICES
FILM LIBRARY SERVICE
NEWSLETTER
PREPARATION OF LABORATORY HANDBOOK
MUSEUM IDENTIFICATION SERVICE FOR PRIMATE SPECIMENS

FIGURE 2.

tions be revised in a meaningful way. Many of these lists are half a century or more old and include species and subspecies that, in the light of modern theories, are quite invalid. The use of computers and advanced statistical techniques are providing new and more accurate means of zoological classification. A recently (Groves, 1967) completed study of gorilla populations using these techniques is an example of the sort of results that can be obtained. Evolutionary studies are a necessary component of systematic revisions; for example, the arrangement of higher categories of Old World monkeys depends on understanding of the phylogenetic relationships among the *Macaca-Papio* ground-living group of Old World monkeys, the arboreal colobine monkeys, and the curiously intermediate *Cercopithecus* and *Cercocebus* groups.

Inasmuch as modern systematics is based on the total biology of populations, a program of revision must be broadly based and must involve research into many diverse fields of primate biology such as anatomy, paleontology, behavior, serology, and genetics. Thus, the systematics program undoubtedly will provide a considerable mass of fall-out information in these special fields of study in addition to providing taxonomic revisions of the genera.

Priority from the point of view of early revision will be given to those genera most commonly used in scientific research. The marmosets are undergoing revision at present (Hershkovitz, 1966, and in litt.) as are some of the macaque species (Fooden, 1964, 1967). *Papio* recently has been restudied, principally from the viewpoint of osteology and paleontology (Jolly, 1965).

The genus *Cercopithecus,* on the other hand, has not been fully revised since Schwarz' (1928) study, although Hill (1964, 1966a, 1966b) has contributed much toward our knowledge of the taxonomy of these animals, particularly from the point of view of gross anatomy. Certain species and species-groups such as the Mona monkeys have been reviewed recently by Booth (1955); and the *aethiops* group, by Dandelot (1959). Verheyen (1962) has studied the skull osteometrically and osteologically; Chiarelli (1966) has supplied a great deal of information on chromosome numbers. Jacob and Tappen (1957, 1958) have studied haemoglobins. Booth (1956, etc.) has studied the ecology of certain West African representatives, and Haddow (1952) has supplied detailed information for a single subspecies, the redtail (*C. ascanius schmidti*). Few behavior studies have been published; Hall and Gartlan (1965) have observed the social behavior of *C. aethiops* on Lolui Island, Lake Victoria, and Cynthia Booth (1962) and Brain (1965) have studied the behavior of certain species of *Cercopithecus* in captivity. These studies must be extended to include all twenty-one species and sixty-seven subspecies now recognized. It must also be extended to the closely related forms *Miopithecus* (the talapoin, a species potentially of great value to research on account of its small size), *Allenopithecus* (the swamp monkey), and *Erythrocebus* (the patas monkey) with a view to determining whether these forms are congeneric with *Cercopithecus*. The *aethiops* species-group of *Cercopithecus* are another potentially source of laboratory primates. The aspects of the biology of this group needing particular study are serology, ecology, and behavior. Evolutionary studies, which should provide the basis of any classification, are also most important (see Jolly, 1966); fortunately, the fossil material of the Cercopithecidae is moderately common, particularly in the Pleistocene (Jolly, 1965). A zoogeographical study of the group after the manner of Hershkovitz on *Callicebus* (1963) is also imperative for the full understanding of their origin and dispersal (see also Tappen, 1960). It is proposed, therefore, to initiate a revision of the genus *Cercopithecus*. Other genera to be studied early in the program will include *Saimiri* (the squirrel monkeys) and *Presbytis* (the langurs).

Taxonomic Teams: Revisions of the systematics of any group cannot, and should not, be carried out by any one individual. Essentially, these are team projects that should reflect the multidisciplinary approach of primate biology. For the proposed fundamental revision of the genus *Cercopithecus*, a team consisting of specialists in the following fields will be co-opted and will operate under the general direction of the author:

1. Osteometric and osteological studies.
2. Serology.
3. Locomotor adaptations.
4. External characters.
5. Ecology.
6. Behavior.
7. Evolution and zoogeography.

Other scientists will be co-opted on an ad hoc basis to study various special aspects of the program, i.e., parasitology.

Duration of Project: In view of the proposed depth and breadth of the revision of *Cercopithecus*, it seems likely that the project will last at least three years, possibly four or even five. Since the systematics team will be drawn from suitably experienced scientists working in different parts of the world, it is considered essential that they should be in constant communication in order that the products of their different viewpoints can be closely coordinated. As far as is possible, a new systematics project involving a separate team will be initiated every second year. Thus, at the end of a five-year period the revision of three important primate genera will be underway.

Study Conferences: The majority of the scientists comprising a "taxonomy team" will be employed on a consultant basis. In order to facilitate close coordination on the project, annual study conferences will be held to bring together the scientists concerned either in Washington or in London.

Publication: During the course of the project, publication of the results of individual studies will be encouraged. At the conclusion of the project, the revision will be published as part of a monograph on the biology of the *Cercopithecus* group.

NOMENCLATURE. Revision is needed also in primate nomenclature. As more and more medical research laboratories utilize primates, the more urgent becomes the problem. The present nomenclature of primates is neither adequate nor sufficiently stabilized for scientists to communicate with one another without considerable danger of misunderstanding. The common laboratory primate, the crab-eating macaque, is a classic inmate of the nomenclatorial madhouse. It is widely and incorrectly known as *Cynomolgus* and less widely, and correctly, known as *Macaca fascicularis,* although most current systematic lists refer to it as *Macaca irus*. It is understandable that harassed research workers should throw up their hands at such an impossible situation and end by using its unequivocal common name, the crab-eating monkey. The stability-loving primate biologist asks nothing more than that he should be able to retire at night with a name on his lips that is still valid when he wakes up in the morning.

A Study Group for Primate Nomenclature and Systematics Research will be established at the Smithsonian under the aegis of the Primate Biology Program. Its purposes will be twofold: immediate and long-term. The immediate aim will be to prepare, in the light of present knowledge, the best possible working list of primate species for use in the Primate Centers and other research laboratories; its long-term function will be to determine the areas of primate biology where systematic research is most urgently needed, to foster such research, and to revise critically the nomenclatorial list from time to time as new, irrefutable evidence becomes available. In this way it is to be hoped that primate nomenclature will achieve a *uniformity* in primate research that it has never before enjoyed. Total *stability* of nomenclature is something that cannot be guaranteed; to advocate such a procedure would be to deny the ebb and flow of scientific opinion. Stability, nevertheless, will be the watchword of the Study Group and purely technical name changes will be examined very critically before the status quo of the working list is disturbed.

LABORATORY IDENTIFICATION. The identification of animals at specific and subspecific level is a fundamental need in both the research laboratory and in the museum. The simplest method is by means of external characters. In the event, considerable reliance is placed on coat coloration. The only means by which this can be achieved other than by direct comparison with known specimens is by reference to published descriptions. Many of the current descriptions antedate the introduction of the Ridgway color system and are, therefore, unstandardized. The earlier Munsel system has been little used in mammalian identification. Even post-Ridgway descriptions with their innumerable subtypes (1115 in all) of the named colors of the spectrum are so complex as to be almost useless in practice for the taxonomist and non-taxonomist alike. At best, all qualitative systems are subjective.

It is proposed to investigate the feasibility of developing a quantitative method of determination of coat colors using the technique of "reflectance spectrophotometry" (Dice, 1947; Hill, 1960). There are a number of techniques available for color specification: the spectrophotometric curve, the tricolor reflectance value, and the C.I.E. (Commission Internationale de L'Eclairage) system, which provides evidence of the dominant wave length of samples.

A pilot study of *Saimiri* is already underway. Hopefully, this technique will provide a method that can be used by nonprimatologists and primatologists alike to aid in the identification of the species under investigation.

POPULATION DYNAMICS. Information is urgently needed on the population numbers of free-ranging primates, particularly the most popular laboratory species, in order to guide future policies on importation of primates and the establishment of breeding colonies in temperate climates. We have little or no precise knowledge of current wild population numbers or of population dynamics in the countries of origin of these animals.

Primate population studies should provide information on population levels, population trends, export problems, holding stations, transport mortality, as well as local attitudes and customs involving primates that might affect exportation.

This is a major project and will need to be developed in two phases: (1) The basic background knowledge of the distribution, abundance, and population dynamics will be gleaned from what is already published in the literature on primates. Much of it is archaic and imprecise, but, nevertheless, there is much that is of value that should be collated as a first step. It will be possible to extract much information on distribution, less on abundance, and very little on population dynamics. (2) Following library research, there should be corollary field studies of several of the important species. Primary emphasis would be on the definition of ecological factors most critical in limiting population growth and those factors favoring population expansion and maintenance. Means of carrying out censuses of populations in various situations would be sought. Finally, model studies of the population dynamics of one or two important species should be undertaken.

Much of the field work in the preliminary stages could be carried out in certain of the soft-currency countries under Smithsonian's Foreign Currency Grant Program.

STUDIES OF THE HUSBANDRY AND WELFARE OF CAPTIVE PRIMATES. One approach to the problem of diminishing stocks discussed above is obviously the increase of breeding and holding programs in artificial environments. Much more basic research is required before such programs can supply all the animals of different species that scientists require. One must know, for example, the normal diet of the primates concerned, as well as its seasonal variations, and the typical locomotor habits and resting postures of the primates in order that appropriate cages, enclosures, holding chairs, etc., can be designed. One must understand the social composition of the species concerned; each species has its own pattern of social behavior that must be understood if the animals are to be kept in captivity as healthy breeding units. One must know the technical details of the microclimate, the temperature-ranges, and the humidity. One must know the physical nature of the environment: Do these monkeys live among the small flexible branches of the canopy, on the stout branches near the trunk, or on the trunk itself? Only by finding the answers to these questions can one hope to provide, artificially, something approaching a realistic (though obviously not a normal) environment for the animal concerned. To provide a captive animal with an adequate, suitable environment is not only humane but sound common sense. Many of these problems are now being tackled in the Regional Primate Centers in the United States, but the basic research necessary for a full awareness of the welfare and husbandry of a wide range of primates will take many years of detailed and imaginative research.

Boredom in captive primates is another very serious, but generally unappreciated, problem. In the wild, most of the primate's working hours are spent in search of food. If, in captivity, it is deprived of this occupation, it has no normal substitutes. It develops behavioral aberrations such as coprophagy, masturbation, and stereotyped behavior patterns like staring into space for long periods, clasping the head or body and rocking to and fro, and hopping from one foot to another. These are typical withdrawal patterns seen in deprived primates, human or nonhuman. It has been said that "a solitary chimpanzee is no chimpanzee at all." Much of the boredom can be alleviated by caging monkeys in social groups so that normal social interactions, such as grooming activities among adults and play among infants and juveniles, can help to compensate for the lack of active food-getting. Ideally, some type of food-getting activity should be devised; for example, it should be possible to mix food pellets or natural food objects into the deep gravel or sandy floor surface of the day cage in order that the animals can spend many hours of the day digging and hunting for food. In this way an element of uncertainty and variety can be introduced into the daily life of the animal. Higher primates need, above all, intellectual employment and the stimulation of unusual objects or events.

The principal aim of the research will be to obtain measurements of tolerance of monkeys to captive conditions in laboratories, zoos, and in "free-ranging" captivity. The following aspects of tolerance should be considered:

1. Climatic: Response to high and low temperatures and humidity levels; habitus changes associated with different climatic conditions.
2. Physical Environment: Responses to altered environmental situations demanding changes in locomotor habits, resting habits, spacing behavior, sexual behavior, aggressive behavior, etc.
3. Dietetic: Responses to wide range of food and feeding patterns, with particular reference to changes in the skeleton.
4. Social Organization: Study of ideal group size in differing captivity situations and its relation to cage size.
5. Diversionary: Investigation of the value of "spare time" activities in the general welfare of the captive.

An essential correlate of this program will be a field investigation of certain basic behaviors of primates in the wild, e.g., diet, locomotion, climatic tolerance, resting posture, etc. (see "Field Studies" below). Captivity studies are clearly a long-term project that will be based both in the United States and the United Kingdom. Informal talks already have held with a pharmaceutical research center in England that is interested in the possibility of setting up primate research of this general nature on its estates in the South Midlands.

FIELD STUDIES. Field studies of free-ranging primates are pivotal to the systematics, captivity, and population studies discussed above, and they will constitute an important part of the program.

It is hoped that it will be possible to establish junior and senior field-study studentships for graduate as well as post-doctoral scientists. Senior studentships normally would be held for five years and the junior appointment for three years. This period will ensure that the post-doctoral worker will, on the completion of his field work, be available to contribute to the systematics and captivity research projects and to the teaching and other activities of the Primate Biology Program. A policy might be adopted whereby the holders of these two studentships would act as senior and junior members of a field-research team.

The possibility of establishing a field primate research training program at the Smithsonian Tropical Research Institute, Barro Colorado Island, Panama, in connection with the award of the junior field-study studentship will be investigated.

FUNCTIONAL ANATOMY. Collection of data on sound biometric principles is still an important part of primate biology. There is no better example of this type of work than that provided by Adolph Schultz, whose lifetime study of growth and variability in the skeletons of higher primates has contributed so much to our knowledge. Statistical techniques such as that of multivariate analysis will in the future provide an even better method of assessment of such data; furthermore, it is expected, as a fall-out from such projects as systematics research, that new information on the anatomy and physiology of primates will become available. The field of primate anatomy has been developed industriously for the past hundred years by authorities too numerous to mention. A synthesis of a century's work is admirably recorded in the monumental treatises of Dr. W. C. Osman Hill of the Yerkes Regional Primate Center. The physiological, or functional, anatomy of primates has attracted less attention. Because of its relevance for primate behavior, the anatomical and physiological whys and wherefores will rate special attention. The "new" science of Lorenzian ethology, in particular, seems to the writer to require an injection of what Elliot-Smith called the "illumination of comparative anatomy"; it is somewhat paradoxical to study the evolutionary significance of facial expression in primates, for instance, without a detailed understanding of the function of their facial musculature.

Over the years a number of projects in functional anatomy have occurred to the writer and are listed below. These are random ideas and are in no sense a definitive list of research proposals.

1. Significance of cheek pouches in primates.
2. Phylogeny and physiology of sexual swelling.
3. Anatomy, social significance, distribution, and phylogeny of sexual dimorphorism.
4. Odaptive significance of the bulla tympanica.

5. The relationship of the fat pad under the heel of primates to ecological adaptation.
6. The anatomy and behavioral significance of swimming in primates.
7. The functions of the primate tail.
8. Adaptations of the vertebral column in relation to primate locomotor patterns.
9. Adaptations of the nails and their phylogenetic significance.
10. The carriage of infants in relation to the locomotion of primates.
11. The functional morphology of ischial callosities.
12. The neonatal coat color; its significance in natural selection.

Education program

In the earlier part of this paper considerable emphasis has been laid on the multidisciplinary approach of primate biology and on the need of its students to acquire a versatile attitude of mind. Primate biologists, for instance, who possess a working knowledge of systematics are to be preferred to systematicists who have a working knowledge of primates, for the systematics of primates should be based on the sum total of their biology, past and present.

The greatest deterrent to subject-oriented research in primate biology is, undoubtedly, the lack of primate biologists. The Smithsonian will not only supply grist for its own mill, but also it will provide a service for other museums and research institutions by developing an education program in this field.

Cooperative Graduate Programs: It is anticipated that the Smithsonian will be seeking education agreements for cooperative graduate programs with certain universities in special relation to centers of primate research. Schemes of this nature would involve praticipation by staff specialists in lectures and seminars held at the graduate school in question and the admission of graduate students to internships at the Smithsonian for a period of a year or less under the supervision of staff members.

Crash Courses: Short and intensive courses on the principles of primate biology will be arranged for institutions and research centers for the benefit of professional employees and technicians.

Undergraduate Courses: Lectures and seminars will be arranged under educational agreements with universities in association with anthropology and zoology degree courses. In order to implement such educational agreements, the permanent professional staff, term appointees, graduate students, and consultants in specialist fields would be expected to play a professorial as well as a research role. Although the academic level of the different courses will vary with the status of students concerned and with the nature of their scholastic background, the subject content will be fairly constant and will embrace the following fields of study:

Principles of evolution, systematics, classification and evolution of primates. Zoogeography and ecology. Anatomy, physiology and behavior with particular reference to habitat (anatomical and ecological basis of behavior). Molecular biology and genetics. Zoonoses, welfare and husbandry of the captive primate. Conservation.

Courses will comprise some lectures but principally seminars and practical classes. Motion picture film will be used extensively (see "Film Library" p. 213). An essential corollary of a teaching program is the production of a comprehensive textbook. This obviously cannot be conjured up overnight and it may be several years before a satisfactory student manual can be produced. As an interim measure, the author is preparing a short student text that should be available, modestly priced, in 1969.

Collection programs

The nature of the program outlined above will necessitate, above all, large and adequately cataloged study collections of primate skins, skulls, skeletons, and wet specimens.

Data Processing: Participation in the Automatic Data-Processing System for cataloging and retrieving information relating to specimens, a system already in use in the Museum of Natural History, is a possibility to be investigated. It is questionable whether the size of the present collection of Primates in the Division of Mammals would justify the high cost involved. Considered in terms of the international orientation of this program, however, such a participation would seem highly desirable; accordingly, the Primate Biology Program will consider the feasibility of processing data relating to primate collections in the major museums of the world. A project of this sort would be inconceivable for such organizational units as the Department of Invertebrate Zoology or the Division of Ornithology, but for the Primate Biology Program, which is concerned with relatively fewer species, a world-wide catalog is not out of the question. Such a catalog housed in one institution would be of immense value to primatologists.

Augmentation of Collection: Few museums possess sufficient duplicate material to allow synoptic loan-kits of skulls and postcranial bones to be made available to accredited institutions or to permit wet specimens to be dissected by graduate students; yet, such facilities would form an important part of an education program. Efforts will be made to augment the Smithsonian's already extensive collections by various means so that the following services can be implemented:

1. *Specimens for Dissection:* At present there is no adequate collection of embalmed specimens suitable for detailed anatomical dissection. Many requests for such material reach the Smithsonian annually. In the course of building up systematic reference collections, stocks of properly preserved anatomical material should be developed. These stocks would serve as a "bank" from which specimens could be drawn for study.
2. *Whole Specimens for Loan:* It is proposed to build up a "library" of the common varieties of primates. The animals preserved in their entirety would be stored in polythene envelopes without fluid and would be available for loan to scientific institutions.

3. *Synoptic Osteological Collections:* For temporary loan to primate centers and other scientific institutions.
4. *Film Library:* For certain fields of study, motion pictures are the essential correlate of more formal methods of instruction; for example, in primate biology, with its emphasis on behavior, films should comprise a major part of the course. It is not easy with large classes to demonstrate behavioral experiments on primates in the laboratory, but the identical experiments can be presented to any number of students simultaneously through motion pictures. Ecological and behavioral studies in the wild are assuming great importance in primate biology and naturally constitute a major part of student instruction; it is clearly impossible to transpose a group of students to the rain forest but perfectly feasible to bring the rain forest to them—on film. Locomotion studies are pivotal to the understanding of primate biology for the primate is structurally a locomotor machine. Locomotion can be illustrated theoretically in a biomechanical diagram of forces, but its behavioral significance, in relation to feeding, etc., can be understood only in dynamic terms where posture, movement, and environment are brought together in one demonstration. It is proposed to develop a library service lending films to laboratories and university departments for educational use. This is substantially the procedure that is followed at the present in the Smithsonian Unit of Primate Biology in London.
5. *Identification Service:* The existing collections of the Division of Mammals would make it possible to provide an identification service for outside organizations.
6. *Identification Manual:* There would appear to be an urgent need in many laboratories that use for a short and concise identification manual; preparations for such a publication are already underway. The manual would incorporate a number of color plates of the skins of certain common laboratory primates.

POSTSCRIPT

A long time has elapsed since 130 A.D., when the anatomist Galen of Pergamum, discovering that, of all living things, the ape is "likest to man," proceeded to practice what he preached by using monkeys as substitutes for human cadavers. Eighteen centuries later—although the correctness of Galen's pronouncement has long since been proven up to the hilt—we are still somewhat chary of admitting the full potential of this relationship.

REFERENCES

Booth A. H. 1955. Speciation in the Mona monkeys. *Journ. Mammal,* 36: 434–49.

———. 1956. The Cercopithecidae of the gold and ivory coasts: Geographic and systematic observations. *Ann. Mag. Nat. Hist.* 9, no. 12: 476–80.

Booth, C. 1962. Some observations on the behaviour of *Cercopithecus* monkeys. *Ann. New York Acad. Sci.* 102: 477–87.

BRAIN, C. K. 1965. Observations on the behaviour of Vervet monkeys, *Cercopithecus aethiops. Zool. Africana,* 1: 13–27.

CHIARELLI, B. 1966. Marked chromosome in catarrhine monkeys. *Folia Primat.* 4: 74–80.

DANDELOT, P. 1959. Note sur la classification des cercopithèques du groupe Aethiops. *Mammalia,* 23: 357–68.

DEINHARDT, F., and DEINHARDT, J. 1966. The use of platyrrhine monkeys in medical research. *Symp. Zool. Soc. London* 17: 127–59.

DICE, L. R. 1947. Effectiveness of selection by owls of deer-mice (*Peromyscus maniculatus*) which contrast in color with their background. *Contr. Lab. Vert. Biol.* Univ. Michigan, Ann Arbor, no. 34, pp. 1–20.

FIENNES, R. T-W., ed. 1966. Some recent developments in comparative medicine. *Symp. Zool. Soc. London,* no. 17.

———. 1967. *Zoonoses of primates.* London: Weidenfeld and Nicholson.

FOODEN, J. 1964. Rhesus and crab-eating macaques: Intergradation in Thailand. *Science* 143: 363–65.

———. 1967. Identification of the stump-tailed monkey, *Macaca speciosa* I. Geoffroy, 1826. *Folia Primat.* 5: 153–64.

GOSWELL, M. J., and GARTHLAN, J. S. 1965. Pregnancy, birth and early infant behaviour in captive Patas monkey, *Erythrocebus patas. Folia Primat.* 3: 189–200.

GROVES, COLIN P. 1967. Ecology and taxonomy of the gorilla. *Nature* 213: 890–93.

HADDOW, A. J. 1952. Field and laboratory studies on an African monkey, *Cercopithecus ascanius schmidti* Matschie. *Proc. Zool. Soc. London,* 122: 297–394.

HALL, K.R.L., and GARTLAN, J. S. 1965. Ecology and behaviour of the Vervet monkey, *Cercopithecus aethiops,* Lolui Island, Lake Victoria. *Proc. Zool. Soc. London* 145: 37–56.

HARLOW, H. F., and HARLOW, M. K. 1961. A study of animal affection. *Nat. Hist.* 70: 48–55.

———. 1962. Social deprivation in monkeys. *Sci. American* 207: 136–46.

———. 1965. The affectional systems. In *Behaviour of nonhuman primates,* ed., Schrier, Harlow, and Stollnitz, New York and London: Academic Press.

———; and HANSON, E. W. 1963. The maternal affectional system in Rhesus monkeys. In *Maternal behavior in mammals,* ed. Rheingold. New York: Wiley.

HARLOW, H. F., and ZIMMERMAN, R. R. 1959. Affectional responses in the infant monkey. *Science* 130: 421–32.

HERSHKOVITZ, P. 1963. A systematic and zoogeographic account of the monkeys of the genus *Callicebus* (Cebidae) of the Amazonas and Orinoco river basins. *Mammalia* 27: 1–80.

———. 1966*a*. Taxonomic notes on Tamarins, genus *Saguinus* (Callithricidae, Primates), with descriptions of four new forms. *Folia Primat.* 4: 381–95.

———. 1966*b*. On the identification of some marmosets: Family Callithricidae (Primates). *Mammalia* 30: 327–32.

HILL, J. E. 1960. The Robinson collection of Malaysian mammals. *Bull. Raffles Mus.* 29: 1–112.

Hill, W. C. Osman. 1964. The external anatomy of *Allenopithecus*. *Proc. Roy. Soc. Edinburgh* 68, no. 4: 302–26.

———. 1966*a*. Laboratory breeding, behavioural development and relations of the Talapoin (*Miopithecus talapoin*). Mammalia, vol. 30, pp. 353–70.

———. 1966*b*. Cercopithecoidea. in *Primates: Comparative Anatomy and Taxonomy*. Edinburgh: University Press.

———. In press. The use of primates in biomedical studies: A review of suitable species.

Hinde, R. A. 1967. *Animal behavior*. New York: McGraw Hill.

Hooton, Earnest. 1954. The importance of primate studies in anthropology. *Hum. Biol.* 26: 179–88.

Jacob, G. F., and Tappen, N. C. 1957. Abnormal haemoglobin in monkeys. *Nature* 180: 241–42.

———. 1958. Haemoglobins in monkeys. *Nature,* 181: 197–98.

Jay, Phyllis. 1965. The common langur of northern India. In Primate behavior, ed., DeVore. New York: Holt, Rinehart and Winston.

Jolly, C. J. 1965. The origins and specializations of the long-faced Cercopithecoidea. University of London: Ph. D. dissertation.

Jolly, D. C. 1966. Introduction to the Pithecoidea with notes on their use as laboratory animals. *Symp. Zool. Soc. London* 17: 427–57.

Landsteiner, K., and Wiener, A. S. 1940. An agglutinable factor in human blood recognized by immune sera for Rhesus blood. *Proc. Soc. Exp. Biol. Med.* 43: 223.

Leaf, Alexander. 1968. Government, medical research and education. *Science* 159: 604–7.

Levine, P.; Vogel, P.; Katzin, E. M.; and Burnham, L. 1941. Pathogenesis of erythroblastosis fetalis: Statistical evidence. *Science* 94: 371–72.

Manley, G. H. 1966. Prosimians as laboratory animals. *Symp. Zool. Soc. London* 17: 11–39.

Martin, R. D. 1966. Treeshrews: Unique reproductive mechanism of systematic importance. *Science* 162: 1402–4.

Mason, W. A. 1965. Determinants of social behavior in young chimpanzees. In *Behavior of nonhuman primates,* ed. Schrier, Harlow, Stollnitz. New York: Academic Press.

Montagna, W. 1967. The use of subhuman primates in the study of disease. *Primate News* 5: 3–10.

Moor-Jankowski, J. 1967. In *Progress in Primatology,* ed. Starck, Schneider, and Kuhn, Stuttgart: Gustav Fischer.

———. 1965. The primate centers and taxonomy. *Science* 148: 734.

Morris, Desmond. 1967. *The naked ape*. London: Jonathon Cape.

Napier, J. R., and Napier, P. H. 1967. *A handbook of living primates*. London: Academic Press.

Ruch, T. C. 1959. *Diseases of laboratory primates*. New York: W. B. Saunders.

Schwarz, E. 1928. Notes on the classification of the African monkeys of the genus *Cercopithecus* Erxleben. *Ann. Mag. Nat. Hist.,* ser. 10, no. 1: 649–63.

Southwick, C. H.; Beg, M. A.; and Siddiqi, M. R. 1961. A population survey of Rhesus monkeys in villages, towns and temples in northern India. *Ecology* 42, no. 3: 538–47.

Stare, F. J.; Andrus, S. B.; and Portman, O. W. 1963. Primates in medical research with special reference to New World monkeys. In *Research with primates,* ed. Pickering. Beaverton, Ore.: Tektronix Foundation.

Tappen, N. C. 1960. African monkey distribution. *Curr. Anthrop.* 1: 91–120.

Thomas, O. 1903. Notes on South American monkeys. *Ann. Mag. Nat. Hist.,* 1, ser. 7: 455–57.

Tiger, Lionel, and Fox, Robin. 1966. The zoological perspective in social science. *Man* 1: 75–81.

Vagtborg, H. 1965. *The baboon in medical research.* Austin: University of Texas.

Verheyen, W. N. 1962. Contribution à la craniologie comparée des primates. Mus. Roy. Afrique Centrale, Tervuren, Belgique, ser. 8, *Sci. Zool* 105: 1–256.

SUPPLEMENTARY READINGS

DeVore, Irven, ed. *Primate Behavior.* New York: Holt, Rinehart & Winston, 1965.

Jay, Phyllis C., ed. *Primates: Studies in Adaptation and Variability.* New York: Holt, Rinehart & Winston, 1968.

Morris, Desmond, ed. *Primate Ethology.* Garden City, N.Y.: Doubleday, 1969.

Napier, J. R. and Napier, P. H. *A Handbook of Living Primates.* New York and London: Academic Press, 1968.

Schaller, George B. *The Mountain Gorilla: Ecology and Behavior.* Chicago: University of Chicago Press, 1963.

seven

HUMAN GENETICS

As Washburn stated in the introductory article, the essential change in physical anthropology was produced by the innovation of modern genetic theory. From 1900 to the present, this change has been slow but inevitable. As the geneticist gained more knowledge of the chemical determinants of human growth and development, another approach was revealed which contributed toward a clearer understanding of the unique nature of human evolution. This concept is well illustrated in the following selections by Dobzhansky and Simpson. Stern, meanwhile, takes a look into our genetic future.

The Concept of Heredity as it Applies to Man

T. G. Dobzhansky

A century ago, in 1858, Charles Darwin and A.R. Wallace published their twin essays containing the fundamentals of the theory of evolution. The theory asserted that organisms now living on earth are the descendants of very different creatures which lived in the past. One of the notable effects of this theory was to throw into confusion, for a time, the basic "law" of heredity: children tend to resemble their parents.

"The whole subject of inheritance is wonderful," wrote Darwin in 1868. But it was not until the twentieth century that a solid basis for experimental studies of heredity was found with the rediscovery of Mendel's laws. Heredity is one of the basic determinants of human personality development, but there is little agreement, even to this day, about the nature and the extent of this determinism. Not only is the matter evidently important to biologists and anthropologists, but it has sociological and even political implications. Yet the concept of heredity, especially as it is applied to man, is now considerably clearer than it was in Darwin's day.

Since the times of Sir Francis Galton, heredity has been referred to, especially in popular writing, as "nature," and environment as "nurture." To at least some people, the word "nature" subtly conveys a sense of fatalist renunciation. "Nature" is surely not to be trifled with, and one must be audacious to hope to change in oneself or one's neighbors something which is due to the innermost "nature." The point easily overlooked is that human "nature," or any biological "nature" is quite powerless except when it interacts with some environment, and that the outcome of the interaction always and necessarily depends upon both interacting variables. In fact, the

From Columbia University Forum *I, no. 1 (Winter 1957): 24–27; Reprinted by permission of the author and publisher.*

action of heredity consists basically in transforming a susceptible component of the environment, food, into a living body. Before all else, genes reproduce themselves. The sum total of genes which an idividual receives from his parents is his *genotype;* the genotype interacts with the environment and makes the body grow and develop; the state or appearance of the body at a given moment is its *phenotype.* In a sense, our bodies, and hence our phenotypes, are by-products of the process of self-reproduction of the genes.

Now, the genes are chemical molecules, fairly large ones to be sure, so that they are courteously referred to as macromolecules. Just how these molecules manage to translate their reproductive activities into manufacturing a human body out of simple groceries is far from sufficiently known, and in any case cannot be discussed here. We must leave this matter with only the remark that self-reproduction is a fundamental property of living molecules. It may be the property which sets apart the living from the nonliving.

The English language, and most other languages, use the same word for biological inheritance and for inheritance of property. This leads to confusion. To say that skin or eye colors, intelligence, or pernicious anemia is inherited does not mean the same thing as the statement that somebody inherits real estate or money. The sum total of biological heredity, which is handed down from the parents to their child, is contained in two sex cells which unite at fertilization. Sex cells have no skin or eyes of any color. Yet many people are surprised to find that Negro infants are born with skin of a lighter color than it will eventually become. Has nature temporarily cheated Negro infants of their inherited color? The answer is, of course, that they do not inherit color but only a capacity to form a pigment at a certain stage of the development of their bodies.

The idea that intelligence, temperament, and certain behavioral tendencies, such as tendencies towards criminality, are conditioned by heredity evokes powerful aversion in many people, because it wrongly suggests to them that man's destiny is fixed in the composition of his genes. In his excellent and deservedly successful book on *Genetics and the Races of Man,* my friend W. C. Boyd lists me among those who deny the inheritance of mental traits in men. To this, I plead not guilty. I merely submit that genes do not work in the way some people believe they do. Your genes certainly have determined your intelligence, but only in the sense that a person with a different genotype might have developed differently if his life experience were approximately like yours. On the other hand, if you had an identical twin he might have acquired a personality different from yours if he had lived differently.

What we inherit are genes, not characters or traits. The genes interact with the environment in which they are placed. By so doing they determine the direction, the path, the trajectory which the development of a given person takes from conception, to birth, to maturity, to senescence, to death. We geneticists often speak or write as though the genes determined merely final states of various characters, especially those of the adult body. This is unrealistic; the development is never completed and the processes of senescence are just as much a part of the normal development pattern as are growth and organ formation. The genes, accordingly, do not determine any particular stage or goal of the development; they bring about *the development as a whole,* both the ascending portion in youth, and the descending part of the trajectory known as aging and senility. In short, the genes determine processes, not states.

A human sex cell contains many genes; the best guess is that the number of genes in a sex cell is of the order of tens of thousands. These genes are units of inheritance because they are units of selfreproduction, in other words because they can synthesize their own copies. It is probable that genes are also units of cell chemistry, since there is fairly good evidence that each of them is responsible for the formation of an enzyme or enzymes. Whether there exists a one-to-one correspondence between genes and enzymes, as some people have thought, is open to question. However that may be, one fundamental fact is certainly clear: that development of an individual does not take place by gradual accretion or summation of traits produced each by a single gene or by a group of genes. The heredity is particulate, since it is the sum total of the genes inherited; the development is unitary, since it represents a single and nonrecurrent process of an individual's life. For descriptive purposes, we may consider "traits" and "characters" in isolation. It should be kept in mind, however, that "characters" are no more than aspects of a single process of living, and that the life of an individual is brought about, jointly and severally, by all the genes which the organism has. Are, then, the genes or the environment more important as determinants of the process of living? Clearly, this is the wrong way to ask a question. There is no organism without genes or without environment; both are absolutely necessary to life, for life is interaction of genes and environment.

True, it would simplify matters if we could distinguish traits due to heredity from those due to environment. We often speak and write as though such a distinction were possible. The color of your skin is hereditary, but the language you speak is environmental. Head cold is due to infection, hence it is an environmental disease, but diabetes mellitus and pernicious anemia are hereditary diseases; hence they cannot, many people would automatically assume, be cured by environmental changes.

But the traditional dichotomy of hereditary vs. environmental traits is invalid. This is easily demonstrated. No doubt, one's skin color has something to do with those of one's parents, but at least some people can modify their skin pigmentation quite appreciably by taking a long vacation on a sunny beach or by staying indoors. Most children and some adults can learn to speak any language, but in some low grade mental defectives the learning is uncommonly difficult and the defect may be hereditary. Besides, one has to be human to learn any human language, hence the learning presupposes a human genotype. Not even the most clever ape or the best trained parrot can manage to learn more than enough to be merely amusing to their human masters. Similarly, the virus of human head cold does not, as far as we know, infect dogs or cats or other domestic animals; and it is probable that some persons resist the infection more than do others. Head cold is a hereditary disease, in the sense that it afflicts carriers of human heredity. Diabetes mellitus, though hereditary, is cured by insulin injections, and pernicious anemia, though caused by possession of a dominant gene, is relieved by vitamin B_{12}. Most certainly, vitamin B_{12} does not change the gene which causes pernicious anemia.

The question at issue is: what are the relative weights of the genotypic and environmental variables in causing differences among men? No single or simple answer to this question is possible, because these weights are not the same for different traits. For example, the observed variance in blood groups is, as far as known, wholly genetic. The diversity of languages which people speak is very largely or entirely environmental. Other traits form a spectrum, mostly between these extremes. Unfortunately, the location in this spectrum of numerous human characteristics and qualities which we regard as important in our fellow men is known only sketchily or not at all.

Much research is needed in this field. In planning and evaluating such research, two fundamental principles should be kept in mind. First and most obvious: a demonstration that a given trait is conditioned by heredity does not in the least exclude the possibility that the *variation* in this trait is controlled also by environmental influences. This may sound a bit too commonplace, and yet an understanding of the compatibility of genetic and environmental causations might at least diminish, if not eliminate entirely, some polemics concerning the origins of certain mental disorders—schizophrenia, for example.

Secondly, the observed degree of heritability of a given character difference may be valid only for the time, place, and material studied. Simple examples will illustrate this. Consider the variability of weight in man. In a group of subjects living together and receiving a uniform diet, the observed variation will probably be smaller than in a group whose diet is not controlled. Ideally, if the diet and other environmental conditions were kept quite uniform the observed variance would be entirely genetic; the greater the environmental diversity the more the genetic components of the variance is eclipsed by the environmental component. It has been found that among nineteen pairs of identical twins reared apart, differences in IQs (Binet) ranged from 1 to 24 points. When the social and educational environments of the twins were evaluated it was found that the magnitudes of the observed IQ differences were positively correlated with the magnitudes of the environmental differences; better environments resulting in general in higher IQs. The degree of heritability of that capacity which is measured by means of IQ testing is, accordingly, a function of the quality or inequality of opportunity which prevails in a given society or social stratum. The heritability is not a constant which can be established once and for all.

Man's environments are capable of rapid change. The environments may become more uniform in some respects, more diversified and complex in other respects. In modern industrial societies men are exposed to environments which were not encountered by our remote and even by our close ancestors. Furthermore, new environments are constantly created by man's ingenuity and man's follies. The phenotypes which result from reactions of human genotypes to their environments are, therefore, changing in time. At this point it is necessary to make clear that the "environment" and especially, the human environment, is an inclusive concept. It is much broader than merely physical, geographic, or climatic environment. Indeed, man as a species has contrived to become progressively more and more independent of his physical environment, which he can alter according to his preferences and desires.

More important are the intellectual, social, economic, and technological environments. Animals and plants become adapted to their environments by, in the short run, changing their phenotypes within the bounds established by their genes—and, in the long run, by changing their genotypes. Man as a species possesses, in addition, a novel adaptive mechanism, unprecedented on the biological level except for mere vestiges from which the human estate has probably developed. This novel mechanism is culture. Human genes make an infant, and indeed a person of any age, receptive to training and conditioning by other members of the society or the group to which the person belongs. It is this conditioning, acquired in the process of socialization and acculturation, which is chiefly responsible for the molding of the aspects of the phenotype which are the personality and the character of a human being.

The genetically established capacity to absorb, transmit, modify, and create the body of learned tradition known as culture sets our species apart from all other biological species. Herein lies the biological uniqueness of man. This unique character of our species has become established in the evolution of our ancestors because it equipped them with an adaptive mechanism of an overwhelming potency. A human individual became able to profit not only by his own experience but also by that of others, to change his behavior accordingly, and even to add to or subtract from the cultural heritage of his group. It is tempting to say that man has two heredities, the biological and the cultural, while all other species have only the former. The profound differences between the two "heredities" call, however, for caution. Biological heredity is transmitted through sex cells; it is passed only in the direct line of biological descent. Transmission of culture is subject to no such limitation. With modern means of communication, it can be independent not only of biological descent but of space and time as well. Biological heredity does not transmit characters acquired by the body in the individual's lifetime. Cultural heredity *does* transmit acquired cultural characters, indeed it is wholly acquired by learning in every individual, never inherited in the sex cells. It is the part of the environment transmitted from generation to generation by teaching and learning instead of by genes.

The evolutionary pattern of the human species is unique in the living world because it involves interactions of the three variables, heredity, environment, and culture, instead of the usual two, heredity and environment. The triangular interaction makes the situation complex, so much so that students of man have again and again succumbed to the temptation to simplify things by ignoring some of the variables. The scientific monstrosities of biological racism and diaper anthropology are among the consequences.

The concept of heredity evolved in modern biology can make a contribution towards a clearer understanding of the unique aspects of human evolution. It is the simple consideration that human phenotypes result from interactions between human genes and the cultural as well as physical environments in which people grow up and develop. At a certain stage of its evolution our species gradually became human—a "political animal" in Aristotle's words. From then on, the evolution of this species acquired and preserved a singular character. The genotypes which evolved and became established by natural selection facilitated the acquisition and transmission of culture. The establishment of these genotypes made possible rapid growth and development of culture. The sequence closed and became circular: the evolution of culture, of the human society, of technology and science, modifies the adaptive values, the Darwinian fitness of human genotypes. The process of natural selection is, therefore, channelled more and more toward adaptation to man-made environments. The purely "natural" or "biological" man has become an imaginary creature; not even the genius of Rousseau was able to conjure this creature into existence. Most certainly, this does not mean that human genetics has evaporated; human genes became an important component of the human man. Thomas Jefferson wrote: "I consider man as formed for society." We may add that man was formed in and by society, and that he continues to evolve as the only existing "political animal."

Darwin once described the natives of Tierra del Fuego, whom he saw during his voyage on the "Beagle," when they were still little touched by contacts with white men. These natives constructed only sketchy and, from our point of view, inadequate shelters, and had only scanty clothes. Yet they apparently withstood the murderous climate of their island with ease. I visited Tierra del Fuego some 123 years after Darwin. It was February, the warmest season there, but I shivered most of the time with two woolen sweaters and a woolen suit on. Naturally, I wondered whether the great resistance to cold of the Fuegians, and my relative lack of such resistance, were to any appreciable extent genetically conditioned. Then it occurred to me that this was not a matter of great consequence. After all, I was there, enjoying the sights despite the cold; the Fuegians were not there—except for a very few hybrid individuals now living white man's lives and wearing white man's clothes.

Does Natural Selection Continue to Operate in Modern Mankind?

T. G. Dobzhansky / Gordon Allen

THE PROBLEM

The purpose of the present article is to examine the validity of the assertion, frequently made in medical, biological, and sociological writings, that natural selection has been relaxed or even done away with altogether in modern mankind, particularly in advanced industrial societies. With this assertion as a premise, dire predictions of biological decadence of the human species have been uttered, especially in popular scientific literature. It is of course not our intention in this article to grapple with this immense problem in its entirety, and we mean neither to affirm nor to refute the predictions of decadence. We feel, however, that the thinking in this field may gain in clarity from a re-examination of the concepts of natural selection and adaptation, particularly as they apply to man. Such a re-examination is the more needed since these concepts have not remained stable even in biology since they were advanced by Darwin. Particularly rapid change has taken place in recent years in connection with the development of population genetics.

Natural selection is regarded in modern biology as the directing agent of organic evolution. The process of mutation yields the genetic variants which are the raw materials of evolutionary change. Sexual reproduction then gives rise to innumerable gene combinations or genotypes. However, which mutants arise, and when, has nothing to do with their possible usefulness or harmfulness to the species. Natural selection, nevertheless, so maneuvers the genetic variability that living species become fitted to their habitats and to their modes of life. Organic evolution consists of a succession

From American Anthropologist *58, no. 4 (1956): 591–604; reprinted by permission of the authors and publisher.*

of threatened losses and recapturings of the adaptedness of living matter to its environment. But the environment does not change the genotype of a living species directly, as some evolutionists of the past have wrongly assumed. The role of the environment consists rather in that it constantly presents challenges to the species; to these challenges the species may respond either by adaptive modification or by extinction.

It would be an exaggeration to say that the above view of the evolutionary process is universally accepted. Few biological theories really are. However, the importance of natural selection, at least as an agent which guards against degenerative changes in populations, is denied by scarcely anyone. We need not labor the point that the evolution of the ancestors of the human species was brought about by the operation of the same fundamental biological processes which act elsewhere in the living world. A new situation has arisen with the advent of the human phase. Species other than man become adapted to their environment by changing their genes. In man, the adaptation to the environment occurs in part through development and modification of his learned tradition and culture. Man is able to adapt by changing either his genes or his culture, or both.

Another innovation has also occurred in the evolutionary pattern of the human species. Owing to the protection conferred upon certain weaker genotypes by civilization, natural selection against these genotypes has become weakened or removed. Individuals and populations which would die out under allegedly "natural" conditions survive and procreate in civilized societies. A large share of the blame for this interference with "normal" evolutionary processes is laid at the door of modern medicine. Although man possesses methods of adaptation which are peculiar to his species, he is still subject to general biological laws. Biological evolutionary processes operate in the human species within the unique evolutionary pattern conditioned by human intellectual powers; yet it would certainly be a dangerous matter to abolish the controlling influence of the processes of selection.

STRUGGLE FOR EXISTENCE AND SURVIVAL OF THE FITTEST

According to Darwin's own testimony, the theory of natural selection was suggested to him in 1838, when he "happened to read for amusement" Malthus's "Essay on the principles of population." And living species is able to multiply in geometric progression, and hence to increase in numbers until it outgrows its food supply. In reality this happens quite rarely, and populations of most species are stable within relatively narrow limits. The causes which bring about the relative constancy of numbers are by no means well-known even at present.

Nineteenth-century authors said simply that excessive production of progeny was balanced by wholesale destruction in the "struggle for existence," in which "famine, war, and pestilence" were the principal factors. Actually, things are more complex. Thus, with many species of birds, the number of eggs in a clutch is such that under average environmental conditions the greatest number of young survives to maturity. Larger clutches produce fewer, not more, survivors, since the parents are unable to take proper care of their brood. Among insects, starving females, or females that develop from underfed larvae, deposit fewer eggs than do well-fed females. Scarcity of food, destruction by predators, disease, unfavorable weather conditions, and accidents of every kind are all involved. One or more of these factors may occasionally be decisive in different species or at different times and places in the same species. Struggle, in the sense of actual combat, is a rare occurrence among members of the same species, although it doubtless exists. To give just one example: adults and larvae of lady-bird beetles, which normally feed as predators on other insects, resort to cannibalism when the food is scarce.

Destruction of a large proportion of the progeny certainly does not by itself guarantee that natural selection will take place. The contrary may be the case. When death or survival, and production or nonproduction of offspring are due mainly to chance, large scale destruction actually hampers selection for anything except fecundity. Selection as an evolutionary force is most effective where each individual's success or failure in life is a consequence of his over-all excellence or imperfection. In precisely this situation, most nearly approached by higher animals, the number of young produced is usually small and survival rates are high.

To put it simply, in order to be effective natural selection must be selective. On the average, survivors must be better fit to live than nonsurvivors. The survivors must be stronger, or more intelligent, or better able to get along on little food, or more resistant to weather, or better able to escape from diseases, parasites, or predators. But not even all these virtues combined will improve the quality of the progeny unless the fitness of the survivors and the unfitness of the nonsurvivors are due to their genes. This proviso is obviously most important in human evolution. In man, individual and group success is often due to better means rather than to better genes.

Natural selection is, then, brought about by the survival of the genetically fit, not of the genetically fittest. Spencer's "survival of the fittest" was an effective slogan in the struggle for acceptance of the evolution theory. But the rhetorical superlative misrepresents the actual situation by overstating the ferocity of the struggle for existence. Nietzschean superman is biologically a dubious foundation on which to build the future of the species. In nature, even under most stringent conditions, the survivors are usually fairly numerous and possess a variety of genetic equipment. Without going into the details of this matter, it can be stated that too severe a selection is likely to be less effective than a moderate one, because severe selection tends to deplete too soon the reserves of genetic variability.

REPRODUCTIVE SUCCESS

The version of the theory of natural selection, which invokes survival of the fittest in the competitive struggle for life, was remarkably well suited to the intellectual climate of Darwin's times. It has often been pointed out that the popularity of Darwinism had more to do with the social and political implications which some people read into the theory than with its scientific validity. Those who believed that limitless progress will inevitably result from unrestricted competition of private enterprise were beguiled to learn that their economic views found support in a universal law of nature. With colonial empires in the expansion stage, it was a comforting thought that the exploitation of the weak by the strong was merely a part of "the stern discipline of nature which eliminates the unfit." An eminent anthropologist was able to advocate withholding education from most people, in order that competition might occur under "natural" conditions. This "social Darwinism" continues to exist even today, and it has recently been given a modern biological dress by Darlington (1953).

With the development of genetics, and particularly of population genetics, the theory of natural selection has been recast in a more exact, though emotionally less impressive form. Consider a population of a sexually-reproducing and cross-fertilizing species, such as man. A Mendelian population of this sort consists of individuals which differ from one another in certain genes. The population has a gene pool, in which different gene variants are represented with different frequencies. Now, in any one generation, the carriers of the different genes are likely to make unequal average contributions to the gene pool of the next generation. Therefore, the gene frequencies in the gene pool will change from generation to generation. Some genes will be perpetuated at rates greater than their alternative genes. The former are, then, favored by selection, and the latter are discriminated against. The genes which are selected for may eventually be established in the population, while those selected against may be lost.

Selection consists in differential perpetuation of genetic variants in the gene pool of a population. Selection success is reproductive success. The Darwinian fitness, or adaptive value of a genotype is measured by the mean contribution of the carriers of this genotype, relative to other genotypes, to the gene pool of the succeeding generations. The highly fit genotypes are those which transmit their genes most efficiently; the less fit ones have a mediocre reproductive efficiency; the unfit ones leave no surviving and fertile progeny.

Under this sober appraisal, the "fittest" is nothing more spectacular than a parent of the largest family. He is no longer the mighty conqueror who has subdued countless competitors in mortal combat. He need not necessarily be even particularly hale and hearty; strength and toughness increase Darwinian fitness only insofar as they contribute to reproductive success. Mules are at least as vigorous and resistant to harsh conditions as their parents, horses and donkeys. But the Darwinian fitness of mules is zero, because of their sterility. Conversely, a hereditary disease which strikes after the close of the reproductive period does not diminish the adaptive value of the genotype. An example of this is Huntington's Chorea. This is a dominant disease due to a single gene, the incapacitating effects of which do not usually appear until its carrier has passed most or all of the reproductive period. There has even been a suspicion that the carriers of this gene have on the average a greater number of children than their normal siblings. The infirmities of old age are easily accounted for by the theory of natural selection. What happens to the organism after the reproductive age is of no concern to natural selection, or only insofar as the condition in old age is correlated with some traits which appear during the reproductive age. In a social organism like man, natural selection may, however, control survival in later years, because what happens to the older members of the family or community also affects the welfare of its younger members. The tendency of this control might be to shorten the interval between the close of the reproductive period and death because, as Haldane has pointed out, in some societies the oldsters prove a useless drain on the resources of the group. But comparison of the post-reproductive years in man with those in other primates would probably show that the net effect of selection has been to lengthen this period.

SELECTION AND ENVIRONMENT

The question whether modern man is subject to natural selection can now be answered. He certainly is. Natural selection would cease only if all human genotypes produced numbers of surviving children in exact proportion to the frequencies of these genotypes in the population. This does not, and never did, occur in recorded history. Quite apart from the hereditary diseases and malformations for which no remedies are known and which decrease the reproductive fitness, the inhabitants of different parts of the world have different reproductive rates.

The selective forces which now act on the human species are natural, rather than artificial, selection. It is of course conceivable that natural selection may some day be replaced by artificial selection. Indeed, "To replace natural selection by other processes that are more merciful and not less effective" the original theme of eugenics was. To make this dream a reality, the contributions which various genotypes made to the gene pool of the next generation would have to be decided on the basis of genetic considerations either by parents themselves or by some outside authority. An alternative idea has been developed, especially by Osborn (1951); instead of substituting artificial selection for natural selection, he suggests a reorganization of social and economic institutions so that natural selection could be relied upon to favor intelligence and social adaptability.

The frequent allegation that the selective processes in the human species are no longer "natural" is due to persistenece of the obsolete nineteenth-century concept of "natural" selection. The error of this view is made clear when we ask its proponents such questions as, why should the "surviving fittest" be able to withstand cold and inclement weather without the benefit of fire and clothing? Is it not ludicrous to expect selection to make us good at defending ourselves against wild beasts when wild beasts are getting to be so rare that it is a privilege to see one outside of a zoo? Is it necessary to eliminate everyone who has poor teeth when our dentists stand ready to provide us with artificial ones? Is it a great virtue to be able to endure pain when anesthetics are available?

The words "fitness" and "adaptedness" are meaningless except in relation to some environment. Natural selection involves interaction between the genotype and the environment, and this interaction leads to furtherance of congruity between the interacting entities. For this reason, organic evolution has on the whole been adaptive. It is, nevertheless, a function of an imperfect world. One of its limitations is that it is opportunistic. Selection enhances the adaptedness of genotypes only to the currently existing environments. Therefore, the direction and the intensity of natural selection are as changeable as the environment. Selection in modern man cannot maintain our fitness for the conditions of the Old Stone Age, nor can it prepare us for novel conditions of the distant future except by increasing our general adaptability.

Man's environments are decisively influenced by his cultural developments. For good or for ill, natural selection fits man to live in the environments created by his own culture and technology. In these environments, the ability to subsist on uncooked foods is probably now less important than it once was; the ability to resist certain infections prevalent in crowded towns is probably more important than it was. So is the ability to learn, to become educated, and to live in reasonable accommodation with one's neighbors. Natural selection now works in what some may call unnatural conditions, but it is still natural selection.

RELAXATION OF SELECTION

The hoary fallacy which is perpetuated by some modern writers is that for a genetic variation to be selected it must be important enough to decide between the life and death of the creature. In reality, even a slight advantage or disadvantage which increases the probability of one genotype leaving more offspring than another will be effective in the long run. It has recently been found that the proportion of people with blood group O is slightly higher among patients suffering from duodenal ulcer than it is in the general population. This does not mean either that everybody with O blood gets a duodenal ulcer, or that those with other blood groups are immune. But the possibility that the frequencies of O bloods in human populations may be influenced by the greater susceptibility of O persons to duodenal ulcer is a real one.

The fitness, the adaptive capacity of the carriers of a given genotype, is continuously changing. Suppose that the contribution of one genotype to the gene pool of the following generation is equal to unity. The contribution of a different genotype may then be represented as $1—s$. The value s is the difference in reproductive success between the two genotypes and is called the selection coefficient. Now, the magnitude of the selection coefficient depends upon the environment. Selection coefficients grow larger as selection becomes more stringent and they diminish as selection is relaxed. When s is zero, the genotypes are equal in fitness, and selection does not operate upon them.

There can be no doubt that modern technology, and especially modern medicine, have greatly mitigated the disadvantages of many genetic weaknesses and disabilities. In other words, in an environment which includes modern technology and medicine, selection coefficients operating against certain human genotypes are smaller than in a primitive environment. But this amounts to saying that the fitness of the carriers of these genotypes has increased. A person afflicted with hereditary diabetes mellitus can live reasonably happily and may even raise a family if his environment includes proper doses of insulin administered at proper intervals. Genetically considered, a disability, that can be corrected by environmental means so that it no longer causes an impairment of reproductive efficiency, ceases to be a disability when a suitable environment is provided.

This reasoning applies also to any relaxation of selection that may result from sociological progress. There is supposed to exist a danger of loss or "erosion" of genes for high intelligence, owing to the higher reproductive rates of the social classes in which such genes are supposedly rare. Cook (1951) describes this danger in the following way:

> As this process continues...the average level of intelligence and the proportion of gifted individuals declines. Should the feeble-minded level be reached, most of the plus-genes will have been eliminated. But before that time growing inefficiency and incompetence would cause the collapse of modern industrial society. The Dark Ages which spread over Europe with the fall of Rome were a cultural blackout that lasted for a thousand years. The Dark Ages which would be caused by continued gene erosion could last five to ten times as long.

It would not be appropriate here to discuss how far this eschatology is justified by available evidence. It should, however, be pointed out that the fearsome process, if it actually occurs, means that in our society high intelligence decreases the average biological fitness of its possessors, while less intelligent people tend to be more fit. This appalling circumstance would be due not to the cessation of natural selection, but to the relative intensification of selection for personality traits other than intelligence. It would be unfortunate only insofar as the most favored genotypes gave rise to certain characteristics which could be regarded as undesirable on other grounds. If the humble and the meek inherit the earth, it will mean simply that in modern industrial civilizations social conditions which obtain humility and meekness will be favored by natural selection, while pride and egotism will be discriminated against.

It should be noted that relaxation of natural selection does not by itself change the genetic composition of populations; it does so only in conjunction with mutation. The process of mutation constantly and irresistibly generates genetic variations, and most of the mutants are deleterious to the organism. Increase of mutation rates would, then, lower the fitness of the population even if the selection pressure remained constant. But the relaxation of selection would necessarily mean that the "bad" genes will have become rather less dreadful than they were.

SELECTION AND ADAPTEDNESS

More than half a century ago, in the heat of polemics, Weissmann wrote about the "omnipotence of natural selection." This unfortunate exaggeration is not wholly absent in the writings of some modern authors. Natural selection is a remarkable enough phenomenon, since it is the sole method known at present which begets adaptedness to the environment in living matter. But it has its limitations. As pointed out above, it is opportunistic and lacking in foresight. Moreover, any genotype which possesses a higher net reproductive efficiency has a higher Darwinian fitness, and is, by definition, favored by natural selection. Higher Darwinian fitness usually goes together with superior adaptedness to the environment; however, the correlation is not perfect.

A single example will suffice to illustrate the occasional miscarriages of natural selection. Dunn (1953) found a recessive gene in the house mouse which is lethal when homozygous. A population of mice in which this gene occurs in a certain proportion of individuals produces, then, some inviable embryos. The gene is clearly deleterious. But this gene possesses the curious property that a male which is heterozygous for it and for its normal allele yields more spermatozoa carrying the abnormal than the normal gene. This automatically confers upon the abnormal gene an advantage in the population, and causes it to spread until its lethal effect in homozygotes checks its propensity to increase in frequency. Dunn has found that the lethal is actually common in many "normal" mouse populations, outside of genetic laboratories. Up to a point, therefore, natural selection favors the spread of a lethal gene in mouse populations because this gene happens to be able to subvert the male reproductive processes in its own favor. The reproductive success of a genotype is, in this case, opposed to adaptive success of the population.

This discrepancy between reproductive and adaptive success arises because the former has but one dimension: the rate of perpetuation of a gene from generation to generation relative to that of an alternative gene. Adaptation is multidimensional, and herein lie some unresolved problems about natural selection, particularly as it occurs in the human species. The pioneers of Darwinism were already aware that, in a social animal, the qualities which promote success in an individual are not necessarily those which are most useful to the society in which the individual lives. A gene for altruism (if such existed) might be discriminated against by natural selection on the individual level, but favored on the population level. The outcome of selection would, therefore, be difficult to predict. One might speculate that it would depend on the population structure of the species. A gene for altruism might be lost in large, undivided populations, but might become frequent in a species subdivided into numerous competing colonies or tribes. Moreover, adaptedness to a certain environment, however perfect, need not go together with adaptability to changeable environments (flexibility, according to Thoday, 1953). For example, it is to be expected that of all the genotypes which are successful in times of abundant food supply, relatively few will be adaptable to periodic starvation; genotypes which can resist a large variety of infections are not necessarily the most successful ones in disease-free environments.

It can be granted that some genotypes which were being eliminated under primitive conditions are enabled to survive and to perpetuate themselves in civilized environments. As pointed out above, this necessarily means that the Darwinian fitness of these genotypes under civilized conditions has risen relative to what it was under primitive ones. The possessors of such genotypes, if they take proper care of themselves, may even be able to secure their share of the joy of living. Does it follow, however, that these genotypes may now be considered desirable in the human species? The answer may, unfortunately, be in the negative. Muller (1950) has portrayed the state of mankind which might result from failure to eliminate weakening mutant genes in the following way: "This means that despite all the improved methods and facilities which will be in use at that time the population will nevertheless be undergoing as much genetic extinction as it did under the most primitive conditions. In correspondence with this, the amount of genetically caused impairment suffered by the average individual, even though he has all the techniques of civilization working to mitigate it, must by that time have grown to be as great in the presence of these techniques as it had been in paleolithic times without them. But instead of people's time and energy being mainly spent in the struggle with external enemies of a primitive kind such as famine, climatic difficulties and wild beasts, they would be devoted chiefly to the effort to live carefully, to spare and to prop up their own feeblenesses, to soothe their inner disharmonies and, in general, to doctor themselves as effectively as possible. For everyone would be an invalid, with his own special familial twists."

The outlook seems grim. Natural selection under civilized conditions may lead mankind to evolve towards a state of genetic over-specialization for living in gadget-ridden environments. It is certainly up to man to decide whether this direction of his evolution is or is not desirable. If it is not, man has, or soon will have, the knowledge requisite to redirect the evolution of his species pretty much as he sees fit. Perhaps we should not be too dogmatic about this choice of direction. We may be awfully soft compared to paleolithic men when it comes to struggling, unaided by gadgets, with climatic difficulties and wild beasts. Most of us feel most of the time that this is not a very great loss. If our remote descendants grow to be even more effete than we are, they may conceivably be compensated by acquiring genotypes conducive to kindlier dispositions and greater intellectual capacities than those prevalent in mankind today.

SELECTION OF WHOLE GENOTYPES

The propensity of evolution to produce unfavorable changes in plants and animals may at first sight appear astonishing. Consider the absurd difficulty which the human female has in giving birth to her young. Here is a process which is assuredly essential for the perpetuation of the species. Natural selection could be expected to make it pleasant, or at least painless. Instead, childbirth is attended with intense pain, and often imperils the life of the mother, of the fetus, or of both. Although the later stages of pregnancy and parturition are to some extent incapacitating in all mammalian females, they are much more so in the human species. This and the other flaws in our biological organization Mechnilov called "the disharmonies of human nature." We cannot but suppose that these disharmonies have arisen during the natural course of human evolution.

The situation will appear less incomprehensible if the mechanics of natural selection are considered. Natural selection cannot develop this or that organ apart from the rest of the body, nor can it foster this or that gene apart from the rest of the genotype. What is selected in the process of evolution is the genotype as a whole. It is the whole organism which survives or dies, and successfully reproduces or remains barren. The genotype is a mosaic of genes, but it is wrong to think of the organism as though it were a mechanical sum of parts, each determined by a single gene. In the process of individual development all genes act in concert. The whole genotype, not just some genes, decides what an individual will be like as a fetus, in childhood, in adolescence, in maturity, and in old age. Moreover, the development of different individuals takes place in different environments; any genotype may be required to adapt its carrier to any one of the possible environments. Certain differences between individuals (such as differences between some blood groups) are ascribable to single genes, but even the expression of these differences may vary; what an individual is like is always due to all the genes this individual carries.

The evolutionary success or failure of a species is determined by the fitness of its entire genotype, and of its entire developmental pattern, in those environments which the species inhabits. An observer may discern, however, that some particular feature or aspect of the organization is most instrumental in bringing about success or failure. Thus with man: his body is remarkable neither by its strength nor by its endurance. The evolutionary success of our species has been due to brain power, not to body power. Evidently, some genotypes which enhance brain power have been selected in spite of their tendency to decrease body power. Darwinian fitness is the resultant of all the advantages and disadvantages which one genotype may have compared to other genotypes. In man, the ability to learn and to invent and use tools influenced this balance more significantly than did muscular strength or resistance to inclement weather, although these were not negligible.

It is certainly reasonable to suppose that genotypes which combined the greatest brain power with the greatest body power would yield the highest fitness. Why then, is man not always as wise as Socrates, as strong as a lion, and as hardy as a dog? If we had unrestricted power to plan the evolution of the human genotype, we would probably equip it with all these qualities and some others besides. But natural selection does not work according to any plan. Selection is opportunistic; whatever can survive does. Man's evolution was not designed or arranged beforehand. It took the course which it did because man's genotype, imperfect as it was, was good enough to survive, and in fact good enough to make our species a tremendous biological success.

Specialization is a common feature of the evolutionary pattern in many kinds of organisms at the expense of all-round perfection. The former is evidently more easily achieved than the latter. This is true not only of unplanned evolution which occurs in the state of nature but also of evolution under domestication, which to some extent is planned. Among cattle, there exist dairy breeds and beef breeds; there exist also some unspecialized breeds, but no breed combines the maximal performances of the best dairy and the best beef breeds. Why this is so is hard to tell; it may be that a combination of the above sort is a physiological impossibility, since the qualities which one may wish to combine may be antagonistic. On the other hand, it may be that a perfect breed of cattle is simply yet to be obtained.

Perhaps the most impressive examples, other than man, of an organism whose biological success appears to be due to an outstanding development of just one ability, and a mediocre development of others, is the man-of-war bird (Fregata). Those who have had the opportunity to observe these superb fliers procure their food from the tropical seas can hardly imagine a more perfect flying machine. Yet, the legs of these birds are so weak that they cannot rise into the air from a flat surface, nor can they alight on water since their plumage becomes waterlogged. Man is certainly the best thinking machine which protoplasm has produced. This confers upon him a biological adaptedness so great that he continues to prosper as a species despite his relatively weak body, his several biological disharmonies, and his many follies. He need not fear biological extinction so long as his genotype as a whole enables him to live in some environments, either "natural" or devised by his own ingenuity.

EVOLUTIONARY PROCESSES ACCENTUATED BY CIVILIZATION

Many traits that were essential for bare survival in a paleolithic culture are unnecessary in New York City, but we have emphasized that natural selection is not restricted to the struggle for survival. For all organisms, reproduction is the essential step in selection, and reproduction in man involves not only bearing children, but rearing them to maturity. In modern civilization, furthermore, parental influence may often be decisive in determining the success of children in their own marriage and reproduction. If so, the reproductive success of an individual may be more adequately gauged by the number of his grandchildren than by the number of his children. Also, if parental influence is so important, the existing negative correlation between intelligence and family size may be compensated in some cultural groups by a positive correlation between intelligence and successful preparation of one's offspring for adult adjustment. This extension of parental functions appears to represent a trend in human cultural evolution; in our own society, as class differentials in fertility diminish, it may restore some of the biological value which intelligence seems to have lost.

Under civilization reproduction and successful child-rearing have come to depend more upon individual adjustment patterns and less on survival or reproductive capacity. Individual and family adjustment is the modern theater of the "struggle for existence." In our culture biological adaptedness, that is, optimal reproduction and childrearing, seems to bear no direct relation to economic or educational status, but probably depends in part upon personal and social adjustment patterns. Though physical and mental handicaps rarely eliminate persons completely, they probably affect such adjustment. Among the traits capable in this way of influencing reproduction, the relative importance of physical health is presumably diminished and that of mental health magnified in comparison with selection in primitive man. In addition, some physiological defects would appear to contribute to personal maladjustments more frequently in a modern than in a primitive culture. Likely examples of such defects are color-blindness, left-handedness and allergic diathesis. With respect to genetic factors underlying these traits, present-day natural selection may be reinforced both relatively and absolutely. Finally, the capacity to compensate for gross physical or sensory handicaps probably has more selective value now than it did under conditions of existence which eliminated most cripples completely.

Further speculation is unwarranted here, but it seems safe to assume that most sensory or mental characteristics that were developed in our primate ancestors in response to the demands of an increasingly complex, variable environment, are even more important to civilized man. If so, they surely play some role in determining which persons shall marry, which shall have stable families, and which shall raise more children. When handicapped individuals defy these determinants and become parents, their children pay the price in a relatively severe selection by the adverse physical and social environment. As a result of this stringent selection in such families, on the average, survivors in the third generation are probably superior to the grandparents genetically.

Selection for many traits at once always makes slower progress than selection for one or a few traits. Insofar as natural selection formerly maintained genetic traits that have now become useless, civilization has eliminated a probable source of interference that impeded selection for cultural adaptability. Whether selection in the latter respect is in an absolute sense stronger or weaker than formerly, it is probably operating more efficiently.

Whatever emphasis is placed here on the positive aspects of natural selection under civilization is not intended as a denial of all negative aspects. Man's increasing physical dependence on his cultural heritage, beginning with cooked food and clothing, can be taken as a historical fact, and accelerated specialization in this direction is to some extent inevitable. Conflicts in our present culture between reproduction and higher education, or between reproduction and self-control, are almost completely new selective forces in human evolution. It is not at all apparent how these conflicts would be resolved in the natural course of cultural progress. On the other hand, artificial attempts to counter such selection by "eugenic" support of culturally desirable types would inevitably lead to another tpye of dangerous specialization; the very need of these types for such support, insofar as the need exists, proves their failure to adapt biologically to civilization. Dependence of society upon complex reproductive controls seems to be a higher order of specialization, whether better or worse, then dependence of the individual on medical and technical aids.

From a long-term point of view, another effect of civilization may be more important than changes in selection pressures per se. Individual genetic variation is the basis for selection, and this has been accentuated in modern man for several reasons. First, relaxation of selection in any respect immediately increases the proportion of minor and extreme abnormalities in the surviving population. Second, new environments, as well as the increasing proportion of deviant individuals, permit fuller expression of genetic differences formerly masked in uniform phenotypes. An example of this is perhaps to be seen in some childhood reading disorders, which would make little or no difference in an illiterate population. Third, migration and intermarriage of formerly separate races or groups produce a great new diversity of genotypes. Fourth, increased survival of mutations results, to a small extent, in greater prevalence of genes that raise the mutation rate.

Even if selection should be reversed for a brief period of time the above sources of increased genetic variation will, in Schmalhausen's words, mobilize the variability of the species. Thus, civilization is now preparing man for rapid evolution in whatever direction long-term selection may determine. As long as populations remain large, and as long as competition exists in any form, degenerative evolutionary trends are likely to be outweighed by adaptive changes, but the direction of these changes is uncertain.

CONCLUSIONS AND SUMMARY

The idea explicit or implicit in many writings, that all would be well with the human species if obstructions to natural selection were removed, does not stand critical examination. Man, like any other biological species, is constantly subject to natural selection. The genotypes which possess the highest Darwinian fitness in the environments created by man's inventive genius are, however, not the ones which were most favored by selection in the past. Natural selection cannot maintain the adaptedness of modern human populations to environments which no longer exist, nor can it pre-adapt them to environments of the future.

Natural selection is opportunistic; it does not always lead to improved adaptedness. After all, extinction has been the fate of countless biological species which lived in the state of nature and which were at all times subject to natural selection. It would be folly for our species to risk the same fate for the juggernaut of blind biological force. One of the causes of extinction is too narrow an adaptedness to circumscribed biological opportunity which proves only temporary. Man has reached a solitary pinnacle of evolutionary success by having evolved a novel method of adapting to the environment, that by means of culture. Having ventured on this biological experiment, our species cannot any longer rely entirely on forces of natural selection as they operate on the biological level. Man must carefully survey the course that lies ahead and constantly study his genetic progress. He can then prepare to take over the controls from Nature if it should become necessary to correct the deficiencies of natural selection. Only thus can he insure for himself continued evolutionary advance.

REFERENCES

DARLINGTON, C. D. 1953. *The facts of life.* New York: Macmillan.

DUNN, L. C. 1953. Variations in the segregation ratio as causes of variations in gene frequency. *Acta Gen. Stat. Med.* 4: 139–51.

MULLER, H. J. 1950. Our load of mutations. *Amer. Journ. Hum. Gen.* 2: 111–76.

OSBORN, F. 1951. Preface to *Eugenics.* 2d ed. New York: Harper & Row.

THODAY, J. M. 1953. Components of fitness. *Symposia Soc. Exper. Bio.* 7: 96–113.

Organisms and Molecules in Evolution

George Gaylord Simpson

It is universally recognized that molecules of biological importance may evolve—that is, they may change in the course of time as have the organisms in which they occur. Some molecules, like adenosine triphosphate, are so

From Science *146 (18 December 1964): 1535–38. Copyright © 1964 by George Gaylord Simpson; reprinted from his volume* Biology and Man *(New York: Harcourt Brace Jovanovich, 1969) by permission of the author and the publisher, Harcourt Brace Jovanovich, Inc.*

nearly universal and invariable as to suggest no evolutionary sequence, but many others surely have evolved, notably groups of proteins and, obviously, DNA. Before the importance of DNA was known, Florkin (1949) had alread discussed the systematics and evolution of various families of molecules. In such instances evolutionary interpretation of the biochemists' findings requires information from paleontologists and systematists, information especially on the time scale involved and the phylogeny and relationships of the species in which varying molecules are to be compared. An example is the hypothesis that serum proteins or cytochromes have changed in a regular if not linear manner with respect to time—that they have evolved by some sort of internal constant-rate mutational process and not in an irregular or a specifically adaptive way. In fact, when the data are replotted with what seem to be the most probable time coordinates they indicate that the hypothesis is incorrect or, at least, that these data do not support it. Williams now tells me that the hypothesis has been modified, but it exemplifies the clarifying confrontation of molecular and organismal data.

Other interesting examples of such confrontation arise from further studies of serum proteins, such as that by Goodman (1963). Phylogenetic relationships of the animals concerned, primates in this case, are inferred from the apparent degrees of homology is their various serum proteins. The lineages thus inferred then permit conclusions as to the evolution of the proteins themselves. Similar inferential methods have been applied to the evolution of hemoglobins, also in primates, by Hill and the Buettner-Janusch (1963). When phylogeny is inferred from the molecular data and molecular evolution is inferred in turn from that phylogeny, there is an element of circularity, which does not wholly invalidate the method but does warrant some reservations. A necessary cross-check is to arrange the molecular data in the framework of a phylogeny based entirely on nonmolecular evidence. It should be mentioned in passing that this, too, has sometimes led to semi-circular reasoning when molecule-based phylogeny has been compared with phylogeny with other bases: agreement between the two has been taken as the requisite validation of the molecular approach to phylogeny, but nonagreement has been taken as evidence of the greater reliability of the molecular method.

However, the most important reason for relating organismal and molecular evolution to each other is not simply the testing of hypotheses or the validation of methods. It is the balancing of points of view and the achievement of more complete explanations. Wald (1963) has said that "living organisms are the greatly magnified expressions of the molecules that compose them." Anfinsen (1959) believes that "we may almost define the life sciences as those concerned with the elucidation of the mechanisms by which molecules exert their specific actions in living cells." In fact there are many respectable and even eminent students of the life sciences who have no concern whatever with molecules or their actions. Concentration on one level of organization to the practical exclusion of others is often a necessity of specialized research, but nowadays almost everyone agrees that eventual understanding of relationships between levels is also necessary. Sonneborn

(1963) has emphasized the fact that molecular genetics could only have arisen through, and would now have little meaning apart from, "classical" or Mendelian organismal genetics. Weiss (1961) has pointed out that there is a "cellular control of molecular activities" as well as a molecular control of cellular activities. There is also an organismal control of cellular activities, and, for that matter, a populational control of organismal activities. Indeed both Wald and Anfinsen, in the works from which one-sided aphorisms have been quoted, were concerned with relationships of molecules to higher organizational levels in evolution.

The sort of problem that can arise from a limited approach is exemplified in a recent article by Mora (1963). He points out that living organisms have a teleological or purposive aspect which he proposes to label "urge." He finds that this aspect is inexplicable at the molecular level as hitherto studied. He proposes, but does not describe, a new approach, to be frankly permeated by teleology. Although he seems to think or hope that this may still be naturalistic, he does not clearly state what a naturalistic teleology might be. Now, this is precisely the problem with which organismal biologists have been coping for generations. Unknown, it would seem, to some biochemists, they have achieved a naturalistic (or, in a sense, materialistic) explanation of what is now often called [after Pittendrigh (1958)] the teleonomic aspect of organisms. The teleonomic, or *apparently* teleological or purposive, characteristics of organisms are adaptations. They include "urge" itself in Mora's sense, its manifestations, and its results in the activities of individuals and the evolution of populations. Teleonomic adaptations arise in the course of evolution, and the factor governing their origin and maintenance is natural selection. That is surely as true at the molecular level as at any other. However, the ramifications of natural selection at various levels are far from simple.

NATURAL SELECTION

The process of natural selection, as now understood, is complex rather in its concrete working and its interactions than in its basis. That basis is simply differential reproduction correlated with genotypic constitution. If some individuals in a population have more surviving and breeding offspring than others, and if there is a consistent average difference, however small, in the genotypes of those who have more and those who have fewer, that is natural selection at work. The actual selection—that is, the determination of which individuals have more or fewer offspring that survive to breed in their turn—is an interaction between environment, in the broadest sense, and the population, in all its individuals throughout their complete ontogenies. Aspects of this process are discussed at length in recent works which supply many details not given here.

Natural selection requires, first, reproduction and, second, hereditary variation of such a kind as to influence the success of reproduction under existing circumstances. When those factors are present, natural selection *necessarily* occurs. In precellular evolution [a principal concern for Mora (1963)] it necessarily began when there were replicating molecules that differed in the rate or efficiency of replication. However, the pertinent unit is not the replicating molecule but the reproducing system. This was presumably a molecule at first but became a cell at the protistan level, and is a dynamic unicellular-to-multicellular ontogenetic individual at metaphytic and metazoan levels. Selection acts on the whole phenotype and can single out genes only to the extent that they have phenotypic effects separable both phenotypically and genetically from those of other genes. Although selection apparently does act in an analytically separable way on some particular molecules, it evidently does not do so as a rule. It usually acts on supramolecular phenotypic characters, on whole complexes of them, or indeed on all of them at once. Since most genes are pleiotropic and most characters are polygenic, it follows that selection usually is not concentrated on single genes, as might appear from the necessarily oversimplified models first formulated by population geneticists. Although the connection is not yet well understood, this presumably means also that it is unusual (it may even be impossible) for intermediary molecules such as enzymes and other proteins to be selected for or selected against independently of other molecules.

EFFECT OF SELECTION ON PARTICULAR FEATURES

In considering the effect of selection on particular features of an organism, it is important to judge how far these are in one direction from the genes and in the other direction from the phenotypic characters directly subject to selection. Behavior is subject to particularly strong selection, and it is probably farthest removed from the genes and also most elaborately polygenic as a rule. Some single-gene determinants of behavior are known, but they are exceptional. Proteins or, at least, intracellular enzymes are believed to be almost directly and uniquely determined by one or a few particular genes. The effect of selection will surely be influenced by the length of the functional chain from the genes to the character selected for or against. As a rule, with exceptions, the effect becomes more, not less, diffuse and less, not more, direct as the level of the gene is approached.

Zuckerkandl (1963) has argued that a molecule like hemoglobin is preferable to most "structural," or more remotely phenotypic, characters for the determination of affinities because it is so near the genes, so nearly a direct reflection of part of the DNA code. It may be added that hemoglobin is so literally vital that natural selection may here act at a level near the gene. Those are advantages in certain respects, but they are accompanied by disadvantages, and the more distantly phenotypic approach also has advantages, as Zuckerkandl notes but possibly understresses. Zuckerkandl has shown that, "from the point of view of hemoglobin structure, it appears that gorilla is just an abnormal human, or man an abnormal gorilla, and the two species form actually one continuous population." From any point of view other than that properly specified, that is of course nonsense. What the comparison seems really to indicate is that in this case, at least, hemoglobin is a bad choice and has nothing to tell us about affinities, or indeed tells us a lie. (It does show that men and gorillas are rather closely related, but that has long and more accurately been known from traditional morphological comparisons.) Of course, as Zuckerkandl points out, we should use not just one kind of molecule but many, preferably proteins. However, if one can be misleading, so can many! (Let me add that Zuckerkandl's discussion of the phylogenetic interpretation of molecular data is invaluable and, unfortunately, almost unique.)

In some respects it is a drawback that hemoglobin, various enzymes, and some other proteins are so near to the genes in the functional chain. It means that each sample is genetically determined by, and therefore provides a sample of, only an extremely minute part of the whole genetic system—apparently only two genes in the case of hemoglobin and probably only one for many enzymes. The farther a character is from the genes, the more likely it is to sample a number of genes or a really significant part of the whole genetic system. The complexity of the genetic determination of a characteristic is a positive advantage, not a disadvantage, when the purpose is to determine affinities of whole organisms. Moreover, such characters are in almost all cases those which were in fact subject to selection. On an average, the farther we are from genes the nearer we are to the action of selection, and thus the better able we are to interpret the adaptive processes involved.

When, as is usual, selection is on the phenotype and well removed from the genotype, all that matters is that the genotype should in fact result in the selectively favored phenotype under the existing conditions of development. In this sense, or beyond that point, it really can be said that the genotype does not matter in adaptive evolution. There is ample evidence, that genotype-phenotype determination is not unique in either direction. Phenotypes that are apparently identical and that seem to be equal in the fact of selection can have markedly different genotypes. There are also many systems—genetic, ontogenetic, and selectional—that tend to channel phenotypic development in the fact of considerable change or variation in genes and hence, presumably, also in many families of macromolecules. I am arguing not that any one kind of evidence on evolution—genetic, molecular, phenotypic, or other—is superior but, on the contrary, that no one kind suffices in itself.

SPECIAL PROBLEMS

The evolutionary study of molecules has raised a number of special problems, not always seen in the same way by molecular and organismal biologists. The phenomenon that has caused most trouble in attempts to determine evolutionary affinities is convergence: the development of similar characteristics by organisms of different ancestry. Any addition of evidence would be most welcome, especially if it involved characters unlikely to converge. Here the molecular biologists do not agree; Wald (1963), for example, says that convergence is much more likely at the molecular level, while Zuckerkandl (1963) independently maintains that it is less likely. To me, as an organismal biologist, it seems that Wald is probably right. Convergence to the point of identity or of seriously confusing similarity would appear to be more likely in a single kind of molecule, even one as complicated as a protein, than in such phenotypic characters as are end results of the interactions of a very large number of such molecules. Anfinsen (1959) cited an example (from the work of Sanger et al.) indicating from insulin composition that sperm whales are identical with pigs and quite different from sei whales! To be sure, a sequence of only three amino acids is involved, and both differences and resemblances could be incidental without even true convergence, but the lesson is there. Fortunately, the fact that protein and morphological convergence may be independent of each other gives a double check if the evidence of both is available.

Another problem, discussed at some length by Anfinsen (1959), arises from the evidence that proteins have parts that can vary greatly or even be removed altogether without seeming to affect function. There is also the concept of "dormant genes" [discussed by Zuckerkandl (1963), among others, and in studies which he cites; see also Zuckerkandl and Pauling (1962)]. This concept is, again, related to the hypothesis of regular, secular change in molecules, mentioned in the opening paragraph of this article. Essentially the same question has long been discussed by evolutionary biologists, in this form: Can a gene (or allele) be neutral with respect to selection? It is impossible to establish complete absence of exceptions, but so far every supposedly neutral gene that has been adequately investigated has turned out not to be neutral. There is a strong consensus that completely neutral genes or alleles must be very rare if they exist at all. To an evolutionary biologist it therefore seems highly improbable that proteins, supposedly fully determined by genes, should have nonfunctional parts, that dormant genes should exist over periods of generations, or that molecules should change in a regular but nonadaptive way.

This unsettled question could have far-reaching significance, for instance through the hypothesis [suggested but not fully supported by Anfinsen (1959)] that the invariable or fully homologous parts of proteins in different animals are the functional, or at least the most significantly functional, parts. It would then seem to follow that the actual specific differences in proteins may be little or not at all adaptive, and this again seems unlikely to an organismal biologist. However, Anfinsen also points out (and the examples could be largely multiplied from other sources) that, for instance, serum proteins with no immunochemical similarity at all may be fully and identically functional. It is certainly not true as a generalization that molecular differences among species are commonly nonfunctional or nonadaptive, and indeed I think no molecular biologist would go to that extreme.

It is undoubtedly on questions related to adaptation that an evolutionary synthesis of molecular and organismal viewpoints and data will be most useful. I shall here give briefly two further examples from work by Wald (1963 and earlier papers cited therein), not because I happen to disagree with his interpretations but because his brilliant studies provide such ideal data on the molecular basis of organismal adaptation. He shows that freshwater vertebrates generally have retinal pigments containing vitamin A_2, while marine and land vertebrates generally have A_1. He interprets this as a phylogenetic phenomenon, with A_2 in ancestral (true) fishes, supposedly freshwater forms, and A_1 developed in progressive phylogeny by marine and land descendants. He finds it inexplicable and almost an unnecessary complication that, for instance, reptiles, primitively having A_1, "revert" to A_2 when they adapt to fresh water. To an organismal biologist, the picture, including the apparent anomalies and supposed reversions, suggests interpretation in terms of adaptation, primarily, and phylogeny only secondarily. Many, but perhaps not quite all, of the observations would be explained if we assumed that A_2 is adaptive in freshwater forms and A_1, in land and saltwater forms —so much so that selection usually produced these adaptations rapidly and tended to erase purely phylogenetic effects. I have no idea what the difference in adaptation might be, but suggest that study from this point of view might clarify the molecular function involved.

A second example from Wald is his demonstration that tadpoles resemble fishes in a number of biochemical characteristics, whereas adult frogs have a biochemistry more like other land vertebrates. Amphibians were of course derived from fishes, and Wald interprets these changes as "the most striking instances we know of recapitulation." In my opinion there is no reason to invoke recapitulation and definite reason not to. As regards the species in question, it would appear that tadpoles are adapted to live in the water and adult frogs to live on land. In spite of some complications, this is the plausible explanation for nitrogen excretion: ammonia in water, urea out of it. Other changes may be less clearly adaptive but are likely, at least, to be adaptive. Some of the evidence, also given in part by Wald, is that when amphibians go from land to water, as some do, the changes tend to go in the opposite direction; they antirecapitulate!

THE ADAPTIVE SYSTEM

Finally, let us turn (or return) to the structure of the whole adaptive system, its causations, and the place of molecules in it. The most basic of all molecules, in this context at least, is DUA. Its influence is exerted, in part if not altogether, through RNA. Recognizing the RNA as an agent of DNA in this sequence, we conclude that RNA is not the cause of the eventual action: synthesis of a protein. (One could raise some delicate semantic problems here, but I think the statement can stand as written for present purposes.) Then is the DNA the causative agent in a really explanatory sense? It carries, as we say, a message (another semantic problem!) and is indeed a messenger and an agent just as much as messenger RNA is. In following the chain back we reach a really significant point of causation not when we locate the message, which is in the DNA, but when we learn where the message came from to begin with, what composed it. Any messeage composed, so to speak, by the DNA itself would be in the language of mutation. But mutations are predominantly inadaptive, and the message, beyond doubt, is almost entirely adaptive. Mutations form what may be called letters or words, to continue the now somewhat shopworn metaphor, and in that way they supply materials that permit something new to be said and that limit what can be said. However, they certainly do not compose the message in any meaningful sense.

The message, or at very least the greater part of it, relates to interaction of organism and environmemnt. The interaction involves the whole organism, and hence arises and expands from the molecular level. There must be some sort of feedback from the organism-environment interaction into DNA, and hence into the other molecules. There are, as is well known, innumerable feedback mechanisms at the molecular level itself, and many or most of these are responsive to interactions with the environment. The Neo-Lamarckians, before much was known about feedback or anything at all was known about molecular genetics, supposed that evolutionary feedback was of the same kind, within individuals and into the genetic system, whatever that might prove to be. Now, however, we do know about DNA and other essentials of the genetic system, and we know beyond serious doubt, even though it seems rather odd, that DNA is not subject to feedback within individuals. That is, as Pontecorvo (1963) has put it,

> the *structure* of the genetic material is not subject to regulatory change... although the *expression* of the genetic material...is subject to regulation—qualitative and quantitative—at all levels of organization....

Changes in individual expression—to put it figuratively, the way the message is read—do not affect the message itself. The necessary message-constructing feedback is not here but in a system of higher order: in the population and not the individual. It operates through natural selection, which operates in populations, just as populations are what really evolve. Thus, through a different approach we come again to natural selection and now see it as the most truly causative (although not the only) element in the adaptive system. Viewed in this way, it is the composer of the genetic message, and DNA, RNA, enzymes, and the other molecules in the system are successively its messengers.

REFERENCES

Anfinsen, C. B. 1959. The molecular basis of evolution. New York: Wiley.

Blum, H. F. 1961. On the origin and evolution of living machines. *Am. Scientist* 49: 474.

Caspari, E. 1958. Genetic basis of behavior. In *Behavior and evolution,* ed. A. Roe and G. G. Simpson. New Haven, Conn: Yale Univ. Press.

FLORKIN, M. 1949. *Biochemical evolution,* trans. S. Morgulis. New York: Academic Press.

GOODMAN, M. 1963. Man's place in the phylogeny of the primates as reflected in serum proteins. In *Classification and Human Evolution,* ed. S. L. Washburn. New York: Wenner-Gren Foundation.

GRANT, V. 1963. *The origin of adaptations.* New York: Columbia Univ. Press.

HILL, R. L.; BUETTNER-JANUSCH, J.; and BUETTNER-JANUSCH, V. 1963. Evolution of hemoglobin in primates. *Proc. Nat. Acad. Sci.* 50: 885.

MARGOLIASH, E. 1963. Primary structure and evolution of cytochrome c. *Proc. Nat. Acad. Sci. U.S.* 50: 672.

MAYR, E. 1963. *Animal species and evolution.* Cambridge Mass.: Harvard Univ. Press.

MORA, P. T. 1963. Urge and molecular biology. *Nature* 199: 212.

PITTENDRIGH, C. S. 1958. Adaptation, natural selection, and behavior. In *Behavior and Evolution,* ed. A. Roe and G. G. Simpson. New Haven, Conn.: Yale Univ. Press.

PONTECORVO, G. 1963. Microbial genetics: Retrospect and prospect. *Proc. Roy. Soc. London* B158, no. 1.

SIMPSON, G. G. 1964. *This view of life.* New York: Harcourt Brace Jovanovich.

SONNEBORN, T. M. 1963. Implications of the new genetics for biology and man. *Am. Inst. Biol. Sci. Bull.,* no. 22.

WALD, O. 1963. Phylogeny and ontogeny at the molecular level. In *Evolutionary Biochemistry,* ed. A. I. Oparin. London: Pergamon.

WEISS, P. 1961. From cell to molecule. In *The molecular control of cellular Activity,* ed. J. M. Allen. New York: McGraw-Hill.

WILLIAMS, C. A., JR., and WEMMYSS, C. T., JR. 1961. Experimental and evolutionary significance of similarities among serum protein antigens of man and lower primates. *Ann. N.Y. Aca. Sci.* 94:77.

ZUCKERKANDL, E. 1963. Perspectives in molecular anthropology. In *Classification and human evolution,* ed. S. L. Washburn. New York: Wenner-Gren Foundation.

———, and PAULING, L. 1962. Molecular disease, evolution and genetic heterogeneity. In *Horizons in biochemistry,* ed. M. Kasha and B. Pullman. New York: Academic Press.

Man's Genetic Future

Curt Stern

Whatever fate may be in store for our civilization, one assumption must underlie all thoughts about the future: Man will continue to exist on this globe. Assuming the human species is here to stay, what is likely to happen to us genetically? Will the human stock improve, deteriorate or remain the same? Is the future predestined, or can we direct it?

To answer such questions we must consider mankind's hereditary endowment as a whole and the distribution of this endowment among individuals. When a human being begins existence, he is compounded of an egg produced by his mother and a sperm furnished by his father. The egg and the sperm each contain thousands of different genes. Let us assume, as we may for the purpose of this discussion, that the human germ cell has exactly 20,000 genes. The individual genes can be identified by the numbers 1 to 20,000. The egg contains 20,000 genes and the sperm has the same number, each a counterpart of the corresponding gene in the egg. Thus, when egg and sperm unite, the new human being starts out (as a fertilized egg) with 20,000 pairs of genes, or a total of 40,000. Some of the pairs are identical; for example, the number 7 gene from the egg may be exactly the same as number 7 from the sperm. Other partners are slightly different; thus the sperm's number 8 gene may be distinguished by minor peculiarities from the egg's number 8, so that we may call one 8_1 and the other 8_2. We can designate the differently numbered genes (e.g., 7 and 8) as species, and the different kinds of genes of the same species (e.g., 8_1 and 8_2) as varieties.

As the fertilized egg develops, the genes multiply. Each gene builds up

From Scientific American *186, no. 2 (1952): 68–72; reprinted by permission of the author and publisher.*

next to itself a faithful reproduction of its own structure, and as the cells divide each new body cell is provided with a complete endowment of the two sets of 20,000 genes with which the fertilized egg started (except that in male children a few genes lack partners).

Every one of the more than two billion people alive on our globe today has the same 20,000 species of genes. Some of the species probably have only one variety, so that gene 7, for instance, may be exactly alike in everyone. Other species may occur in two, three four, and perhaps up to as many as 100 varieties. In any case, the total pool of genes in the earth's population at present is some 80 trillion (two billion people times 20,000 pairs of genes each). This is the storehouse from which the genetic future of man will be furnished.

The number of different possible combinations of the varieties of genes is very large. When a new individual draws on the genes that he has received from his mother and father to make a new set in his own germ cells, he may reshuffle the genes in a multitude of different ways. Take, for instance, just two genes, each of which is present in two varieties. Suppose the individual receives 8_1 and 9_1 from his mother and 8_2 and 9_2 from his father. From these he can form four different combinations to transmit to his children—8_1 and 9_1, 8_2 and 9_2, 8_1 and 9_2, or 8_2 and 9_1. With many gene pairs and varieties to choose from, vast numbers of different combinations are possible. The number is so huge, indeed, that of the hundreds of billions of sperms one man produces during his lifetime, no two are likely to be identical in the combination of genic varieties. The shuffling of the genic cards makes it unlikely that any person on earth (with the exception of identical twins) has ever exactly duplicated any other person in genic make-up, or ever will in the future.

This does not mean, however, that our inheritance is an entirely random affair. If men and women were completely promiscuous in mating—socially, racially, and geographically—then one genic combination would be as likely as any other, and people might vary individually much more than they actually do. There are times and places where man does approach such random mating, for example, during great migrations and large military occupations, when one group may sow its genic varieties among those of another group. As a rule, however, a potential child within a given group does not draw on the whole storehouse of mankind's genes. Usually his genes will come from a socially, nationally, and racially segregated part of the store.

Yet for thousands of years the barriers separating the store of human genes into compartments have been progressively lowered, and with the increase of human mobility in our era of world-wide transportation many barriers will undoubtedly disappear. Tribes, minor races, and other subgroups will vanish. How far this process of joining the genetic endowment of mankind into large pools will go, we can only guess. A diffusion of genes from one group to another is bound to occur, however slowly and gradually, and in time it will tend to eliminate all partitions in our storehouse.

Will this be good, bad, or immaterial for mankind? We cannot answer this question without evaluating the racial differences of the present. Have the present combinations of genic varieties originated in a haphazard way, or are they the result of selective forces in the earliest prehistory of mankind which adapted the different races to specific environments? It is probable that both chance and design have played a role. Thus, the racial differences in blood types (Rh and so on) seem to be just accidental and of no adaptive significance. On the other hand, it is likely that the differences in pigmentation and breadth of nose between the Africans and the Caucasians were evolved to fit the differing climates in which these peoples lived. Does this mean that the leveling of the genic partitions will make the world's peoples less fit to cope with their respective environments? Such a conclusion might be justified if we could assume that the originally adaptive traits have the same significance today as they had 100,000 years ago. But has not man created new influences which effectively alter his environment in such a fashion that the external physical factors continuously decline in importance? Housing and clothing, food and medicine, occupation and training have changed radically, and it may well be that these new factors have superseded the old ones.

What of mental differences among races? Whether such differences exist has not been established; exact knowledge of the genic distinctions between groups is most lacking where it most matters. This is not only because psychologists have found it difficult to invent standard tests to measure the inborn capacities of different races, but also because there is great variability in mental traits within any one group.

The 20,000 pairs of genes in the fertilized egg control a multitude of interactions whose full complexity far transcends our understanding. In every trait of the individual numerous genically induced reactions are involved. There is no absolute, one-to-one relation between a specific gene and a specific trait—no gene for dark hair or for height or for "mental endowment." Each gene is only a link in the development of a trait; it is necessary for the process that results in the specific trait, but it does not invariably produce the trait in question. A gene for clubfoot, for instance, makes for an inclination, a potentiality, toward the appearance of clubfoot, but whether this potentiality will become reality depends on the interplay of life processes. A slight variation in timing or in the environment may decide one way or the other. The clubfoot defect may appear in one foot, in both feet, or in neither.

The amount of variation in some life prepocesses is small, in others large. A man's blood type, for example, remains the same throughout his life, but the color of his hair changes. Are the traits that distinguish different races variable in expression or invariable products of their genic endowments? It seems as a first approximation that genes for physical traits are more rigid in expression than those for mental traits. The Caucasian's hair remains straight or wavy and the Negro's kinky, regardless of any change in environment or training. It is otherwise with mental traits. A normal man's genetic endowment provides him with a wide potential for mental performance, from very low to very high. As with a rubber balloon, the state of expansion of his mind at any given time is hardly a measure of its expansibility. In human evolution those genes that allow the greatest mental adaptability, that possess the greatest plasticity of expression, seem to have undergone preferential selection in all races. If this is actually so, then the different genic varieties for mental traits may be comparably distributed among all human groups, and the disappearance of the present barriers subdividing man's genic storehouse would not greatly affect mankind's mental potentialities.

What role will differences in reproduction play among the various socio-economic groups within populations? It is well known that the lower socio-economic layers of Western societies have higher birth rates than the upper ones. Do these layers differ in their stocks of genes? We cannot say with any certainty. The difficulties of research in this important field are great. We do not know, for instance, to what extent intelligence scores reflect true genetic factors in addition to education and environment, which they certainly reflect to a large degree. Nevertheless, the evidence strongly suggests that hereditary mental differences between socio-economic groups do exist. The mean intelligence scores of children at the higher socio-economic levels are consistently higher than those of lower groups, whether the tests are made in the U.S., in the U.S.S.R., or in any other country. That environment is not the sole reason for such differences is indicated by comparative studies on comparable groups of children, particularly twins reared together and separately. It is hard to avoid the conclusion that there are mean differences in the genetic endowment of different socio-economic groups, although the individual endowments within each group cover the whole range from very low to very high.

If there are genetic differences between groups, then the differences in their birth rates will result in selective increase of some genic varieties and decrease of others in the population as a whole. Since the groups that seem less well-endowed intellectually produce the most children, a deterioration of the genetic endowment of the population should result.

This large-scale difference in reproduction rates is a rather recent phenomenon. It is primarily the result of birth control, which did not become an important social practice until the second half of the 19th century. So far the upper and middle groups of Western countries have adopted birth control much more widely than the lower ones. But there is reason to believe that the use of contraceptive measures will spread through the whole population, and that the group differentials in fertility will be diminished, although perhaps not obliterated.

Before we become too alarmed over the possibility that the genetic stocks of Western peoples may deteriorate, it would be well to obtain an estimate of the rate of this suspected deterioration. Such analyses as have been made suggest that the decrease of valuable genic varieties is probably much smaller than a naive consideration would suggest. High intelligence undoubtedly is based not on single varieties of genes but on the cooperation of many genes. The valuable varieties must be present, singly or in partial combinations, even in the great mass of individuals who score low in intelligence. From there they can, in the course of a single generation, reconstitute an appreciable number of the "best" combinations. In other words, the population at large constitutes a great reservoir, and the possible loss of valuable genic varieties possessed by the small upper layers of the population tells only a part of the story.

Those who consider man's genetic future usually lay emphasis on the possibility that the human race is preserving and accumulating genes that cause physical and mental defects. In former times, it is argued, most of the unfortunates who inherited these defects died an early death, often before they could transmit their unfavorable genes to another generation, whereas now medical and social care keeps these people alive and permits them to pass on the bag genes to the next generation. There is some truth in this argument, but the case is overstated. The most severely handicapped individuals, such as idiots and complete cripples, usually do not reproduce, either because they cannot or because they are kept in confinement. Furthermore, civilization has neutralized some of the so-called defects; thanks to the development of clothing, for example, the naked modern man is able to live in cold climates as well as his hypothetical furry ancestor. In other words, the survival of "bad" genes in modern times is often possible because the ingenuity of modern man provides for environments in which the "bad" genes lose their adjective.

Nevertheless, there *are* many defective genes in the human storehouse that are loading man's genetic future unfavorably. They are the anomalies, such as the inherited juvenile cataract, the cleft palate, the predisposition to schizophrenia, which are not serious enough to prevent reproduction but cannot be remedied readily or completely by medical treatment. It would seem desirable to exclude the bearers of such unfavorable genic varieties from reproduction. But this is a matter of some difficulty: even assuming we could adopt feasible measures for doing this, how are we to identify all those who should be prevented from reproducing? Many, indeed the majority, of the bearers of bad genes do not themselves show any abnormality; they are merely carriers, and the defect appears only in their descendants.

Any consideration of man's genetic future must also, of course, take account of sudden changes, or mutations, that may produce new varieties of genes, and of the possibility that the 20,000 species man now possesses may increase or decrease in number. Most mutations, however, seem to produce genic varieties not very different from those already in existence, and the processes that might add to or subtract from the basic set of 20,000 genes are so rare that their significance for the future of man appears very limited. Most likely man's future will be determined by recombinations and changes in the proportions of the known varieties of genes, rather than the creation of new varieties.

The changes in mankind's genic substance proceed more or less automatically. The eugenics movement proposes to make the process less haphazard in the future by applying nationally designed population policies, looking toward the elimination of genetic misfits and an increase in the number of those with superior genetic endowments. The difficulties of such a program are great, and the enthusiasm of its proponents, who have often been motivated by race or class prejudices, has been a drawback rather than a help to the success of the movement. It is now clear that we need very much more knowledge before a far-reaching blueprint can be designed. Fortunately, it is also clear that the problem is not as urgent as it seemed to past generations. The storehouse of human genes is so immense that neither mankind as a whole nor any of its groups is likely to undergo any serious genetic deterioration within the next century or two. If the threatened breakdown of our civilization on the cultural level can be avoided, we shall have time to work out the tasks of the genetic future.

These still utopian tasks will be threefold—biological, political, and ideological. In the biological realm we need first to learn how to recognize the presence of undesirable and desirable genic varieties even when they are borne by apparently normal carriers. We may attempt to suppress bad genes, not only by controlling reproduction but, better still, by identifying and separating the desirable germ cells from the undesirable ones, which are likely to be present in every individual. We may attempt to improve our endowment of genic varieties by artificial mutation with radiation and chemicals. Mutations are usually toward the worse, but the future may well place specific tools in our hands with which we can change less desirable into more desirable genic varieties. We will also make further progress on the road toward the artificial culturing of human ovarian and testicular tissues and the rearing to maturity of human embryos obtained by fertilization in such cultures.

Progress in these biological fields very likely will run ahead of our social and political thinking. When the biologists have discovered how to put together combinations of genes for given traits, they will have to be told what traits are desirable and what undesirable. And when they can grow human beings in culture vessels, society will have to decide what use should be made of that feat.

The decisons to be made will be revolutionary for man's thinking, his private life, and his social organization. They will carry with them the danger of his loss of freedom. They will force man to a reconsideration of the problems of free will *versus* determinism, in a more urgent form than ever before. Shall we be glad that we do not have to decide all these problems in our time?

SUPPLEMENTARY READINGS

DOBZHANSKY, T. *Genetics and the Origin of Species*. New York: Columbia University Press, 1951.

LIVINGSTONE, F. B. Anthropological implications of sickle-cell gene distribution in West Africa. I. M. F. Ashley Montagu (ed.), *Culture and the Evolution of Man,* pp. 343–354. New York: Oxford University Press, 1962.

MOURANT, A. E. *The Distribution of the Human Blood Groups*. Oxford: Blackwell Scientific Publications, 1954.

eight

HUMAN VARIATION

Our civilization has been plagued with a number of social problems supposedly based on biological differences among the members of our species. The division of mankind into phenotypic segments was originally a taxonomic device which represented a preliminary step to the study of geographic variation. However, what was originally a biological aid to the scientist became a tool of the unscrupulous. Emotional attitudes became confused with biological fact, and the true nature of such factors as environmental influences were totally ignored or misrepresented. The following articles attempt to cover the many facets of a voluminous literature on this subject.

Race as an Evolutionary Episode

Frederick S. Hulse

An examination of living human groups shows that we have not been exempt from the normal processes of local evolutionary change. It would be difficult to mistake a Chinese for a Dane, or a Hottentot for a Sioux. Genetic differences between these groups have accumulated throughout the thousands of generations during which they have shared only a minute portion of their ancestry. Certain constellations of characteristics have become typical of the people of East Asia, others have become just as typical of Europeans. It is a matter of interest and importance that evolutionary diversification has not proceeded still further among humans, and that by all biological criteria, we remain members of a single species.

Since we are all members of a single species today, and since the human fossils from very early times are, in many respects, so different from any modern skeletal material, it has become a very common opinion that racial diversity postdates the appearance of Homo sapiens. The phylogenetic tree which has been most popular among anthropologists is shown in Figure 1. In this type of arborization the various fossils antedating those of the Upper Paleolithic are ordinarily shown as side branches which suffered termination through extinction rather than through evolution. As a rule, they have been given specific or even generic status, at least by their discoverers. Only one central line ascends triumphantly to the very peak of the tree, upon which twigs represent whichever racial stocks suit the fancy of the designer. It would appear from an examination of such a diagram that we have never succeeded in digging up our grandfathers, but only our great uncles, who were childless.

From American Anthropologist *64 (1962): 929–45; reprinted by permission of the author and the American Anthropological Association.*

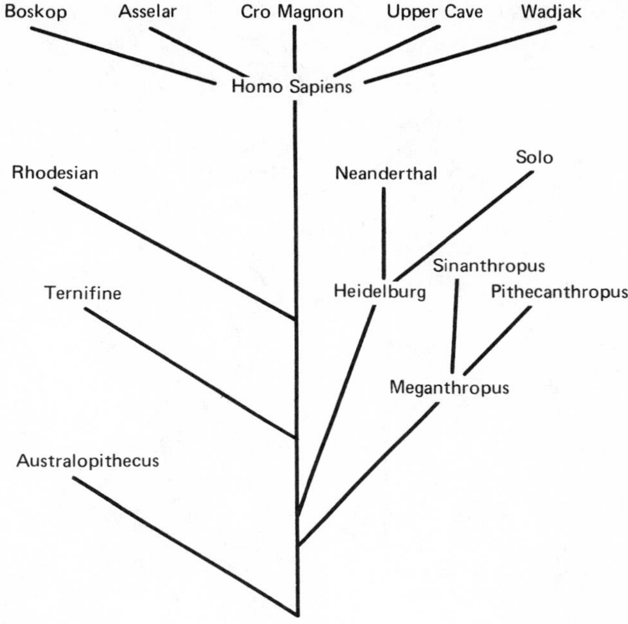

FIGURE 1. *Phylogenetic tree. (Adapted by Jacquelyn Hetrick from drawing by S. M. Nagoda.)*

Not all students of human evolution, of course, have accepted this scheme in all details. Hrdlicka, for example, maintained that Neanderthal man was ancestral to ourselves. Hooton could not bring himself to believe that hybridity had not taken place between our unfound ancestors and at least some Neanderthaloids. And a few authors, going to the opposite extreme, assumed a total separation between the so-called major racial stocks dating back to the Pliocene or earlier. This extreme opinion, however, has no evidence of any nature to support it. The different sorts of people whom we find in the world today just are not that different.

At the same time there is an inherent improbability in the notion that only a small proportion of the earlier populations of men left any offspring at all. It would seem strange that the bones of our direct ancestors elude us, while we continue to find those of their close relatives. Perhaps the standard design of the ancestral tree, so useful in representing the descent of different species, has misled us. Is such a design appropriate as a representation of sub-specific diversification? Do all the Middle and Lower Paleolithic human fossils differ enough from one another to deserve separate specific names?

In my opinion, the answer to both questions is: No. Weidenreich, a number of years ago, proposed a design to represent the immediate phylogeny of Homo sapiens, not in the form of a branching tree, but of a grid or trellis, similar to that shown in Figure 2. Hooton showed a vine of which

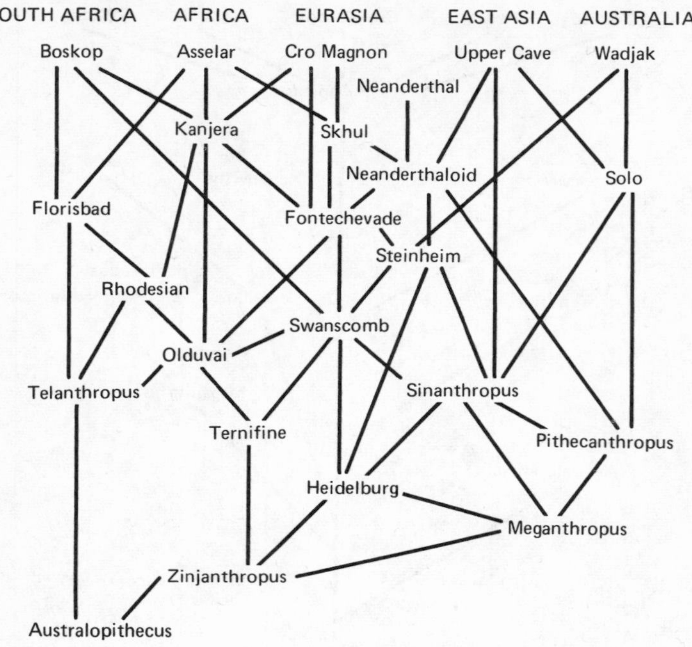

FIGURE 2. *Phylogenetic trellis. (Adapted by Jacquelyn Hetrick.)*

the branches coalesced, as well as separating, to indicate what he believed to be the relationship between the living human races. Both of them realized that, within a species, genetic continuity exists, and that any diagram which does not show this fact is bound to be misleading. Weidenreich even pointed out certain characteristics of Sinanthropus, especially in the teeth, which he believed foreshadowed some of the characteristics of the living inhabitants of eastern Asia. Many of his colleagues refused to see any significance in these resemblances, but on grounds of chance alone one would expect to find a greater concentration of genes derived from Sinanthropus in East Asia than in Europe or Africa. This does not mean, of course, that Sinanthropus, when alive, looked like a modern Chinese. An examination of the fossil remains of this early type demonstrates that he did not. Mankind as a whole has evolved to a very considerable degree during the last five hundred thousand years, and we have no evidence to suggest that any contemporary of Sinanthropus could be mistaken for any contemporary of ours. Although, except for Sinanthropus and Pithecanthropus, the fossil evidence from this period is slim, we find all taxonomists agreed that the human beings of that time should be classified in another species than our own. Confirmed splitters speak of different genera. Indeed, until a generation ago, Sinanthropus and Pithecanthropus were given separate generic status. It is interesting to note that Ashley Montagu, who denies the existence of races within Homo sapiens, was a fervent advocate of generic distinction between the Chinese and Javanese forms, on the basis of the diastema found in the latter, but absent in the former.

Since we are fortunate enough to have several indivduals from both of these groups, it is possible, and therefore necessary, to say that they do appear to represent separate populations. The available remains of their western contemporaries, found at Heidelberg and Ternifine, are so scanty as to demand great caution in our conclusions concerning them, yet the small size of the teeth in the large Heidelberg jaw is suggestive, at least, of a certain degree of difference between this form and the others. Would it not be more reasonable, however, to think in terms of population differences in different parts of the world during the lower Paleolithic of the same order of magnitude which we find among populations living in different parts of the world today? It may well be that the accumulation of evidence in the future will lead us to the conclusion that mankind was then divided into separate geographic species; or that, on the contrary, people then resembled one another much more closely than is now the case. The evidence which we have at present, however, leads me to infer that then, as now, human populations living in various parts of the world could reasonably be classified as races, but not as species.

What is implied by the term "race"? To some people it is just another nasty four-letter word, not to be uttered in decent company, with the hope that it may thus be conjured out of existence. This abhorrence is easy to understand, for the word has been badly misused in many ways and has carried varied implications. But so has another four letter word: Love. In neither case does banning the word appear to be the type of action which will assist in solving the problems connected with its use. Ashley Montagu raises a more serious problem in stating that the word does not correspond to any reality in the actual world and is therefore dangerously misleading. To him, the word race contains the implication of eternal unchangeability, so that it cannot be made to fit into an evolutionary framework. It is true, of course, that the use of the term is rather older than the demonstration by Darwin of how evolution is brought about. But Darwin does not appear to have felt it necessary to avoid the use of the word species, which in earlier days had carried the implication of eternal unchangeability as well as separate creation. No matter what the origin and destiny of species may be, the word represents a valid taxonomic category. In the same way, recognizable subspecific categories are known to exist within many, but not necessarily all species. According to Simpson, the recognition of subspecific taxa is appropriate if this happens to be useful to the taxonomist, which it will certainly be if there is some nonarbitrary element in the definition of the groupings concerned. A grouping may be considered as real, and as existing in nature rather than in the taxonomist's mind, if three-quarters of the individuals in adjacent subspecies are unequivocally determinable.

Subspecific categories, whether we call them races, breeds, varieties, subspecies, demes, breeding populations, isolates, or anything else, are likely to lack the sharp boundaries which characterize species. In the absence of artificial hindrances, genetic communication between any one of them and its neighbors is open and is likely to be frequent, in direct contrast to the lack of genetic communication between adjacent species. Breeding between members of separate species, although often technically possible, is likely to take place only when artifically encouraged, as for instance in the case of captive animals which have no other sexual partners available. Hybrids between valid species are therefore as rare, in the natural world, as hybrids between subspecific categories are common.

Despite this fact, it is sometimes easier to distinguish members of one breed of a species from members of another breed of the same species than it is to distinguish members of one breed within that species from members of another species. An Alsatian, for example, looks more like a wolf than it looks like a Dachshund. Variety within a species, clearly, can proceed to a remarkable degree with no break in the chain of genetic continuity. So long as this chain is not broken, the subspecific taxa are always capable of merging with one another, and vanishing: animal breeders must exercise constant care to maintain those genetic characteristics which they happen to favor. In the wild, only geographic isolation can be depended upon to keep naturally existing subspecies distinctive from one another. One would expect then, in the history of any species, that subspecific taxa should be evolved from time to time within it, but that most of them would eventually disappear, as such, because of random mating, as the opportunity arose, between the members of the various natural groupings.

Dobzhansky in his article, "Species after Darwin," states that

> Races are sometimes referred to as incipient species...it does not, however, follow that every race will at some future time be a species.... When the interbreeding of populations does not lower the fitness, the stimulus for the development of reproductive isolation is lacking.

He is writing, in this instance, about genetic mechanisms enforcing, or at least promoting, reproductive isolation; he is not writing about external circumstances, such as geographical barriers, which may lead to such isolation for a certain period of time. Among living human populations, all the evidence at our disposal would indicate that interbreeding between populations whose ancestors had long been isolated from each other does not lower the fitness. Europeans, after their invasion of the Americas, interbred freely with the Indians, producing offspring who appear to be at least as fit as either parental stock. Our knowledge of prehistory would suggest that these two groups had shared no ancestry whatever for at least one thousand generations. A great many millions of Latin Americans today are of such mixed ancestry, and the birthrate in that part of the world indicates adequate fertility. Scientific studies of European-Hottentot hybrids in South Africa and of European-Polynesian hybrids in the South Pacific demonstrate that fitness has been preserved, and perhaps even enhanced, by such mixtures. It would certainly seem that human races show no signs whatever of being incipient species. On the contrary, some of the populations which are classed as races by Coon, Garn, and Birdsell have come into existence as a result of mixtures which took place within the last few score generations. Within the genetic continuum of any species, the genesis of a new race by means of hybridization may be anticipated whenever the circumstances are opportune. Human fossil remains indicate that this sort of diversification between contemporary populations took place during quite remote as well as more recent times.

It is also clear, however, that long continued free interchange of genes on a random basis must result in the complete merging of such previously distinctive populations as may have existed earlier. In the absence of historic documentation, whether in the form of written records or of skeletal remains, any attempt at description of the biological characteristics of such now submerged racial groupings is hazardous at best. It is often alleged, for instance, that separate races such as Nordics, Alpines, and Mediterraneans once existed in Europe. At present, there are clines of frequency for such characteristics as blondness of hair and eyes, various series of blood-types, brachycephaly, stature, and numerous other items within that continent. It must be noted at once, however, that clines divide frequencies of characters, not sorts of organisms: the clines which we find in Europe are not racial boundaries in any sense. Blondness is most frequent in the north, red hair along the Atlantic Coast, brachycephaly in the east, short stature in the south, and so on. If we draw clines for the frequency of as many as half a dozen characteristics on a map of Europe, a crazy-quilt pattern is seen, and nothing more. To reconstruct racial history on the basis of such data would be out of the question, and the notion of separate races within this region was exploded by Huxley and Haddon. Fortunately, for this continent historic and prehistoric documentation does exist. Some, but far from all, of the data concerning living people can be made to fit with what we learn from a study of European history. But to all intents and purposes, breeding in Europe has been random enough to submerge any previously existing distinctive populations. Any classification of Europeans, purporting to show subspecific or racial differences, is really arbitrary rather than natural and would have to be abstracted from such a diagram as is shown in Figure 3, derived from Simpson's *Principles of Animal Taxonomy*. As can be seen, any one of a number of groupings would appear to be equally valid. Of course, different types may be rather more frequent in some areas than in others. Individuals of so-called Nordic type—tall, leptorrhine, dolichocephalic, and blond—are rare in Italy, Greece, and Spain; whereas, in Norway and Sweden as much as 10 percent of the population of some valleys may combine all of these features. But types within a breeding population are by no means races, and the inclusion of such types among the 31 races listed by Coon, Garn, and Birdsell is incongruous with the rest of their seminal book, *Races*. Only a few minor populations, such as the Basques and the Lapps, appear to differ at all sharply in gene-frequencies at several loci from their neighbors. Indeed, as far back as the Upper Paleolithic, the range and variety among the European skeletal remains which are available for study indicate the lack of racial divisions among them.

Yet these early skeletons do appear to be those of Europeans rather than those of Orientals or Negroes. They closely resemble skeletal remains

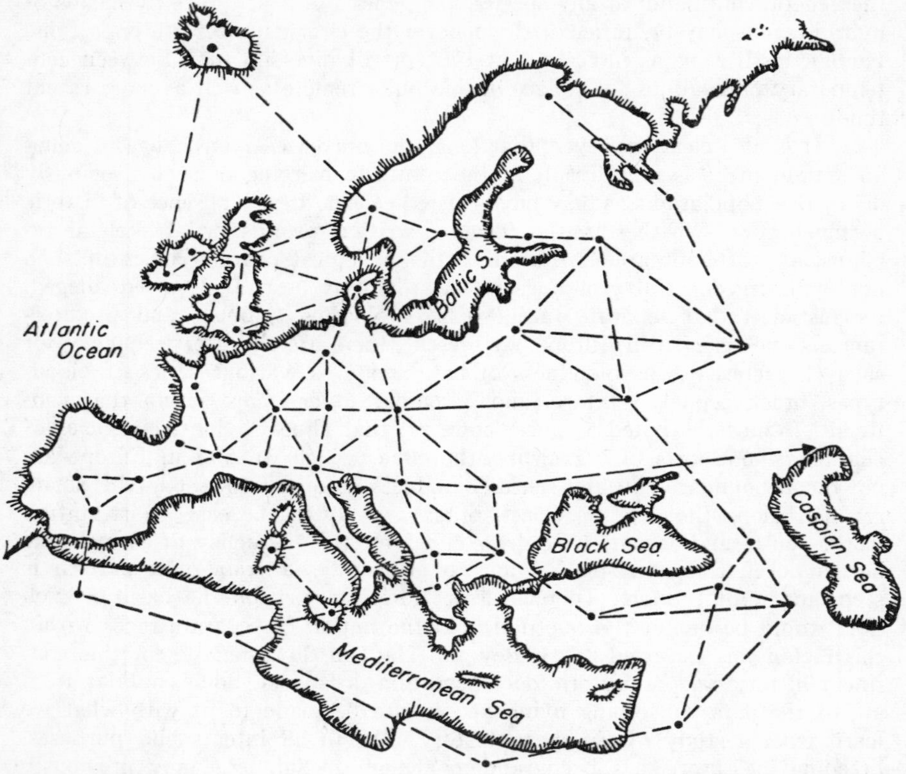

FIGURE 3. *Lines of genetic communication in Europe. (Adapted by Jacquelyn Hetrick.)*

from North Africa and the Middle East, but are much less similar to those from Boskop, Asselar, Kanjera, and others from Africa south of the Sahara. At the same time, as Weidenreich has pointed out, the Wadjak specimens have strong affinities to modern native Australians, and those of the Upper Cave at Choukoutien show some characteristics typical of the present inhabitants of northeastern Asia. The earliest remains from the Americas do not differ to any great extent from much later or even recent American Indian skeletons. Unfortunately, our data from places other than Europe and the Mediterranean area are still far too scanty. Yet what is avaliable would suggest that during the Upper Paleolithic, as during earlier times, different parts of the world were inhabited by populations having different bodily characteristics. Most, but not all, of these ancient specimens are more rugged in build than is the bulk of the world's population today. Since modern Europeans are, on the average, distinctly less pedomorphic than are most non-Europeans, this fact tends to obscure the extent of divergence, among early populations, which would otherwise be apparent. Evolution within the various populations has certainly been proceeding since, just as it had been before, and differing circumstances have led to selection pressures in different directions.

The South African Bushmen and the aboriginals of Australia are among the few living peoples who still pursue their livelihood in a manner reminiscent of that which characterized all peoples five or six hundred generations ago. Selection (or drift?) among the former has led to the still further development of the pedomorphic qualities foreshadowed by Boskop. Among the latter, however the contrary has been the case. Many of their skeletal characteristics have remained similar to those which most men possessed in earlier times, with the result that numerous skeletons from as far apart as Lagoa Santa and Afalou have been misleadingly labeled Australoid. Why the Australians have remained conservative while the Bushmen have not we do not know. It is interesting to note that the Bushmen and the Australians are divergent in such characteristics as blood-types and dermatoglyphics as well as in skeletal structure and general hirsuteness: gene-flow between their ancestors must have been infinitesimal for a very long time indeed.

In Paleolithic times communication between widely separated parts of the world was certainly difficult and probably slow. Hunters and collectors may range over a considerable territory, but for sound practical reasons are reluctant to move beyond the range to which they are accustomed. There is ample evidence that some migrations did take place, but to extrapolate from this and jump to the conclusion that our Old Stone Age ancestors were busy milling around all over the world is quite unjustified. As an explanation of assumed similarities between populations in different parts of the world, the hypothesis of widespread migration is to be received with profund skepticism, unless it is accompanied by supporting data from archeology and linguistic distribution. It seems more cautious to assume gene-flow by means of mating between adjacent groups as the more ordinary means for spreading hereditary characteristics. From Ajit's study of the Juang, an aboriginal tribe in Orissa, we learn that the average distance of movement in marriage is, at present, only three kilometers. He has calculated that, at this rate, a new mutation might be expected to travel about 50 kilometers in one hundred generations. From Peking to Paris is more than ten thousand kilometers, so that four hundred thousand years might be expected to elapse before a mutation in one place reached the other. Doubtless settlements were much further apart during the Paleolithic, so that, with an equal degree of deme exogamy, genetic transmission would have been very much speeded up, but it would certainly have been very slow during the time when walking was the only available means of transportation. It is not, therefore, strange to find that the Swanscombe skull is so different from those of Sinanthropus, although both of them date from the Mindel-Riss interglacial. Distances within Europe are minimal compared to distances between France and China, or either of these with South Africa. It would be perfectly reasonable to expect that such natural geographical barriers as oceans, glaciated mountain ranges, or deserts would channel such gene-flow as existed along specific routes. If this indeed took place, the proper diagram to represent the relationships between peoples in the world after the end of the Würm Glaciation would be one such as is shown in Figure 4, also modified from Simpson.

This is in sharp contract to the European-Mediterranean situation, since it shows a natural rather than arbitrary set of divisions into subgroups within the genetic continuum. At other times during human history, existing lines of communication would certainly alter: old ones might vanish and new ones appear. But at all times some barriers would be bound to exist to channel gene-flow. Thus the conditions which might be expected to promote the evolution, and the fluctuation, of perfectly valid sub-specific taxa have been in existence during most, if not almost all of human history. A number of things should be noted in the clustering of populations which is apparent on this chart. In the first place, not all are of equal dimensions: racial groups need not be equal in population, or even of the same order of magnitude. Population size is totally irrelevant to the degree of genetic distinctness: small groups are not necessarily branches of big ones. In the second place, some are intermediate between other clusters: racial groups may be intermediate in gene-frequencies between other such groups. Nor need this be the result of hybridity: it may be a response to intermediate conditions. In the third place, some clusters are in communication with only one other, some with two, and some with even more than that. This chart does not represent a neatly ordered filing system: it simply attempts to represent lines of genetic communication.

Within this framework, of course, selective pressures have been at work since the beginning. The necessity to adapt to the circumstances of the time and place, and natural selection of those best fitted for survival and reproduction, continues among humans as among nonhuman organisms. But

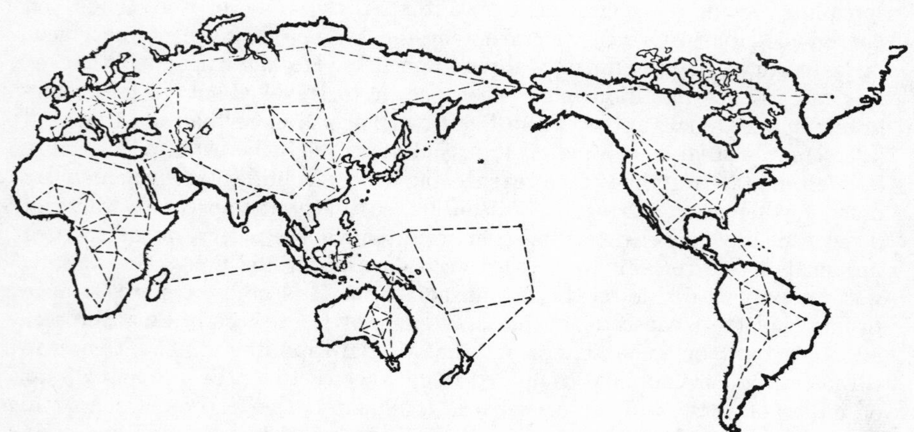

FIGURE 4. *Lines of genetic communication in the world. (Adapted by Jacquelyn Hetrick.)*

as time has gone on, our ancestors, in developing culture, have succeeded in modifying the surrounding circumstances to a greater and greater degree. The ability to do so has of course proved advantageous in all parts of the world and at all times, with the result that orthoselection has tended to develop the mental abilities of mankind to an equivalent degree in all populations, as was pointed out by Dobzhansky and Ashley Montagu. Adaptation to the requirements of culture must have become necessary at a very early time among all proto-human populations, and since these requirements are similar in all societies, parallel evolution towards increased intelligence, increased emotional adjustability, and increased motor skills in dealing with tools presumably took place. Adaptation to the requirements of culture is very probably dependent upon the well-known plasticity of man, which is one aspect of his individual versatility: a characteristic which has had high survival value for our species. As Thoday points out, a high degree of heterozygosity within any population tends to enhance this useful characteristic, which is often considered to be a sign of evolutionary progress.

Furthermore, at some time, perhaps rather early in the development of human culture, an idea concerning sexual behavior arose which has, since then, become a cultural universal and had a universal effect. This idea is the incest taboo, and its effect has been to promote gene flow. We do not know to what extent other primates mate outside their group of origin, but during his careful and prolonged studies of baboons, Washburn observed only two successful cases of intergroup migration. Since they lack ideas, there is no abhorrence among them to mating within such a group. All field studies of nonhuman primates agree on this point. Insofar as any close kinfolk become unavailable as sexual partners, however, gratification must be sought elsewhere. Rules concerning availability vary a great deal among different peoples today, but there are always rules of some sort, so that there is a greater amount of pressure favoring the exchange of genes between different human groups than exists among nonhuman creatures. The lines of genetic communication within the human species have been kept open, because of this universal habit, to a greater extent than is true of any other species, and the result must always have been to minimize the differences which would otherwise have developed between populations.

As time went on and technology improved, our ancestors began to build—although very slowly at first—a new environment within which they lived, sheltered to some degree from the conditions of the outside world. The division of labor, tools, fire, language, and many other aspects of culture began to form a protective screen which reduced the effect of differences in natural circumstances existing in different parts of the world. These aspects of culture also have tended to result in orthoselection and the minimization of divergent evolutionary trends within the species. During the last few thousand years technological revolutions have taken place earlier among some societies than among others, so that among some populations the protective screen of culture has become much more effective, but by far the greater part of human evolution took place before this divisive influence came into existence. Thus, for many thousands of generations, the influence of culture must have tended to guide the course of human evolution in the same direction wherever men lived, even though not necessarily at the same speed in all places.

A few aspects of culture may have tended in the other direction, and these should certainly be mentioned. For instance, the division of labor in itself should have made the emphasizing of secondary sexual characteristics easier than it would otherwise have been; and we find in all peoples that differences in appearance due to sex are of the same sort. However, ideals of desirability differ from one society to another, and Darwin suggested that, as a result of this fact, racial characteristics began to develop by means of sexual selection. This is a dubious proposition, but it is possible that existing differences may have been reinforced in this way. Linton believed that he had found evidence of this among the Tanala in Madagascar. Even if all adults in preliterate societies marry, not all of them produce or raise the same number of offspring. Among civilized peoples, Spuhler and Clark have found in Michigan a higher fecundity among males with large heads and women with narrow noses. Henriques has found that, in Jamaica, females having some approximation to physical characteristics of Caucasians are able to attract males who will assume more responsibility for their offspring. Elston has found definitive positive correlations in physical features such as eye color and lip thickness between mates in Sweden, but has not indicated whether their marriages are more or less fecund than are others. Unfortunately, no one has bothered to collect data concerning possible relationships between fecundity and physical characteristics among preliterate peoples.

Furthermore, human culture makes it possible for very small groups indeed to maintain an existence, and to do so even when completely out of contact with the rest of the species. Under such conditions genetic drift can become effective in determining the relative frequency of alleles in future generations. Examination has shown that peoples in remote places, and those who are known to have had a relatively high number of their ancestors in common, are the ones most likely to have unusual gene-frequencies. It is perfectly possible that a number of the ways in which races differ from one another are, under these circumstances, nonadaptive insofar as biological survival value is concerned. This idea, which used to be considered orthodox, has recently become a bit unfashionable. It should not for that reason be discarded.

At the same time it is clear that climatic and other factors of the environment have played a great part in guiding the evolution of human races. Correlations between nasal index and climate were documented on a large scale more than a generation ago. More recently, Roberts has demonstrated correlations between climate and both weight and basal metabolism. The peculiar utility of Mongoloid facial features for hunting under frigid conditions was noted by Coon, Garn and Birdsell. Marrett suggested iodine economy as an explanation of the hair-characteristics of Mongoloids. The function of heterozygosity at the sickle-cell locus, as a protection against malaria, has been demonstrated by Allison and others. Brues has pointed out that the greatly skewed distribution of ABO blood-types must indicate some selective advantage for heterozygosis at this locus as well. The studies of Vogel suggest that the relative frequency of blood-type O in different parts of the world may be due to the fact that the bubonic plague bacillus contains the H antigen; he also finds that smallpox is more severe among persons of type A, at least in India. Selection by contagious disease has obviously become increasingly important since the Neolithic, and it is possible, at least in the case of pulmonary diseases, that this might have resulted in some depression of stature by eliminating those who were growing most rapidly during adolescence.

Body build which, together with pigmentation, is among the most obvious ways in which various populations differ from each other, appears also to be among those traits which can most plausibly be explained as a climatic adaptation, and climate is clearly an aspect of the environment which has been important from the very beginning, and in all parts of the world. All of our ancestors have had to adapt to climatic stress, whereas most other stresses have been less universal. At the same time, we must remember that different adaptations to similar forms of stress may come into existence. The Neanderthal people of Europe during the Würm Glaciation do not seem to have had a Mongoloid facial appearance at all. Deep orbits may have served to protect their eyes from freezing, and their enlarged maxillary sinus—a feature lacking in all living races—may have served to warm the air they breathed in. Among living peoples, the natives of Tierra del Fuego do not have the same mechanisms to protect their bodies from chilling as have the natives of Australia, though both appear to get along equally well in cold, but not constantly frigid, weather without clothing. The Papago and other Indians of the southwestern desert in the United States are far from skinny, as many other desert-dwellers tend to be, but their limbs are frequently long. As Baker points out, climate must always be considered in relation to culture. Melanesians are alleged to suffer fewer ill effects from malaria than do their Polynesian neighbors, yet they lack the abnormal hemoglobins which appear to confer some immunity against this disease among Africans. It is not unlikely that blondness among northwest Europeans is an adaptation to the necessity of synthesizing vitamin-D in a rather sunless climate, but the Northwest Coast Indians, under the same conditions, have much darker skins: their diet includes plenty of oil from the fish which has been their staple food.

Selection can only work on the material which is available, and the conditions under which the remote ancestors of any racial group lived are bound to affect the way in which such a group adapts to new conditions. We all have ancestors as well as necessities. American Indians, most if not all of whose ancestors arrived via the Arctic, tend to retain some characteristics which are best explained as Arctic adaptations, even though they now dwell in the Amazon Valley. All too many of us, no matter what our racial origin, are capable of storing up excess fat when food is plentiful; this must have been a useful ability when meals were less easily available. Light eyes and fair skin have by no means been eliminated from the gene pools of the middle Eastern and North African peoples. During the Würm Glaciation, this part of the world apparently had a climate somewhat similar to that of northern Europe today, so that selection for blondness ought to have taken place among the populations which lived there at the time, if indeed blondness is adaptive in such a climate. It may be noted that there is no archeological evidence of the consumption of sea food in this part of the world until rather late in this period.

Racial characteristics are not eternally unchangeable, but neither does the selection which causes evolution take place overnight. Race is an evolutionary episode, and racial evolution proceeds at a slow pace. As conditions change, no matter how the change may be brought about, new selective forces replace old ones, and individuals who might earlier have been successful now die. But the constant flow of genes from one population to another may either speed up or slow down any shift of gene-frequencies due to local adaptation. Travel to great distances has become so rapid and so easy by now, that such gene flow is a more important factor in human evolution than is adaptation to purely local circumstances. During most of human history, however, this cannot have been the case. Even when racial mixture takes place, one cannot expect that gene-frequencies among the resulting offspring will be predictable without taking selection into account: and, in the present state of our knowledge, this will be difficult to do. If, in fact, the smallpox virus contains the antigen of blood-type A, which is frequently found among Europeans, and if Europeans introduced smallpox among American Indians, as well as mating with them, would one expect an increase of blood-type A in American Indian populations? We do not know the answer. But among several tribes in the Northwest the degree of intermixture calculated from RH frequencies is much higher than that calculated from ABO frequencies.

Many of the barriers which impede gene flow between adjacent populations, or populations sharing the same territory, are man-made, the products of our imaginations. This is another of the objections raised by Ashley Montagu against the use of the word race. His contention is that the only lines of division separating mankind today are cultural ones: he therefore comes to the conclusion that we should speak and think only in terms of castes and ethnic groups. Yet the power of the human imagination is such that the barriers which it raises against gene-flow are as much a part of our environment as is the incest taboo which acts in the opposite direction. Xenophobia, religious prejudice, caste snobbery, and linguistic diversity may well be even less amenable to our efforts at amelioration than are deserts, oceans, malarial swamps, high plateaus, and contagious diseases. Any psychiatrist knows that few cures are affected by telling a patient that his delusions are imaginary. All of these factors, the man-made, the man-modified, and those as yet unchanged by man, have had effects upon the fluctuating pattern of racial diversification and resubmergence. Gene frequencies have changed, and are changing, in response to selective pressures, some of which tend towards separation and others which do not. All the evidence available to us suggests that the differences in gene-frequencies between human populations living in different parts of the world have been of the same order of magnitude in prehistoric as in historic times. We cannot devise a neat filing system in classifying these populations, but we cannot avoid observing that some of them have highly distinctive gene-frequencies: such groups are valid subspecific taxa. Some of them may be ethnic groups as well: this will depend upon whether or not they are distinguishable by cultural as well as biological characteristics. The Andaman Islanders, for instance, might be considered both as a race and as an ethnic group. The Jews, on the other hand, although they have shared a common cultural tradition and so are properly thought of as an ethnic group, are so internally diverse in a biological sense that they could scarcely be classified as a race. Others may be castes as well: this will depend upon their social status. The Ghetto-based Jewish population of Europe was certainly a caste, as is the American colored population today. The latter, however, may properly be called a race because of its distinctive gene-frequencies.

Races are populations which can be readily distinguished from one another on genetic grounds alone. They are not types, as are a few of the so-called races within the European population, such as Nordics and Alpines. It is the breeding population into which one was born which determines one's race, not one's personal characteristics. Central Africans are equally Negroes whether or not they have the sickle-cell trait; Hopi are equally American Indians whether or not they are albinos or have shovel-shaped incisors. One cannot change one's race, but, by mating with someone of another race, one can produce offspring who may fall into a different classification: only the future can tell. Populations with distinctive gene frequencies tend to be more long-lasting than political and other social units: perhaps it is this fact which has given the illusion of permanence to racial groups.

But in fact, races are simply episodes in the evolution of a widespread species. Without the ability to diversify in response to existing circumstances over a wide range, a species could scarcely be considered successful. Such diversification is useful insurance against environmental changes which are bound to occur; it enables the species to become numerous; it promotes the heterozygosity which appears to confer added vigor to its members. Whether our improving ability to modify our environment will abolish the advantages of diverse racial adaptations remains to be seen: such adaptations have certainly been useful in the past.

How Man's Genes have Evolved

K. F. Dyer

When man diverged from the primates his brain increased in size and became more efficient, his bodily dimensions altered and he diversified into a large number of distinct races. The physical difference between races visible today, and even those preserved in fossils, are largely due to the expression of genetic changes; it is therefore the genetic changes themselves which we must examine if we want a complete understanding of human evolution.

The problems of tracing gene changes are much greater than of investigating physical change alone. Genes, unlike bones or teeth, are not preserved as fossils. The genetic evolutionist therefore has to use indirect and comparative methods to assess rates of change. Unfortunately, rarely is there accurate knowledge of the time intervals involved in racial or other separations and it is therefore not often possible to determine rates of genetic change. The time of divergence of man's ancestors from other primates is variously dated—between 4 million years and 14 million years (see "Man's earliest ancestors", *Science Journal,* February 1967). Even in cases where dates are reasonably accurately known—for example, the transport of large numbers of Negroes from West Africa to the Americas, creating a new isolated Negro population—the genetic constitution of the founding population has usually subsequently become mixed to a greater or lesser extent with the indigenous population. In the case of US Negroes, this amounts to anything up to 25 per cent white gene admixture. Therefore what genetic change has occurred in the immigrant population, when it is compared with that in its country of origin, may be due to such gene flow rather than to selective changes indicative of true evolution.

From Science Journal *6, no. 7 (1970): 27–34; reprinted by permission of the author and publisher.*

Another objection can often be raised even in cases where the isolation of two populations is known to have been relatively complete and even when the times of isolation are also known. This is when the populations involved are usually so small as to have been subject to the effects of genetic drift and therefore also to be of a very insignificant size compared with the size of the total human gene pool. Such cases—which include the well-studied Tristan da Cunha people and many small religious isolates—can therefore hardly be regarded as being typical in any study of the nature of speed of normal human evolution. Nevertheless, despite these difficulties there are now several areas in which a reasonably accurate assessment of genetic evolution in man can now be made, and these, taken together, are remarkably informative.

Jewish populations offer a particularly good example of genetic change. Today it is possible to recognize at least three culturally and ethnically distinct Jewish groups. These date back as far as the 1st century AD, when the conquest of Jerusalem by the Romans instigated the mass exodus of Jews from Palestine. One group, the Ashkenazi, are those Jews who dispersed in central, eastern and western Europe (and subsequently went to North and South America, South Africa and Australia). Another group, the Sephardi, lived in the countries round the Mediterranean including the European part of Turkey. A third group, the Oriental Jews, live in Asia Minor, Iraq, Iran, and the Yemen. The three groups have been genetically isolated from each other and from non-Jews, to varying extents, for a period of 2000 years—that is, between 60 and 70 generations. The three groups of Jews have different frequencies of many well known genes; the Ashkenazi Jews, in particular, have a very high frequency of certain genetic disorders as compared with the Sephardic and Oriental Jews and also with non-Jews. This provides a fine opportunity to investigate genetic evolution in fairly well defined circumstances.

The gene table (Table 1) shows the results of surveys carried out

TABLE 1. GENE FREQUENCIES (PERCENTAGE)

	blood group genes						*other genes*			
Jewish groups	A	B	O	M	N	RH⁻	phenly thiocarbamate (PTC) tasters	colour blindness	glucose 6 phosphate dehydrogenase deficiency	haptoglobin (Hp) gene
Ashkenazim	26	12	62	64	36	9	21	8	0.1	30
Sephardim	32	15	53	50	50	7	22	6	2	38
Oriental										
Kurdistan	32	14	54	53	47	4	13	6	58	31
Iraq	30	20	50	50	40	6	16	4	25	27
Iran	20	19	55	60	40	5	16	6	15	29
Yemen and Aden	18	10	72	76	24	10	18	5	5	25

indicating the type of genetic divergence which has occurred between these populations. Presumably the original Jewish population in Palestine was fairly homogeneous for most of these genes. Of course, some of this divergence may be due to a degree of intermarriage with local non-Jewish populations; and it is therefore especially relevant that certain characters found in the Ashkenazi Jews are significantly different in their frequency both from other populations of Jews and from non-Jews, thereby excluding this possibility. The most noteworthy of these characters are Gaucher's disease, Tay-Sachs disease and Niemann Pick disease—three fat storage diseases possibly sharing similar polymorphich properties and subject to the same selective forces.

Tay-Sachs disease (TSD) also known as infantile amaurotic familial idiocy, is a hereditary disease of fat storage, resulting in a progressive degeneration of brain function which commences soon after birth and ends in death, usually within the first or second year of life. The disease is due to the homozygous (two copies of the gene present in the cell—one inherited from the father and one from the mother) condition of a single autosomal recessive gene. It occurs once in approximately 6000 Jewish births in the United States and once in approximately 500,000 non-Jewish births, indicating that one in 40 Jewish persons and one in 380 non-Jews is heterozygous (only one copy of the TSD gene present), such a person being a carrier who passes on the disease but shows no symptoms. The birth incidence of TSD among the Sephardic and Oriental communities of the Middle East and North Africa appears to be even lower than that found in non-Jewish Europeans and Americans.

It appears therefore, as if a selective advantage exists among the Ashkenazi for heterozygous carriers of the TSD gene. This advantage has been sufficient to raise the frequency of the gene from .0013 at the end of the 1st century AD, when the mass emigration of the Jews began, through 60 generations to a new figure of .0126 in the 20th century.

Calculations suggest that a selective advantage of about 4.5 per cent in heterozygotes (carriers of the gene) would be sufficient to raise the gene frequency to its present level among Ashkenazi Jews. The advantage of the TSD gene to carriers has been sufficiently great to overcome the disadvantages of having the increased frequency of the TSD disease in the population. Studies on the relative fertilities of grandparents of children showing Tay-Sachs disease, and who must therefore have been heterozygotes, suggest that they have a net reproductive advantage which amounts to six per cent. In this case, therefore, demographic studies provide a neat confirmation of a genetic hypothesis.

The problem still remains, however, as to whether the incidence of Tay-Sachs disease is at equilibrium among Ashkenazi Jews or whether it is still increasing in frequency. In fact, a selective advantage of about five per cent will, as Figure 1 shows, lead ultimately to an equilibrium value of more than 2000 per million births, indicating that the incidence of the disease at present must be increasing rapidly among Ashkenazi Jews. It appears that the rate of change in the incidence of the disease today is about 7.5 per cent per generation—this is, between .25 and .33 per cent each year. A change

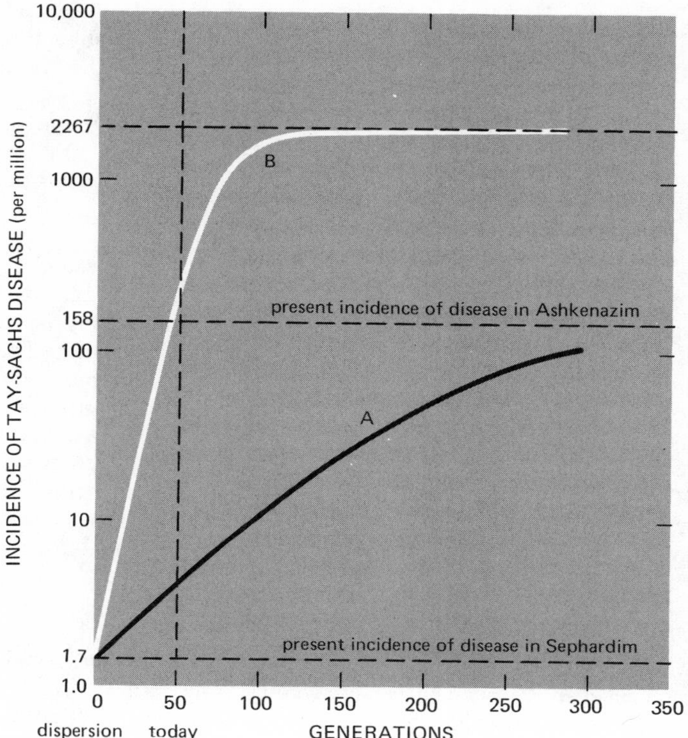

FIGURE 1. *Ashkenazi and Sephardic Jews have different incidences of certain genes and different susceptibility to disease. Tay-Sachs disease—a form of infantile idiocy—is almost ten times as frequent in the Ashkenazim than in the Sephardim and is very rare amongst non-Jews. Assuming that the gene was equally frequent in both types of Jews before they dispersed 50 generations ago, it can be calculated that individuals heterozygous (two different copies) for this gene must have a selective advantage of about five or six per cent. If this is the case then the gene must be increasing rapidly in the population and it can be predicted that the disease may reach a calculated incidence of two per cent of births. Graph A shows the increase in Tay-Sachs disease amongst Ashkenazi Jews, assuming that heterozygotes have 1.2 per cent more offspring than average. In graph B the heterozygotes are assumed to have 5.3 per cent more offspring than average.*

of this magnitude should be measurable in an appropriate study. In other words, it seems possible to detect evolution occurring in large human populations by measuring individual gene frequencies using demographic means.

The second example of evolution occurring in human populations is the sickle cell gene in American Negroes. This example is less clear cut, partly because the genetic constitution of the founders—unlike that of the Jews—is not accurately known and also—again unlike the Jews—racial amalgamation and gene flow has occurred on a fairly large scale. One of the functions of the sickle cell gene is probably to confer some protection for its carrier against the malarial parasite. This deduction has been made after the study of the way in which the frequencies of these genes are changing in populations removed from areas of endemic malaria, and in populations in areas where malaria has been eradicated.

The sickle cell gene produces an altered form of haemoglobin. Ever since the work of J. V. Neel in 1949 it has been known that individuals heterozygous for the sickle cell gene show no morbid effects because half their haemoglobin is normal and carries oxygen efficiently. Individuals homozygous for this gene, however, develop severe anaemia and almost always die young from distortion of their red cells by crystallized haemoglobin. Despite this almost inevitable elimination of the gene in the homozygous condition, it appears that the frequency of heterozygotes is stable at about 40 per cent of the population in certain African tribes. It seems certain that the reason for this high frequency of genes is that the heterozygotes have a much greater resistance to certain forms of malaria than those without the gene at all.

If 75 per cent of the homozygotes for the sickle cell gene die without reproducing, it can be calculated that the heterozygotes must have a "fitness" of about 1.26 times that of the normal homozygote in order to maintain an equilibrium level of 40 per cent heterozygotes. The term "fitness" is taken from Darwin's concept which is summed up by the phrase "survival of the fittest"—but it can be given a precise meaning in the modern theory of evolution. Statistically the fitness of an individual is measured by his or her contribution of offspring to the next generation as compared with the average for the population. Clearly the sickle cell gene will only remain at this high frequency in the population if the greater fitness of the heterozygote remains. If these populations are removed from malarial areas, or if malaria is eradicated, then this stable situation will be upset and gene frequency changes can then be expected to ensue.

This is precisely what has happened among Negroes removed from Africa to the United States during the slave trade. The average incidence of the sickle cell gene in the original slave population was about 22 per cent, according to calculations made by A. C. Allison of the National Institute for Medical Research, London. These Negroes, in the United States at least, have now been diluted by between 20 and 25 per cent European and Indian admixture; a sickle cell frequency of perhaps 16–17 per cent would therefore be expected. But the actual overall incidence of the sickle cell trait in American Negroes is about nine per cent. According to Allison, such a change between expected and observed gene frequencies would have taken about 12 generations (300 to 350 years). This fits well with the known details of the slave trade—from malarial Africa to the comparatively non-malarial western hemisphere—which commenced during the 16th century.

The opposite direction of change—an increase of the sickling gene—

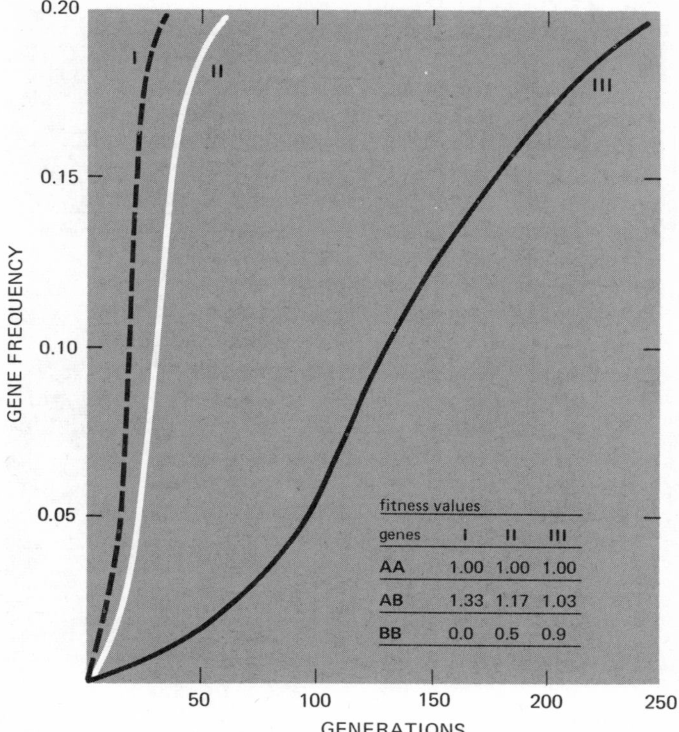

FIGURE 2. *Homo sapiens is a species more than 300,000 years old and must therefore have passed through some 10,000 generations. Changes in the frequency of genes may occur over small or large numbers of generations depending on the selective advantage of the genes in question. In the graph right 'fitness' values for the homozygotes AA and BB and the heterozygote AB have been chosen such that they will have the same final equilibrium values but will take different lengths of time (from 40 to 250 generations) to reach final equilibrium.*

has occurred in parts of West Africa and has been related to man's destruction of the tropical rain forest. Such an alteration of environment has provided new habitats for the mosquito vector *Anopheles gambiae* and the plasmodium parasite of falciparum malaria.

Although I mentioned that this example was less clearcut than that of gene frequency changes in various Jewish populations, there is one confirmatory piece of evidence which is just as striking. Between the 16th and 17th centuries, the two Dutch territories Surinam and Curacao imported Negro slaves for a rather short period from what was then the Gold Coast. These two territories have broadly similar environments, except that malaria is absent in Curacao but highly endemic in Surinam. The present frequency of the sickle cell gene in southern Ghana, where malaria is prevalent, is 20

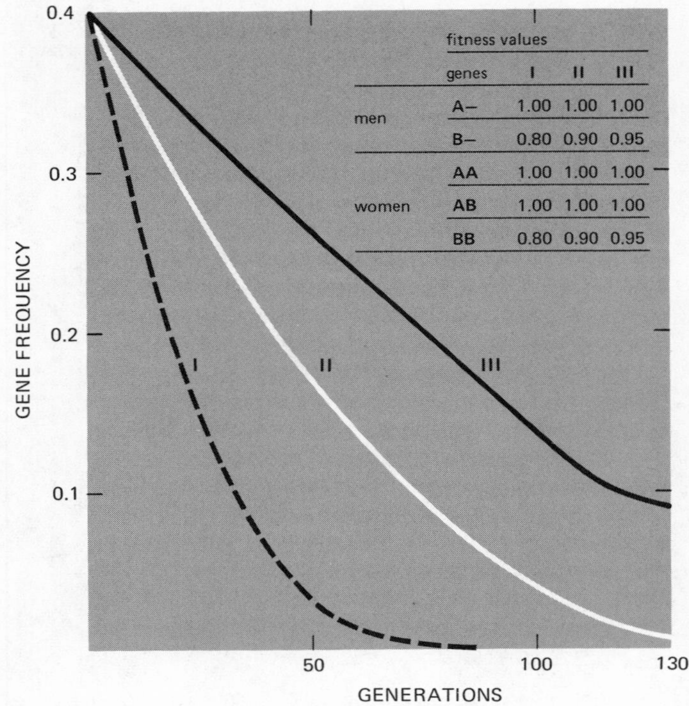

FIGURE 3. *Harmful genes are eliminated from the population by selection. A harmful gene (B in the graph left) may reach a high frequency in a particular population because it confers some advantage on the heterozygotes which possess one copy of the harmful gene and one copy of the normal gene. When conditions in the environment change the gene may then confer no advantage. In the graph above, the curves show the way in which the frequency of a sex linked gene is reduced by selection, assuming three different lowered values for 'fitness' (as defined by Darwin) conferred by the gene. Men (B–) have only one copy of the harmful gene on the X chromosome and women (BB) have two copies of the gene, one on each of their X chromosomes.*

per cent. In Surinam this frequency has remained at 20 per cent. But in Curacao, where in the absence of malaria the selective superiority of the heterozygote is obviously removed, the sickle cell gene has dropped to five per cent. Selective gene frequency change—in other words, evolution—has occurred in one of the two localities.

The gene which codes for a deficiency of the enzyme glucose-6-phosphate dehydrogenase (G6PD) is also thought to protect its carriers against malaria. In this case, differential selection can also be shown to have occurred in North American Negroes after their transportation from Africa. In fact, of up to 15 genes which have been investigated by P. L. Workman and others with the object of discovering gene flow between whites and blacks in the United States, it appears that five show evidence of selective alteration of overall frequency, while the remainder show only changes compatible with up to 20 per cent white gene mixture. These genes (see Table 2) can be arranged into two groups — those in which selection is thought to have altered the resulting gene frequencies in a systematic way, and those in which it has not. Unfortunately, no accurate assessment of the degree of selection operating can be made, because of uncertainties and possible errors in the original estimates of gene frequency in the contributing populations.

Because of the malarial eradication programme which is now achieving some success—especially in Mediterranean countries—the G6PD gene, which shows marked changes in frequency over short distances in Sardinia, Italy and Greece, among other places, is likely to prove a sensitive measure of future evolution.

A large number of genes, both blood group genes and genes affecting bio-chemical reactions, can be used in characterizing human populations. Each human population has its own unique combination of these genes. Thus, for example, the ABO blood group system has a mean world-wide frequency of 23 per cent A, 11 per cent B and 66 per cent O. The A gene frequency

TABLE 2. GENE FLOW AND SELECTION IN A US WHITE AND NEGRO POPULATION

genes		*West Africa negro* percent	*Southern USA negro* percent	*Southern USA white* percent	*total amount of gene flow (white to Negro only)* percent	*Comment*
Rhesus-system	R^0	59	54	4	11	
	R^1	7	11	43	10	
	r	21	23	36	13	
Duffy system	Fy^a	0	5	42	11	No selection of these genes can be detected
P system	P	78	76	53	9	
Kidd system	JK^a	78	74	54	17	
MNS system	S	13	16	28	14	
ABO system	B	15	13	5	22	
	A	15	16	25	11	
phenyl thiocarbamate (PTC) tasting		80	67	53	46	
haptoglobin[1] (HP)		60–78	52	41	42–70	selection believed to have increased frequency of these genes
glucose-6-phosphate dehydrogenase		18–21	12	0	34–44	
haemoglobin S (sickle cell)		8–14	4	0	46–69	
transferrin D[1]		35–88	5	1	50	

can, however, vary from zero in South American Indian tribes up to nearly 30 per cent in parts of western Europe and the B gene between zero in South America to nearly 40 per cent in northern India. Other populations show most of the different possible intermediate combinations between these limits.

Clearly by using information from other blood groups—such as Rhesus with eight alleles (alternative forms of the gene such as ABO), MN with four alleles and other less familiar blood groups also having four or more alleles—each population can be described and differentiated in genetic terms, despite the fact that there are no hard and fast barriers or sudden jumps in gene frequency between adjacent populations or races.

As sufficient information is gathered from human populations all over the world it is possible to arrive at an estimate of the number of completed "gene substitutions" which have occurred between different races of Man. Such an estimate is, in effect, a sum for the values of all the partial gene substitutions in the individuals of each population. The fact that one population has, say, five per cent of the A allele at the ABO locus while another has 25 per cent indicates partial gene substitution at this locus. Rather complex calculations then allow an overall total figure to be obtained taking into account partial substitutions at a large number of different genes. Using methods developed by Drs L. L. Cavalli-Sforza of the University of Pavia, Italy, and A. W. F. Edwards of Cambridge University "family trees" of human evolution can be constructed; the diagrams on page 279 show two such reconstructions of human evolution, together with estimates of the number of gene substitutions involved. In both cases, the solutions arrived at are obviously compatible with normal anthropological conclusion. In fact, in the case of the evolution of 15 populations, Cavalli-Sforza and Edwards point out that when the tree is projected on a world map, ignoring distances, it follows what might have been reasonable routes of migration.

The development of techniques such as this have made it possible to investigate another situation immensely informative to the student of human evolution: the differentiation of the various tribes of American Indians. The ancestors of all these tribes crossed the Bering land bridge from Asia about 20,000 years ago and it is likely that there was a greater homogeneity in the founding stock than is true for any other large population. In the case of the South American Indian, there was a second constraint in time—namely, the passage through the Central American isthmus some 15,000 years ago.

Among the many South American tribes, there are 12 which have been surveyed in fairly large numbers with respect to at least seven different sets of genes. The blood groups ABO MN Rh, Kidd, Duffy and Diego, and the haptoglobins of these tribes, have been investigated by J. V. Neel and others at Michigan University, and analysis of the results shows that they have a non-Indian admixture of less than five per cent.

They found that the maximum divergence between any two tribes for six of these gene sets (the ABO genes cannot be used because the Indians are almost universally blood type O) is 1.37 gene substitutions. This figure of 1.37 gene substitutions is a sum of partial substitutions at six different genes. The average rate of genetic divergence is only one-sixth of this. If the antiquity of Man in Central and South America is 15,000 years, then the maximum time taken for a substitution to occur at one gene when any two human groups are diverging is 6 × 15,000/1.37 or approximately 66,000 years. It would therefore require at least twice this or 130,000 years for two substitutions in the two genes of each individual of a race to occur. It must be emphasized that, because of the uncertainties as to whether all these tribes trace back to a common ancestral population 15,000 years ago, this estimate is the maximum for the rate of genetic divergence.

The speed of genetic change and the degree of genetic variability encountered naturally raise questions as to how this fits in with the history of the human species. It is generally accepted that *Homo sapiens* evolved from *Homo erectus* more than 300,000 years ago—a period which represents between 10,000 and 15,000 generations.

The set of curves (see Fig. 4) shows the overall increase of variation of individual gene frequencies with time—a representation of the fact that genes increase in frequency in some races and decrease in others—on the assumption that genetic drift alone and not selection is responsible for the observed variation. Comparing these curves with the world variances for

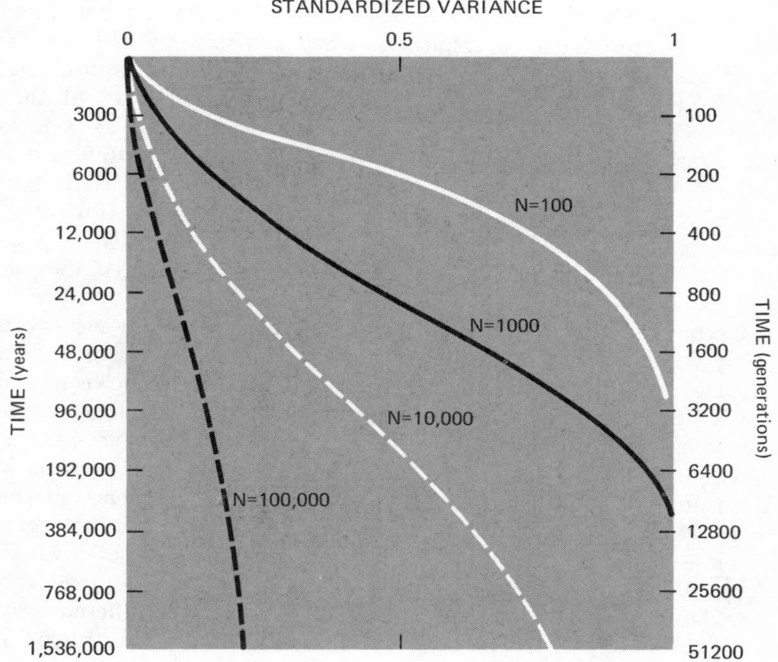

FIGURE 4. *Populations diverge genes which have little or no selective advantage vary in frequency by chance. When the population size (N) is smallest the gene frequencies vary most. The graph shows the increase of the standardized variance—a measure of variability between diverging populations—for different sized populations.*

many genetic markers, it is apparent that even the greatest variance observed would be compatible with a large isolate size (N) of 10,000 and a separation time of 300,000 to 400,000 years—the duration of existence of our species, *Homo sapiens*.

Of course natural selection is known to play some part in fixing equilibrium values of many of these genes; for instance ABO blood groups and the genes which determine ability to taste phenyl thio carbamide (PTC) have low variances and are probably true 'balanced polymorphisms'. In such cases it seems to be advantageous for the different genes—for example AB and O—all to be present in the population, although it is difficult to identify exactly why this is so. Some genes with high variances in different populations most probably have been subject to other selective conditions in different environments in the past and also may have acquired extra variance as a result of genetic drift. Another gene GN for instance, which affects the character of serum proteins, exhibits a correlation of gene frequency with latitude, suggesting that temperature conditions may be affecting the selective advance of some of these alleles.

Evidence so far available on genetic evolution in Man is not sufficient in itself to answer the many pressing questions of anthropology and social biology which face us today.

In many cases rates of genetic substitution may be very rapid and the degree of substitution and diversification which has occurred within 15,000 or 20,000 years in American Indians is of the same order of magnitude as that which characterizes many of the universally recognized races of the universally recognized races of Man. Even among a group as supposedly homogeneous as the Jews significant diversification at many different genes has taken place. But Man is still one species; there are no barriers to the successful and fertile mating between, say, an Eskimo and a Hottentot, and by slowly passing through intermediate populations no doubt some genes are exchanged between all human races, no matter how separated they are in distance and environment.

During the course of human evolution some races are lost by interbreeding and disappear or lose their identity during successive migrations. Other races are of recent origin, as for example the American Negro and the South African 'coloured'. With increasing opportunities for travel and intermarriage the world-wide mixing of genes will become much more pronounced. And on a local level increasing education and urbanization is likely to produce social changes which will reduce the frequency of consanguineous marriages (marriages between first and second cousins and other fairly close relatives) and hence will also make more genetic variability available. With this genetic variability much more widely spread through the population many of the genetic characteristics of the different races of Man will be totally lost. The rapidity of genetic change illustrated in this article shows that this process could be rapid.

By looking around us we see that Man has evolved an enormous range of physical and physiological characteristics to enable him to survive in environments as diverse as the African tropics or the arctic tundra, the monsoon forests or the dry sandy desert. Future trends appear to suggest a

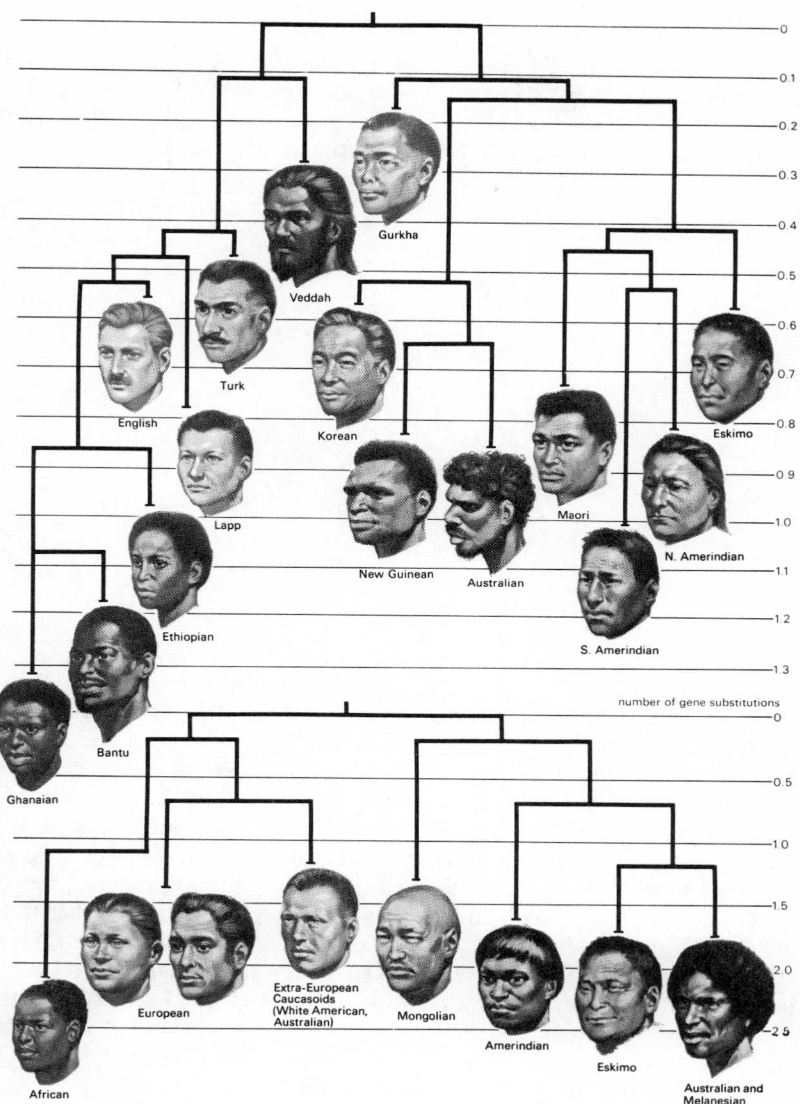

FIGURE 5. *Human evolution can be reconstructed from observations of gene frequency in present day human populations. In upper diagram (right) a comparison of five sets of genes in 15 different populations have been used to reconstruct the relations between human groups. The lower diagram shows a similar comparison of 13 genes in seven ethnic groups. The scale shows the overall number of substitutions for the genes considered which has occurred in the evolution of the races. Both diagrams show the calculated point of divergence of two or more races, and also the calculated number of gene substitutions which has occurred since divergence of a race (length of line). On the basis of estimates of evolution in diverging indian tribes in North and South America, one substitution in any gene is likely to occur once in 130,000 years.*

much greater mixing of the total human population, and it seems likely, therefore, that the mixing together his great genetic diversity will lead to many novel and advantageous genotypes being created and therefore a rate of evolution possibly more rapid than has occurred hitherto.

Climate and Race

Carleton S. Coon

Three-quarters of a century ago, in 1877, J. A. Allen, a zoologist at the American Museum of Natural History, wrote, in an article reprinted, like this one, in a Smithsonian Annual Report: "The study of man from a geographical standpoint, or with special reference to conditions of environment, offers a most important and fruitful field of research, which, it is to be hoped, will soon receive a more careful attention than has as yet been given it." Allen's paper dealt with geographically correlated variations in North American animals and birds, on three axes: color, general size, and the relative size of the peripheral parts; or more simply, color, size, and form. The first of these had already been studied in 1833 by Gloger, the second by Bergmann in 1847. Only the third was new with Allen. Wholly apart from the study of man, few scientists in the zoological field have concerned themselves, since Allen's day, with the subject of geographical variations within species. An outstanding exception is Rensch who, during the late twenties and thirties tested these rules and added several observations of his own; but even with this work available, Ernst Mayr was moved to state: "The study of these ecological correlations and the establishment of definite rules is such a new field that we may consider ourselves at the beginning of the work."

If, 64 years after Allen's statement, an authority of Mayr's stature could say that we were at the beginning of the work, it is clear that up to 11 years ago this aspect of biology had been greatly neglected, and such is still the case. During those 64 years the study of biology passed through

From Climatic Change, *ed. H. Shapley (Cambridge: Harvard University Press, 1954), pp. 13–34; reprinted by permission of the author and publisher.*

several phases of emphasis. First was the Darwinian epoch, in which Allen's work could clearly be rejected as Lamarckianism, and then came the era of genetic orthodoxy, during which it could be tossed into the bin of discredited interests, for at this time it was fashionable to call people interested in taxonomy, naturalists. Mayr himself, probably more than any other man, has brought taxonomy back into the biological social register. He has shown how essential the study of systematics is to a comprehension of the total life process. Although his interest in ecological rules does not represent a complete rediscovery, as Morgan rediscovered Mendelian genetics, yet his emphasis on this aspect of biology may turn out to be an equally important landmark in biological history.

If the study of ecological rules has been neglected by biologists, physical anthropologists have slighted it even more. The study of race in man has been influenced not only by biological fashion but also by current political ideologies. In each country of Europe, as in America, and in some African and Asiatic nations, a small but persistent group of men has continued to pile up objective data on the metrical and morphological characters of human beings. In some European and Asiatic countries, before World War II, politicians and propagandists concocted theories of racial superiority and inferiority with which to bolster their political schemes. In other European countries corresponding politicians and propagandists interested in internationalism brewed up opposite theories: first, to the effect that all races are equal in every respect, and second, to deny the existence of races at all. In America we have followed both of these fashions in turn. Each has served the political motives of its period. The second movement, unfortunately for the progress of science, is still with us. So strong is the feeling against thinking or talking about race that the study of the facts of race itself is nearly at a standstill. But fashions come and go. What is laughed at in one decade becomes the rage in another. Perhaps our turn will come.

Just as Rensch was the only voice crying in the zoological wilderness, the combined plea of three men, Garn, Birdsell, and myself, raised, in 1949, a feeble noise in the desert of physical anthropology. In our small and conceptually indiscreet book *Races* we suggested that some of the racial variations in man may be due to adaptations, by mechanism or mechanisms unknown, to extremes of environment. At the time we wrote it I, at least, had never heard of Allen, Gloger, Bergmann, or Rensch. It was only in a review of our book by Dr. M. T. Newman that I learned of their work. Since then I have found a little time to read what these zoologists have written, and to think about how their findings may possibly apply to man. Just this small amount of contemplation has made it abundantly clear that if a person is to study the racial variations in man in terms of ecology, he must be a superscientist, thoroughly conversant not only with his own subject, including anatomy, but also with physiology, particularly heat-and-sweat physiology, nutrition and growth, radiation physics, optics, body mechanics, genetics, and cultural anthropology in time and space. With all due respect to my colleagues I know of no one individual who can meet these qualifications. Hence it looks as though Allen's prediction would have to be still further delayed.

Still the problem can be stated. According to the modern concept of species formation expounded by Mayr and others, most animal species are polytypic—that is, they extend over a varied geographical range, and in a number of observable characteristics the local populations vary gradually from one end of the spatial range to another. A minority of species is monotypic—that is, lacking in geographical variation in any known character. Monotypic species are usually confined to small and isolated areas. Man is a polytypic species. Cases of genuine isolation, like that of the Polar Eskimo, are rare and probably of short duration. Like other polytypic species man varies from place to place, and the different forms which his variations take seem, in some, but not all, instances, to follow the same ecological rules as do those of those of other warm-blooded animals. Three of these rules, the longest known, concern us here.

1. GLOGER'S RULE. "In mammals and birds, races which inhabit warm and humid regions have more melanin pigmentation than races of the same species in cooler and drier regions; arid regions are characterized by accumulation of yellow and reddish-brown phaeomelanin pigmentation." "The phaeomelanins are subject to reduction in cold climate, and in extreme cases also the eumelanin" (polar white).

2. BERGMANN'S RULE. "The smaller-sized geographic races of a species are found in the warmer parts of the range, the larger sized races in the cooler districts."

3. ALLEN'S RULE. "Protruding body parts, such as tails, ears, bills, extremities, and so forth, are relatively shorter in the cooler parts of the range of the species than in the warmer parts."

The rest of this paper will be devoted to an inquiry into the possible application of these three rules to man. They cannot be called laws in the sense of Newton's Law or the Second Law of Thermodynamics, although these two, and other well-established physical principles, no doubt contribute to whatever validity they may be shown to possess. That no one simple law is involved in any instance is shown by Rensch's discovery that these three rules, along with several others of his own formulation (Rensch's clutch rule and hair rule, for example) are subject to 10 to 30 percent of exceptions. They cannot be called laws, because controls have not been sufficiently established to eliminate outside functions, and because not enough experiments have been made. However, a hibernating animal that defies Bergmann's rule is no more a valid exception to it than a helicopter is to the law of gravity; if all exceptions were run to the ground and all leads followed, the physical basis for these observations could in each case be established, or the rule refuted.

With man we have several advantages, and one disadvantage. We are dealing with a single species, or *rassenkreis,* to use Rensch's term, that is extremely numerous for a mammal and that covers a larger geographical area than that of almost any other mammal. More human beings have been "collected" than any other kind of fauna. Our measurements, while far from adequate, are relatively numerous. Another advantage is that we know quite a lot about the history of man. One principal disadvantage is that man possesses culture. In addition to his enormous capacity for physical adjustment to many climates, he has developed artificial adaptive aids, such as the use of fire, shelter, clothing, food preservation, and transportation, which have permitted him to occupy every single part of the land surface of the world except the Greenland and Antarctic icecaps, and by means of which he is already looking for further conquests in other planets and outer space. There neither Gloger, nor Bergmann, nor Allen can help him.

For the best part of a million years, some kind of man has existed, probably occupying not one but several environments, and during his evolutionary life span the climates of most, if not all, of the regions in which he has lived have been altered, in most cases more that once. As part of the cultural growth of man, two principal evolutionary shifts have been achieved. The brain has gone through two major changes in size, quite independently of body size, by means of two consecutive doublings of the cortical area. This means that two major steps in human evolution may have taken place since the ancestors of man became erect bipedal primates feeding themselves with their hands. This further means that some, if not all, of the climatically adaptive changes which distinguish modern races from one another may have been acquired in stage 1—or stage 2 of this process, rather than in stage 3, the modern level of potential cerebration. The late Franz Weidenreich postulated that the Mongoloid face began with *Sinanthropus* in stage 2. Whether or not he was correct, that anatomist was prepared to accept the thesis of presapiens raciation, and the concomitant thesis of multiple evolution from an earlier evolutionary level. Whether or not one or several human stocks made this jump, we do not know, but for present purposes the latter possibility must be taken into consideration.

We must not, however, assume that any or all stocks which passed through the first two cerebral size stages to the third were any more apelike in many respects than the reader. Schultz has shown that some of the features which distinguish man from his fellow occupants of the great primate house are more conservative and ancient in man than in the apes. For example, the heavy hair on the human scalp is also present in the newborn chimpanzee, which has hair elsewhere only on its eyelids, eyebrows, and arms. The erect position of the head on the top of the spine, with the position of the face and orbits below the brain case, is another example of what Schultz calls ontogenic retardation, or conservatism, rather than using the less palatable and perhaps less truthful, if commoner, word, fetalization. The human position of the great toe falls also in this class of phenomena, while the smaller size of the other toes is due to shortening rather than to an increase of the length of the big toe itself. Furthermore, we cannot assume that all earlier human types had big teeth and prognathous jaws. The gibbon's face is no larger in proportion to its brain and body than that of man. The siamang, in a few examples, has a chin.

In the basic evolutionary characters all men are equally human as far as we can tell; if some races resemble one or another of the anthropoids in some particular feature, that may mean only that that particular race is more specialized, more differentiated from the common stock, than the others. No earlier evolutionary status is necessarily implied, at least until we know all the pertinent facts.

Schultz has shown that among the apes just as much variation is seen as among men, if not more. He says that the

> skin color of the chimpanzee varies from black to white...the writer has the body of a young chimpanzee, born of black haired parents, which had straw-colored hair at birth, and later this color changed to a reddish tint. ...Giants and pygmies have developed among chimpanzees and orang-utans, and long-armed and short-armed varieties among gorillas.... Of the great apes...each has a very limited distribution, in contrast to man, yet each has produced several species or subspecies which are morphologically but not geographically as different from each other as the main races of man.

Schultz's statement shows that many of the differences between men which we consider racial also occur individually and racially among the apes. This means that the early human forms must have possessed the capacities for these same variations, some of which can, therefore, be very ancient and can go back to the earlier evolutionary stages. In other words, a Negro may have become black before he became a man, a Nordic's ancestor blond and blue-eyed while his brain was still half its present cortical surface size. The evidence used in this paper does not favor any such interpretation, but neither does it render it impossible.

Taking up Gloger's rule, first, we find that it was originally formulated to account for the color of feathers and fur, rather than skin. Birds and beasts of humid forested regions, in the cooler latitudes as well as in the Tropics, tend to adopt sombre colors; the association is with humidity and shade, rather than with temperature. Since individual birds and animals have been seen to grow darker or lighter when carried from one environment to another, it is clear that whatever influence produces this effect reflects a genetic capacity of considerable latitude. At any rate, it does not apply to man. His color variation is primarily concerned with the skin, which in a precultural state must have been wholly, except for the scalp, exposed to the elements, as in some racial and cultural situations it still is.

Speaking very broadly, human beings have three kinds of skin. One is the pinkish-white variety that burns badly on exposure to the sun and fails to tan. Such skin is found in a minority of individuals in the cloudy region of northwest Europe, among descendants of the inhabitants of this area who have migrated elsewhere, and among albinos anywhere. It is quite clearly defective skin; and causes its owners trouble anywhere anytime they step out of the shade. Clothing, lotions, wide-brimmed hats, and sun glasses help to mitigate its deficiency. Luckily for the rest, relatively few of mankind possess it.

At the opposite extreme is black or chocolate-brown skin, familiar as the integumental garb of the full-blooded Negro. Persons who wear skin of this type are the same color all over, except for their palms and soles.

As I discovered in Ethiopia, the unexposed skin is sometimes even darker than the portions exposed to the sun such as the hands and face, perhaps owing to an increased thickening of the horny layer in contact with solar radiations. Once this layer has thickened, man with this kind of skin can travel anywhere without fear of the sun; he can roll up his sleeves, toss off his shirt, or run naked in any climate where he or any other human would not be hindered by the cold. Negroes have gone to Alaska and to the North Pole.

In between is the range of integumental color possessed by the majority of mankind, belonging to skins which, although appearing as white, olive, yellowish, reddish, or brown, have one feature in common. The skin that is covered by clothing, if any, is relatively light. Exposed areas, if the light is strong enough, tan. In some populations this tanning can approach the darkness of the black-skinned peoples. However, skin that can tan can also bleach. Peoples who live in mid-latitude regions where the air is dry and the sky cloudless in summer, while in winter dampness and clouds are the rule, can shift their skin color with the seasons. This capacity for developing pigment in response to light and losing it when the light is gone is probably the original genetic situation with man.

The physiological advantages of the second and third types of pigment are easy enough to see. They concern entirely, as far as we know, ultraviolet radiation. The UV scale runs from about 2400 to 3900 Angstrom units, where it joins the lower end of the range of visible light. Actually, although shorter waves are produced artificially by lamp makers, all solar radiation under about 2900 units is filtered out by the earth's atmosphere and has nothing to do with the adaptive character of the human skin. Through the remaining thousand-unit range, UV radiation penetrates exposed skin to irradiate some of the subcutaneous fats, thus producing vitamin D, which is of benefit to the system.

However, those rays which are concentrated in an extremely narrow peak near the short end of the range, and centered at 2967 units, can damage the unpigmented skir if the sky is clear, the sun overhead, and if the exposure is prolonged past a critical time limit. Sunburn, erythema, prickly heat, and sunstroke can follow. However, the hazard carries its own cure, for if the skin is exposed for short periods it will tan. The pigment so acquired absorbs the UV radiation concentrated at this critical peak and converts it into radiant heat, which the skin then loses through the normal processes of radiation, convection, and sweating, along with other heat produced by the metabolism of food within the body. The pigment granules do not interfere with UV penetration along the rest of the scale, and thus vitamin D production can continue. Tanned skin is thus useful in regions where the peak of UV radiation is seasonal, since in the season of reduced light the skin bleaches and permits the maximum of irradiation.

In contrast to the genetic capacity for change inherent in skin that tans, black skin is constant. In the distant and naked past, it must have had a clear advantage in the Tropics over tannable skin. That advantage remains to be discovered experimentally. Geographically speaking, peoples with black skin who are known to have lived in their present habitats since the rather mobile dawn of history live in regions close to the Equator where UV is strongest. They inhabit the forests and adjacent grasslands of central Africa. The second great center is Melanesia, including Papua and northern Australia. They also include the extinct (in the full-blooded state) Tasmanians. In between Africa and Melanesia fringes of land and islands hold connecting links; southern India, Ceylon, the Andamans, the Malay Peninsula, and the Lesser Sundas contain black-skinned peoples, as do some of the islands of the Philippines.

Except for Tasmania, whose inhabitants had obviously migrated there from a region of lower latitude, these areas are all within 20° of the Equator, and most of them are within 10°. In all of them there is little seasonal change. Aside from these uniformities, they represent a variety of environments, including shady forests, grasslands, deserts, and coast lines. Since we have a good idea what black skin is good for, we can discover no particular reason for it in the forests. Bright equatorial sun is, however, a problem in grasslands, deserts, and on the water.

Returning to the rest of the animal kingdom, we find that grassland and desert mammals are generally light or tawny colored. This is true of animals whose skins are protected by hair. A few animals, however, are naked like man, and these are black or dark gray. They include the elephant, rhinoceros, hippopotamus, buffalo, and certain types of pig. These animals reach their peak of numbers and development in the grasslands or desert fringe; except for the rhino they enter the forest, where they are fewer and less favored. Their color, carried in from the sunlight, is neither an advantage nor a disadvantage in the shade.

In Africa the blackest Negroes live in the grasslands. In the forest we find two kinds of people: Pygmies, who are not completely black, and Negroes. The Pygmies hunt, the Negroes farm. The two exchange products. Since the Negroes make the arrowheads and nets with which the Pygmies hunt, the latter would have a hard time living without either these implements or the plantains which the Negroes give them for food. Furthermore, the food plants which the Negroes cultivate are of southeast Asiatic origin, and they could hardly have been introduced later than the first millennium B.C. Since southern India got iron during this same millennium, and the motive which brought people across the Indian Ocean to Africa was a search for iron, it is unlikely that the Negroes entered the forest to live much before the time of Christ. If we look at Melanesia we see again that the forest is poor in game, the principal animal being the pig, escaped from domestication. The pig came in with agriculture, and neither can have been introduced much before the first millennium B.C. Therefore, the present black-skinned populations of these two tropical forest areas must be historically recent; black skins go with grasslands or deserts and have entered forests in numbers only with agriculture. In the Belgian Congo the forest Negroes are decreasing in numbers while the Pygmy population remains constant. If we look back to the Pleistocene, we see that the glacial advances and retreats in the north were accompanied by a succession of pluvial and interpluvial periods in the Tropics. At least once the Sahara was blooming with grass and flowers, and at other times the forest was reduced to a fraction of its present area.

Why, one may ask, did not black skins develop in the Americas, where land within 10° of the Equator runs along a course of 4,000 miles? The answer, which is geographical, confirms our interpretation of black skins in the Old World. The coast of Ecuador is heavily forested. Open country begins at the Peruvian border, 4° south of the Equator, whence it continues to the forest zone of Chile. The coastal desert averages only 20 miles wide. Owing to the combination of the mountains behind and the cold Humboldt Current in front, the air is cool, the humidity high, the sky usually overcast, and little solar radiation gets through. Moving up into the highlands, we should expect a double concentration of UV at 10,000 feet, where one-sixth more solar radiation penetrates the atmosphere than at sea level. However, the region of Quito, which is on the Equator, is frequently cloudy; the year has two rainy peaks. Thunder, Brooks says, is heard on 99 days each year. Since the air is also cold, the Indians cover up as much of their skin as possible. At 17° farther south, on the shores of Lake Titicaca, less rain and clouds appear, but the humidity is moderately high. Americans with untannable blond skins suffer intensely. The Indians, who wear broad-brimmed hats as well as the usual heavy clothing, tan to a deep reddish brown on exposed parts.

Moving eastward we find most of the Amazonian countryside heavily forested. Indians, Negroes, Whites, and all shades between get along with equal ease as far as UV is concerned. However, between the great river system in Brazil, the Guianas, and Venezuela are patches of savannah, precisely the kind of country in which black-skinned animals and men luxuriate in Africa. However, these patches are small and not long ago may have been smaller. They support no tempting animal life as in Africa, and the few Indians who got out there are refugees from the forests that line the streams. There is no evidence of any earlier population in this region at all. From all these considerations no reason appears for a black-skinned population to have developed in the Americas. The relative antiquity of man in the two hemispheres is therefore beside the point.

While Gloger's rule appears to cover variations in the response of the human skin to UV, both Bergmann's and Allen's rules are cut to fit the other end of the scale, radiant heat. Unlike UV, radiant heat both enters and leaves the body, which is physiologically well adapted to maintain an even temperature under extreme environmental conditions. Clothing, shelter, and fire also help, but not to the exclusion of physiological adaptation.

Bergmann's rule, that warm-blooded animals of a given polytypic species will be larger in the colder and smaller in the warmer portions of its ecological range, is based on the physical fact that the larger a body, all else, including shape, being equal, the smaller the ratio of skin surface area to bulk, one being a square, and the other a cube. Since most of the heat loss comes through the skin, the larger the animal, all else being equal, the easier the process of keeping it warm. Other factors, some of which will be dealt with presently, enter into this picture, and if they and others still to be determined did not, it would be more than a rule.

The simplest test of Bergmann's rule is to compare mean body weight of different human populations with climate as expressed by latitude. In Europe a regular cline is found between the peoples of the northwest, as the Irish with 157 pounds and the Finns with 154, down to the Spaniards with 132 and the racially white Berbers of Algeria with 124 pounds. In Asia the Mongoloid peoples show the same tendency, with the North Chinese weighing 142 and the Annamites 112 pounds, respectively. In America the Eastern Aleuts average 150 pounds, a level maintained by most of the Indians of the northern United States and Canada, while the Maya of Central America tip the scales at only 119 pounds. In South America weight rises with altitude and latitude to a peak among the bulky Indians of Patagonia and the grasslands of Tierra del Fuego. The equatorial Andamanese weighted only 98 pounds, the Kalahari Bushmen 89. The Baluba, a non-Pygmy Negro tribe of the Belgian Congo, average only 118 pounds, which seems to be par for tropical rain forests. In Polynesia, where offshore breezes make heat loss no problem, weights are high, as they are in cool New Zealand. Polynesian figures range from 140 pounds upward. Indonesians, to whom Polynesians are supposed to be related, are 20 to 30 pounds lighter. Their islands are hotter.

It can be easily demonstrated that changes in body size may take place in a single generation. Whatever genetic mechanisms control weight permit a useful capacity for variation. Man's size is as plastic as his tannable skin color and as automatically regulated. Anyone who has visited the Lower Amazon country has seen that the Brazilian citizens in that tropical forest are of one size, whatever their hair form, skin color, or cast of facial features. At least three racial stocks are concerned, the Mediterranean, Negro, and American Indian. All come out the same size. Farther south representatives of these same three stocks are much larger.

One other environmental factor affects body size, causing different populations within a given climatic zone to vary within their limits of tolerance. That is nutrition. In my North Albanian series I found that the tribesmen living on food raised on granitic soil were significantly smaller than those who walked over limestone, thus confirming the results of French investigators more than half a century earlier. Trace elements are important, and so are feeding habits. In a Moroccan village studied by Schorger the boys were given almost no meat until they reached the age of 14, at which time they were expected to work. From then on they ate with the men, whose diet included animal proteins. At that point their growth was relatively rapid. A main diet of polished rice goes with small people; we do not know how big they would have been if they had eaten other foods in a hot climate.

Most striking of all the size differences in man are those between the Pygmy peoples of Africa, the Indian Ocean countries, Indonesia and Melanesia, and normal human beings. However, the Pygmies are not much smaller than some of the people of the Amazon Valley. In all these selvas the leaching of the soil through excessive rainfall is held responsible, through the agency of washing out of trace elements. But man is not the only pygmy in the forest. In Africa the elephant, hippopotamus, buffalo, and chimpanzee all have pygmy counterparts. What affects man there cannot be cultural; it is of universal mammalian application, since the animals mentioned eat the whole range of available foodstuffs and are exposed to the same range of temperature, humidity, and solar radiation.

Along with size comes the question of basal metabolism. Although questions have arisen about coordinating techniques, still the geographical distribution of the results follows a Bergmannian pattern. The norm is set for Europe and the northeastern United States; rates more than 10 percent above normal are found among the Eskimo, who reach 30 percent of excess, the Ojibwa Indians of the Great Lakes region, and the Araucanians of southern Chile. Rates 10 percent and more below the norm are found among Australian aborigines and inhabitants of the hotter parts of India, Australia, and Brazil. Americans in New Orleans are also below par. This needs a lot of checking and controlling, but despite two exceptions the trend is clear. Furthermore, like alterations of pigment and gross size, changes in basal metabolism can in some cases be acquired.

That basal metabolism should change with climate makes sense, as does the whole mechanism of heat control in man. Here we enter a field where many physiologists have brutalized themselves and their friends for the sake of science; one investigator writes that he and his team even took the rectal temperatures of porcupines in the Talkeetna Mountains of Alaska at −22° F. Others thrust thermocouples into their own flesh, piercing their palms and wrists to the depth of the bone. Still others consented to be locked in sealed chambers from which heat and oxygen, alternately, were withdrawn, while a few pedaled themselves nearly to death on bicycles. As a result of this self-sacrifice we are in a position to evaluate Allen's rule in man.

Being a warm-blooded animal is a great advantage. It permits one to move and act at nearly all times in nearly all places, instead of scampering feverishly for shade or waiting for the chill to burn off before moving. However, the process of keeping the internal organs at a temperature of 98.6° F. has its problems too. This temperature can fall to 77° F. or rise to 110° F. before death intervenes, but variations of half these magnitudes are serious, particularly on the high side, for man can lose heat more safely than he can gain it. Even when he is trying to keep warm, man loses a certain amount of heat functionally in evaporation of moisture through the palms, soles, axillae, and public regions, just to keep tactile and hinge areas ready for action.

As long as the temperature of the outside environment is below 83° F., the body normally loses heat by radiation and convection. At 83° F. it begins to sweat, and the surface of the body grows increasingly moist, until at 93° F., in a saturated atmosphere, the whole body is covered, water is dripping off the surface, and the perspiration fails to do its work, which is to cool the surface of the skin by evaporation. At this point, if the temperature rises without a drop in humidity, trouble is near. However, in dry air only 40 percent of the body surface is normally wet at 93° F.; at blood temperature the ratio is 50 percent, and a complete coverage, in the American human guinea pig, is not attained until 106° F.

The evaporation of sweat is the principal means by which the body loses its radiant heat. Experiments have shown that a resting man at 122° F. and a humidity of 44 percent will lose 1,798 grams of sweat per hour; a working man, in a humidity of 35.6 percent saturation, will lose 3,880 grams per half hour, or half his normal blood volume, at a cooling potential of 25 to 30 times the normal resting metabolism. Needless to say such a liquid turnover requires him to drink gallons of water and also taxes his heart. It is greatly to the advantage of human beings living under conditions of extreme heat to avoid this circumstance as much as possible.

Such heat is found largely in the deserts of the world which lie on either side of the Equator, on the Tropics of Cancer and Capricorn. Chief among them are the Sahara, the Arabian, Persian, Thar, Kalahari, Australian, Argentine, Chilean, and Colorado deserts. Of these the Turkestan, Gobi, Argentine, and Colorado deserts lie farthest from the Equator. Characteristic of deserts is a great diurnal variation in temperature, and often a seasonal one as well. On a hot day the mercury may fall to 71° F. at 5:00 A.M., reach the critical sweating point of 93° F. at 10:15 A.M., hit a peak at 108° F. at 2:00 P.M., and fall to 93° F. again at 7:45 P.M. A hunter, who has nothing to work with but his own body and a bow and arrows or a handful of spears, will be up before daylight, and he will be on his way by the time the coolest point of the daily cycle will have been reached. He will be able to go out to his hunting ground before the heat bothers him, and if he is lucky he can make his kill early and take his time on the way home before or during the heat of the day. If he is on a 2- or 3-day hunting trip, he can nap under a bush in siesta time, and return on another morning. An Arab who is herding camels or conducting a caravan will travel by the light of the moon and stars and sleep under a lightproof black tent in the middle of the afternoon. In Middle Eastern desert countries even truck drivers prefer to work at night, to save their tires as well as their own systems. If forced to do so, a desert-dwelling human being can walk in the heat of the day, but if he confines his traveling to the nighttime he can go three times as far, without water, before collapsing.

Animals that live in the desert belong to two classes, those that can do without water and those that use it to cool the body through evaporation. The first category includes especially a number of rodents, which derive water from desert vegetation and can even extract it metabolically from dry seeds. Such animals have no water to spare; they hide behind or under rocks or bushes during the heat of the day, or burrow far underground, in some cases pulling stoppers of earth in behind them. When the surface ground temperature is 122° F. it may be only 83° at a depth of 1 foot 3 inches, while at 6 feet it may fall as low as 68° F., with considerable humidity. Animals that hide during the day to save water will die when forced to spend a few hours in the bright sun in the heat of the day.

The other class of animals is composed of larger forms, such as the camel, oryx, and addax, which are able to hold up to a fifth of their body bulk in stored water and to utilize it gradually. In this sense they are no better off than a man weighing 120 pounds carrying a 5-quart canteen. In cool spring weather they are at an advantage over the man, however, for they can derive their moisture from herbage; only in the hot and barren season do they depend on their speed to carry them to water. In addition to their water-holding capacity, these animals have something else in common. They all have long legs and necks and are extremely gracile for their weight. Their bones are long, fine, and hard; their musculature light. In treeless country they can make high speeds. Even the cat famliy has its desert representative, the long-legged cheetah, which is said to be the fastest runner of all living things.

Man in the desert is also light and gracile. He too needs to be able to travel far on a small heat load. But his animal companions have buff-colored hairy coats, which reflect solar light; it is unlikely that they lose their heat in this fashion. Man must lose it through his skin surface, and the more surface he has per unit of weight the better. The more he can lose through radiation and convection the less he has to sweat, and the more skin surface he can use for evaporation the higher the temperature he can stand. The smaller his bulk, the less the load on his heart. The shape of his body takes on added importance as we realize that all parts of its surface do not lose heat equally. The back of his hand has about 400 sweat glands to the square centimeter, the forehead 200, and the cheek as few as 50. The hands, which comprise 5 percent of the body surface on normal Americans, lose 20 percent of the heat of the body by evaporation.

When a man begins to perspire, moisture appears first on his forehead, neck, some of the larger areas on the front and back of his trunk, the back of the hand, and the adjacent part of the forearm. The head and neck must lose heat rapidly for they have the brain to keep in thermal equilibrium, and if the head is globular in form, it has the worst possible shape for heat loss. Old World hot-desert peoples are narrow headed. After this the cheek, the lateral surfaces of the trunk, and the rest of the extremity surfaces begin, but these regions sweat much less. Sweating is always slight to moderate on areas rich in subcutaneous fat, such as the cheek and the gluteal and mammary regions. The inside of the thighs and armpits sweat even less, since they face in and not out and are in a poor position for heat loss. The palms and soles, which perspire at lower temperatures, lose the least of all in periods of stress.

The chief burdens then are on the neck and head, which have purely local duties, and on the hands and forearms, which act as radiators for the whole body. It has been shown that the average human body (American) loses heat after the fashion of a cylinder averaging 7 cm. in diameter. While the head and trunk are bulkier than this, the forearms and hands resemble even smaller cylinders, and the fingers and toes even smaller yet. Now heat loss increases as the square of the diameter of the cylinder decreases. Hence the survival value of long, tapering forearms and fingers in a dry, hot place becomes self-evident.

One of the racial peculiarities of Negroes is long arms, with particular emphasis on the length of the forearm, and large hands with long fingers. Forest Negroes often have relatively short legs, but we have seen that the legs have much less to do with heat regulation than the arms. The Nilotics and Somalis and Masai and other black-skinned peoples of the Sahara, Sudan, and the Horn of Africa have long skinny legs and long gracile necks; no case of adaptation to a given environment situation could be clearer. The same is true of South Indians, Ceylonese Vedda, most Melanesians, and the Australian aborigines of the desert, as well as of white Australians from Queensland. The Bushman of the Kalahari is extremely slender; of the inhabitants of the American deserts information is defective. At any rate, as far as we know, the desert portion of Allen's rule holds for man, for obvious reasons. The mechanism of change is less obvious.

The other end of Allen's rule applies to adaptation to cold. Naked savages can live without much clothing in temperatures down to the freezing point. Several technical experiments have been performed on Australian aborigines sleeping naked in the desert when the night temperature fell to the frost point. These people keep rows of small fires burning and sleep between rows. Parts of their skin surface become quite cold, others hot. They seem to be able to absorb radiant heat from the fires on some parts of their skin surface in all of which the venous blood is at a minimum. Thus they survive until morning. In the daytime the air temperature rises rapidly.

The Yaghans, canoe Indians of Tierra del Fuego, paddle nearly naked in their boats in foggy channels, in an environment where year-round temperatures hover above and about freezing point. Darwin saw a naked woman nurse a naked baby while sleet melted on her body, and a group of Yaghans who drew up to the outer glow of the explorers' fire sweated profusely. The Ona, foot Indians of the plains on the northern part of the island, wore guanaco skin robes and moccasins, and slept behind skin windbreaks in the snow. The Chukchi of Siberia, who wear Eskimo-style clothing, like to remove their shirts to cool off, and Bogoras saw Chukchi women thrust lumps of snow between their breasts for the same purpose.

The mechanism of heat loss in cold conditions will explain this. When the environmental temperature falls the body stops sweating at 83° F., and heat loss is accomplished wholly by radiation and convection. Venous blood, which has been returning from the back of the hand through superficial blood vessels on the arm, is rerouted; vasoconstriction shuts off this road, and vasodilation opens alternate channels through deep-lying veins which surround the artery. The chilled venous blood returning to the heart cools the arterial blood, so that it will have less heat to lose, and the heat gained by the venous blood is carried to the heart. Thus heat loss through the hand and arm is reduced to but 1.5 percent of the body's total at higher temperatures. The amount of blood that flows through 100 cc. of fingertip tissue falls from a maximum of 120 cc. to .2 cc. per minute. The arm itself becomes an insulator in depth.

At an air temperature of 73° F. a naked American with a rectal temperature of 97° will show the following skin temperatures: head, 94°;

trunk, 93°; hands, 86°; feet, 77°. Deep thermocouple work has shown that the hands and wrists chill to the bone literally. However, when the temperature of the extremities falls below a point between 41° and 50° F., vasoconstriction ceases, and peripheral bloodflow is accelerated, to keep the extremities from freezing. What this means racially is that a person of north European ancestry can afford to have big bony hands which help keep him cool in hot weather, because at the winter temperatures at which he operates, particularly when clothed, the size of his hands makes no difference in heat economy; they are simply shut off from the heat system, like an empty room.

It is a matter of casual observance that most Mongoloids have small and delicate hands and feet, short distal segments of both upper and lower limbs, and short necks. However, recent studies of the Eskimo have shown that despite expectation these people have large hands. It is believed, although the material proving this has not yet been published, that racial differences in venous patterns exist, which would account for the Eskimo hand as well as for the ability of the Australian aborigine to sleep in the cold without clothing.

Turning to the Eskimo foot, which is small as expected, it is commoon knowledge that his excellent boot keeps this extremity warm, as long as it is dry. Water can leak in through the stitch holes if the sinew is not preswollen, and it can also come from sweat induced through exertion. A wet boot affords little insulation, and some Eskimos freeze their toes. Similarly the hand is here a liability; as Quartermaster Corps researchers have shown, it is almost impossible to keep a hand warm in the best of mittens when the body is at rest outdoors in very low temperatures. Eskimos bring their arms and hands in next to the body skin, leaving sleeves dangling, when they can.

Ears, nose tips, and other protrusions need special protection; with the fall of the glass the amount of blood sent to the ears increases greatly, and a relatively great loss occurs at this vulnerable point. Polar and subpolar people are invariably described, in the prime of the individual, as being well equipped with subcutaneous fat. This fat is especially well developed on critical spots, such as the cheek, wrist, and ankles. One centimeter of fat is given the same insulation rating as a complete suit of winter clothing. The healthy Negro living in a hot country carries almost no subcutaneous fat. His superior performance in the desert, compared to Whites of the same age and weight, has been demonstrated.

In summary, adjustment to the cold requires large body mass, short extremities, much fat, deep vein routing, a high basal metabolism, or some combination of these five features. Adjustment to the heat requires small body mass, attenuated extremities, little fat, extensive superficial vein routing, a low basal metabolism, and a greater number of sweat glands per unit of surface area. Possibly the role of melanin in starting the skin to sweat at a lower threshold by conversion of UV to radiant heat may be added. Any combination of these seven may be involved. The type or types of physique most suited to cold resistance are exactly those which, the doctors tell us, are most likely to suffer from heart trouble, and so it is a lucky thing that adjustment to the cold does not place an extra load on the heart. Heat-adapted physiques are those best calculated to stand the extra heart load which they receive.

So far we have been thinking about heat loss from the skin, but calories also leave the body through the lungs. In hot weather the heat loss from the lungs through respiration is negligible and of little help to the suffering organism, but as the mercury drops this source of leakage becomes serious, reaching 50 kg. calories per 1,000 liters of expired air in extreme cold. Not only does this affect the total heat load of the body, but it subjects the nasal passages to heavy chilling. To what extent the Mongoloid face, inside and out, may compensate for this by its special architecture remains to be discovered.

One other climatic hazard which human beings have faced and overcome is that of reduced oxygen at high altitudes. Dill and his associates have found that the inhabitants of the Andes have become able to live and work at 17,500 feet and more, through the fact that their blood carries a much higher concentration of red corpuscles than of people at sea level. At the same time they need more air, which they obtain through more efficient automatic breathing control as well as the larger lungs. The requirements for physique in high altitude resemble those for cold. Perhaps it is no coincidence that the two great high-altitude plateaus of the world, the Andean and the Tibetan, are inhabited by Mongoloid peoples who greatly resemble each other.

This paper does not pretend to cover, even in outline, all the more obvious adaptive variations in man in the fields of color, size, and form. No attempt has been made to deal with the eye or the hair. Little attention has been paid to genetics, in the belief that before we can discover the biological techniques by which a set of variations is inherited we should first describe the variations themselves. Since blood groups are believed to be nonadaptive, they have been temporarily ignored.

Since I started this racial heresy in 1946, when I wrote the first draft of what was to be expanded into the book RACES, with the help of Garn and Birdsell, many others who possess special technical skills, and whose interests are focused in other than purely racial channels, have been working on important aspects of the problem. Garn is conducting experiments with metabolism and body heat at the Fels Institute, Yellow Springs. Ancel Keys and Josef Brozek, in Minneapolis, have independently studied the basic components of the human body, with special emphasis on its fat content. Russell Newman, Phillip Wedgewood, and Paul Baker have been devising techniques for the same purpose in Lawrence, Mass., and conducting interracial studies of physiological tolerance for the Armed Forces. Various other Army and Air Force scientists, and their Canadian colleagues, have been working on basic differences in anatomy and physiology between Eskimos, Indians, Whites, and Negroes.

Our subject is acquiring dignity, and results are being produced. We are now on the road to learning the basic facts about race in man, facts of which no one should be proud or ashamed. In an atom-age world in which men of all races are coming into increasing contact with one another on a basis of equality and cooperation, a knowledge of what a wonderfully adaptive thing the human body is, is a much healthier commodity than the recently traditional hide-race point of view.

Human Adaptation to High Altitude

Paul T. Baker

Stretching along western South America from Colombia to Chile lies a large section of the Andean plateau, or *Altiplano,* which rises above 2500 meters (about 8250 feet) (Fig. 1). This area is suitable for human habitation up to the permanent snow line, which is generally above 5300 meters (17,590 feet). There are now more than 10 million people living in this zone, and the historical and archeological records indicate that it has been densely populated for a long time. Indeed, before Europeans arrived, the Inca empire, which had its center in this zone, formed one of the two major civilizations of the Western Hemisphere and, in A.D. 1500, probably contained about 40 percent of the total population of the hemisphere.

With such a history, one would assume this to be an ideal environment for man and the development of his culture. Yet, in point of fact, modern man from a sea-level environment ("sea-level man") finds this one of the world's more uncomfortable and difficult environments. The historical records show that such was the case even in the 1500's, when the Spanish complained of the "thinness of the air," moved their capital from the highlands to the coast, and reported that, in the high mining areas, the production of a live child by Spanish parents was a rare, almost unique, phenomenon. Today this environmental zone remains the last major cultural and biological center for the American Indian. The population has an extremely low admixture of genes from European peoples and virtually none from African peoples.

From Science *163 (1969): 1149–56. Copyright by the American Association for the Advancement of Science; reprinted by permission of the author and publisher.*

The few cities are Hispanicized, but the rural areas retain a culture which, in most aspects, antedates the arrival of the Spaniards.

It would be far too simplistic to suggest that this unique history is explicable entirely on the basis of the effects of altitude on sea-level man. Yet, there is sound scientific evidence that all sea-level men suffer characteristic discomfort at high altitudes, the degree of discomfort depending upon the altitude. There is evidence, also, of long-term or permanent reduction in their maximum work capacity if they remain at these altitudes, and evidence that they undergo a number of physiological changes, such as rises in hemoglobin concentrations and in pulmonary arterial pressure. In a few individuals the initial symptoms develop into acute pulmonary edema, which may be fatal if untreated. On the basis of less complete scientific evidence, other apparent changes are found for sea-level man at high altitudes: temporary reduction in fertility, reduction in the ability of the female to carry a fetus to term, and a high mortality of newborn infants.

With these problems in mind, a group of scientists from Pennsylvania State University, in collaboration with members of the Instituto de Biología Andina of Peru, decided to investigate the biological and cultural characteristic of an ecologically stable Peruvian Quechua population living in traditional fashion at a high altitude. We chose for study the most stable population known to us at the highest location reasonably accessible. It was hoped that some insight could be gained into the nature of this quite obviously successful and unusual example of human adaptation. In this article I review some of the results available from this continuing study.

The general problem may be defined by three questions: (i) What are the unique environmental stresses to which the population has adapted? (ii) How has the population adapted culturally and biologically to these stresses? (iii) How did the adaptive structures become established in the population?

Our basic method of study, in attempting to answer these questions, was a combination of ecological comparisons and experimental analysis.

THE STUDY POPULATION

The population chosen for study lives in the political district of Nuñoa, in the department of Puno in southern Peru. In 1961 the district had a population of 7750 and an area of about 1600 square kilometers. Geographically, the district is formed of two major diverging river valleys, flat and several kilometers broad in the lower parts but branching and narrow above. These valleys are surrounded by steep-sided mountains. In the lower reaches of the valley the minimum altitude is 4000 meters; the higher parts of some valleys reach above 4800 meters. The intervening mountains rise, in some parts, to slightly above 5500 meters.

The climatic conditions of the district are being studied from weather stations on the valley floors and on the mountain sides at different altitudes. From present records, the pattern seems fairly clear. The lower valley floor appears to have an average annual temperature of about 8°C with a variation of only about 2°C from January, the warmest month, to June, the coldest. This is much less than the diurnal variation, which averages about 17°C. The seasonal variation in temperature is due almost entirely to cloud cover associated with the wet season. Some snow and rain fall in all 12 months, but significant precipitation begins around October, reaches its peak in January, and ends in April. Since the diurnal variation is high, some frost occurs even in the wet months. Mean temperatures fall in proportion to increases in altitude (by about 1°C per 100 meters), but, because of the sink effect in the valleys, minimum temperatures on the valley floors are usually somewhat lower than those on the lower mountain sides.

Except for two small areas of slow-growing conifers, almost all of the district is grassland. Because of the existing climatic and floral conditions, herding has become the dominant economic activity. Alpaca, llama, sheep, and cattle, in that order, are the major domestic animals. Agriculture is limited to the cultivation of frost-resistant subsistence crops, such as "bitter" potatoes, *quinoa,* and *cañihua* (species of genus *Chenopodium*). Even these crops can be grown only on the lower mountain sides and in limited areas on the lower valley floors. In recent years, crop yields have been very low because of drought, but they are low even in good years.

A single town, also called Nuñoa, lies within the district and contains

FIGURE 1. *The high-altitude areas of South America and the location of Nuñoa. Shading indicates altitude of 2500 meters (8200 feet) or more.*

about one-fourth of the district's population; the other three-fourths live in a few native-owned settlements called *allyus,* or on large ranches or *haciendas,* which are frequently owned by absentee landlords. The social structure may be loosely described as being made up of three social classes: a small (less than 1 percent) upper class, whose members are called *mestizos*; a larger intermediate class of individuals called *cholos*; and the Indians, or *indígenas,* who constitute over 95 percent of the population. Membership in a given social class is, of course, based on a number of factors, but the primary ones are degree of westernization and wealth. Race appears to be a rather secondary factor, despite the racial connotations of the class designations: *mestizos,* of mixed race; *cholos,* transitional; *indígenas,* indigenous inhabitants. Biologically the population is almost entirely of Indian derivation.

By Western economic and medical-service standards, this district would be considered very poor. If we exclude the *mestizo,* we find per capita income to be probably below $200 per year. The only medical treatment available in the district is that provided by a first-aid post. The upper class has access to a hospital in a neighboring district. Yet repeated surveys suggest that the diet is adequate, and that death rates are normal, or below normal, for peasant communities lacking modern medicine. Indeed, this population must be viewed as being one nearly in ecological balance with its technology and its physical environment.

Superficial archeological surveys reveal that the central town predated the Spanish conquest, and suggest that the district population has been fairly stable for at least 800 or 900 years.

From this general survey of the Nuñoa population and its environs we have concluded that the unusual environmental stresses experienced by this population are hypoxia and cold; other stresses, more common to peasant groups in general, which the Nuñoa population experiences are specific infectious diseases, the problems of living in an acculturating society, and, possibly, nutritional deficiencies.

HYPOXIA

At elevations such as those of the district of Nuñoa, the partial pressure of atmospheric oxygen is 40 percent or more below the values at sea level. As noted above, such a deficiency of oxygen produces a multitude of physiological changes in sea-level man, at all ages. We therefore attempted to evaluate the native Indian's responses to altitude at all stages of the life cycle.

Demography

A survey of more than 10 percent of the population revealed an average completed fertility of about 6.7 children for each female. This is quite a high fertility by modern standards, but there was no evidence of voluntary birth control, and cultural practices appeared in many ways designed to provide maximum fertility; under these conditions, 6.7 children is no more than average. This same survey, partially summarized in Table 1, did not show

TABLE 1. STATISTICS ON REPRODUCTION AND VIABILITY OF OFFSPRING FOR THE DISTRICT OF NUNOA, BASED ON A SAMPLE OF APPROXIMATELY 14 PERCENT OF THE POPULATION OF THE DISTRICT.

	Total sample	*Sample of postmenopausal individuals*
Married Women		
Number in sample	136	31
Mean age (yr)	36.2	45±
Mean age at first pregnancy (yr)	19.5	20.1
Offspring (no.)	608	207
Mean number of offspring per woman	4.5	6.7
Mean number of surviving* offspring per woman	3.2	4.4
Sex ratio (males to females) of offspring		
At birth	124	113
Surviving*	129	146
Mortality of offspring during the period of growth (in percent)		
Male	30	27
Female	33	44

* "Surviving" refers to time of census.

an unusually high rate of miscarriage but did reveal two unusual features. (i) The earliest age at which any woman gave birth to a child was 18 in the low valleys and something over 18 at higher elevations. The average age of first pregnancy was also higher for women at the higher altitudes. (ii) The sex ratio was highly unusual in that there was a large number of excess males. Furthermore, there was a higher mortality of females than of males throughout the period of growth. In an associated study of newborns it was found that, for Quechua mothers in Cuzco (altitude, 3300 meters), placenta weights at childbirth were higher and infant birth weights were lower than corresponding weights for comparable mothers near sea level. Finally, an analysis of the Peruvian census showed that, as in the United States, the mortality of newborn infants is higher at higher elevations; this does not appear to be primarily a socioeconomic correlation. From the results so far obtained, we conclude that fecundity and survival through the neonatal period is probably adversely affected by high altitude, even in the native populations of high-altitude regions. However, it is clear that the Nuñoans can still maintain a continuing population increase. Our data do not provide a basis for deciding whether, at high altitudes, fecundity and survival of offspring through the neonatal period are greater for natives than they are for immigrant lowlanders.

Growth

Intensive studies on growth were carried out on over 25 percent of the Nuñoa-district children, from newborn infants to young people up to the age of 21. A number of unusual growth features were apparent shortly after birth. Thus, as shown in Table 2, a slower rate of general body growth than is standard in the United States is apparent from a very early age. In addition, developmental events such as the eruption of deciduous teeth and the occurrence of motor behavior sequences occur late relative to U.S. standards. For example, the mean number of teeth erupted at 18 months was 11.5 for Nuñoa infants as compared with 13 for U.S. infants. The median age at which Nuñoa children briefly sat alone was 7 months, and the median age at which they walked alone was 16.2 months. These data were collected by means of the technique developed by Bayley, who reported that the median ages at which U.S. children sat and walked alone were 5.7 months and 13.2 months, respectively.

Some of the growth characteristics in later development are shown in Figures 2 and 3. In these growth studies it was possible to compare our results with cross-sectional data for groups from lower elevations (Huánuco and Cajamarca, 2500 meters; Lima and Ica, 300 meters). We have also collected some semi-longitudinal data in order to evaluate growth rates. These combined data showed, for Nuñoa children, (i) lack of a well-defined adolescent growth spurt for males, and a late and poorly defined spurt for females; (ii) a very long period of general body growth; and (iii) larger chest sizes, in all dimensions and at all ages, than those of children from lower elevations.

In explanation of the unusual growth aspects of the Nuñoa population, at least three hypotheses may be suggested: (i) all Quechua have an unusual growth pattern, genetically determined; (ii) malnutrition and disease are the prime causes; (iii) hypoxia is the major factor. Our present data are not adequate for testing these hypotheses. However, a number of observations suggest that hypoxia is a major factor. As discussed below, we have been unable to find any evidence of widespread malnutrition or of unusual disease patterns. What data are available on the growth of other Quechua show growth patterns different from those found for the Nuñoans. Finally, hypoxia has been shown to affect growth in a number of animals other than man.

TABLE 2. STATURE AND WEIGHTS OF NUÑOA INFANTS AND OF INFANTS IN THE UNITED STATES.

Age (months)	*Stature, males (cm)*		*Stature, females (cm)*		*Weight, males (kg)*		*Weight, females (kg)*	
	Nuñoa	U.S.	Nuñoa	U.S.	Nuñoa	U.S.	Nuñoa	U.S.
6	62	66	61	65	6.9	7.6	6.6	7.3
12	71	75	69	74	7.9	10.1	7.3	9.7
24	76	87	75	87	9.9	12.6	9.0	12.3

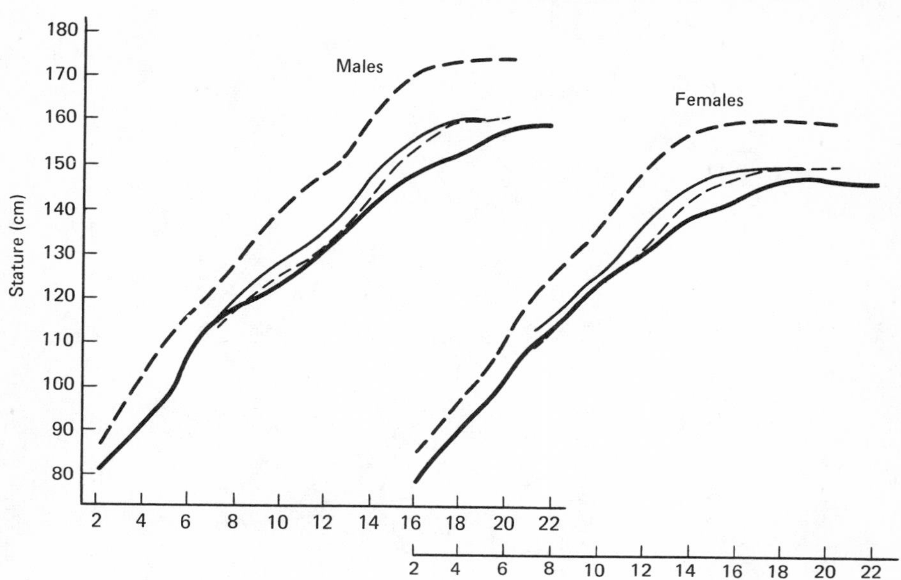

FIGURE 2. *The growth of Nuñoa children as compared to that of other Peruvian populations and of the U.S. population. (Heavy dashed lines) U.S. population; (light solid lines) Peruvian sea-level population; (light dashed lines) Peruvian moderate-altitude (1990 to 2656 meters) population; (heavy solid lines) Nuñoa population (altitude, 4268 meters).*

Work physiology

The most striking effect of high altitude (4000 meters) on newcomers, apparent after the first few days of their stay, is a reduced capacity for sustained work. This reduction is best measured through measurement of the individual's maximum oxygen consumption. For young men from a sea-level habitat, the reduction is in the range of 20 to 29 percent; the men who had received physical training generally showed a greater reduction than the untrained. Some rise in maximum oxygen consumption occurs during a long stay at high altitudes, but studies extending over periods of as much as a year have failed to show a recovery to even near low-altitude values for adult men.

Maximum oxygen consumption for any individual or group is controlled by a large number of factors, among which the level of continuing exercise is of major importance. Among young men of European descent, mean values for maximum oxygen consumption range from below 40 milliliters of oxygen per kilogram of body weight for sedentary groups, through 45 milliliters per kilogram for laborers, up to more than 55 milliliters per kilogram for highly trained runners. The high degree of variability in this parameter makes it difficult to determine whether the native of a high-altitude region has a work

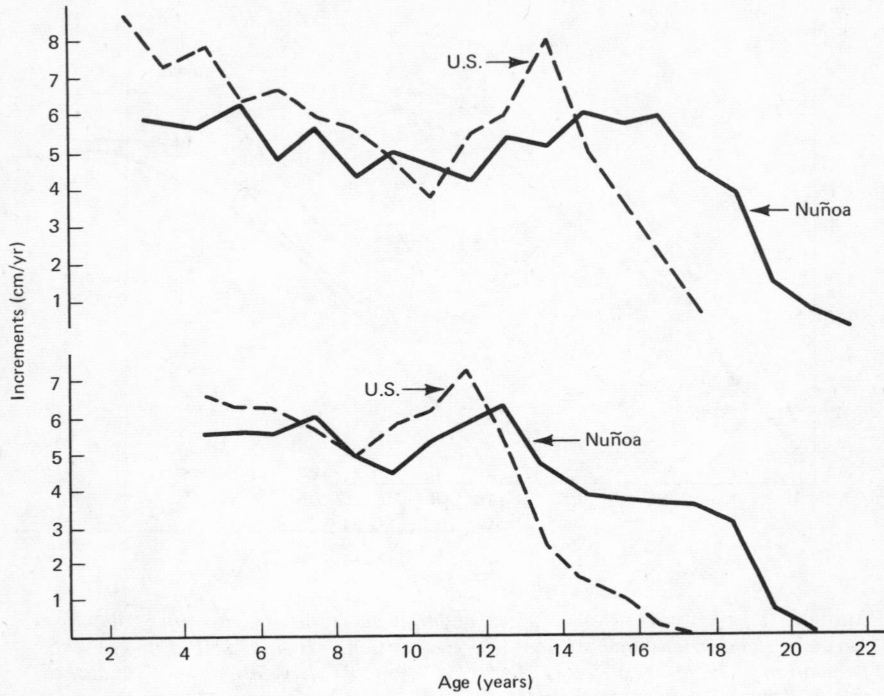

FIGURE 3. *Rates of general body growth for children in Nuñoa as compared with that for children in the United States. (Top) Males; (bottom) females.*

capacity different from that of an individual from a low-altitude habitat, and makes it even more difficult to determine whether the complex physiological differences between groups from high and low altitudes have resulted in a better adaptation, with respect to work capacity, for the high-altitude Quechua.

In order to help clarify these questions, we determined maximum oxygen consumption for a number of carefully selected samples of contrasting populations; in all cases the method of determination was the same. Some of the results of these studies are presented in Table 3. It should be noted that the individuals referred to as White Peruvian students are so classified on the basis of morphology, and it is quite possible that they contain some admixture of native Quechua genes.

On the basis of results obtained for students alone, one investigator surmised that the differences in maximum oxygen consumption for high-altitude and low-altitude groups might be only a matter of life-long exposure, plus a high state of physical fitness in the highland Quechua. In an article based on partial results, some of the investigators, including myself pointed out that trained athletes from lower altitudes could, at high altitudes, achieve the

TABLE 3. SOME DATA FROM TESTS OF MAXIMUM OXYGEN CONSUMPTION (MAX V_{O_2}) AT HIGH AND LOW ALTITUDES FOR CONTRASTING POPULATIONS.

			Subject					*Responseo*				
Group of subjects	*Altitude at which tested (m)*	*Duration of exposure to high altitude*	*Number*	*Mean age (yr)*	*Mean height (cm)*	*Mean weight (kg)*	*Max V_{O_2} (liter/min)*	*Aerobic capacity† (ml/kg/min)*	*Maximum ventilation (liter/min)*	*Ventilation equivalent‡ (V/V_{O_2}/min)*	*Maximum heart rate (beat/min)*	*Oxygen pulse (ml/beat)*
Nuñoa Quechua	4000	Life	25	25	160	57	2.77	49.1	75	27.3	171	16.0
U.S. white researchers	300		6	30	183	79	3.92	50.4	131	33.7	185	21.2
U.S. white researchers	4000	4 weeks +	12	27	181	75	2.78	38.1	91	32.9	173	16.6
U.S. white athletes	300		6	20	179	71	4.58	64.2	131	28.8	175	26.5
U.S. white athetes	4000	4 weeks	6	20	179	71	3.14	46.6	105	33.7	172	19.4
Quechua from sea level	100		10	22	160	62	3.01	49.3	108	36.2	187	16.7
Quechua from sea level	4000	4 weeks	10	22	160	62	2.67	44.5	87	33.4	190	14.5
Peruvian students												
Quechua	3830	Life	10	23.8	162	60	2.79	46.8	72	25.8	188	15.1
White	3830	Life	13	23.5	169	61	2.62	42.8	74	28.2	186	14.2

* The measurements were made by means of a bicycle ergometer in 10-minute progressive exhaustion tests.

† Aerobic capacity is the maximum oxygen consumption per kilogram of body weight and, as such, is the most significant measure available of the success of the individual's (and, by inference, the group's) biological oxygen transport system. It is also assumed to be one of the best measures available for judging an individual's work capacity relative to his body size.

‡ Ventilation equivalent is the ventilation volume per unit oxygen uptake per unit time. The lower the value, the greater the relative efficiency in supplying oxygen.

same oxygen consumption per unit of body weight as the Nuñoa native. While the data now available support the idea that physical training and life-long exposure to hypoxia act to increase maximum oxygen consumption, these two factors appear insufficient to explain the total results. The data, instead, suggest that a fairly random sample of Nuñoa males between the ages of 18 and 40 have a vastly greater maximum oxygen consumption than a group of reasonably physically fit researchers from the United States. The oxygen consumption of the Nuñoans also significantly exceeded that of young native students from lower altitudes, and equaled that of a group of highly trained U.S. athletes who had spent a month at high altitude. Furthermore, the heart rate and ventilation rate for the Nuñoans remained low. The Nuñoans do walk more than people from the United States, but nothing in the personal history of the Nuñoa subjects suggested that they had experienced physical training or selection comparable to that involved in becoming a college track athlete. To me, the data suggest that a high-altitude Quechua heritage confers a special capacity for oxygen consumption at 4000 meters. In the absence of more precise data, such a conclusion remains tentative. However, the data can certainly be interpreted as showing that the Nuñoa native in his high-altitude habitat has a maximum oxygen consumption equal to, or above, that of sea-level dwellers in their oxygen-rich environments. This conclusion is in agreement with the results obtained by Peruvian researchers.

COLD

The microenvironment.

By the standards of fuel-using societies, the temperatures in the Nuñoa district are not very low, and we would consider the typical daily weather equivalent to that of a pleasant fall day in the northern United States. However, the lack of any significant source of fuel made us suspect that at least some segments of the population might suffer from significant cold stress. As mentioned above, few trees grow in the district, and those that do are slow-growing. At present, these trees are used primarily as rafters for houses; only an occasional member of the upper class uses wood for cooking. The fuel used almost universally for cooking is dried llama dung or alpaca dung. This dung provides a hot but rapid fire, and is burned in a clay stove, which provides little external heat. Since cooking is done in a building separate from the other living quarters, only the women and children benefit from the fire. Bonfires are lit only on ceremonial occasions; the winter solstice is celebrated by a pre-Hispanic ceremony in which many bonfires are lit all over the district. The use of fires during solstice ceremonies throughout the world is often considered an act of sympathetic magic to recall the sun. For Nuñoans it may also recall the warmth.

The houses of the native pastoralists, with walls of stacked, dry stone and roofs of grass, provide no significant insulation. Measurements made within the dwelling units generally showed the temperature to be within 2° or 3°C of the outdoor temperature. This is in sharp contrast to the situation in the adobe houses used by the upper classes, by some agriculturalists in the Nuñoa district, and by all classes in slightly lower areas of the Altiplano. Adobe houses provide good insulation, and indoor temperatures are frequently 10°C above outdoor temperatures during the cold nights of the dry season.

From this analysis and other observations we concluded that the Nuñoa native depends upon his own calories for heat, and relies, for heat conservation, primarily upon his clothing and upon certain customs, such as spending the early evening in bed and having as many as four or five individuals sleep in the same bed. His clothing is layered and bulky, with windproof materials on the outside. Thus, it provides good insulation for his body. However, the Nuñoa native's wardrobe does not include gloves, and the only foot coverings are sandals occasionally worn by men. The insulating effect of native clothing was tested under laboratory-controlled cold conditions. It was found that at 10°C the clothing increased mean body temperature by about 3°C and raised the temperature of hands and feet despite the lack of gloves and shoes.

From the total assessment we concluded that the Nuñoa native probably experiences two types of exposure to cold: (i) total-body cooling during the hours from sunset to dawn and (ii) severe cooling of the extremities, particularly in the daytime during periods of snow and rain. To assess the degree of stress due to cold we took measurements of rectal and skin temperatures of individuals in samples selected by sex, age, and altitude of habitat. These studies indicated that at night the adult women experience very little stress from cold, whereas adult men showed some evidence of such stress. During the day, women, because they are less active than men, may experience slight stress from cold, whereas men do not, except for their extremities. Active children show no evidence of such stress; however, during periods of inactivity, as at night, their skin temperature and rectal temperature are low. Indeed, at these times, all indices show an inverse relationship between age, size, and body temperatures.

Physiological responses

In order to characterize the Nuñoa native's responses to cold, we used three types of laboratory exposures: (i) total-body cooling at 10°C with nude subjects, for 2 hours; (ii) cooling of the subject's hands and feet at 0°C, for 1 hour; (iii) cooling of the feet with cold water. The subjects were Nuñoa males and females, North American white males, and Quechua males from low-altitude habitats.

Some results of the studies of total-body cooling are summarized in Table 4. Since the Nuñoa Indians are smaller than either the coastal Indians or U.S. whites, the data are presented in terms of surface area. Viewed in this way, the data show that the native Quechua from a high-altitude habitat produced more body heat during the first hour than individuals from low-altitude habitats, but produced amounts similar to those for such individuals during the second hour. By contrast, heat loss was much greater for the Nuñoans than for members of the other groups during the first hour and

TABLE 4. EXCHANGE OF BODY HEAT AS EXEMPLIFIED IN HEAT PRODUCTION AND HEAT LOSS. THE VALUES ARE AVERAGES FOR TWO EXPOSURES AT 10°C, EXPRESSED ON THE BASIS OF BODY-SURFACE AREA.

Subjects	*Number in sample*	*Heat production* ($kcal/m^2$)			*Heat loss** ($kcal/m^2$)		
		1st 60 minutes	2nd 60 minutes	Total time	1st 56 minutes†	2nd 60 minutes	Total time
Whites	19	51.5	62.2	113.7	29.6	11.8	41.4
Nuñoans	26	58.1	65.5	123.6	51.0	12.9	63.9
Lowland Indians	10	54.7	65.5	120.2	30.1	14.7	44.8

* Heat not replaced by metabolic activity.

† Because perfect equivalence in body temperature prior to exposure to cold was not achieved, heat loss in the first 4 minutes of exposure has been excluded from this calculation.

similar during the second hour. The findings on heat loss are perhaps the more interesting, since they conform with results of two other studies of cooling responses in native Quechua from high-altitude habitats.

When the source of the greater heat loss was closely examined, it proved to be almost entirely the product of high temperatures of the extremities, and these temperatures, in turn, seem to be produced by a high flow of blood to the extremities during exposure to cold. When a comparison was made, as between Nuñoa males and females, of the temperatures of the extremities, the women were found to have warmer hands and somewhat colder feet. In both sexes the temperatures for hands and feet were significantly above corresponding values for white male subjects. The specific studies of hand and foot cooling made with exposures of types ii and iii shed further light on the subject, showing that the maximum differences between populations occurred with moderate cold exposure; that the high average temperatures of hands and feet were the result of a slow decline in temperature, with less temperature cycling than is found in whites; and that the population differences were established by at least the age of 10 (the youngest group we could test).

Since the oxygen exchange between hemoglobin and tissue bears a close positive relationship to temperature, it is clear that, when the temperature of the peripheral tissues remains high, more oxygen is available to these tissues. Therefore, the high temperatures of the extremities of the Nuñoans at low atmospheric temperatures may be considered not only an adaptation to cold but also a possible adaptation to hypoxia.

NUTRITION AND DISEASE

In the complex web of adaptations that are necessary if a peasant society is to survive, adequate responses to nutritional needs and prevalent diseases are always critical. For a people living at high altitude, these responses are important to an interpretation of the population's response to altitude and cold.

Nutrition

The analysis of nutritional problems in the Nuñoa district has proceeded through a number of discrete studies, including a study of dietary balance in individuals, a similar study for households, an analysis of food intake by individuals, and a study of the metabolic cost, to the community, of food production. Of these studies, the first two have been completed, the third is in the analysis stage, and the fourth is in the data-collection stage. The results to date suggest that the Nuñoa population has a very delicate, but adequate, balance between nutritional resources and needs.

The dietary-balance study was carried out with six native adult males, chosen at random. Food requirements were predicted from U.N. Food and Agriculture Organization standards, on the basis of weight and temperature. The food used in the study consisted wholly of native foodstuffs and was prepared by a native cook. The results showed that, for these individuals, protein, caloric, and fluid balance remained good, and indicated that caloric and protein balance was good prior to the time of the study. The household survey suggested that nutrition for the population as a whole was generally adequate, although the method did not permit conclusions on the adequacy of nutrition for special subgroups, such as children and pregnant women.

The household survey also suggested that the diet might be somewhat deficient in vitamin A and ascorbic acid. Subsequent, more detailed surveys of individuals now cast doubt on the validity of this conclusion and suggest that, if malnutrition exists, it is probably no more common than in U.S. society. Indeed, in the light of the modern concept of "overnutrition," we might even say that the Nuñoans have a better dietary balance than the U.S. population. As noted above, the balance is delicate, and there must be years and times of the year when certain dietary deficiencies exist. Furthermore, the balance is subtle. To cite an example, the basic foods available are very low in calcium, yet adequate calcium is obtained, primarily by use of burned limestone as a spice in one type of porridge.

Disease

Our data on infectious disease are particularly inadequate. Health questionnaires are almost useless, since native concepts of health are only partially related to modern medicine. The *indígenas* attribute over 50 percent of all illness and death to *susto,* a word best translated as "fright." As noted above, no regular medical treatment is available, so records are lacking, even for a subsample. In our general survey we encountered the usual variety of infectious diseases and had the impression that respiratory ailments, such as tuberculosis and pneumonia, were common. On the other hand, we did not find evidence of deficiency diseases—not even goiters.

Perhaps the most striking results of the survey were those relating to cardiovascular disease. In the survey, heart murmurs were common among children, but no evidence of myocardial infarction or stroke was seen. Casual blood pressures of individuals from age 10 to 70+ were taken. They revealed a complete absence of hypertension, the highest pressure encountered was 150/90 mm-Hg. Other researchers have reported similar results for high-altitude populations, and it has been suggested that hypoxia may directly reduce the incidence of hypertension. In an attempt to trace the etiology of the low blood pressures, we subdivided our sample into a series of paired groups, first into lower- and higher-altitude groups, next into urban and rural groups, finally into more acculturated and less acculturated groups.

Significant differences in the effect of age on blood pressure appear when the sample is divided on the basis of any of these three criteria. However, it is not possible to assess the extent to which the environmental factors are independently related to blood pressure, since the total sample is too small to provide six independent subsamples large enough to give meaningful analytical results. It is our present belief that acculturation is the most

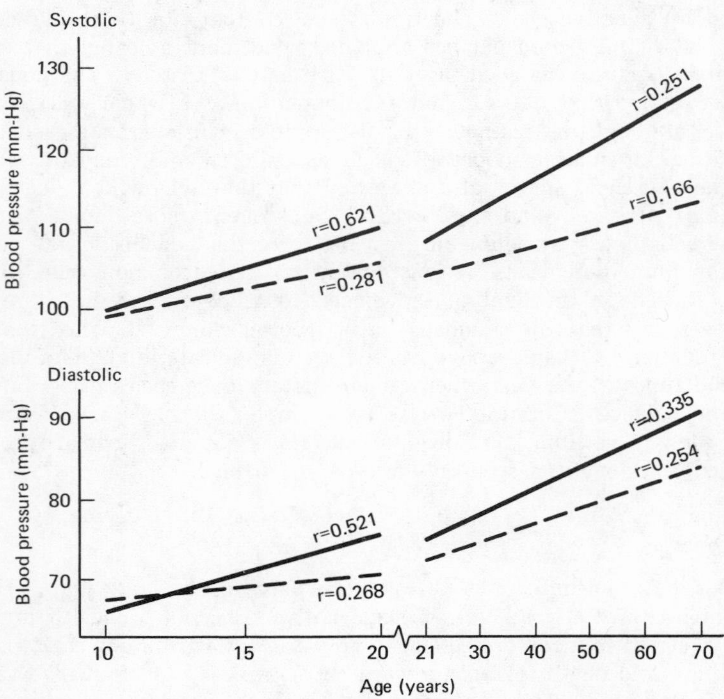

FIGURE 5. *Changes with age in the blood pressure of male Nuñoa natives, according to level of acculturation. (Solid lines) More acculturated; (dashed lines) less acculturated;* r, *Pearson correlation coefficient.*

significant of the factors, since altitude, urban residence, and acculturation are interrelated within the Nuñoa district population and the group differences are most striking when acculturation is taken as the criterion of subdivision. Children aged 10 to 20 years were classified as "acculturated" if they were in school, whereas children in the same age bracket who were not in school were classified as "unacculturated." Among adults, evidence of schooling, knowledge of Spanish, and use of modern clothing and specific material items, such as radios, were taken as signs of acculturation.

The results of these comparisons are shown in Figures 5 and 6. Certainly the regressions cannot be taken as evidence that altitude does not affect blood pressure, since none of the Nuñoa males, even those in the

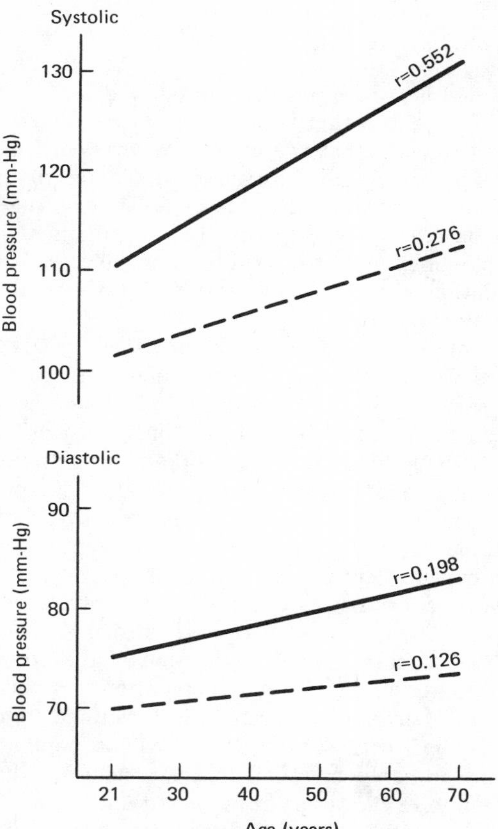

FIGURE 6. *Changes with age in the blood pressure of female Nuñoa natives, according to level of acculturation. (Solid lines) More acculturated; (dashed lines) less acculturated;* r, *Pearson correlation coefficient.*

acculturated group, have high blood pressures in old age. However, the analysis does show that, within a native population living at high altitude, something associated with the process of acculturation into general Peruvian society leads to significant increases in systemic blood pressure with age. Similar results have been reported for peasant and "primitive" populations at low altitudes, and some researchers have attributed the increase to psychological stress associated with modern culture. Such an explanation might apply to the results of our study, but it does not appear safe to conclude that this is the case before carefully examining nutritional and disease correlates. The available nutritional data are being examined for evidence of possible nutritional differences between the groups.

DISCUSSION AND CONCLUSIONS

From earliest recorded history it has been recognized that men from different populations vary in physical (that is, anatomical) characteristics and in cultures, but it is only recently that the variety of *physiological* differences has been revealed. The physiological differences so far shown are of the same general magnitude as the anatomical variations. That is, the available information suggests a basic commonality with respect to functions such as temperature regulation, energy exchange, and response to disease, but comparison or different populations has revealed a number of specific variations in response to environmental stress.

Probably the most controversial aspect of these new findings concerns the mechanisms underlying the physiological differences. Because of the time and expense involved in studying the problem, population samples have often been small. Thus, with respect to specific findings, such as the high oxygen-consumption capacity reported by some workers for natives living at high altitudes, it has been suggested that biased sampling explains the difference. Other differences have been explained in terms of short-term acclimatization or of variations in diet or in body composition. Of course, genetic differences and long-term or developmental acclimatization have also been suggested, but the short-term processes have been more commonly accepted as explanations because they are based on known mechanisms.

We believe that a more general application of the extensive and intensive methods used in studying the Nuñoa population is a necessary next step in the search for the sources of differences in functional parameters in different populations. Thus, with respect to the Nuñoa population, a study of growth alone would probably have led to the conclusion that the observed differences in growth were the result of malnutrition.

On the other hand, the results of the growth study considered together with results of detailed studies of nutritional and other responses suggest hypoxia as a better explanation. Similar examples could be cited, from other aspects of the program, to show that a set of integrated studies of a single population can provide insights not obtainable with data pertaining to a single aspect of population biology.

In general, the data are still not adequate to treat the third question originally posed, on the sources of adaptation. Indeed we cannot even clearly differentiate genetic factors from long-term and developmental acclimatization. For this purpose one would require comparable data on several populations that vary in genetic structure, in altitude of habitat, and in other aspects of environmental background. Fortunately, collection of such data is contemplated as part of the Human Adaptability Project of the International Biological Programme. The importance of understanding the sources of population differences seems obvious in a world where the geographical and cultural mobility of peoples is greater than it has ever been throughout history.

It seems clear that the native of the high Andes is biologically different from the lowlander, and that some of the differences are the result of adaptation to the environment. How well and by what mechanisms a lowland population could adapt to this high-altitude environment has not yet been adequately explored. Moreover, almost nothing is known about the biological problems faced by the highlander who migrates to the lowlands.

SUMMARY

The high-altitude areas of South America are in many ways favorable for human habitation, and they have supported a large native population for millennia. Despite these facts, immigrant lowland populations have not become predominant in these areas as in other parts of the New World, and lowlanders experience a number of biological difficulties on going to this region.

In order to learn more about the adaptations which enable the native to survive at high altitudes, an intensive study of a native population is being carried out in the district of Nuñoa in the Peruvian Altiplano. In this area hypoxia and cold appear to be the most unusual environmental stresses. Results to date show a high birth rate and a high death rate, the death rate for females, both postnatal and prenatal (as inferred from the sex ratio at birth), being unusually high. Birth weights are low, while placenta weights are high. Postnatal growth is quite slow relative to the rate for other populations throughout the world, and the adolescent growth spurt is less than that for other groups. The maximum oxygen consumption (and thus the capacity for sustained work) of adult males is high despite the reduced atmospheric pressure at high altitude. All lowland groups brought to this altitude showed significant reductions in maximum oxygen consumption. The Nuñoa native's responses to cold exposure also differ from those of the lowlander, apparently because blood flow to his extremities is high during exposure to cold. The disease patterns are not well known; respiratory diseases appear common, whereas there seems to be almost no cardiovascular disease among adults. Systemic blood pressures are very low, particularly those of individuals living in traditional native fashion. Nutrition appears to be good, but analysis of the nutrition studies is continuing.

The results of these studies are interpreted as showing that some aspects of the natives' adaptation to high altitudes require lifelong exposure to the environmental conditions and may be based on a genetic structure different from that of lowlanders.

SUPPLEMENTARY READINGS

Barnicot, N. A. Climatic factors in the evolution of human populations. *Cold Spring Harbor Symposia in Quantitative Biology,* 1959.

Coon, C. S. *The Origin of Races.* New York: Knopf, 1962.

Garn, S. M. *Human Races.* Springfield, Ill.: Charles C. Thomas, 1961.

nine

GROWTH AND DEVELOPMENT

Evolution means change. And it is the evidence of change in the physique of modern man that not only demonstrates that man is a product of evolution, but also that man is still subject to the influence of ongoing evolutionary processes. Recorded measurements and observations of various populations over the last few generations have indicated certain progressive physical changes. By researching the developmental mechanisms responsible for such changes, we can advance the scientific study of man and add to our knowledge of the nature of man's present evolution as well as gain clues to probable future developments. Tanner provides us with a more informed view of the great biological variability of our species, while Hunt analyzes some of the known metric changes that have been recorded during the past several decades.

Growth and Physique in Different Populations of Mankind

J. M. Tanner

The physique of a population—whether its members are tall or short, long- or short-limbed, broad or slender, muscular or slight, fat or lean, round-headed or long-nosed—depends on the distribution in it of numerous genes, on the mutual interaction of the products of these genes during development, and on the further interaction of these products with a wide variety of continuously changing environmental stimuli during the whole process of growth.

Such a system can respond very flexibly to alterations in the environment. Short-term alterations, such as a transient period of starvation, are met by homeorrhetic responses on the part of individuals; long-term alterations, such as an increase in solar radiation, by selective or evolutionary responses on the part of the population as a whole. These two types of response are not entirely separable, for they interact on each other. During a period of starvation a child may slow down in growth, and promptly catch up onto his previous growth curve when food again becomes freely available. This represents the individual homeorrhetic response. However, children whose growth regulation in the face of transient starvation is poor will be selected against. Such selection may occur either by a higher mortality at the time or by more subtle mechanisms such as reaching breeding age later, having narrower pelves (females, at risk in childbirth), or being smaller and less powerful (males, at disadvantage in competitive mating). The general ability to regulate growth in the face of a variety of environmental difficulties

From The Biology of Human Adaptability, *ed. P. T. Baker and J. S. Weiner (Oxford: The Clarendon Press, 1966), pp. 45–66; reprinted by permission of the author and The Clarendon Press, Oxford.*

will be selected for in all populations. All children everywhere must be able to depart from and return to the lines of growth that characterize them.

The lines of growth themselves differ, however, from one population to another. We must suppose that in each of the major populations of the world the growth of its members was gradually adjusted, by means of selection, to the environmental conditions in which they evolved. The remnants of this process we should be able to see in modern populations—the remnants only, because relatively recent migrations have much altered the distributions of peoples, so that many no longer live in the areas in which they evolved.

These two aspects, the response of the individual and the response of the population, each have their separate counterpart in the study of growth. The first takes us into medical, social, and economic studies; the second into ecological physiology, human evolution, and history. Both have their place in the International Biological Programme, and both need continuing study and coordination, as I shall argue later, in some permanent International Bureau for Growth Studies.

In regard to the first aspect, growth is one of the best indices of child health that we have, and a continuous monitoring of the growth and development of children in under- and over-nourished populations is, or should be, a major concern of all public health authorities and governments. If we compare the growth of members of a single population under differing social, nutritional, and medical conditions we can see to what extent their present environment falls short of supplying those stimuli and substrates which are necessary if all members of the population are to fulfil the potentialities of their gene complex. If we continue to study different social groups in the population as social and economic development or regression occurs we can see clearly whether or not we have really advanced and whether we have favoured one social group at the expense of others.

As for the second aspect; if we study healthy, fully developed children and adults, or as near to them as we can find, in a variety of populations, we can arrive at some notion as to the elements in physique which have been adaptive and we can obtain a more informed view of the great biological variability of our species. In other words, we can advance the scientific study of man and the understanding of his evolution. It is true that only family studies will throw light on the genetic mechanisms concerned in the control of growth, but the physiological mechanisms can be investigated in populations, and so too can the effects of selection. In all that follows population, rather than family, studies are considered. Wherever possible, however, family studies should be made concurrently.

THE EFFECT OF STARVATION AND DISEASE ON GROWTH AND PHYSIQUE

To begin with, we must get as clear a notion as we can of the effects of starvation and disease upon growth and physique. These are the environmental stimuli we hope to reduce or eliminate, in contrast to other more permanent aspects of the environment, such as climate and altitude.

It is convenient to distinguish clearly between effects on (1) rate of growth, (2) growth in size, (3) growth in skeletal shape, and (4) growth in tissue composition. These four effects may all occur together, or they may occur separately. If a child suffers an overall reduction in rate of growth at age 5, then clearly his size at age 5.5 must be affected, but not necessarily his size at 20 or adulthood. His shape and tissue composition may or may not be affected at 5.5 depending on whether the rate change is an overall one or peculiar to certain areas. It is perfectly possible for growth in size to be affected at all ages without the rate of maturation being slowed down; puberty and cessation of growth would occur at the usual age but at a smaller size than usual. Growth in skeletal shape could be affected without growth in size being changed, provided we took care that our definitions of skeletal size and shape were made so that the two were independently measured; and growth in tissue composition could, of course, be affected without growth in size or skeletal shape being necessarily involved.

In fact starvation seems usually to cause effects in a certain order, so that shape changes seldom, if ever, occur before size and rate changes are far advanced. Differences in gene complex on the other hand seem most frequently to affect shape and tissue composition. Thus we have already some guide as to the likelihood of a given population difference being due mostly to gene differences or to starvation and disease.

Besides distinguishing possible effects in this way, we must also clearly distinguish different causes. The effects of acute temporary, and chronic persistent, starvation may be very different. We must also remember that all the effects depend upon the age of the child, and all or many depend also upon sex, boys in general being more easily affected than girls.

Acute temporary starvation occurs from time to time in many populations. It may be associated with war, or temporary economic collapse, or physical disaster. In some populations it may occur fairly regularly at a certain time of year, so that the condition is a sort of half-way house between acute temporary and chronic persistent starvation. We can observe individual children from time to time with acute starvation due to psychological or medical causes. Unless the starvation is severe, all that happens is that the child's growth and development slow down, and when food is again available speed up to a rate above normal until the child has quite caught up again to its previous growth curve. Mild temporary starvation has clearly no lasting effect. But we do not know exactly how severe and how long-lasting starvation has to be before it produces a permanent effect, that is, a reduction in size of the adult. Probably this depends on the age at which it occurs, permanent effects being more rapidly produced in young children and possibly adolescents than in children in the mid-growth years. Possibly for a given degree of malnutrition, the critical time is proportional to the natural velocity of growth. One can imagine a sort of metabolic debt signifying 'unsatisfied growth potential' being built up as time passes and no growth occurs; I have elaborated elsewhere a hypothesis of how such a mechanism might operate (Tanner, 1963).

If rats are partially starved from birth to 21 days and then allowed to eat as much as they like, they at once have a catch-up spurt of growth, but it is insufficient to restore them to the normal curve of their litter-mates and they remain small all their lives (Widdowson and McCance, 1960; McCance, 1962). If rats are partially starved from 14 to 21 days they catch up better but still not entirely; if they are partially starved from 21 days to 40 days they are capable then of catching up completely. The rat is born at a much earlier stage of development than man, so that the birth-to-21 day period corresponds to the latter part of the foetal period in man. Malnutrition of the foetus is probably quite rare in man, but the rat experiments do show that, if we are seeking to explain some of the differences in size between populations as due to malnutrition, we should scrutinize most carefully the first two or three years, for it is influences at that time which are mostly likely to produce manifest and persistent effects.

Both temporary and permanent effects of periods of malnutrition are much less upon skeletal shape than on size. The answer to the question, "Are Nilotics linear because they eat too little at some particular time or throughout growth?" is clearly in the negative. At one time it was thought that acute or chronic malnutrition could change body proportions, and by analogy with some early results in cattle, it was suggested that short legs relative to the trunk length was a sign of malnutrition at an early age, as it may be in calves. Later work on rats and pigs has shown that the cattle results are not of general application and indeed the early results have not been uniformly repeated even in cattle. Widdowson's starved small rats had the same proportions of tail to body length, and of femur length to femur breadth, as the well-nourished larger rats, and also the same bone composition at each age. Apart from fat (and hence body weight) the only difference in shape seems to have been in the relation of head size to body length. As the head was much nearer adult size than the body at birth to 21 days, when starvation occurred, it remained relatively large in the starved small animals.

One good piece of evidence on this point in man comes from Greulich's (1957) study of Japanese children reared in California compared with those reared in the worse environment of Japan. The California-reared children were bigger at all ages, by the relationship of sitting height to leg length was practically the same throughout growth under both conditions (as shown by plotting Greulich's data on standard sitting heigh/stature charts). In general the proportion of limb to trunk, which varies so much from one population to another, is strongly regulated by genetic programming, in a way that overall body size is certainly not. This regulation can be seen very clearly in children who are severely dwarfed due to lack of growth hormone. They maintain normal proportions of limbs to trunk not only while they are dwarfed but even while they are catching up at four times the normal rate of growth when given human growth hormone (Tanner, unpublished). Similarly, there are recorded a number of cases of identical twins, one of whom has been malnourished or has had a chronic disease. This one has always been smaller than the healthy twin, but of the same skeletal proportions.

An exception to this rule may occur in hypothyroidism. Hypothyroid children are said to have legs which are relatively shorter than their trunks, even for their small overall size. This does not seem to be true of juvenile hypothyroids, whose disease starts after age 3 or 4. But in children who are hypothyroid at birth this disproportion may well exist, and may even be persistent, especially if therapy is not begun immediately after birth. Here again we see that it is disturbances in the early stages of growth which are least readily put right. A recent paper (Stock and Smythe, 1963) has in fact suggested that undernutrition during infancy may cause decreased brain growth and subsequent intellectual damage. Twenty-one very undernourished children in South Africa were followed, from 1 year of age to about 5 years, and the growth of their head circumference was compared with that of a control group whose parents had the same head circumference as the parents of malnourished children, but who lived in good circumstances. It appears that the head circumference of the malnourished was indeed less than that of the controls even at the time when the growth in both groups was nearing completion. The malnourished children also scored less in tests of mental ability, but this means very little since their homes were appalling and their parents non-existent or hopelessly improvident: in these circumstances the stimuli necessary for the development of mental ability are well known to be lacking. However, it is clear that research should be concentrated upon the early growth of the brain, particularly in areas where undernutrition is rife.

Whether growth of tissues, such as muscle, may be differentially affected by starvation or disease is not known. Here again we need data, and particularly data in the early years, and at adolescence when a new spurt of muscular growth occurs. The technical means of measuring widths of fat and muscle and bone in the limbs is at hand in simple X-rays (see Tanner, 1962) which can be used even in remote field conditions. Until this is done we cannot really be sure how much of the characteristically slender muscles of some East African Negroes are due to inheritance or to starvation. We do know, however, that the amount of muscle in Europeans is largely governed by inheritance, just as is bone (Hewitt, 1958; and see Osborne and De George, 1959). It seems likely that the shape of the muscle covering the bones and also the shape of the fat covering the muscle are both chiefly gene-determined. However, the amount of the muscle is governed, to some extent, by exercise, and the amount of fat is governed, to a far greater extent, by diet and sloth.

As for chronic malnutrition, there is little in practice that we can say to distinguish its effects from those of acute food shortage, although the distinction is of much theoretical importance, and will certainly be of practical importance when our data are better. In this respect it is important, for the IBP and later, to collect data on the best nourished and most healthy children in the population in underdeveloped countries so as to determine their growth potential. Knott (1963) has recently given figures for well-off Puerto Rican children which show them to be as large as Middle-West Americans from 7 years onwards and larger than the Spaniards from whom they are chiefly descended. Burgess and Burgess (1964) have likewise given "healthy" figures for East Africans, and Tanner and O'Keefe (1962) for Nigerian girls from 12 years onwards.

Acheson and others have maintained that the trend towards greater height that has occurred in the adult, as well as the child, population of Europe, America, and Japan during the last 80 to 100 years reflects better nutrition and less disease. He asserts that even relatively mild disease or subnutrition will cause chondrogenesis to stop while permitting osteogenesis —the turning of cartilage to bone—to continue. If this did occur it would certainly cause ultimate stunting. However, the evidence for such dissociation is very poor, since in most illnesses it seems that the two processes are retarded or advanced together. A degree of special pleading has tended to enter this discussion. Recently Acheson and Fowler (1964) have estimated that the sons of well-off men in London would, when fully grown, exceed their father's height by 1.9 inches; the sons of miners in the Rhondda Valley whose fathers grew up in conditions of unemployment and often misery were estimated to exceed their fathers by 2.3 inches. The hypothesis to be tested is that the differences between the circumstances of fathers and sons during the growing period—small for the London group, large for the Rhondda—have brought about a differential effect on growth. This the authors declare to be shown, despite themselves saying that the difference of .4 inch between the means is far from significant. But the facts are in themselves very interesting and remind us that we have at present no sure explanation of the secular trend. Probably in certain areas it is chiefly due to better nutrition and less disease; probably in others chiefly to heterosis and the breaking of isolates. We lack data on this from tropical and underdeveloped countries and it is much to be hoped that the IBP will lay the foundation on which continuing studies of the trend may be built (see Tanner, 1962, p. 143; Milicer, 1962; Craig, 1963.)

There is also a well-defined social class difference in European countries, the children of well-off parents being larger at all ages, and as adults, than children of poorly-off ones. The better-off also appear to have a lower weight for the same height. They seem to be a little more linear, less squat, and less muscular. This may be due to their being better nourished, but it could also be due to some inherent relation between size and/or shape and ability to rise in a European-type society, combined with assortative mating. Children with many siblings are significantly less in height and weight at each age and have a later puberty than children with few, presumably for similar nutritional-care reasons (see Tanner, 1962, p. 142; Valsik et al., 1963). These social class differences are a good example on a microscale of the differences between populations that we are trying to explain. They may be due to environment, and chiefly nutrition; but there may be also a genetic differential involved. The two interact inextricably.

Disease and growth

All that has been said about malnutrition applies equally to the effects of disease. A short and mild disease in a well-nourished child produces such a transient effect that if it exists it cannot be detected (see Tanner, 1962, pp. 130–134; Meredith and Knott, 1962). More severe diseases cause slowing of growth followed by a catch-up if the disease is cured. Probably critical periods for the effects of disease on growth exist, as they do for malnutrition, and certainly disease and undernutrition interact, not necessarily in an additive fashion.

Chronic disease, however, is our chief concern, and we are just beginning to have reports on the effects on growth due to eradicating malaria or hookworm or other similar diseases in areas in Africa and South America. In general the effects seem to be not spectacular. Thus reduction of the incidence of malaria in a heavily parasitized population in Tanganyika did not result in any significant increase in the weights of children during the first 18 months after birth (Draper and Draper, 1960); and children with repeated heavy malarial infections in the Gambia were no smaller by age 3½ than those protected by chloroquine (McGregor et al., 1956). Similarly being heterozygous for sickling haemoglobin S, even in malarious areas where its possession is supposed to confer an advantage in mortality, does not affect growth in height or weight (Garlick and Barnicot, 1957; Roberts, 1960). Diseases which cause a large reduction in regular haemoglobin content of the blood have a larger effect.

Neither disease nor malnutrition should be accepted uncritically as the cause of differences in growth between, for example, African and European populations. McGregor, Billewicz, and Thomson (1961) studied the growth of 187 children in rural Gambia from 9 months onwards. Though 43 per cent died before age 7, the heights and weights of these in the year previous to death were no different from the heights and weights of survivors. Growth was similar to that of Europeans in the first 6 months, then slowed until 2 years, when it resumed at the European rate. The authors say this slowing is not nutritional in origin in this area of rural Africa and think that undernutrition in certain children more likely follows disease than is the cause of it. They lay the chief blame on the inefficient development of active immunity.

DIFFERENCES BETWEEN POPULATIONS IN GROWTH AND PHYSIQUE

Anthropologists have documented some of the physical differences between populations with a zeal that approaches the excessive; but other aspects of physique such as muscle width have been less well studied, and the all-important question of how members of each population grew during childhood so as to attain their characteristic size and shape has been studied least of all. This is the field in which studies, internationally planned but nationally conducted, could contribute immensely to an understanding of the genesis of human variation.

What follows is not an exhaustive catalogue of studies of growth and physique in non-European populations—useful though that would be at the present time—but a selection and discussion of a number of the chief attempts to explain adult differences in physique by reference to differential growth rates.

One of the best of such studies is that of Hiernaux (1964) on the growth of the Tutsi and Hutu peoples of Rwanda. The Tutsi are tall, linear people, with an average adult male height and weight of 176 cm and 57 kg. The Hutu are shorter and stockier, with averages of 167 cm and 58 kg. There are two ways by which the Tutsi could grow to be taller. Either they may be longer at birth or shortly after and grow slightly more in length throughout their childhood; or they could grow at the same rate, but for a longer period, adding their extra 9 cm after the Hutu had stopped growing. The former is in fact the case. Both Tutsi and Hutu grow slowly compared with European children, probably because their nutrition is suboptimal, but both cease growth at about the same age (being 93–94 per cent of mature height at age 17), have menarche at the same age (about 16.5 years) and show the reversal of boys-taller to girls-taller at the same age (14 years). Hiernaux's data start at age 6 only, so we cannot tell exactly when the characteristic height-weight differences first were obvious. They are clear enough at age 6, however, Tutsi averaging 4 cm taller than Hutu, with almost identical weights. They probably start immediately after birth and reflect genetic differences of the same sort as those which cause boys' forearms to grow, from birth onwards, relatively a little faster than girls' (see Tanner, 1962).Tutsi and Hutu were growing up in a similar environment (the survey was made in 1957–8) but the Tutsi were better nourished, being the ruling caste. Despite this the Tutsi weight for given height was considerably lower than that of the Hutu. In the same paper Hiernaux gives figures for a group of Hutu reared from birth in Congo mining camps, where they were somewhat better nourished than in Rwanda. Only boys aged 6 to 9 are adequately represented and these are taller, by 2 to 2½ cm, than the Rwanda Hutu. They are also about 4 kg. heavier.

This study raises virtually all the problems that we need to discuss in planning the IBP studies. They are as follows.

1. CHRONOLOGICAL AGE. In this study age was known. When age is unknown, differentiation between the growing-faster and the growing-for-longer hypotheses is impossible. Except in special circumstances, there seems to be virtually no way out of this impasse. Certain pairs of measurements change their relationship during growth; for example the head circumference, which is relatively advanced at birth and grows little later, and the leg length, which is relatively retarded at birth and grows much later. Hence the ratio, leg length/head circumference, increases as the child gets older; or, better, the figure for leg length adjusted to head circumference by a regression increases as the child grows. This ratio, or the position in the regression chart, could therefore be used to estimate the child's age, but only within a given population under given conditions. If we have to compare two populations we would have first to be sure that in whatever other aspects of physique they differed, in the relation of leg length and head circumference they were the same at all ages. This seems virtually impossible even if both populations are equally well nourished. If one population's growth is retarded in all respects, perhaps by malnutrition, then the argument breaks down completely. A more accurate estimate of age can be made from combining

a whole series of measurements—this is called 'shape age' and is currently under statistical investigation in my laboratory and others—but again this only works within, not between, populations.

Given a single population under stable environmental circumstances, the chronological age of the children could be 'reconstructed' at the end of a 5-year longitudinal study perhaps, starting with groups at birth, 5, 10, and 15 years. Either through measurement ratios or perhaps better by taking hand and wrist X-rays for skeletal age the appearance of known 1-, 2-, 3-, 4-, and 5-year-olds is secured and then those children who were, on this criterion, 4, 5, etc., five years ago located. The skeletal ages of the whole child population could be reconstructed in this way, but no allowance could be made for the variation between skeletal and chronological age in individual children older than 5 years. Reconstruction by reference to tooth eruption has the same difficulties but perhaps to a lesser degree.

We need to find something which is entirely unaffected by malnutrition and disease, and absolutely the same for all populations. Only age satisfies this criterion. Perhaps amongst physical measurements the one which most nearly approaches the criterion is the number of erupted teeth. The eruption of teeth seems to be less affected by malnutrition than maturation of the skeleton or physical growth. This is particularly the case for the primary dentition (Voors, 1957; Voors and Metselaar, 1958) which also seems, in our relatively scanty data, to vary less from one population to another than does the secondary. In eruption of secondary dentition East African and South African Bantu and Dutch New Guinea children are ahead of Europeans; in primary dentition this is not the case, but American Negroes are somewhat ahead of American Whites (see Tanner, 1962, p. 71).

We may say, then, that in IBP surveys so far as possible only children of known age should be included and much ingenuity and time may have to be expended getting parents to date their children's birth accurately by reference to remembered local events. Secondly, so that we may investigate further the possibilities for the future, tooth eruption should be recorded on all children, particularly those in the stage of primary dentition. If X-rays are available more sophisticated methods for dental maturity should also be used. Radiographs of the mandibular teeth will give a dental maturity rating at all ages.

2. CROSS-SECTIONAL AND LONGITUDIAL STUDIES. Hiernaux's study is cross-sectional and this has not been detrimental for the purposes for which the study was designed. We have to keep in mind, however, exactly what cross-sectional studies will and will not do. They tell us the attained heights, weights, etc., at each age. They tell us, up to but not during adolescence, the mean velocity of growth from year to year in each measurement. They enable us to compare two populations for size and shape at a given age. They enable us to say something about differences in rate of change of size and shape before adolescence, though we cannot make a significant test of population differences since we do not know the standard errors of the mean velocities. However, we can approximate them by a general knowledge of the results of longitudinal studies. Cross-sectional studies do not tell us how

much a population varies in growth rate. They give us an idea of the average age at which the adolescent acceleration reaches its peak (though a slightly biased one) but little idea of the magnitude of the average peak velocity. They do not give a true figure for the average age at which growth ceases, since the latest-finishing subjects affect the height-achieved averages. We may wish to know whether two populations which differ in some measurement as adults were the same before adolescence, one having a greater adolescent spurt in the measurement; or if the differences arose before adolescence, the quantities added in the spurt being the same. A general notion of which has occurred may be obtained from cross-sectional studies, but not a precise answer. If menarcheal age is available as a guide to when adolescence occurs, this improves the tentative answer; the same is true of skeletal age.

Thus in the IBP cross-sectional studies are useful, but should be supplemented where possible by longitudinal studies particularly of infancy and adolescence. These longitudinal studies should extend over a minimum of 5 years.

3. AGES REPRESENTED. In Hiernaux's study the first age represented is 6 years. For this reason we cannot say whether the increased rate of growth in height of the Hutu begins at birth or later. In the IBP all ages from birth to maturity, i.e., at least 25, should be represented. For the first year 3-monthly groups should be used and from 1 to 2 years 6-monthly groups. This implies that there should be three or four times as many 0- to 1-year-olds and twice as many 1- to 2-year-olds measured as 3- to 4-, 4- to 5-year-olds, etc.

4. BOYS AND GIRLS. In Hiernaux's study both boys and girls are represented. Hence we can see at what age girls' height begins to exceed boys', which is a valuable guide to the age of beginning of the girls' adolescent spurt. The same is true of the age at which this trend reverses. Secondly we can see whether there is any significant sex-population interaction. This may be important. The response of girls to a variety of environmental disturbances is less than that of boys; girls seem to be better canalized (see Tanner, 1962, p. 127). Hence a lesser growth of boys in one population compared with another, in the presence of equal growth of girls in both, points to an environmental difference between the populations (as for example in Graffer, Asiel, and Emery-Hanzer, 1961). This is not an absolute criterion since sex-limited genes may differ between the two populations, but less usually.

For the IBP then, girls and boys should be studied simultaneously.

5. MEASUREMENTS OF DEVELOPMENTAL AGE. Without some measure of developmental age we cannot answer accurately the basic question as to whether the Tutsi grow for longer—whether they are the same height as the Hutu at each skeletal age, for example, but have a lower skeletal age for each chronological age—or grow more. Hiernaux answered this in his paper by reference to menarcheal age, which was known, and by reference to the percentage of adult height reached by his oldest age groups, that is 17-year-olds. Both methods are useful; obtaining figures for menarche may

be easier than obtaining a sample of healthy 25- to 30-year-olds for the adult mature measurement. Neither technique tells us whether the situation in height relative to stage of development changed between 6 and 17. It might be that at 6 the Tutsi had a more advanced skeletal age than the Hutu and that their superiority of height at that age corresponded simply to faster growth and development; the height of the two groups for skeletal age might be the same. This might have gone on till adolescence was approached. Then the Hutu might have had a more rapid advance during adolescence, catching up to the Tutsi in skeletal age by the time of menarche, without having a correspondingly greater increase in their adolescent height spurt. Such would be the picture of population-age interaction for rate of growth. Admittedly such a thing is less likely than the more simple situation, and it probably does not occur in the Tutsi-Hutu comparison. But as between Chinese and Europeans (see below) it seems to be present, just as the analogous interaction takes place between different individuals in the same population.

Thus in IBP studies some measure of developmental age should be included. Menarche is by far the easiest. All that is necessary is to ask a large sample of girls of known age from about 9 to 17 whether or not they have yet begun to menstruate and fit the resulting percentage incidence curve by logits or probits (see Burrell, Healy, and Tanner, 1961). The presence of secondary sex characters such as public hair, breasts, and male external genitalia can be dealt with in the same way, though less accurately. (Good examples are the papers of Lee, Chang, and Chan (1963) on the maturation of Chinese girls in Hong Kong as related to social class and of Bottyán and associates (1963) in Hungary.) Pictorial standards for judging development are given in Tanner (1962). Skeletal ages should be done where possible also, using the left hand and wrist and either the Greulich-Pyle or the Tanner-Whitehouse assessments.

In the IBP therefore menarcheal age should always be investigated, and secondary sex character age and skeletal age where possible.

In passing it may be noted that menarche may not occur at the same place on the height curve in all populations. Its position is rather constant in European groups, but in Nigerians it may perhaps occur later, that is nearer the point of cessation of height growth (see Tanner and O'Keefe, 1962). Hong Kong girls mature early, but have the same relation of menarche and mature height as Europeans. However, in Hong Kong girls the relative timing of appearance of breasts and public hair differs from that observed in Europeans and white Americans; public hair appears relatively later in the Chinese (Lee, Chang, and Chan, 1963).

Chinese-European differences

Another interesting difference of rate occurs in Hong Kong children. From 6 to 15 years in boys and 6 to 12 years in girls, the skeletal maturity of Hong Kong children is retarded relative to the American Greulich-Pyle standards. However, at adolescence a change occurs and the Chinese pass more rapidly through the standards than the Americans, so that they are advanced after 12 in girls and 15 in boys (Low, Chan, Chang, and Lee, 1964). Here then is our example of the population-age interaction in rate of growth (or non-parallelism, to use another biometrical analogy) discussed above. It is not possible to tell from the cross-sectional studies whether this rapid adolescent skeletal development is accompanied by a stature spurt with a higher peak velocity than in Europeans; the figures suggest it may be so in boys. When plotted on the 1954 standard British charts the Hong Kong girls' average height lies at the 25th percentile from 9 to 11, reaches the 30th at 13 and 14, and drops to the 10th at 15, 16, and 17. It seems here that the adolescent spurt was of average European intensity, occurred early, and finished more rapidly than in Europeans. The best-off members of the Hong Kong population showed similar timings, though a different size level. The girls were at the British 50th percentile for height at 9 to 11, rose to the 65th at 12, had menarche at 12.5 compared with the British 13.1, and fell to the British 15th percentile by age 15. Well-off boys were at the 40th percentile at 9-11, 50th at 12 rising to 60th at 14, and dropping back to the 20th at 17. Clearly there are many interesting timing differences, but their full extent can only be elucidated by longitudinal study.

Negro-white differences

There are, of course, many differences in build between Negroes and Whites. The Negro has long legs and arms relative to the trunk length, narrow hips, less muscular calves, and heavier bones. Not only is this true of the average American Negro student compared with Whites, but it even holds in Olympic athletes, amongst competitors at each type of sport (Tanner, 1964). Hurdlers, for example, have long legs, but Negro hurdlers have longer legs than White hurdlers. Weight-lifters, both White and Negro, have short legs, but the White lifters are shorter than the Negro.

We know very little of how these differences come about. One very well attested difference, however, is in the rate of maturing. Negroes, whether in America, West or East Africa, are ahead of Whites at birth in skeletal ossification, even compared with Whites living in better economic circumstances. This probably reflects an inherited difference in hormone secretion during the late foetal period, for their permanent teeth also erupt earlier, and the basis of these teeth is laid down in the uterus, though later than the laying down of the primary teeth, whose eruption date differs less between the races (see Tanner, 1962, pp. 66 and 77; Massé and Hunt, 1963). The Negro child maintains his advancement for about 2 to 3 years if living in good economic circumstances; it is reflected in a greater rate of growth in length and weight and a greater maturity of motor development and behavioural milestones. But after this age even in good circumstances the African child appears to decelerate in growth curve of the two races having a different shape, just as do the velocity and development. This may well be a natural occurrence, the velocity curves of males and females, in both races. The same thing is seen between members of the same population. Hewitt (1958) has shown that sibs resemble each other in having either a rapid growth of calf muscle from 6 months to 3 years followed by a relatively slower growth from 3 to 5 years, or the reverse pattern. This is a fairly complicated problem in growth velocities, and can only be satisfactorily solved by longitudinal studies on various populations living under good nutritional circumstances.

Indian-Asian differences

Berry and Deshmukh (1964) have recently shown that the somatotype distribution of Indian students differs greatly from that of European ones and probably even more from Asians (Heath, Hopkins, and Miller, 1961). Indians are less mesomorphic and more ectomorphic. This difference has also a genetic component, and starts early in childhood. In Singapore, Indian children had a lower weight for height than Chinese and Malayan children living in similar circumstances at all ages from 3 months to 5 years (the oldest studied), though by 5 years they were actually taller (Millis, 1957, 1958). More studies of children of different ethnic groups living in a similar environment are very desirable.

Primitive Populations

None of what has been said so far refers to primitive populations, and one of the avowed tasks of the IBP is to study these so as to have records of them before they disappear or are assimilated. Few primitive populations have been adequately studied from the point of view of either physique or growth. There is little on the Eskimo or the Andean, little on the Pygmy or the Australian Aboriginal. We have heights and weights, but no chronological ages, on Shilluk and Dinka in the Sudan (Roberts, 1961), but this has actually led to a probably incorrect interpretation of the genesis of their linearity (see Hiernaux, 1964). A few studies on American Indians have been done (see Kraus, 1954), but nothing on Tibetans or dwellers in Himalaya. Yet we know there are vast differences between these populations, not only in adult physique but in childhood. Margaret Mead, Tony Schwartz, and I studied somatotype pictures of all members, adults and children, in a Sepik River village community in New Guinea. Both men and women were strikingly mesomorphic compared with Europeans, and the children seemed to show the same type of build. Certainly between many primitive communities there is no overlap at all in physique. It takes no great anthropologist to distinguish any one Dinka from any one Manus even if the facial features, skull contour, and skin colour are all obliterated. The techniques developed in the study of more advanced cultures are mostly quite easily applicable to these groups, and we must hope that in the IBP their children's growth will be studied now before it is too late.

Climate and altitude

We do not at present know to what extent the differences between populations are due to climate and altitude. We must presume that these geographical features originally governed the selection of growth-controlling genes and hence led to the emergence of the differences we see now. The adaptative significance of the various features can only be assessed by physiological studies, and at least some of these should if possible be carried out on children as well as adults, for the adaptation may be relevant to the growing period rather than adult life. Most selection takes place before the reproductive age is reached. It seems less likely that many of the differences in growth pattern are directly due to the action of climate and altitude on the growing child, except in such instances as emphysematous chests in very high altitude dwellers. A test of this is provided by people of one race who grow up in the area mostly inhabited by another. Europeans reared in the Sudan do not grow up with the Dinka physique, nor do Africans reared in Liverpool grow thick European-type calves. Englishmen who pass their youth in Japan are not, so far as we know, characteristically short-legged. Nevertheless a study of persons reared in a *milieu* very different from that of their parents would be a very desirable addition to the IBP programme. Italian migrants to Boston are being studied intensively by Boutourline Young. Few results have yet been published. Greulich's (1957) excellent study of Japanese migrants to California has already been mentioned. Two great difficulties are presented by all migrant studies, however: first migrant parents seem never to be a random sample of the nation they leave, being usually larger and more intelligent than the stay-at-homes (even if they only migrate from one English county to another); and secondly food habits and opportunities are very seldom the same for migrants as for sedentes. Thus the effects of climate and altitude are hard to assess by this means. A similar difficulty beset Wurst's (1961) study of the growth of Austrian children in relation to altitude. The higher the villages, the poorer were the people, the worse was the food and the greater the calories expended on walking to school. Thus though the high-altitude children were smaller at all ages, the reasons for this cannot be disentangled.

SUMMARY

1. A summary is given of present knowledge of the effects of malnutrition and disease on growth and physique. Disturbances of the environment affect first rate of growth, then, if prolonged, final size. Only very severe disturbances affect shape. It is likely that malnutrition in the early years has a more lasting effect than malnutrition later.
2. Differences in patterns of growth between different populations are then considered, an attempt being made to distinguish those which are inherited from those which occur as a result of malnutrition or disease. A comparison of two African populations is cited and used as an example for the development of a list of guiding principles to be observed when making growth studies in the IBP. The limitations of cross-sectional and longitudinal studies are discussed and the usefulness of such landmarks as menarche, whose mean and variability can be assessed even on cross-sectional data.
3. It is proposed that a small International Bureau for Growth Studies be set up, to co-ordinate present and future knowledge, which at the moment is widely scattered and collected with little reference to existing work. The function of such a Bureau would be somewhat similar to those of the International Blood Group Centre.

REFERENCES

Acheson, R. M. and Fowler, G. B. 1964. Sex, socio-economic status and secular increase in stature. *Br. J. Prev. Soc. Med.* 18: 25–34.

Berry, J. N. and Deshmukh, P. Y. 1964. Somatotypes of male college students in Nagpur, India. *Hum. Biol.* 36: 157–76.

Bottyán, O.; Dezso, Gy; Eiben, O., Farkas, Gy; Rajkai, T.; Thoma, A.; and Veli, Gy. 1963. Age at menarche in Hungarian girls. *Annls Hist. Nat. Mus. Natn. Hung.* 55: 561–71.

Burgess, A. P., and Burgess, H. K. L. 1964. The growth patterns of East African schoolgirls. *Hum. Biol.* 36: 177–93.

Burrell, R. J. W.; Healy, M. J. R.; and Tanner, J. M. 1961. Age at menarche in South African Bantu girls living in the Transkei reserve. *Hum. Biol.* 33: 250–61.

Chang, K. S. F.; Lee, M. M. C.; Low, W. D.; and Kvan, E. 1963. Height and weight of southern Chinese children. *Am. J. Phys. Anthrop.* 21: 497–509.

Craig, *J. O.* 1963. The heights of Glasgow boys: Secular and social influences. *Hum. Biol.* 335: 524–39.

Draper, K. C., and Draper, C .C. 1960. Observations on the growth of African infants with special reference to the effects of malaria control. *J. Trop. Med. Hyg.* 63: 167–71.

Garlick, J. P. and Barnicot, N. A. 1957. Blood groups and haemoglobin variants in Nigerian (Yoruba) schoolchildren. *Ann. Hum. Genet.* 21: 420–25.

Graffar, M.; Asiel, M.; and Emery-Hauzeur, C. 1961. La taille et le périmetre cephalique pendant la première année de la vie. *Acta Paediat. Belg.* 15: 61–74.

Greulich, W. W. 1957. A comparison of the physical growth and development of American-born and native Japanese children. *Am. J. Phys. Anthrop.* 15: 489–515.

Heath, B. H.: Hopkins, C. E.; and Miller, C. D. 1961. Physique of Hawaii-born young men and women of Japanese ancestry, compared with college men and women of the United States and England. *Am. J. Phys. Anthrop.* 19: 173–84.

Hewitt, D. 1958. Sib resemblance in bone, muscle and fat measurements of the human calf. *Ann. Hum. Genet.* 22: 26–35.

Hiernaux, J. 1964. Weight/height relationship during growth in Africans and Europeans. *Hum. Biol.* 36: 273–93.

Knott, V. B. 1963. Stature, leg girth and body weight of Puerto Rican private school children measured in 1962. *Growth* 27: 157–74.

Kraus, B. S. 1954. *Indian Health in Arizona.* Tucson: University of Arizona Press.

Lee, M. M. C.; Chang, K. S. F.; and Chan, M. M. C. 1963. Sexual maturation of Chinese girls in Hong Kong. *Pediatrics* 32: 389–98.

LOW, W. D.; CHAN, S. T.; CHANG, K. S. F.; and LEE, M. M. C. 1964. Skeletal maturation of southern Chinese children in Hong Kong. *Child Develpm.* 35: 1313–36..

MCCANCE, R. A. 1962. Food, growth and time. *Lancet* 2: 621–26.

MCGREGOR, I. A., and BILLEWICZ, W. Z. 1961. Growth and mortality in children in an African village. *Br. Med. J.* 2: 1661–66.

———; GILLES, H. M.; WALTERS, J. H.; DAVIES, A. H.; and PEARSON, F. A. 1956. Effects of heavy and repeated malarial infections on Gambian infants and children. *Trans. R. Soc. Trop. Med. Hyg.* 2: 686–92.

MASSÉ, G.; and HUNT, E. E. 1963. Skeletal maturation of the hand and wrist in West African children. *Hum. Biol.* 35: 3–25.

MEREDITH, H. V., and KNOTT, V. B. 1962. Illness history and physical growth: III. Comparative anatomic status and rate of change for schoolchildren in different long-term health categories. *Am. J. Dis. Child.* 103: 146–51.

MILICER, H. 1962. Investigations on the physical development of youth. In *Physical Education in School,* eds. W. Missiuro and J. Sadowska, Warsaw: Institute of Physical Culture.

MILLIS, J. 1957. Growth of pre-school Malay infants in Singapore. *Med. J. Malaya* 12: 416–22.

———. 1958. Growth of pre-school Chinese and Southern Indian children in Singapore. *Med. J. Malaya* 12: 531–39.

ROBERTS, D. F. 1961. Körperhöhe und Gewicht nilotiden Kinder. *Homo* 12: 33–41

STOCK, M. B., and SMYTH, P. M. 1963. Does undernutrition during infancy inhibit brain growth and subsequent intellectual development? *Archs. Dis. Childh.* 38: 546–52.

TANNER, J. M. 1962. *Growth at Adolescence.* 2d ed. Oxford: Blackwell.

———. 1963. Regulation of growth in size in mammals. *Nature, Lond.* 199: 845–50.

———. 1964. *Physique of the Olympic Athlete.* London: Allen and Unwin.

———, and O'KEEFE, B. 1962. Age at menarche in Nigerian schoolgirls, with a note on their height and weights, from age 12 to 19. *Hum. Biol.* 34: 187–96.

VALSIK, J. A.; STUKOVSKY, R.; and BERNATOVA, L. 1963. Quelques facteurs geographiques et sociaux ayant une influence sur l'âge de la puberté. *Biotypologie* 24: 109–23.

VOORS, A. W. 1957. The use of dental age in studies of nutrition in children. *Documenta Med. Geogr. Trop.* 9: 137–48.

———, and METSELAAR, D. 1958. The reliability of dental age as a yardstick to assess the unknown calendar age. *Trop. Geogr. Med.* 10: 175–80.

WIDDOWSON, E. M., and MCCANCE, R. A. 1964. Some effects of accelerating growth: I. General somatic development. *Proc. Roy. Soc.* B 152: 188–206.

WURST, F.; WASSERTHEURER, H.; and KINNESWENGER, K. 1961. *Entwicklung und Umwelt des Landkindes.* Vienna: Osterreichicher Bundesverlag.

Human Growth and Body Form in Recent Generations

Edward E. Hunt, Jr.

In a discussion of the physical anthropology of white Americans, Kluckhohn (1955) mentions the desirability of making fresh analyses of the statistical data recorded by some of the earlier anthropometrists. The present paper is such an attempt, based on modern concepts of physical growth, body composition, posture and physique.

In some human groups, measurable changes in body build have undoubtedly occurred during the past several decades, and the abundant evidence of these changes has recently been reviewed by Kaplan (1954). One of the best studies of these phenomena is the excellent monograph of Bowles (1932) on the anthropometry of Harvard fathers and sons. These data are to be utilized again here. Bowles's study also included samples of mothers and daughters from four women's colleges in the eastern United States, but this material is too meager for our present purposes.

Unfortunately, somatic measurements taken on college students are only indications of the outcome of growth. These dimensions are only indirect hints as to the metamorphoses which took place earlier. It is therefore necessary to implement our analysis with findings on the physical growth of other human groups—especially when individual children have been repeatedly observed and measured over a period of years.

As a preliminary to a review of Bowles's data, we shall first consider the recent trends of growth and final body size in a few human populations. The next topic is the use of anthropometry for locating specific sites of growth in the body. Finally, we shall deal with Bowles's Harvard series itself:

From American Anthropologist *60, no. 1 (1958): 118–31; reprinted by permission of the author and the American Anthropological Association.*

the methods used in measuring it, and the interrelations among posture, body composition, shape, and size in the paternal and filial generations.

The main thesis of this paper is that a decreased frequency of disturbances of growth has been chiefly responsible for the recent somatic enlargement of Harvard families. In local regions of the body, tissues with the largest specific contributions to total body size have undergone the greatest absolute enlargement in the Harvard sons. The evidence for this hypothesis lies in the great consistency of changes in posture, the sizes of local body regions, and in the fat content and muscularity of the organism.

GROWTH RATES AND FINAL SIZE IN MAN

In considering secular trends of human body size in recent generations, it is becoming clear that some populations have remained metrically stable, and others have changed. One of the most unaltered groups known to me is the Micronesian people of Yap. Six anthropometrists have measured them from 1876 to 1948, and in that time span they have remained unchanged metrically (Hunt, Kidder, & Schneider 1954). This metrical stability has persisted during a severe depopulation, and while Yap was occupied successively by Spain, Germany, Japan, and the United States. In this interval, the Yapese have remained genetically almost unmixed with foreigners, and their diet and culture have changed relatively little. In 1948, cross-sectional data on Yapese of known age revealed that the males reached a maximal stature at 26 years of age, and females at 22 years.

The attainment of this maximum is not, of course, the average age at which the Yapese of each sex stopped growing in stature. It is about the age when the most delayed minority did so, and is perhaps five years later than the mean age of cessation of statural increase.

According to Morant (1948), British men in the late 19th century attained their statural maximum at 26–27 years, while during World War II this level was reached at about 21–22 years. At 20 years of age, modern samples are consequently taller than their ancestors, but this difference vanishes a few years later.

These findings show that accelerated maturation need not increase the final or maximal average statures of human populations. In research on such data, we should attempt to separate growth rates from final size (Randall 1949). Indeed, evidence from animal growth studies in general suggests that the two phenomena may not be controlled by the same genes (Dobzhansky 1955). Furthermore, measurements of college students or military personnel may not efficiently separate growth from final size—especially if most individuals were measured at or below the age of 20 years.

Although data from Yap and Britain show considerable genetic continuity from the 19th century to the present day, national samples from the United States are less unambiguous in this respect. If we are interested in large military samples, we find that measurements of the Union army during the Civil War are based chiefly on men from the Northern states with relatively short stature. Samples from later wars contain progressively smaller percentages of men of "Old American" stock (Kluckhohn 1955).

In 1946, the maximal stature of a large sample of white American enlisted men was reached at 23 years of age. According to Randall (1949), this attainment is probably equivalent to a mean age of completed stature of about 18 years. Like the British, Americans seem to have been maturing at progressively younger ages (Martin 1953). Nevertheless, it is still not absolutely certain whether the completed average stature of the American people as a whole has really increased. From skeletal data on a Midwestern cadaver population, Trotter and Gleser (1951) conclude that Negro and white Americans of the poorer classes did not become taller in the 19th century, but have done so since.

When we turn from national samples to American college students, much more convincing increases in body size have occurred (*cf.* Meredith 1941, and Kluckhohn 1955). In using Bowles's evidence for documenting this trend, we should first consider some of its limitations and advantages.

One complication of sampling in Bowles's series is that the few students who were measured in their twenties tend to be shorter than the majority who were measured in their teens. The data do not indicate an earlier age of maximum stature in the filial generation. The filial samples were also measured at younger mean ages than were their parents, in both sexes. These peculiarities of the data should work against a finding of larger size in the progeny. Nevertheless, the increase of size in both sexes is unquestionable.

A major advantage of Bowles's study is its use of familial material. This plan minimizes the effects of changes in the ethnic composition of the United States on body measurements, which apply equally to college students and to the population at large.

When college progeny of college parents are studied, the only residual source of bias which occurs to me is the possibility that the filial generation may be unrepresentatively energetic or intelligent, relative to their remaining siblings. Confining ourselves to Americans alone, Terman (1925), Terman and Oden (1947), and Hrdlička (1940) have noted some degree of association between large body size and superior intelligence. But there is no reason to think that the filial generation at college was more selected in this respect than was the parental generation.

ANTHROPOMETRY AND THE SITES OF SOMATIC GROWTH

Although stature is a crude overall measure of skeletal growth, it tells us little of local or specific changes in the human body during successive generations. Fortunately, Bowles's monograph contains many other somatic measurements which are far more useful for analytic purposes. But as Krogman and Sassouni (1957) and others have observed, traditional anthropometry was invented mainly to compare racial specimens or samples. It is not necessarily suitable for studies of the specific processes or consequences of growth.

For such developmental investigations, one valuable procedure is to minimize the number of proliferating tissues or growth centers which lie between the boundaries of a measurement (Washburn 1953). We call such dimensions *parsimonious* (Baker, Hunt & Sen 1957). Since growth occurs mainly deep within the body, considerations of parsimony lead us to measure the "inner man" radiographically as well as the "outer man" by external mensuration of the entire individual.

Another justification for parsimony is that some tissues are more liable than others to arrested development—whether in the embryo, fetus, or child. Localized measurements—even in the adult—may indicate where these arrests typically occurred in the members of a population. After a transient cessation of growth, later compensatory enlargement of a tissue may be observed (Greulich & Pyle 1950), but some recent studies have shown that this compensation in the skeleton is negligible in younger children (Acheson & Hewitt 1954), and the final size of the damaged part may be somewhat stunted (Acheson & Dupertuis, 1957).

As research in physical growth centers on the "inner man," we inevitably come to measure chemical growth and body composition (Macy 1942; Hunt & Giles 1956; Macy & Kelly 1956), and also the interrelationships of size among different kinds of tissues (Baker, Hunt & Sen 1957). As a by-product of such internal measurements of the body, equations can be devised to predict body composition from external anthropometric dimensions. One of these equations is used here on Bowles's data.

Another example of the usefulness of radiographs to illuminate outward assessments of the body is the original evidence of Sheldon et al. (1940) relating the postural curvatures of the vertebral column to somatotype. Goff (1951) later verified these findings both from body build photographs and by spinal radiography. When the dimensional trends in Bowles's data indicate changes in posture in the sons, it is important to determine whether body build has changed in the equivalent direction.

ANTHROPOMETRIC TECHNIQUE IN THE HARVARD STUDY

The anthropometry of Harvard undergraduates was initiated in 1870 by Dr. William T. Brigham, former director of the Hemenway Gymnasium. His successor, Dr. Dudley A. Sargent, published a manual in 1887 which describes the techniques and equipment used in this survey, which continued until 1917. Some of Sargent's procedures are described and attributed to him in Martin and Saller (1956), but others are not. Accordingly, in the tables to be discussed later, the dimensions included in Martin-Saller are indicated by their measurement numbers. The remainder are described here, usually in direct quotation from Sargent's manual.

Measurements of height of body parts were taken with a fixed upright wooden anthropometer, mounted on a wooden box. The metal tapes and calipers used for the other measurements are not unlike those used today.

The measurements not listed in Martin-Saller and deviating from modern standards are:

Knee height: "Right foot placed upon the box with the knee bent at a right angle press the sliding arm forcibly upward against the hamstring tendons close to the calf of the leg—read the figures at the top of the slide."

Pubic height: "Figure standing easily erect upon the box, measure to the lower edge of the pubic bone."

Shoulder to elbow length: "From the top of the acromion process to the olecranon; the arm bent sharply at the elbow and held at the side; care should be taken that the measuring rod is parallel with the humerus; not with the external surface of the arm."

Elbow to finger length: "From the olecranon process to the tip of the middle finger, the arm bent sharply at the elbow and the rod resting on the back of the arm and hand."

Neck girth: "Halfway between the head and body or just below the 'Adam's apple,' head erect."

Waist girth: "At the smallest part, after a natural expiration."

Forearm girth: "At the largest part; fist firmly clenched"; elbow fully flexed and abducted about 45° (illustrated), and fist lateral to shoulder.

Wrist girth: "Between the styloid process and the hand, which is held open with the muscles of the forearm relaxed."

Neck breadth: "At the narrowest part: head erect and muscles of the neck relaxed."

Shoulder breadth: "At the broadest part, five cm below the acromion process; standing in a natural position, elbows at the sides, shoulder neither dropped forward nor braced backward."

The chief justification for presenting these details of measuring technique is that some of the interpretation of the data is based on them.

LENGTHS OF BODY SEGMENTS

For purposes of analysis, it is desirable to separate lengths of body segments from transverse diameters and girths. The lengths or heights of the postcranial parts of the body result mainly from epiphysial growth. In a few cases, the number of epiphyses included in a measurement is small enough so that we can evaluate parsimoniously the activity of specific epiphyses. In Table 1, the mean segmental increments or decreases of sons relative to their fathers are expressed in terms of the paternal mean at 100 percent.

In order to produce sufficient detail, it was necessary to subtract some mean measurements from others. The use of subtractive measurements is an unsatisfactory substitute for direct measurements of the living body Howells 1957), but in the present instance was unavoidable.

As Bowles himself stated, some body segments increased appreciably from fathers to sons, and others have been more stable or even decreased. In the limbs, the greatest elongations were at the thigh and distal to the elbow. Unfortunately, we do not have a measure of forearm length which could help to distinguish between lengthening of the hand and that of the forearm. The foot, however, increased only slightly in the sons, and if the hand was similarly stable, still more of the filial elongation from the elbow to the finger tip must have been localized in the forearm.

The subtractive measurement from pubis to knee is also rather unsatisfactory. Experienced anthropometrists are well aware that femoral length cannot be measured accurately on the living subject. In the Harvard series, since the knee height is actually the height of the hamstring tendons in a bent knee, a more bulky filial thigh as well as elongation of the femur may be contributory to the filial increase in thigh length.

Aside from these complications, the interpretation of the findings is based on the mechanisms of elongation of the forearm and thigh. The long bones involved in this growth have very active epiphysial cartilages at their distal ends, whereas the bones of the brachium and calf grow more nearly equally from both ends (Weinmann & Sicher 1955).

When a bone elongates mainly from a growth center at one end, that center must exhibit great metabolic activity—especially if it produces most of the femur, which is the heaviest bone in the body. One of the most general principles of developmental physiology is that the higher the metabolic rate of a tissue at a given age, the greater its vulnerability to developmental disturbances (Stockard 1931).

"Disturbances" in the elongation of bones sometimes leave transverse scars or "Harris's lines" in the metaphysis, and these features can be seen radiographically (Harris 1933). One of the main reasons for using the hand and wrist (Greulich & Pyle 1950) or the knee (Pyle & Hoerr 1955) for assessing the skeletal progress of children is that these lines are so readily observed distally in the broad metaphyses of the radius or femur. If the disturbance and scarring have not been severe, Harris's lines usually disappear as the metaphysis undergoes reorganization in later growth, but it is thought that the final length of the bone is permanently shortened. In some children, it is possible to correlate Harris's lines with known illnesses, but in other cases the reasons for these lines are obscure (Acheson & Dupertuis 1957).

We conclude, therefore, that the paternal generation underwent more frequent arrests of skeletal growth than did their sons, and these arrests were most severe in the distal epiphyses of the femur, radius and ulna.

Table 1 indicates that the limbs were not the only sites of metrical changes in the sons. In the head, neck, and trunk, some of the filial changes are probably related to regional enlargements, and others to changes in posture.

The subtractive measurement from sternum to vertex, as indicated by the difference between stature and sternal height, increased by 0.9 percent in the sons. This increase indicates that the sons underwent more growth in cervical height, head height, or both.

Sitting height is a still more composite measurement of the head, vertebral column, pelvis, buttock muscles and subcutaneous tissues. In the sitting position, however, the curvatures of the vertebral column are likely to be straighter than in the standing pose, and we may suspect that the filial increase of 1.3 percent in this measurement indicates some elongation of the trunk.

If this vertebral elongation occurred, the remaining body heights indicate that increases in lumbar lordosis and thoracic kyphosis have taken place in the sons. Two independent estimates of lower limb length are indicative of changes in the lumbar curve. When sitting height is subtracted from stature, the sons' lower limb length so calculated is 2.8 percent greater than their fathers'. Their increase in public height, however, is only 2.2 percent. This discrepancy suggests that the average position of the filial pubis was lower relative to the thigh in the standing position.

Such a lowering of the son's public region would probably accentuate the lumbar curve, and this accentuation in turn could stretch the height of the lower abdominal wall. The rather sizeable filial increase in the distance from pubis to navel (2.3 percent) is thereby intelligible.

The mechanics of human posture and balance are such that an increase of lumbar lordosis is compensated by more kyphosis of the thoracic spine. If the thoracic spine in the sons became taller but more curved, the distance from the suprasternal notch to the umbilicus might not increase. Actually, the fathers and sons show almost identical averages for this measurement.

Sheldon et al. (1940) observed that men with rounded (endomorphic) physiques tend to have relatively straight thoracic and lumbar spines. In more muscular (mesomorphic) or linear (ectomorphic) men, however, these spinal segments are more curved. Goff (1951) verified these conclusions from both body build photographs and radiographs.

In applying these findings to Bowles' series, it would appear that the filial generation has lost endomorphy and gained in mesomorphy, ectomorphy, or both components. A consideration of body weight, girths and breadths in the two generations will further document these trends.

BODY WEIGHT, GIRTHS AND BREADTHS

Table 1 enables us to make further calculations and inferences on the alterations of physique and body composition in two generations of Harvard men.

The first calculation to be attempted is the estimation of the percentage of extractable fat and the fat-free body weight (lean body mass) in the two generations. The formula to be used here is based on two studies of body composition and basal oxygen consumption. Best and Kuhl (1953) calculated two formulae by which basal oxygen consumption could be predicted from anthropometric measurements. The one based on stature, waist girth and total body weight is used here. This formula was based on data from 22 healthy young men.

Letting

W = total body weight in kg.
H = stature in meters
G = waist girth in meters
O_2 = basal oxygen consumption in ml/minute.

$$O_2 = 5.09\,W - 6.0\,H^3 - 194.0\,G^3 + 3.10 \qquad (1)$$

TABLE 1. PERCENTAGE CHANGES IN BODY DIMENSIONS IN HARVARD SONS RELATIVE TO THEIR HARVARD FATHERS

Measurement	*Measurement Number (Martin-Saller)*	*Fathers*		*Sons*		*Percentage Change in Sons*
		N	Mean	N	Mean	
Lengths of Body Segments						
Foot length	58	477*	25.98	477	26.15	+0.6
Knee height	—	399	46.66	478	47.02	+0.8
Pubic height minus knee height	—	399	40.44	478	42.00	+3.9
Pubic height	—	399	87.10	478	89.02	+2.2
Stature minus sitting height	1 minus 23	—	83.00	—	85.36	+2.8
Navel height	5	399	103.72	478	107.02	+3.2
Navel height minus pubic height	—	399	16.62	478	17.00	+2.3
Sternal height	4	399	141.83	478	145.10	+2.3
Sternal height minus navel height	—	399	38.11	478	38.08	−0.01
Stature	1	399	173.95	480	177.50	+2.0
Stature minus sternal height	1 minus 4	399	32.12	—	32.40	+0.9
Sitting height	23	350	90.95	479	92.14	+1.3
Shoulder to elbow length	—	477*	37.55	477	36.80	−2.0
Elbow to finger length	—	474	90.95	479	92.14	+1.3
Girths						
Neck	—	398	34.70	478	35.64	+2.4
Chest (normal)	61	398	86.88	479	90.88	+4.6
Chest (expanded)	61 (a)	397	91.88	477	94.38	+2.8
Waist	—	397	72.88	478	73.48	+0.8
Hips	64 (1)	479*	89.28	476	91.84	+2.9
Thigh	65 (a)	397	52.12	478	53.94	+3.3
Knee	68 (3)	396	35.52	478	36.62	+3.0
Calf	69	399	35.09	479	35.59	+1.1
Upper arm	65 (1)	479*	29.37	479	30.78	+4.6
Elbow	65 (3)	472*	25.17	472	25.46	+1.2
Forearm	—	479*	25.78	479	26.80	+4.1
Wrist	—	479*	16.23	479	16.42	+1.1
Breadths						
Head	3	396	15.30	475	15.009	−1.9
Neck	—	477*	10.94	477	11.17	+1.9
Shoulders	—	476*	42.69	476	43.68	+2.2
Waist	—	478*	25.33	478	25.90	+2.2
Hips (bitrochanteric)	42	479*	33.06	479	32.92	−0.6
Nipple to nipple	38	476*	20.26	476	20.34	+0.2

Adapted from Bowles 1932.

* Calculated from the correlation tables, so that fathers with more than one son were duplicated.

Equation 1 is identical with that recorded in Best and Kuhl (1953) except that errors in the location of decimal points in the coefficients of H^3 and G^3 have been corrected.

From basal oxygen consumption, Miller and Blyth (1952) derived the following formula for the estimation of the fat-free weight of the body in kilograms from a series of 48 young men:

$$(2) \qquad FFW = 0.2929\ O_2 - 7.36.$$

Combining formulas 1 and 2, we obtain an equation for predicting the fat-free weight of a young man from weight, stature and waist girth:

$$(3) \qquad FFW = 1.49\ W - 1.76\ H^3 - 56.82\ G^3 - 6.45.$$

To be strictly accurate, equation 3 should properly apply to individual data and not group means. If means of the cubes of stature and waist girth were available for the Harvard generations, this limitation of the data would be avoided. When Equation 3 is used on Bowles's original means, it overestimates the fat-free weight, and therefore yields too low percentages of fat in the fathers and sons. On the basis of comparisons with another college male series where fat was calculated from body density (Brožek 1952), it would appear that the percentages of fat in the Harvard groups are perhaps 2 percent too low as recorded in Table 2.

TABLE 2. CALCULATED BODY COMPOSITION IN HARVARD FATHERS AND SONS COMPARED TO DATA FROM UNDERWATER WEIGHING (DENSITOMETRY) OF COLLEGE MEN (BROŽEK, 1952)

Measurement	*Fathers*	*Sons*	*College Series from Brožek (1952)*
N	399	480	21
Mean age (years)	approx. 19.6	approx. 18.5	20.3
Stature (cm)	173.95	177.50	177.0
Total body weight (kg)	63.63	68.19	68.7
Fat-free body weight	57.17	62.84	61.9
Weight of extractable fat	6.46	5.35	6.9
% fat in total body weight	10.2	7.9	9.9

Despite the preceding errors in our use of equation 3, the generational trend is clear enough: that the average son is less adipose than the average father. This trend agrees well with the changes in filial posture which were shown earlier.

If the Harvard sons have lost fat, it is reasonable to infer that some of the decrease was in the subcutaneous layer. The rationale of this inference is that in young (but not old) adults, the subcutaneous and inner adipose deposits are in harmonious relationship to one another, so that skinfolds rather efficiently predict the total fat content of the body as determined from body density (Brožek & Keys 1951; Škerlj, Brožek & Hunt 1953). The predictive efficiency of skinfolds in older subjects declines because of great individual differences in the rate of accumulation of inner fat.

If the decline of total body fat in the sons was about 2 percent of total body weight, we should expect decreases of skinfolds even in highly adipose regions such as the belly to be no more than 3 mm. (Brožek & Keys 1951). Elsewhere the decline should be 2 mm. or less. These postulated decreases can be used in further interpretations of the metrical trends in Table 1.

The width of the head in the sons is diminished by over 2 mm. This narrowing is probably more than a simple adipose loss, but further deductions on this measurement are not possible.

The estimated decrease of less than 2 mm. in adiposity in the filial arm is not nearly enough to explain the marked decrease in the sons' upper arm length (7.5 mm.). This measurement, which was taken with the elbow flexed, shows a reduction whose nature is still obscure.

The two girths of the upper extremity taken with tensed muscles (upper arm and forearm) show very considerable increases, whereas girths encompassing relaxed muscles and loosely extended elbow and hand joints (elbow and wrist circumferences) show much smaller increases. In addition to the increased relaxation, the elbow and wrist measurements encompass relatively more bone and fewer muscle fibers than do the other girths of the upper limb.

In the neck and chest, the girths are more enlarged percentagewise than are the transverse dimensions. These trends indicate that the sons have deepened dorsoventrally in these regions more than they have broadened transversely. The very small increase in the nipple-nipple dimension shows that the sons have probably acquired more flaring musculature lateral to the rib cage.

This lateral flare is still clearer in the waist, where the breadth is increased percentagewise more than the girth. The filial decrease in abdominal skinfolds may have been an additional reason for this trend. The increases in neck, shoulder, and waist breadths are about equal, but the width of the hips (bitrochanteric) is actually smaller in the sons. These trends contribute to a more "masculine" outline of the body as seen from the front or rear in the filial group. Hip girth, however, is appreciably increased in the sons. We can therefore conclude that the sons have acquired more prominent buttocks than their fathers.

This prominence of the buttocks may partly result from muscular development, but it may also reflect the increased lumbar lordosis in the sons which was shown earlier.

The girths of the sons' hips, thigh, and knee have all increased more than that of the calf. The increments of the proximal muscle masses in the lower limb seem greater than those of the distal segment.

These trophic responses of various muscle groups in the sons are not unlike the effects of body building exercises on young men. According to Tanner (1952), if a young man is not too scrawny to begin with, the brachium, forearm, and chest can often be measurably increased by such training. In ten young men whom he studied during this kind of program, the maximum segmental girths of the upper limb uniformly increased. The thigh showed variable responses, and the calf decreased in all members of the group.

DISCUSSION

The main theme of this paper is that in local regions of the body, the tissues with the largest contributions to final body size have shown the greatest enlargement in the filial generation. In the skeleton, these growth centers are the distal epiphysial cartilages of the thigh and forearm.

This argument applies also to the skeletal musculature. The postnatal enlargement of these tissues is considerably greater than that of total body weight. At birth, muscle weight is about 23 percent of total body weight, whereas in an average adult man this percentage is about 45 (White House Conference 1933). Postnatally, the musculature increases fortyfold, while body weight increases only twentyfold.

Skeletal musculature, then, has a sizeable growth potential, and is perhaps sensitive to growth arrests in the same manner as the largest and most active epiphyses in the body. Except for the muscles in the calf, the evidence suggests that the largest muscles in the body may have increased more markedly than did the smaller ones. Furthermore, the muscles which grow most during a program of body building seem to have been rather similar to those which increased the most in the Harvard sons. The data on the whole indicate that a single developmental process was at work in most of these trends of body form and composition, along with a corresponding change in posture.

Lest these findings be attributed too hastily to environmental changes, it would be well to compare Bowles's findings with the abundant data in the literature on the anthropometry of related persons. Bowles himself published correlations between the generations, using the basic measurements discussed here, and on a smaller scale, those between brothers as well. Some—but not all—of the most highly correlated measurements in kinsmen are the ones which increased most in the sons. This partial agreement also occurs if one compares Bowles's data with findings on the most "heritable" body measurements in twins (Clark 1956). The great complexity of this topic and abundance of the relevant literature preclude further discussion here.

The few contradictions and the consistency of the pattern of somatic changes which emerge from this study are a tribute to the thoroughness and skill of Bingham, Sargent, and Bowles. These findings are a powerful argument for the biological study of human groups on a generational basis, and for making use of well-executed somatic measurements, even long after the completion of the original investigation.

SUMMARY

Some human populations, such as the Micronesians of Yap, have remained metrically unchanged since the late 19th century, and are characterized by a late attainment of mature stature. During this interval, the Yapese have not changed appreciably in genetic composition, diet, or culture.

Accelerated maturation seems to have occurred in Britain without an increase in final stature. In the United States, acceleration has been striking, and a statural increase has been apparent in at least some segments of the population. In anthropometric studies of successive human generations, each phenomenon should be analyzed separately. A major difficulty in studies of growth and final size in the United States is in separating these trends from metrical changes produced by the newer ethnic strains in the country.

Bowles's study of college parents and progeny satisfactorily controls both accelerated maturation and genetic diversification in a study of Americans. The parental and filial generations at Harvard and several eastern women's colleges show no difference in the age of attainment of mature stature, and the familial nature of the data helps to limit the genetic differences between the generations whose body measurements are analyzed.

In Bowles's sizeable samples of Harvard fathers and sons, dating from 1870 to 1917, the greatest elongation of body regions probably occurs in the thigh and forearm. Calculated trends of body build and body composition are in the direction of less fat and more muscularity and linearity in the sons. These changes correspond with greater thoracic and lumbar curves in the vertebral column, both of which are known to be less straight in the less adipose body types. The local patterns of muscular enlargement are not unlike those produced by body-building exercises in young men.

Both the local and general somatic trends in the sons appear to be exaggerated responses of tissues which are especially vulnerable to disturbances in growth during childhood. Paradoxically, however, some of these same dimensions are also the most strongly "heritable" in kinsmen, according to a number of relevant studies in the literature.

REFERENCES

Acheson, R. M., and Dupertuis, C. W. 1957. The relationship between physique and sexual maturation in boys. *Human Biol.* 29: 167–93.

Acheson, R. M. and Hewitt, D. 1954. Stature and skeletal maturation in the pre-school child. *Brit. J. Soc. Prev. Medicine* 8: 59–65.

Baker, P. T.; Hunt, E. E. Jr.; and Sen, T. 1957. The growth and interrelationships of skinfolds and brachial tissues in man. *Am. J. Phys. Anthrop.* (in press).

Best, W. R.. and Kuhl, W. J. 1953. Estimation of active protoplasmic mass by physical and roentgenological anthropometry. *Med. Nutr. Lab. Report* 114, Surgeon General's Dept., U. S. Army.

Bowles, G. T. 1932. *New types of Old Americans at Harvard.* Cambridge, Mass.: Harvard Univ. Press.

Brožek, J. 1952. Changes of body composition in man during maturity and their nutritional implications. *Fed. Proc.* 11: 784–93.

Brožek, J. and Keys, A. 1951. The evaluation of leanness-fatness in man: Norms and interrelationships. *Brit. J. Nutrition* 5: 194–206.

Clark, P. J. 1956. The heritability of certain anthropometric characters as ascertained from measurements of twins. *Am. J. Human Genetics* 8: 49–54.

DOBZHANSKY, T. 1955. *Evolution, genetics and man.* New York: Wiley.

GOFF, C. W. 1951. Mean posture patterns with new postural values. *Am. J. Phys. Anthrop.,* n.s. 9: 335–46.

GREULICH, W. W. and PYLE, S. I. 1950. Radiographic atlas of skeletal development of the hand and wrist. Stanford, Calif.: Standford Univ. Press.

HARRIS, H. A. 1933. *Bone growth in health and disease.* Oxford: Oxford University Press.

HOWELLS, W. W. 1957. Variations of external body form in the individual. Cambridge, Mass.: Peabody Museum. (Multilithed).

HRDLIČKA, A. 1940. Observations and measurements on the members of the National Academy of Sciences. *Mem. Natl. Acad. Sci.* 23: 1–108.

HUNT, E. E., JR., and GILES, E. 1956. Allometric growth of body composition in man and other mammals. *Human Biol.* 28: 253–73.

HUNT, E. E., JR.; KIDDER, N. R. and SCHNEIDER, D. M. 1954. The depopulation of Yap. *Human Biol.* 26: 21–51.

KAPLAN, B. A. 1954. Environment and human plasticity. *American Anthropologist* 56: 780–800.

KLUCKHOHN, C. 1955. Physical anthropology. *American Anthropologist* 57: 1280–95.

KROGMAN, W. M. and SASSOUNI, V. 1957. A syllabus in roentgenographic cephalometry. Philadelphia: Philadelphia Center for Research in Child Growth.

MACY, I. G. 1942. Nutrition and chemical growth in childhood. Springfield, Ill.: C. C. Thomas.

———, and KELLY, H. J. 1956. Body composition in childhood with reference to *in vivo* chemical analysis of water, fat and protoplasmic mass. *Hum. Biol.* 28: 289–308.

MARTIN, R., and SALLER, K. 1956. Lehrbuch der Anthropologie in systematischer Darstellung. 3d ed. Stuttgart: Gustav Fischer.

MARTIN, W. E. 1953. Basic body measurements of school age children. U. S. Dept. Health, Educ. and Welfare, School Housing Sect., Office of Education.

MEREDITH, H. V. 1941. Statures and weights of children of the U. S. with reference to the influence of racial, regional, socio-economic and secular factors. *Am. J. Dis. Childr.* 62: 909–32.

MILLER, A. T., JR., and BLYTH, C. S. 1952. Estimation of lean body mass from basal oxygen consumption and creatinine excretion. *J. Appl. Physiol.* 5: 73–78.

MORANT, G. M. 1948. Applied physical anthropology in Great Britain in recent years. *Am. J. Phys. Anthrop.,* n.s. 6: 329–39.

PYLE, S. I. and HOERR, N. 1955. Radiographic atlas of skeletal development of the knee. Springfield, Ill.: C. C. Thomas.

RANDALL, F. E. 1949. Age changes in young Army adult males. *Human Biol.* 21: 187–98.

SARGENT, D. A. 1887. Anthropometric apparatus with directions for measuring and testing the principal physical characteristics of the human body. 2d ed. Cambridge, Mass.: Hemenway Gymnasium, Harvard University.

SHELDON, W. H., STEVENS, S. S. and TUCKER, W. B. 1940. Varieties of human physique. New York: Harper & Row.

Škerlj, B.; Brožek, J. and Hunt, E. E. Jr. 1953. Subcutaneous fat and age changes in body form in women. *Am. J. Phys. Anthrop.*, n.s. 11: 577–600.

Stockard, C. R. 1931. The physical basis of personality. New York: W. W. Norton.

Tanner, J. M. 1952. The effects of weight-training on physique. *Am. J. Phys. Anthrop.*, n.s. 10: 427–61.

Terman, L. M. 1925. Mental and physical traits of a thousand gifted children. Stanford, Calif.: Stanford Univ. Press.

———, and Oden, M. H. 1947. The gifted child grows up. Stanford, Calif.: Stanford Univ. Press.

Trotter, M. and Gleser, G. C. 1951. Trends in stature of American whites and Negroes born between 1840 and 1924. *Am. J. Phys. Anthrop.*, n.s. 9: 427–41.

Washburn, S. L. 1953. The strategy of physical anthropology. In *Anthropology today,* ed. A. L. Kroeber Chicago: Univ. of Chicago Press.

Weinmann, J. P. and Sicher, H. 1955. Bone and bones: fundamentals of bone biology. 2d ed. St. Louis, Mo.: C. V. Mosby.

White House Conference on Child Health and Protection. 1933. Growth and development of the child II: Anatomy and physiology. New York: Century.

SUPPLEMENTARY READINGS

Baker, Paul T., and Weiner, J. S. eds. *The Biology of Human Adaptability.* London and New York: Oxford University Press, 1966.

Dill, D. B.; Adolph, E. F.; and Wilber, C. G. eds. *Handbook of Physiology,* Sec. 4, "Adaptation to the Environment." Washington, D. C.: American Physiological Society, 1964.

Harrison, G. A.; Weiner, J. S.; Tanner, J. M.; and Barnicot, N. A. *Human Biology.* London and New York: Oxford University Press, 1964.

Kaplan, B. A. Environment and human plasticity. *American Anthropologist* 56 (1954): 780–800.

ten

APPLIED PHYSICAL ANTHROPOLOGY

After long years of academic preparation, many students aspire to a position in teaching and/or research, where they can disseminate knowledge to the present generation and seek new facts for the next. Increasingly apparent, however, is a trend toward the application of special skills and methodologies in solving modern man's everyday problems. The physical anthropologist is no exception. White's article, originally published in 1952, remains the best available summary of the ways in which some physical anthropologists work to make life a bit more comfortable for all of us. The final selection examines the recurrent need for quick and accurate identification of human skeletal remains.

Some Applications of Physical Anthropology

Robert M. White

Just as some cultural and social anthropologists have adapted their particular fields to contemporary problems, so have some physical anthropologists drawn from their techniques and developed methods by which many problems of every-day living which involve dimensions of the human being may be subjected to scientific analysis and solved in an objective manner. Although the problems generally treated by fields of anthropology other than physical are more subtle and abstract in nature, their very subtlety and abstractness have presented challenges that have enabled professional anthropologists to engage in direct approaches to them, since they present fields of investigation in which no other people are prepared to engage. On the other hand, the physical anthropologist encounters large numbers of "experts" when he approaches any of the numerous problems he may solve or help to solve.

In general, we, as people, have become so well acquainted with all the various implements used by us physically that we suffer from the types of prejudices so well described by Gittler in 1949. Clothing, furniture, automobiles, all are familiar to us from our early childhood. We develop specific ideas about them, aided considerably by advertising claims. Consequently, when we develop tired backs, or we feel cramped, we believe we are in the best furniture or clothing that can be made and so we, as people are at fault. The dissenting opinion of the objective investigator, merely expressed as a viewpoint, immediately arouses our antagonism. "I paid $150 for this suit, so it is perfect." "This automobile cost $2,500, so it cannot be improved upon." Such reactions should be familiar to all of us. Since these reactions are

From Journal of the Washington Academy of Sciences *42, no. 3 (March 1952): 65–71; reprinted by permission of the author and publisher.*

encountered among laymen, it is easy to imagine the attitudes or opinions expressed by designers of clothing and other items with which we come into physical association. Men who have made fortunes in the designing of clothing are hard to convince when we argue that they might improve upon their procedures. One of the greatest handicaps in reaching a mutual understanding with the designer or the engineer is the necessary use of statistical knowledge in explaining the problem. No one professional group attempts to use applied statistics more than does that engaged in clothing design and construction. Grading between sizes and sizes themselves are really applied statistics, but the use made of modern statistical concepts among that group is practically archaic. Although mechanical design engineers have benefited from training in mathematics, little, if any, statistical method has been included.

Since we, as people, are so well acquainted with all the various articles we wear or use every day, it comes somewhat as a shock to us to find that so little consideration has been given to us, as people, in the design of those articles. The common reaction expressed by most persons who are at first confronted by the idea that all is not right with the world is one of perplexed questioning. "How have we gotten along so well, so far, if this situation actually exists?" The answer is simple. The first chair was probably a stone or a log. Trial and error soon indicated its deficiencies. A pad of animal skin or grass considerably alleviated the concentration of pressures on the ischial tuberosities. By further trial and error a back was added, and so we have now a product, called a chair, which has shown little evolution from its primitive ancestor. Sporadically, claims are made that some chairs are functional. Seldom is the function specified. Rarely is it directed at comfort, objectively specified in terms of the human occupant. Claims are often made, but the proof is seldom present. Coincident with this situation in furniture is that existing in clothing. Design and size are considered to be integral. They are, but seldom does size have a known and provable relation to human bodily dimensions. It is of little interest to the designers of clothing that I wear a "size 38 Regular" in this year's style, and next year, even though my dimensions do not change, I wear a "size 40 Regular." The explanation is simple. I am a "38 Regular" in this year's style, and a "40 Regular" in next year's. Opposed to this type of free thinking is the plight of the retailer who stocks next year's inventory on the basis of this year's sales. The equalization occurs with a "stock reduction and clearance sale." Fortunately for the poor retailer, the designer and his style usually stay within three sizes in their variation, so that the retailer can operate at 80–85 percent efficiency.

All this should serve to orient us with the more direct aspects of the field into which physical anthropology has recently entered. Essentially, the scope lies almost within the range of engineering, whether it be termed as such, or whether it is such by method. In clothing, little has been accomplished which would warrant the term "engineering." In what is more commonly accepted as an engineering field, furniture, automobiles, etc., equally negligible accomplishments have been attained with specific reference to human beings. Two factors explain this condition. The first, and fundamentally the most important, is the lack of static and dynamic anthropometric data. Allied with this, although necessarily following it in demand, is the lack of statistical knowledge required to obtain proper application. The second, and of equal practical importance, is the universal attitude that the accommodation of the human being is a factor in the general field of competition. Whole industries are willing to standardize sizes of fittings, such as rims of wheels on automobiles, in order to accommodate tires made by another industry, but the perfectly simple concept of standardization of accommodation for human beings has not yet been accepted. The various commercial airlines are encountering a serious problem as a result of this type of situation. Pilot accommodations vary considerably among various aircraft. Consequently, when the suggestion is made that saving in time and money could be achieved by through-routing of aircraft over different lines, the pilots refuse, and wisely so, to accept responsibility of piloting aircraft that have cockpit arrangements differing markedly from those with which they are familiar. The armed services have been striving for the past five or six years to accomplish some form of cockpit standardization, and have made some progress, but the fulfillment of their efforts has yet to be realized in operational aircraft.

Therefore, when the physical anthropologist carefully measures large series of people, develops objective analyses, and proposes results to be introduced into the design of all types of personal equipment or of equipment which requires accommodation of the human being, only part of his work is done. Two parts remain. He must educate the designers in his way of thinking, and then he must collaborate with the designers in setting up experiments which will convert the anthropometric requirements into terms which will be familiar to them.

The various needs for the objective consideration of bodily dimensions should be obvious, in part, to the casual observer. Beginning with clothing, these needs extend to furniture, both for comfort and for function, automobiles, trains, aircraft, and even housing. From the viewpoint of the applied physical anthropologist a person "wears" a house, in that he gains his greatest comfort and efficiency if the house "fits" him. Tired backs at the kitchen sink and the laundry tub can be just as painful as if they resulted from sitting in an inefficient chair. Bodily motions can be just as inefficient in a small room as they can be in tight gloves or shoes (Callaghan and Palmer, 1944). The main objective, then, in applied physical anthropology is to attain the optimum "fit" and thus the proper "size" for the human beings involved.

Obviously, in most of the problems encountered, 100 percent efficiency is not expected. The degree to which efficiency can be obtained in any one item will be dependent upon its functional characteristics of "fit" and also upon the degree of variability of dimensions which it will be required to accommodate. A secondary factor which enters the picture is the economics involved. All these factors operate to produce a compromise which is considered optimum. For example, the kitchen sink is relatively tolerant of a considerable variation in stature, but not so much as to accommodate a range of 16 inches in stature commonly encountered among housewives. On the other hand, most housewives do not operate on a strict time and motion basis, even though it would be to their advantage to do so, if they could. Finally, building houses in various "sizes" in terms of wear by the housewife is not very economical. Therefore, a compromise between accommodation, efficiency, and cost is necessary. The common compromise is a standard sink height, with the cost at a minimum and the efficiency unknown. It would not seem unreasonable to consider another possible answer; a sink provided with a height adjustment. Cost would rise somewhat, but range of accommodation and increase in efficiency would result.

It is the goal of the investigator to provide information for the designer as to the requirements of accommodation. It is the goal of the designer to meet these requirements. Finally, it is the objective of both to obtain the optimum compromise at the minimum cost.

Thus, in the field of applied physical anthropology, the physical anthropologist occupies three successive positions. Initially, he is an anthropometrist in collecting the metric data. Secondly, he is a statistician in preparing the "specifications" which describe the requirements. Finally, he is an applied physical anthropologist, analyzing the problem of the designer insofar as it relates to human bodily dimensions, and in providing for the designer, in concrete practical terms understandable to the designer, the measure of fulfillment of the requirements by the designer. Many times this last role permits the anthropologist, through his analysis, to suggest revisions in the original design which will improve its efficiency materially and often reduce its cost.

The part played by statistics in applied physical anthropology should not be underrated. It is the essential tool for converting anthropometry to engineering terms. The use made of statistical method by designers is limited at best. More often than not the concept of variability is ignored. Further the concept of accommodation of an optimum percentage (e.g., 90 percent) of a population is usually only estimated. A common design criterion is the accommodation of the "average." Two examples may serve to indicate how this is done. In the design of clothing, a new pattern is usually tested to prove its adequacy. This test is accomplished by construction of an "average" size, 36 or 38 Regular in men's garments. Revision may be necessary, but the final opinion is based upon the adequacy demonstrated by this size of garment tried on "average" men. Following this test, there are certain rules which are followed to develop the other sizes. However, experience has shown that these rules are only, at best, vaguely related to regressions which can be demonstrated by anthropometry and statisics.

In automotive design, considerable use is made of profile manikins. These are constructed as "average men," complete with hat. If space is sufficient to accommodate this "average" man, the design is considered satisfactory. But, consider for a moment. The "average" man is about 69 inches tall and weighs about 150 pounds. Stature ranges between 61 and 77 inches, and weight between 110 and 250 pounds. Further, and apparently totally ignored, at least 33 percent of our automobiles are driven by women as well as by men. Women "average" about 64.5 inches tall and 135 pounds in weight, ranging between 56.5 and 72.5 inches, and 90 to 200 pounds. If the automobile is to accommodate its drivers, the "average" man is too large to be "average" of drivers. Further, if the design is satisfactory for 90 per cent of its drivers, being adjustable for statures between about 61 and 70 inches, and weight between 110 and 210 pounds, it will certainly accommodate "average" drivers, and, consequently, the "average" manikin has only academic interest at best.

Situations such as those described above have been encountered so universally that there is good reason to suspect that the field of applied physical anthropology has considerable room to grow.

As of this writing at least three large and applicable series of anthropometric data have been accumulated in the United States. The first, on some 147,000 children (O'Brien and Girshik, 1939; O'Brien, Girshik, and Hunt, 1941), and the second, on about 14,700 women (O'Brien and Shelton, 1941) were collected by the Bureau of Home Economics, United States Department of Agriculture. The third, on about 135,000 Army men and 10,000 Army women represents a selected military population (Damon and Randall, 1944; Randall, 1948*b*). Some applications of the Department of Agriculture series have been made (Lonie, 1948; Staples and DeLury, 1949). Much wider applications of the military series have been accomplished over the past seven years. Since the Department of the Army and the Department of the Air Force are in a position to include anthropometric findings in their specifications, wide and effective applications are possible. The results can be quickly demonstrated and assessed. It is hoped that demonstrated results of the use of applied physical anthropology in the armed services will serve as stimuli to other agencies to incorporate similar approaches in their activities.

Frequently, such questions as "Why is the Army interested in physical anthropology?" or "How is the Army using physical anthropology?" are asked by laymen and even physical anthropologists as well. It is intended here to summarize present Army research in physical anthropology and to indicate some of the methods currently in use.

In some respects, it would seem that the use of physical anthropology by the military is a relatively new thing, at least in this country. The increasing use of applied physical anthropology, which is perhaps a more accurate term, is a comparatively new development. However, it is interesting to note that a book by B. A. Gould was published by the U.S. Sanitary Commission in 1869, entitled *Investigations in the military and anthropological statistics of American soldiers,* while in 1875 two volumes by J. H. Baxter were issued by the Government Printing Office under the imposing title of *Statistics, medical and anthropological, of the Provost-Marshall-General's Bureau, derived from records of the examination for military service in the Armies of the United States during the late War of the Rebellion, of over a million recruits, drafted men, substitutes, and volunteers.*

The extensive work of Davenport and Love during and following the first World War is familiar to most physical anthropologists. Measurements were obtained on 1,000,000 recruits, and also on 100,000 troops during demobilization. Although the emphasis was primarily statistical and clinical, some applications of the anthropometric data to clothing problems were carried out. Medical and clinical studies were continued through the last war under the Surgeon-General's Office, while the Selective Service System has issued several reports on medical statistics, dealing with such topics as physical examinations and causes for rejections of draftees.

As early as 1942, research in applied physical anthropology was started by the Army Air Forces. This work was carried on throughout the war, with the center of activity at the Aero-Medical Laboratory, Wright Field, Dayton, Ohio, and is being continued there. Several anthropometric surveys were carried out on flight personnel and the data obtained were used in connection with spatial requirements in aircraft and in the development of flight clothing and other types of personal equipment (Damon et al., 1944; Randall et al., 1946; Hertzberg, 1948).

After several years, the Army Quartermaster Corps carried out an anthropometric survey in 1946. Approximately 96,000 Army separatees were processed at separation centers, while a small series of 8,500 inductees was also obtained. A series of about 9,000 women, consisting of WAC personnel and Army nurses, was measured. In conjunction with the anthropometric survey, somatotype photographs of approximately 50,000 men and 550 women were taken. This photographic material has been utilized by Hooton at Harvard University in extensive studies of body builds occurring in the Army population.

More recently, additional data have been secured in the form of smaller Army series. One year ago, a sample of 6,500 men, including draftees, enlistees and reenlistees, was measured at induction centers, while data on 2,000 marines were also obtained in 1949. Numerous smaller series of men have been measured from time to time in connection with various clothing fitting tests.

Since one of the primary responsibilities of the Office of The Quartermaster General is to clothe and equip Army men and women, applications of anthropometric data to clothing problems have received first consideration. However, there are still basic problems in the general field of human biology for which the accumulated Army anthropometric data should and can be used. Consequently, the Army program of research in physical anthropology may be considered to include both basic research and practical applications.

Obviously the human sample comprising the available Army data cannot be considered representative of the total population, since it is a selected group. There are various limiting factors, such as age, physical and medical qualifications, as well as social and economic factors. However, several types of investigation are possible with these data. One for example, is the problem of age change and terminal growth. Sufficient data are available to provide adequate series for each age from 17 through 32 years. Another problem involves the differences between military and nonmilitary populations. How do draftees or enlistees entering the Army for the first time compare with separatees who have been exposed to the military environment for various lengths of time? It is well-known that draftees, and especially 17-, 18-, or 19-year old enlistees tend to gain weight and that their body measurements change upon entering the Army. Do these changes take place rapidly within the first few weeks, do they extend over the whole period of basic training, or is it a more gradual process covering several years? These are questions of practical importance to those responsible for supplying and issuing Army clothing and equipment. Present studies utilizing the anthropometric data are focussed on these problems (Randall, 1949*a*).

Only preliminary reports on the Army work have been issued, since analyses of the extensive data have taken considerable time. A volume of the female data has been published, containing some 98 bivariate charts of 23 body measurements, together with 109 regression tables (Randall & Munro, 1949*b*).

Sorting of the male data and statistical analyses of some 37 body measurements have been completed, giving 72 bivariate charts and 83 regression tables. In addition, the male data have been sorted by age groups from 17 through 32 years, with bivariates and regression tables for each year of age. All this material is now ready for publication and will represent useful reference data.

A certain amount of sociological information is included along with the anthropometric data, such as location of birthplace, national extraction, birthplace and extraction of parents, education, civilian and military occupation, etc. Preliminary sortings on the basis of geographical area of birthplace and national extraction are now in progress.

The more recent data of a year ago are being sorted on the basis of classification—draftees, enlistees, reenlistees—as well as by age groups, for purposes of comparison with the earlier separatee and inductee material. The IBM system of punched cards and electrical sorting machines is used in all this work.

As has been mentioned previously, Army clothing has received first consideration in the applications of anthropometric data. It has been a gradual process, but marked improvements have been and are being made in the fit of Army clothing. The old Army joke to the effect that there were only two sizes of clothing issued—too large and too small—has been disposed of.

Reduced to simplest terms, the aim of the Quartermaster Corps with respect to clothing is to fit the Army population with the best possible clothing in a minimum number of sizes, requiring the least amount of alteration. In addition, there is a further consideration which is the percentage of the population to be fitted with standard sizes. It is desirable to have this percentage as high as possible, since men outside of the range of standard sizes must be fitted with supplementary or special order sizes. These men are usually those whose body measurements fall at the upper or lower ends of the distribution curve, and who comprise the lowest percentage frequencies in the population.

Obviously, the clothing of several hundred thousand men is no small item, especially in terms of the taxpayers' dollars and cents. In this respect, it will be seen that in the proper applications of Army anthropometry with respect to clothing sizes, size systems and tariffs, significant contributions can be made, particularly in the elimination of waste resulting from incorrect sizes. The Army cannot afford the trial and error methods of the clothing industry with respect to size, nor can it afford the cost of frequent or numerous alterations.

The applications of anthropometry to clothing consist, essentially, of relating body dimensions to clothing sizes (Randall, 1948*a*). This procedure has necessitated a definition of the Army population in metric terms in order to obtain a measure of the ranges and variations which occur. The metric definition of the population, together with the establishment of normal distribution curves, is the most useful advance made thus far (Randall, 1949*b*; Randall & Munro, 1949).

Initially, the anthropometric data were used in investigating deficiencies in the size systems of standard clothing items already in use. In several cases, this resulted in recommendations that some smaller sizes be procured, since many smaller men at the lower end of the distribution curve were not being fitted properly.

Another use of the data has been in the preparation of clothing tariffs. A tariff is a listing of the numbers of each clothing size required for the population, in terms of a given ratio, such as number per 1000, or per 100,000, as the case may be. For example, such tariffs for clothing items were prepared when the Universal Military Training program was first under consideration. Tariffs were also prepared when the recent postwar draft went into effect.

Even more profitable applications of anthropometry have been made in the development of new and improved items of clothing. In some cases it has been necessary to investigate various body measurements in order to determine just which dimensions are critical and important in the fit of clothing. It has been found that although upper body clothing, such as coats and jackets, traditionally has been sized on the basis of chest circumference, actually shoulder circumference and even waist circumference are more important than chest with respect to tolerances and fit. For example, a new system of sizing trousers on the basis of the seat dimension rather than the waist may result in a reduction of standard trouser sizes from 95 to only 30 sizes, which would be quite a saving. The sizes and tariffs for the new Air Force blue uniform were developed through the use of anthropometric data.

The applications of anthropometric data are not limited to body clothing by any means. Measurements of the head and face were used during the war in the development of gas masks, oxygen masks, goggles, and helmets (Randall and Damon, 1943). The anthropometry of the foot and the proper fit of all types of boots and shoes is a large problem in itself. A study of the hand and the functional fit of handwear has recently been initiated. It is hoped that the use of anthropometric data eventually may be extended to other types of military equipment: sleeping bags, tents, tanks, etc. The necessity for anthropometric specifications in aircraft and submarines where spatial requirements are critical is obvious.

The criticism has been made that Army anthropometry on such a scale is unsatisfactory from the standpoint of technique. Some anthropologists even feel that as far as clothing is concerned, tailors could do just as well, and that we are wasting time and effort in attempting to apply the methods of physical anthropology to such a problem as Army clothing. The point is that clothing people are basically artists, and not human biologists, and they do not have sufficient knowledge of such topics as normal distributions of body measurements or applied statistics. Here is one field in which the trained professional anthropologist can make a practical contribution.

In closing, mention should be made of the late Francis E. Randall, who, perhaps more than any other, was responsible for the development of applied physical anthropology in the Army. He began his work with the Air Force during the war, and then came to the Quartermaster Corps in 1946 to direct the anthropometric survey. He really believed in applied physical anthropology, to the extent that had he lived, he probably would have found ways to incorporate anthropometric data in the working height of the kitchen sink or the handle of an eggbeater, not to mention automobiles or office furniture.

REFERENCES

RANDALL, F. E. 1948*a*. Applications of anthropology to the determination of size in clothing. *Environmental Protection Section Report* no. 133. Lawrence, Mass.: Quartermaster Climatic Research Laboratory.

———. 1948*b*. Anthropometry in the Quartermaster Corps. *Am. J. Phys. Anthrop.* n.s. 6: 373–80.

———, and DAMON, A. 1943. An interesting application of a basic science to aviation medicine. *J. Aviation Med.* 14: 200–205.

RANDALL, F. E., and MUNRO, E. H. 1949. Anthropometric nomograph of Army women. *Environmental Protection Section Report* no. 148. Lawrence, Mass.: Quartermaster Climatic Research Laboratory.

STAPLES, M. L., and DELURY, D. B. 1949. A system for the sizing of women's garments. *Textile Res. J.* 19: 346–54.

The Secrets that Dead Men's Bones Tell

Sharon S. / Thomas W. McKern

For more than 150 years, Danish spines have tingled over a gruesome horror tale. Legend has it that Giertrud Bodenhoff—one of Europe's wealthiest 18th century women—was buried by mistake while in a state of suspended animation, only to be bludgeoned to death later by ghoulish grave-robbers bent on stealing her jewelry.

Scientists gathered in 1952 at Copenhagen's Assistens Cemetery to determine whether the grisly tale was fact or fiction. Digging into the crypt said to hold Giertrud's remains, they found a skeleton, face downward and convulsively twisted. The skull, heavily dented, bore evidence of a crushing blow.

Scientific age assessment indicated the skeleton belonged to a female aged about 19 at the time of her death; Giertrud was 19 when she was buried. A mandible or jaw bone found among the remains matched perfectly the slightly underhung jaw which characterized Giertrud in contemporary portraits. Science and legend agree: Giertrud was murdered in her coffin.

It may be true that dead men tell no tales. But their bones speak—loud and clear. The skeleton tells its own detailed story, relating the facts of age, sex, race, body build and duration of interment—as well as numerous diseases and injuries suffered during life and, often, the cause of death. When the body dies, the flesh is soon gone, but the skeleton endures long after—an entity as distinctive of its owner as his vanished fingerprint. A comprehensive analysis of bone can lead to personal identification of human remains even in the total absence of clothing, personal effects or human tissue.

Skeletal identification is a specialized sort of work, and few people

From Science Digest *66, no. 2 (1969): 30–34.* *© The Hearst Corporation; reprinted by permission of the authors and publisher.*

are trained to perform it. Because of a background in anatomy, osteology and race studies—and because of much experience in handling large numbers of skeletal remains—the physical anthropologist is uniquely qualified to "read" unearthed bones. He's called in whenever ordinary means of identification fail—in cases of burning, drowning, dismemberment, mutilation and mass disaster. In short, the "bone man" works on bones that are long dead—in archaeological excavations and historical burials—and where decomposition is so advanced that fingerprints and scars are useless for identification.

The anthropologist's interest may be historical, as in the case of Giertrud Bodenhoff, or the bones reputed to represent the remains of St. Peter, which have long been the subject of anthropological speculation (see *Science Digest,* December 1968). The bones of Richard, Duke of York and his brother, Edward V—said to have been murdered in 1483 in the Tower of London—have been positively identified. And the remains of other historical persons—among them, Dante, Bach, Kant, Richelieu, Cromwell and Shakespeare—have been exhumed and examined in order to verify their authenticity. This has been accomplished with varying degrees of success. But the identification of skeletal remains is hardly confined to historical problems. Human bones turn up almost constantly, often under the most curious circumstances. Police are understandably anxious to identify them.

In a routine case, police in a small Massachusetts town found a scattered heap of bones near the local cemetery. No clothing or personal effects were located; the bones were shipped off for expert identification. Examination indicated that the bones were those of a male aged 60–65 years at the time of his death. Living height, determined from the leg bones, was estimated at 5′7″, give or take a half-inch. Elbow and spine bones showed signs of advanced arthritis. An immediate check of missing persons lists revealed the six-month absence of an elderly man, 5′7″ tall, with a crippled left arm and stiff back. Quickly, the dentist of the missing man was located and asked to supply dental records for his former patient. The records matched the teeth of the skeleton and identification was established.

This sort of skeletal assessment is possible because the skeleton, as a living organ, develops with the body. Individual bones support and are supported by the muscles which surround them. Body structure both shapes the skeleton and is shaped, in turn, by skeletal development. This is why sexual differences appear in skeletal remains—the function of childbirth results in characteristic skeletal development for females.

Age is determined through an analysis of the teeth, skull and long bones, as well as consideration of a "combined maturation pattern"—a check of numerous bones to pinpoint biological age events. The skeleton acts as its own timepiece, registering age changes as they occur. Long bones—those of the arms, legs, fingers and toes—begin as three separate pieces: a middle shaft and two ends of *epiphyses*. These grow together at known rates and fuse into single bones at known intervals.

Dr. Wilton M. Krogman, perhaps the greatest of identification experts, has established the facts of identity from skeletal remains alone in literally thousands of cases. He tells of a young Indian-Negro who ran away from his Oklahoma home in the early 1920s, only to be killed a few weeks later while trying to leap aboard a running freight. His remains were buried beside the railroad, and the case was forgotten until, several years later, oil was discovered on lands allotted to the boy. Before his parents could collect funds due the boy's estate, definite identity had to be established for the buried remains. In 1929, the boy's skeleton was exhumed; an investigator for the oil company judged it to represent an adult male over 30 years of age, arguing that it could not then be identified as the missing heir. Dr. Krogman, however, proved through extensive gross examination and X ray analysis that the bones represented a young male aged 18–19 years; even further, he demonstrated, on the basis of skeletal proportions and certain facial traits, that the bones indicated an Indian-Negro ancestry. This evidence resulted in a court verdict in favor of the boy's parents.

In December 1941, the extensively-burned body of an adult male was found at Schiller Park near Chicago. A local black woman positively identified the body as that of her missing spouse in order to collect life insurance benefits. Dr. Krogman showed that the burned bones represented a 50-year-old, white male, 5′7″ to 5′8″ tall and of slender build, a description that could not fit the missing spouse. Dr. Krogman was unable to find a clinical cause of death, but he reasoned that such destruction by fire would require either intense heat over a short period of time, or considerable heat over a longer period. The first condition could not have resulted from an open fire in the woods; the second carried with it a high risk of discovery for someone openly burning a human body. Dr. Krogman concluded that the body might have been burned elsewhere, then placed on burning logs in the park to disguise the murder. The body has never been positively identified. But the missing husband turned up.

Scientists derive identification techniques from detailed study of the few available skeletal samples for which age, race and sex are known. The famous Todd Collection which includes more than 3000 skeletons, has been the source of numerous techniques.

Additional methods have been formulated through studies of American war dead. It's interesting to note that the United States is the only world power which seeks to systematically identify and repatriate her war dead. Other nations, including our allies, favor mass burial, often behind enemy lines. The U.S. tradition of repatriation for humanitarian reasons also has made possible the accurate determination of identity in an overwhelming majority of recovered fatalities. Because each individual receives meticulous and separate attention and because detailed records are kept of skeletal variations, scientists have been able to refine techniques which can also be applied in civilian cases of unidentified remains.

The identification of human remains in any mass disaster or war presents innumerable difficulties. In the American Civil War, almost half the reported fatalities remained forever unidentified. In World War II, however, the Memorial Division, Office of the Quartermaster General, established identification laboratories at various sites in Europe and the Pacific, employing physical anthropologists to assist in classifying war dead remains. Ninety-six percent of the American fatalities were positively identified.

Operation Glory, initiated in 1953 following the Korean conflict, led to

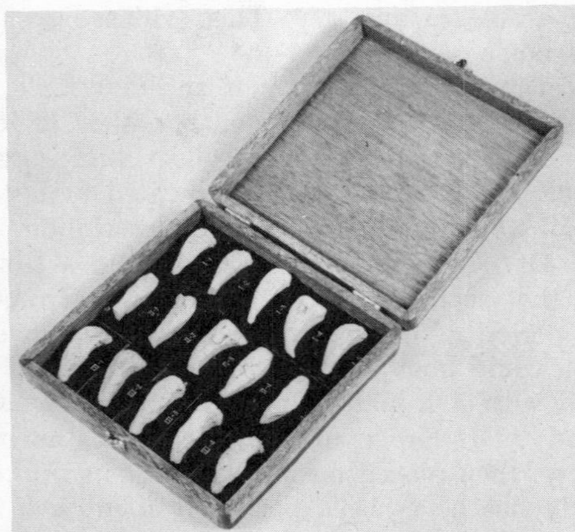

FIGURE 1. *McKern-Stewart system for age identification (left) uses tiny portion of the human pubic bone—pubic symphsis—to establish skeletons' ages. Kit shows casts of public symphysis at various ages. Bone maturity can also be established by examining the femur (thigh-bone). Below are femurs at four stages of growth and development. Condition of the epiphyses—lobe-shaped formations at top of larger bones which are not present at birth but which develop later in life and become fused to the femur at maturity—aids physical anthropologists in determining age. Left to right: A, newborn, no epiphyses present; B, age 4, one epiphysis appears; C, age 12, both epiphyses present but unfused; D, age 20, both epiphyses fused. These two tests are used in combination with other information.*

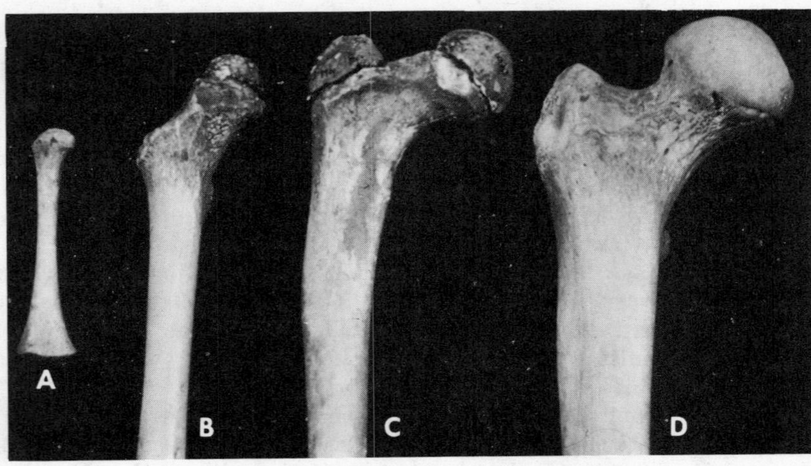

the accurate identification of 97.1 percent of American war dead. Dr. T. Dale Stewart, then curator of physical anthropology at Washington's Smithsonian Institution, established a Central Identification Laboratory at Kokura, Japan; there he worked not only to identify fatalities but also to collect photographs, casts and records of skeletal age changes in more than 400 individuals.

Later analysis of the Korean study enabled scientists to test existing identification techniques and to formulate new methods. From this analysis came the McKern-Stewart system for age identification from a tiny portion of the pubic bone. This system is now in use by law enforcement agencies all over the world.

Because teeth are the most durable of all body parts and because they differ greatly from one individual to another, they provide a means of identification second in value only to fingerprints. Police files are filled with murder cases where the missing element—the *corpus delicti*—was supplied by dentists working with anthropologists.

In one case, John Hamilton, a member of the famous Dillinger gang, was killed by gunfire while escaping from agents who sought to arrest him. His body, first treated with lye to avoid identification, was buried by his friends in an unmarked grave. The lye did its work—except on the teeth. Dental records from the penitentiary at Michigan City coincided exactly with teeth taken from the grave.

Perhaps the most thorough investigation ever attempted followed a Chicago furnace murder in 1956. Some 18,000 bone fragments were taken from the furnace and reconstructed to yield an identification sufficient to name the victim. In order to test his evaluation of the fragments, Dr. Krogman—who was called in to testify—set up a test furnace and burned medical samples until he could predict the extent of damage by fire.

Little in the way of evidence is overlooked when verifying identification in criminal cases. Imprints made by bullets or knives constitute valuable evidence. Certain poisons—lead, arsenic, mercury and others—are recoverable from the bones long after death. Supplementary evidence—microscopic hairs found among bones—is carefully analyzed. Dr. Hamilton Smith of Glasgow University has demonstrated from a few surviving hairs of Napoleon that the emperor was given arsenic some 40 times between 1820 and 1821, the year of his death. On-going research—particularly race, blood and pathology tests—is conducted to enhance existing procedures, and it becomes increasingly obvious that the skeleton provides a rich source of medicolegal evidence.

SUPPLEMENTARY READINGS

BROTHWELL, DON R. *Digging Up Bones*. London: Trustees of the British Museum (Natural History), 1965.

HERTZBERG, H. T. E. Postwar anthropometry in the Air Force. *American Journal of Physical Anthropology* n.s., 6 (1948): 363–71.

Krogman, W. M. *The Human Skeleton in Forensic Medicine*. Springfield, Ill.: Charles C. Thomas, 1962.

Lonie, M. Anthropometry and apparel. *American Journal of Physical Anthropology,* n.s., 6 (1948): 353–61.

Morant, G. M. Applied physical anthropology in Great Britain in recent years. *American Journal of Physical Anthropology* 6 (1948): 329–39.